D1706357

DYNAMICS OF THIRD PARTY INTERVENTION

DYNAMICS OF THIRD PARTY INTERVENTION

Kissinger in the Middle East

Edited by

Jeffrey Z. Rubin

In cooperation with the Society for the
Psychological Study of Social Issues

PRAEGER

PRAEGER SPECIAL STUDIES • PRAEGER SCIENTIFIC

Library of Congress Cataloging in Publication Data

Main entry under title:

Dynamics of third party intervention.

    Includes index.
    1. Near East—Foreign relations—United States.
2. United States—Foreign relations—Near East.
3. Kissinger, Henry Alfred. 4. Mediation, International.
5. Jewish—Arab relations, 1973-   . I. Rubin,
Jeffrey Z. II. Society for the Psychological Study of
Social Issues.
DS63.2.U5D96   327′.0956   80-28763
ISBN 0-03-051061-9
ISBN 0-03-0640733 (pbk)

Published in 1981 (hbk) and 1983 (pbk) by Praeger Publishers
CBS Educational and Professional Publishing
a Division of CBS, Inc.
521 Fifth Avenue, New York, New York 10175 U.S.A.

©1981 by Praeger Publishers

3456789   145   987654321

Printed in the United States of America
on acid-free paper.

Dedicated with love to
my parents, Frances and Zoltan Rubin

CONTENTS

PART III: CONTEXTUAL ANALYSES OF KISSINGER'S INTERVENTION

PART IV: DISCUSSION

SPSSI FOREWORD

Throughout its history, the Society for the Psychological Study of Social Issues (SPSSI) has maintained a program of publishing materials relevant to its goal of applying social science knowledge to improve the understanding of social issues. This publishing program, in addition to the regular appearance of the Society's quarterly, the *Journal of Social Issues*, includes issuing books from time to time under its imprimatur. Because there is no established schedule for such books, nor an organizational requirement that any set number be published, both the publications committee and the Council of the organization are free to commission and select for publication only those manuscripts which meet their most stringent requirements for quality, timeliness, and relevance to important social issues.

It is my pleasure to introduce the present volume to its readership as an outstanding example of the applications of social science knowledge and methods of analysis to both a current broad social issue and to a more narrow example of that broad issue.

Conflict resolution is a wide-ranging topic in the behavioral sciences which has been approached in different ways in many arenas, ranging from resolving two-person marital conflict, to labor negotiations, to racial tensions, to international disputes. Third party intervention as an approach to conflict resolution similarly can have many facets. *Dynamics of Third Party Intervention* is about both those broad topics. But its focus on a single set of negotiations and a single third party provides a concrete anchor for what otherwise might be an abstruse discussion and set of generalizations. By sending each expert contributor the same list of questions to consider in composing his chapter, the book gained further focus and cohesion. The inclusion of authors from a variety of disciplines insured the examination of social science knowledge from more than one perspective and the application of more than one set of methods in analyzing the core data presented. This approach, designed and executed by the book's editor, Dr. Jeffrey Rubin, represents an innovative attack on the dimensions of the "elephant," as Rubin characterizes the focal issues. The organization of the book and the method used to develop it, are at one with the content in embodying the aims and principles of the Society which is sponsoring its publication. Not only does the book address a major social issue, but the mode of its organization makes its own contribution to the field.

Conflicts in the Middle East are far from resolved, so the book has relevance for both current and continuing specific issues. However, as our society moves into the postindustrial period, and as the development of our social fabric more and more weaves institutions and individuals into constant contact, both additional conflict and greater opportunity for third party intervention in its resolution can be anticipated. The material in this book therefore may foreshadow an area of increasing importance to behavioral scientists, and thus it represents an opportunity for SPSSI to make a contribution to future concerns as well as to immediate social and theoretical issues.

I congratulate the authors and editor on the quality of their papers, and I offer sincere thanks and appreciation for their generosity in contributing their work to the benefit of both our society and our Society.

Cynthia P. Deutsch
President (1979–1980), the Society for
the Psychological Study of Social Issues

PREFACE

A PERSONAL HISTORY OF THE PROJECT

Ideas have a way of occurring when one least expects them to, with consequences that could not have been foreseen. So it is with the idea that spawned the project culminating in this book. Back in fall 1977, my colleague Dan Druckman encouraged me to propose a symposium on third party intervention for the 1978 annual meeting of the International Studies Association (ISA). From the outset, the plan was to assemble a small group of experts on the resolution of disputes, each laboring in the vineyard of a different social science discipline, in order to invite exploration of the similarities and differences in assumptions, techniques, and approaches to intervention in conflict. In order to provide the experts with a lens through which points of similarity and departure in outlook could be viewed more clearly, it was decided to select a single illustration of third party intervention in international affairs for common appraisal.

With the kind assistance of Dan Druckman and Herb Kelman, a set of possible case studies was developed. These included the United States' intervention in the aftermath of the Turkish-Greek conflict in Cyprus in the 1970s, the 1954 American-British intervention in the partition of Trieste, the ongoing effort to mediate the conflict between the Dutch- and French-speaking peoples of Belgium, intervention in the conflict in Northern Ireland, the intervention by Japan, Cambodia, and the United States in the 1963–66 confrontation between Indonesia and Malaysia, and the efforts at mediation by Dr. Henry Kissinger in the aftermath of the 1973 Arab-Israeli War (the so-called October or Yom Kippur War). After some deliberation, the last of these cases was chosen for the symposium, not only because it constituted a particularly dramatic instance of intervention in a part of the world that was likely to be of concern for years to come, but also because an unusually interesting, gossipy, informative, and concise paper was available to describe the case: Ed Sheehan's (1976) article in *Foreign Policy*, "How Kissinger Did It: Step by Step in the Middle East."

Armed with an interesting case history and a fine panel of participants—Bill Zartman (a political scientist), Dean Pruitt (a social psychologist), and Tom Kochan (an industrial psychologist)—the roundtable symposium at the 1978 ISA meetings proved to be a success. The panelists were asked to address the following set of questions, basing their answers on the perspective provided by their own particular discipline: What should Kissinger's third party role have been? What did he do "right"? What mistakes did he make? Most generally, what is the unique or special contribution that each discipline can make to an understanding of third party intervention in international relations?

In a hotel corridor later in the day, France Pruitt (Dean's spouse) urged me to broaden the symposium to include representatives of other disciplines and persuasions, and to transform the project into a book. France's words of kind support were all that I needed and hoped to hear. This book thus emerged out of the encouragement of friends and colleagues, as well as the commitment of the symposium panelists to continue on as chapter contributors.

RATIONALE AND OBJECTIVES

Conflict is a ubiquitous phenomenon, arising in virtually all aspects of social life. Moreover, wherever conflict exists, impasses are occasionally likely to result. When such conflictual impasses fail to be resolved by the disputants themselves, this may lead to the intervention of a third party who attempts to facilitate the resolution of conflict. Regardless of whether impasses arise between individuals (as in marital conflict) groups (as in labor-management disputes), or nations (as in border disputes or arms control negotiations), third parties are apt to emerge, filling such widely varied roles as those of marriage counselor, mediator-arbitrator, and diplomat.

Despite the ubiquity of conflictual impasses and the number of third party roles to which these impasses have given rise, virtually no attempt has yet been made to compare and contrast the various approaches taken to third party intervention. Theorists and practitioners working in disciplines as diverse as social psychology, industrial and labor relations, political science, marital counseling, and international relations, have studied, discussed, and implemented various techniques of third party intervention. These efforts usually have occurred in isolation of one another, with little opportunity for interdisciplinary sharing of assumptions and insights. Like the wise men, each attempting to describe an elephant from the vantage point of his own idiosyncratic perspective, experts on third party intervention have tended to study conflict within the confines of their respective disciplines. In doing so, these experts have come to understand a part of the elephant rather than the beast as a whole. A first major purpose of this volume is therefore to provide a forum in which the assumptions and methods of various experts on third party intervention can be shared, and in which the points of similarity and difference in perspective can be better understood.

A second objective of this book is to understand better the process of dispute resolution in international affairs. Despite the best efforts at intervention by peacekeeping agencies such as the United Nations, as well as by representatives for individual nation-states, the record of successful conflict resolution in the international domain remains a rather dismal one; this is evident by the frequency with which international negotiations continue to founder and overt hostilities continue to erupt. Clearly there is room for renewed critical appraisal of the process by which third parties can, should, and actually do intervene in international conflict. This volume provides some of this much needed appraisal by focusing attention on a dramatic and important recent case history of third party intervention in international conflict.

WHY A SINGLE ELEPHANT?

The great virtue of selecting a single case study for critical examination by a group of experts on third party intervention is that it provides a common focus of attention about which experts can comment from the vantage point of their own discipline. The reader should thereby be afforded a unique opportunity to observe the points of similarity and contrast that emerge when each of a number of scholars, working from assumptions that may be strikingly different, is asked to develop an interpretation of a single set of facts. The potential disadvantage of focusing attention on a single case history is that it becomes impossible to develop insights and generalizations that can be applied with confidence to all instances of third party intervention. However, no single case history, no matter how carefully chosen, can realistically serve as an archetype of the more general class it is meant to represent; each account is colored by unique properties and twists, idiosyncrasies that help to make the account interesting and worthy of study in the first place. Therefore, rather than become trapped in the quest for the perfect exemplar(s) of third party intervention, a case history was selected on the basis of its political significance, the richness of detail in which the case was described, and the degree to which it was likely to prove stimulating for authors and readers with diverse backgrounds.

WHY KISSINGER?

The case history selected for examination in this book describes the period of Dr. Henry Kissinger's step-by-step diplomacy in the Middle East. From the outset of the October War in 1973, until the conclusion of the final round of Arab-Israeli disengagement negotiations in August 1975, U.S. Secretary of State Kissinger engaged in a unique and important form of third party intervention. His efforts lasted nearly two years, taking him on over a dozen missions covering more than 300,000 miles of flying back and forth between Washington and the capital cities of the Middle East, requiring thousands of hours of negotiations, and resulting in three disengagement agreements between Israel and its Arab neighbors.

Kissinger's intervention was accompanied by, and no doubt helped give shape to, several important changes in the Middle East policies of the United States, policies whose consequences are being felt even today. The 1973–75 era of step-by-step diplomacy thus constitutes far more than a historical curiosity; it is an illustration of third party intervention in international conflict with dramatic and far-reaching implications for the manner in which the Middle East conflict is being waged today and is likely to be managed in the months and years to come.

Another objective of this book is to understand better one facet of the multimedia performance of the central figure in this Middle East drama: Dr. Henry Kissinger. The style and substance of Kissinger's movements on the world stage for more than a decade have had a way of commanding enormous interest. He is a star whose energy and intensity have continually lit up the sky for all to see. It has therefore proven impossible to write a book that addresses his intervention in the aftermath of the October War without speculating about the nature of Kissinger the man, as well as the motives, intentions, and expectations that organized his mediational efforts. In a sense, Kissinger's mediation between 1973 and 1975 was selected for study precisely because he was so central a figure. Larger than life almost, a caricature of third party intervention technique, Kissinger was by no means a typical mediator. He was and is, however, a figure whose proportions invite the gauge and the measure. In the lingua franca of the wise men parable, Kissinger was and is an elephant of extraordinary palpability, complexity, and subtlety.

THE CONTRIBUTING CAST OF CHARACTERS

The task of assembling the chapter contributors proved to be almost as much fun as working on the book itself. I am proud and delighted to have succeeded in assembling a personal All-Star Team of experts in various aspects of the conflict resolution process. The contributors were deliberately invited from a variety of disciplines. Although no attempt was made to pursue a Noah's Ark arrangement—with one or more exemplars representing every persuasion, practice, or profession—a premium was placed on diversity, and homogeneity of outlook was discouraged whenever possible. Here, then, the All-Star Team:

> From the University of Maryland, Dave Bobrow, a fine political scientist who was armtwisted and cajoled into a contribution on a bus ride late at night in the depths of the Israeli West Bank.
> From the Mathematica Corporation, an experimental social psychologist, Dan Druckman, strategist, analyst of international cable traffic, pundit, and prime mover of this project's prime mover.
> From the Harvard Law School, Roger Fisher, the distinguished scholar and author who provided me with much of the strong support, guidance, and good ideas necessary to transform the symposium into a book-length manuscript.

From the University of Minnesota's Quigley Center, a bright and engaging political scientist, Terry Hopmann, with a long-standing interest in both international relations and the negotiation process.

From the Sloan School of Management at MIT, Tom Kochan, an industrial psychologist with both research interests and practical experience in the domain of public sector negotiation.

From Rutgers University, another social psychologist, Ken Kressel, who has written extensively on labor-management mediation and who has worked for the last several years in a rather different mediation role, that of couple therapist.

From SUNY-Buffalo, my friend and colleague, Dean Pruitt, an experimental social psychologist with long-standing research interest in bargaining and negotiation as well as international dispute resolution.

From the American Arbitration Association, where he retired as president in order to establish and head its Research Institute, Don Straus, an expert on mediation and arbitration in labor-management disputes.

And finally, from New York University, Bill Zartman, a political scientist who has written widely about both dispute resolution in various international arenas and the nature of the bargaining process.

THE CONTRIBUTORS' ASSIGNMENT

I have painfully discovered that an editor, like an effective third party, must learn the lesson of flexibility. The best laid plans have a nasty propensity to go awry, and editors and third parties alike must know when surrender is the shortest route to success—in this case, a completed book. At the project's outset, the contributors were given a background reading assignment, an organizational structure for their chapters, and a set of questions that were to be addressed. Although the authors prepared themselves carefully for this difficult task, they unfortunately did not always choose to follow the format I had recommended or answer the questions I had posed. Rather, like the Boston driver in the presence of a red light, they tended to regard my signal as "advisory."

Background Reading

Apart from the importance of Kissinger's efforts at step-by-step diplomacy in the Middle East, it happens that his work during this period has been described in rich and interesting detail in a number of articles and books. In addition to factual accounts of the events surrounding the October War and its aftermath, there are also several fascinating, behind-the-scenes descriptions of Kissinger's conversations with, and attitudes toward, the principals in the Middle East negotiations. The materials that were to be read by each of the contributing authors consisted of:

Sheehan, Edward R. F. "How Kissinger Did It: Step by Step in the Middle East." *Foreign Policy* 22 (1976):3–70. This is a brief introduction to the events, motives, and attitudes surrounding Kissinger's intervention. Because it is so well written, concise, and fascinating a background account, it has been reprinted in its entirety as Chapter 2 of this book.

Sheehan, Edward R. F. *The Arabs, Israelis, and Kissinger.* New York: Reader's Digest Press, 1976. This is a book-length elaboration of Sheehan's *Foreign Policy* article, as well as a piece that appeared in the *New York Times Sunday Magazine.*

Quandt, William B. *Decade of Decisions: American Policy toward the Arab-Israeli Conflict, 1967–1976.* Berkeley: University of California Press, 1977. Pp. 165–252. This is an excellent historical account of the events of the 1973–75 period, written by a man who served for a period as a member of the National Security Council under President Carter.

Golan, Matti. *The Secret Conversations of Henry Kissinger: Step-by-Step Diplomacy in the Middle East.* New York: Quadrangle, 1976. As the title suggests, this is a largely behind-the-scenes account of Kissinger's actions during the shuttle diplomacy era, written by an Israeli journalist.

Kalb, Marvin, and Kalb, Bernard. *Kissinger.* Boston: Little, Brown, 1974. Pp. 450–542. Another background piece, written by the American journalist brothers, it provides additional information about Kissinger's moves and motives.

Chapter Structure and Organization

The contributors were told that their chapters should consist of two sections, approximately equal in length: in the first section they were to analyze Kissinger's intervention as a third party as specifically and concretely as possible; in the second section they were asked to back away from the details of their critique and present, as explicitly as possible, the assumptions about conflict, conflict resolution, bargaining, and third party intervention that guided their previous analysis.

All the contributors honored this important requirement by critiquing Kissinger's intervention, as well as advancing some of the assumptions that guided their analysis. These sections were by no means equal in length (it proved easier to critique Kissinger than to describe one's assumptions about the nature of conflict), nor were they necessarily addressed in the order intended. It is fair to say, however, that each chapter contains material written both from a proximal and a more distal perspective.

In their analysis of Kissinger's intervention, the contributors were to address the following set of general questions:

- How would you characterize, overall, the distinguishing features (the style and substance) of Kissinger's step-by-step diplomacy? What, in your judgment, did he try to do? What did he accomplish?
- Would you characterize Kissinger's intervention, overall, as effective or ineffective? If effective, how, in what ways? If ineffective, why? What should Kissinger have done? What should his role have been? What could he have done? What advice would you have given him?
- To what extent do you attribute the outcomes of Kissinger's step-by-step diplomacy to Kissinger the person? Would anyone in Kissinger's shoes have accomplished the same results? For that matter, to what extent do you believe that the outcomes of Kissinger's intervention would have resulted even in the absence of any third party intervention? In other words, to what extent was third party intervention unnecessary?

In addition, the authors were asked to address a set of more specific questions regarding Kissinger's intervention. It was simply not possible, without seriously disrupting the ebb and flow of each chapter, to clearly demarcate the authors' answers to these questions. Nevertheless, it is fair to say that in the case of almost every chapter, these specific questions were answered.

In addressing themselves to the following questions, the authors were to indicate not only whether they believed Kissinger's intervention was correct, appropriate, or otherwise, but also what they would have advised him (or someone in his place) to do:

- During the last days of November 1973, as plans were being made for the Geneva conference, Israeli General Yariv and Egyptian General Gamasy began to negotiate a Sinai disengagement directly. According to several reports, Kissinger expressed his displeasure with this experiment in direct negotiations between the disputants. Was Kissinger's intervention appropriate in this instance? What would you have advised him to do?
- On December 7, 1973, Israeli Defense Minister Dayan informed Kissinger of an Israeli proposal to disengage immediately in the Mitla and Giddi passes, in exchange for an Egyptian commitment to reopen the Suez Canal. Kissinger apparently advised against this proposal, urging the Israelis to move slowly in the negotiations and thereby maintain an appearance of strength. Quandt (1977) describes the rationale for Kissinger's position as follows: "It was important for the Arabs to see that it was difficult for the United States to influence Israel, otherwise their expectations would soar"

(p. 221). Do you agree with Kissinger's analysis of this situation? What would you have advised Kissinger to say or do?

• On May 8, 1974, as negotiations were taking place for an Israeli-Syrian disengagement in the Golan Heights, Kissinger met with President Assad in Damascus. Although Israeli leaders had recently discussed with Kissinger a number of concessions they would be willing to make, Kissinger disclosed only some of these concessions to Assad, apparently withholding others so that he would have something to present to Assad on future trips. Quandt (1977) observes: "Kissinger felt that he had to avoid whetting Assad's already substantial appetite for Israeli concessions, while at the same time being able to show continued progress" (p. 241). What would you have advised Kissinger to do in this situation?

• During August 1974, in the immediate aftermath of Nixon's resignation, Kissinger had to decide which of two rather different possibilities for future negotiated settlement to pursue next. One possibility was to continue the use of step-by-step diplomacy in order to push for a Jordanian-Israeli settlement that would deal with the sensitive political issues of the West Bank and Palestinian sovereignty. These issues were (and still are) enormously important, and failure to resolve them to the satisfaction of Jordan and Israel might have slowed the momentum toward settlement that Kissinger hoped to create. The second, less risky possibility for negotiated settlement consisted of a quick move on the Egyptian-Israeli front, leading to a disengagement agreement concerning the Sinai passes and Egyptian oil fields. It was this second possibility that Kissinger elected to pursue. What choice would you have advised Kissinger to make? Why?

Finally, having addressed themselves to several general and specific issues regarding Kissinger's intervention in the wake of the October War, the authors were asked to describe, as explicitly as possible, the assumptions about conflict, bargaining, and third party intervention that guided their critical analysis. In other words, having analyzed Kissinger's assumptions and methods as a third party, they were now to carefully analyze their own assumptions and methods as well. The questions to which the authors were asked to address their attention included: What do you believe to be the attributes of an "ideal," optimally effective third party? What is the role of an ideal third party? What functions should a third party perform? At what point(s) in an escalating conflict should a third party (be called upon to) intervene? What kind of conflict should a third party avoid, lest his or her intervention prove disruptive or inappropriate? What kind of conflict is best suited to the intervention of a third party? These questions were designed not to constrain or otherwise limit the contributors' analysis of assumptions; rather, they were meant to illustrate the sorts of general concerns to which they should direct their attention.

PLAN OF THE BOOK

This book contains four parts, consisting of two introductory chapters, eight core chapters, and a commentary.

Part I: Background

In Chapter 1 I attempt to introduce the reader to the issue of third party intervention: what it is, what is known about the many roles and functions of third parties, and what are some of the remaining unanswered questions about third party effectiveness. In Chapter 2, Edward R. F. Sheehan's 1976 article in *Foreign Policy* is reprinted in its entirety. It is hoped that this paper will provide the reader who is unfamiliar with the details of Kissinger's intervention with the background necessary to follow its many twists and turns. Sheehan's article is true to its title: it is indeed a step-by-step, blow-by-blow recapitulation of much of Kissinger's journey from 1973 to 1975. It outlines the details of the three major disengagement settlements in which Kissinger was instrumentally involved: first, the disengagement between the Egyptian and Israeli armies in the immediate aftermath of the October War; second, the Israeli-Syrian disengagement in the Golan Heights; and finally, the second Egyptian-Israeli disengagement in the Mitla and Giddi passes of the Sinai desert.

A word or two of caution may be in order. Although the Sheehan piece is reprinted here in order to provide necessary background information, the facts presented should not be confused with Sheehan's interpretation of them. When it first appeared, this article generated a considerable hue and cry among Kissinger and his many watchers, and perhaps for good reason. The Sheehan article is spicy, blunt, and thought provoking. As such, I consider it to be a fine introduction to Kissinger's intervention in the Middle East arena. All the more reason, however, for the reader to seek out some of the many other available books and articles for study as well.

Part II: Analyses of Kissinger the Actor

Chapters 3 through 10 comprise the book's core chapters. Rather than present the chapters in simple alphabetical order or in some Noah's Ark array, I have elected to group them according to a simple, post-hoc, organizational plan. Thus, although all the chapters reflect an awareness of both Kissinger's unique role as well as the political and psychological context in which this role was enacted, they differ in the emphasis placed on one of these themes rather than the other. Part II contains the four chapters that come closest to analyzing Kissinger's diplomacy in relation to the particular set of intervention tactics that he chose to adopt.

Chapter 3, by Roger Fisher, develops the position that although Kissinger was most effective at the art of gamesmanship, he may have been playing the wrong game. In Chapter 4, Tom Kochan analyzes Kissinger's intervention from the perspective of the labor-mediation process. Chapter 5, by Dean Pruitt, anchors a detailed analysis of

Kissinger's intervention tactics in the social psychological literature on mediation. Finally, in Chapter 6, Bill Zartman attempts to explain the disengagements that resulted from Kissinger's intervention by analyzing his strategy and tactics in terms of the negotiation process.

Part III: Contextual Analyses of Kissinger's Intervention

The four chapters in this section are fundamentally alike in their appreciation of the importance of the context in which intervention occurs. Chapter 7, by Dave Bobrow, places Kissinger's intervention as a "biased intermediary" in the context of great power foreign policy. In Chapter 8, Terry Hopmann and Dan Druckman analyze Kissinger's mediation in relation to the parties' readiness for negotiation, as well as Kissinger's own inclination to pursue a particular strategy and set of tactics. Chapter 9, by Ken Kressel, develops the position that Kissinger's intervention can be understood as an illustration of the effects of role strain on international mediation. In Chapter 10, Don Straus analyzes Kissinger's diplomacy in the Middle East as an effort to cope with enormous social and informational complexity.

Part IV: Discussion

Chapter 11 concludes the book with a commentary on the preceding material. In this chapter I have attempted to sift through the contributed chapters for points of similarity and departure, overlap and distinction, in the hope of pointing the way toward a more general theoretical statement concerning the nature of third party intervention.

A WORD ABOUT THE BOOK'S SPONSORSHIP

One of the divisions of the American Psychological Association is a nonprofit organization known as the Society for the Psychological Study of Social Issues (SPSSI). Throughout the forty or so years since it was founded, SPSSI has attempted to apply social-scientific theory and research findings to the study of social issues. SPSSI's primary concern is education rather than social advocacy. Its "business," in effect, is the identification and analysis of social issues, particularly those issues whose understanding may be enhanced through social-scientific theory and research. SPSSI's ongoing activities include the publication of a quarterly journal, the *Journal of Social Issues*, the provision of grants-in-aid to investigators engaged in socially relevant psychological research, the award of several annual prizes for distinguished contributions, and the sponsorship of books that the Society believes reflect its interests.

Several of the book's contributors, including the editor, expressed an interest, as active SPSSI members, in seeking the Society's sponsorship. The book's other contributors, although not (yet) SPSSI members, kindly consented to this arrangement, and SPSSI agreed to assume the role of sponsor. In exchange for the endorsement and imprimatur of this distinguished Society, the authors and editor have agreed to have SPSSI receive all book royalties, such as these may be. I therefore wish to take advantage of this moment of access to the printed page to thank my colleagues for their generosity and goodwill.

ACKNOWLEDGMENTS

In addition to reiterating my deep gratitude to Dan Druckman, Herb Kelman, and France Pruitt for their early advice and encouragement, and to Bill Zartman, Dean Pruitt, and Tom Kochan for their willingness to serve as cannon fodder at the initial symposium and then come back for more punishment as chapter contributors, I wish to acknowledge the help and good wishes of the following individuals: Chick Judd who, in the earliest days of the project, was always willing to lend an ear and help shape an idea; Larry Wrightsman, member of the SPSSI editorial advisory board, peripatetic Scrabble player, sage, critic, and dear friend, who nurtured me at every step along the way; Phil Brickman and Frank Stech, the other two members of the SPSSI advisory board, as well as Marilynn Brewer (the cochair of SPSSI's publications committee), who provided the chapter contributors with detailed and constructive comments and suggestions, and provided me with the impetus to finish; Zoltan Rubin, my father, who kindly supplied me with many interesting historical and literary examples of third party intervention in conflict; Bill Smith, who gave me what I needed most in order to finish: time; Bob Miller of the Tufts Department of Religion, who provided many more fascinating illustrations of third parties in the Bible than I could possibly use; Carol, David, Sarah, and Noah Rubin, who made it such fun to come home at the end of a day in the library; Dan Nathanson, who quickly and skillfully provided me with a map of the Middle East; Joel Brockner, Jean Hiltrop, Barbara Kellerman, Sinaia Nathanson, Carol Rubin, Walt Swap, and Dave Swinney, who kindly agreed to read through portions of the manuscript; Jackie Ellis, who spent many an hour transforming chicken scratching into typescript; Joseph Komidar, the Tufts University Librarian, who generously availed me of a faculty study in which the last, lingering touches of this book could be completed in monastic bliss; and Frank Russo, Jr., who kept my means of transportation in running order to the very end.

Without the financial, spiritual, and temporal support of the following institutions, this work would have taken far longer to reach fruition: Tufts University, Harvard University, the John Simon Guggenheim Memorial Foundation, the National Science Foundation, and the Society for the Psychological Study of Social Issues. Finally, I wish to thank the publishers of *Foreign Policy* for their generosity in granting permission to reprint the Sheehan article in its entirety, at no cost.

0 20 40

Miles

ISRAELI BORDERS PRIOR TO 1967 WAR ----------

ISRAELI BORDERS TODAY ——— · ——— · ———

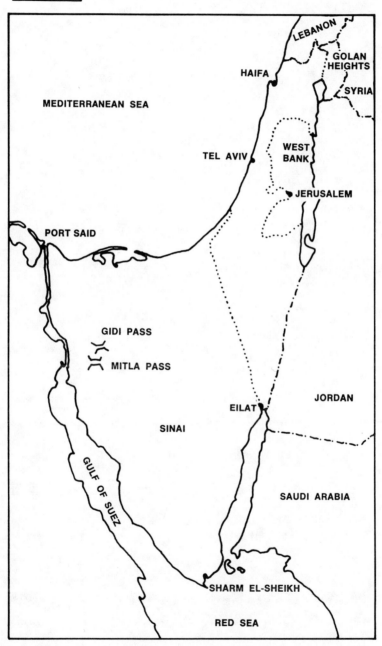

LEBANON

GOLAN
HEIGHTS

HAIFA

SYRIA

MEDITERRANEAN SEA

TEL AVIV

WEST
BANK

JERUSALEM

PORT SAID

GIDI PASS

MITLA PASS

JORDAN

EILAT

SINAI

GULF OF SUEZ

SAUDI ARABIA

SHARM EL-SHEIKH

RED SEA

PART I

BACKGROUND

1

INTRODUCTION
Jeffrey Z. Rubin

The purpose of this chapter is to set the stage for the subsequent case analysis chapters by introducing the reader to the nature, roles, and functions of third parties. Because the following chapter describes the details of Henry Kissinger's two-year tour of duty as a mediator in the Middle East, little effort will be made here to characterize his intervention. Rather, the focus of this chapter is more general and is designed to introduce the reader to some of the properties underlying the many illustrations of third party intervention.

The history of third party intervention in conflict is probably as old as the history of humanity itself. People have always had a nasty propensity for stirring up conflict between and among themselves.* All too often, such conflict has resulted in the extreme solutions of either total domination or total withdrawal by one or more of the parties. The very extremity and long-term unacceptability of these solutions, in turn, has provided the raison d'etre for more integrative alternatives.

THE STORY OF WISE KING SOLOMON

One of the earliest and most dramatic illustrations of a third party's potential effectiveness comes from the pages of the Old Testament (I Kings 3:16–28). King Solomon sat in judgment of two women, each

---

*Merely consider, for example, the large number of words in the English language that begin with the prefix "dis" (discord, disagreement, dissonance, disruption, disunity, dispute, and so forth), thereby denoting a state of conflict.

claiming to be the mother of the same young child. As is often the case in protracted conflict, the issue in dispute was constant-sum in nature: only one of the women could be the child's true mother. Moreover, the only really acceptable outcome to the conflict was constant-sum as well; thus, apart from an awkward, and in those days untenable, shared custody arrangement or the physical division of the child at the expense of its life, there was no way to resolve the conflict other than by awarding the child to one woman rather than the other. Given that each woman claimed the proprietary right to the same child, how could the king render a wise decision?

King Solomon may well have realized that in order to resolve the issue of parentage he would have to move beyond the superficial proprietary implications of being a parent to the underlying implication of parental concern and love. Thus, although a bogus parent might claim ownership of a child as readily as the true parent, only the latter might be expected to demonstrate genuine regard for the child's welfare. It was precisely by pitting parental proprietary rights against parental concern that King Solomon was able to determine the true parent. He called for a sword and commanded that the living child be divided in two, giving half to one woman and half to the other. The true mother then beseeched the king, rather than slay the child, to give it to the second woman—leading King Solomon to award the child to the first woman, its true parent.

Notice that the third party in this account, through the subtlety of his understanding of human motivation, was able to move an apparently intractable conflict to solution. By sorting out the underlying issue from its more superficial counterpart, by testing the disputants' commitment to particular positions and the basis for this commitment, and by transforming the size and scope of the issue in question, King Solomon was able to impose an arbitrated agreement that had the additional virtue of further enhancing his own reputation as a wise and just leader.

Although the intervention of third parties is not always so neat, coherent, effective, and reputation enhancing, the tale of King Solomon is illustrative of the potential of third parties for skilled and insightful behavior. By examining the many roles and functions that third parties provide, and by considering some of the many factors that contribute to their effectiveness, it should be possible to move toward a more general conceptual understanding of the third party process.

BARGAINING AND THIRD PARTY INTERVENTION: SOME DEFINITIONAL CONSIDERATIONS AND ASSUMPTIONS

Once conflict has arisen between two or more parties, it is necessary that they develop integrative solutions to their dispute if they are to avoid the extreme alternatives of total domination or total withdrawal by one side. One of these alternatives, bargaining, functions at the interface of cooperative and competitive interests. For bargaining to occur, the disputants must be sufficiently competitive in their outlook that each wishes and hopes to extract an agreement that is more favorable to oneself than the other is willing to provide, while at the same time being sufficiently cooperative that they are willing to negotiate this relative advantage through the (verbal) exchange of offers and counteroffers. In bargaining each side hopes to do better than the other, but each can do only as well as the other is willing to tolerate through the agreement that is reached. Because bargaining theory and research has been extensively reviewed elsewhere, nothing more need be said here about this important method for achieving conflict resolution. (See Chertkoff and Esser [1976], Druckman [1977], Morley and Stephenson [1977], Nemeth [1972], Pruitt [1981], Pruitt and Kimmel [1977], Rubin and Brown [1975], and Zartman [1978].)

The second major alternative, and the focus of the present inquiry, is third party intervention. Like bargaining, third party intervention also emerges at the interface of cooperative and competitive interests, although in a rather different way. Here the parties' competitive inclinations are presumed to dominate to such an extent that the disputants are unable or unwilling to reach agreement of their own accord; each wants so much and/or is willing to concede so little that a conflictual impasse tends to result. Given this impasse, however, the disputants are sufficiently cooperative that they are willing to invite or accept the intrusion of one or more external (third) parties who may be able to break the conflictual stalemate.

Stated most simply, a third party is an individual who is in some way external to a dispute between two other parties, and who interposes (or is interposed) between them. Were it not for the two others in dispute (the principals in effect), there would be no need for a third party. Indeed, by virtue of its very semantic construction, the term "third party" implies the existence, the reality, of at least two others about which several things appear evident: the principals were there first (namely, first and second). Had they not been there first, there would have been no third; the third party is thus spawned by the relationship between the other two. Additionally, because the principals were there first, their exchange takes precedence over any relationship that the third party might have with either of them. The role and involvement of a third party are thus typically peripheral to the primary relationship. Moreover, should the third party become centrally involved in the relationship between the two principals, thereby transforming a dyad into a triad, the basis of the third party's involvement is necessarily different than that of the disputants. Over time, the third party may become enormously important, even transcendent, so much so that the relationship between the principals could no longer continue without the third; yet even here, the third party must be seen as an outgrowth of the relationship between the first two, and as having a set of relationships that are qualitatively different than that between the principals.

One of the most dramatic and powerful illustrations of the preceding structural analysis can be found in the very basis of New Testament theology. According to the Old Testament, a covenant exists between God and man: follow Torah (God's law) and God will be satisfied; the wicked will suffer, while the righteous will prosper and be saved. According to New Testament theology, however, this covenant between the "principals" cannot be followed because of man's inherent sinfulness, what John Calvin described as "moral color blindness." As a result, ongoing enmity exists between God and man. It is Jesus, the Son of God, whose emergence, sacrifice, and transcendent importance signal the possibility of an end to the conflictual impasse. Thus, it is written in I Timothy 2:5-6, "For there is one God, and one mediator between God and men, the man Christ Jesus; who gave himself a ransom for all, to be testified in due time." °

Quite apart from the fact that the very term "third party" implies the existence of a relationship between at least two others, the term has a second important structural implication: namely, that the stability of the dyad is about to be shaken by the inclusion of a third person. Early in this century, the sociologist Georg Simmel (1902) observed that people prefer, and attempt to function in, one-to-one, dyadic relationships. Given the formation of a triad, there is a powerful tendency for a coalition of two persons to form at the exclusion of the third—with the excluded third constantly attempting to form a dyadic relationship with one of the other two. As Sartre (1955) has demonstrated in his play *No Exit*, and as attested to by the fluidity of changing relationships among such international groupings as USA–USSR–China or USA–Egypt–Israel, the presence of a triad tends to generate movement toward one of several dyadic possibilities.

The inclusion of a third party in a dispute between two principals thus invites the formation of a coalition between one disputant and the third party, as when the third party favors (or is believed to favor) the position of one person over the other; it also invites the development of a coalition between the two principals at the exclusion of the third party, as when the disputants share the belief that the third party has a hidden agenda and is apt to intercede in ways that may be mutually costly. Regardless of whether these possible coalitions are long term in nature or, as is far more likely, are only temporary arrangements, and regardless of

---

° Other biblical passages attesting to the emergence of Jesus as a third party may be found in Romans 3:23–25, 5:6–21, 6:5–8, 8:17, and in John 1:29–36.

whether they are based on actual variations in third party behavior or the disputants' perceptions alone, the inclusion of a third party tends to shake the dyadic system. This is so by virtue of the third party's mere presence and structural inclusion, and is entirely independent of anything that party may say or do.

The inclusion of a third party creates two distinct possibilities for increased turbulence. On the one hand, in a protracted conflict betwen disputants who are deeply entrenched in intransigent pos tions, the mere presence of a third party may generate pressure for movement from the stable stagnation of intractable conflict. On the other hand, in a conflictual relationship that is characterized by rapid escalation—as well as the threat, counterthreat, bluff, deceit, and deployment of resources that accompany such escalation—the third party's inclusion may make it possible to disrupt this pattern of conflict intensification, by shifting the disputants' exclusive focus away from each other. In either case, the effect of the third party's presence is to modify the nature and basis of interchange between the principals, and for this reason alone the intervention of a third party is likely to have powerful, and often enormously helpful, consequences.*

A PARTIAL LISTING OF THIRD PARTY ROLES

Having briefly examined some of the definitional considerations and assumptions that are implicit in the very term "third party," attention should now be paid to third party roles and functions: who they are, in effect, and what they do. Although it is possible to distinguish third party roles from third party functions, as the following analysis will suggest, one should not lose sight of the fact that the distinction is often fuzzy at best. The role of go-between, for example, is descriptive of its function of going between the principals. Simitarly, the occupant of a fact finder role has the function of "finding facts." These illustrations of conceptual fuzziness notwithstanding, it is useful to distinguish the range of variety of roles that third parties occupy from the functions and services they provide.

Although third party roles can be characterized in any number of

---

*An important implication of the preceding analysis is that because of the disruptive effects of a third party's inclusion, that party may not only not facilitate dispute resolution, but also may hinder it. Consider the possibility that a third party's intervention in a conflict that is already on its downward slope, where the principals are already working effectively together on the resolution of their dispute, may have the effect of disrupting this productive momentum and slowing the pace of settlement. If so, it is incumbent upon a third party who wishes to facilitate dispute resolution to judge the size and course of conflict, and to intervene only (or especially) when the conflict is on its upward slope or when an impasse has been reached.

ways, it may be of heuristic value to present these roles in terms of a series of bipolar continua along which third parties tend to lie. Bear in mind that third parties typically occupy several roles simultaneously (for example, the formal, content-oriented, and conflict preventive roles of a baseball umpire), and that in the course of their intervention they may move from one end of a role continuum toward the other (for example, a mediator who is process oriented at first and then becomes innreasingly content oriented). The following listing is presented in no particular order of importance and is meant to be suggestive rather than exhaustive.

Formal versus Informal Roles

Most third parties have their roles defined either legally or on the basis of some formal understanding among the principals. The legitimacy, impartiality, and authority of these formal third party roles may be the result of tradition and/or consensus or, on occasion, may be the outgrowth of licensing or certification procedures. Formal third party roles include those of mediator: a person who attempts to help the disputants reach a voluntary agreement; fact finder: a person who listens to arguments from the principals in order to ascertain the facts surrounding the (potential) dispute in question, and who subsequently makes recommendations for settlement (real estate brokers in Western societies typically occupy this role); arbitrator or referee, umpire, or judge: a person empowered to make binding recommendations for the settlement of a dispute; and ombudsman: a person charged with the resolution of conflicts that arise between individuals and institutions. In sum, formal third parties may be said to be in the business of dispute resolution.

In contrast, more informal third party roles tend to arise not out of tradition, law, or formal agreement, but because of some need to implement rather narrowly defined, short-lived, and informal functions. Thus, one of the disputants may unilaterally appoint a special envoy to convey a particular message to the other, as when President John F. Kennedy asked his brother Robert to indicate U.S. intentions to Soviet Ambassador Dobrynin during the 1962 Cuban missile crisis. A go-between may be enlisted by one of the disputants or may volunteer his or her services in order to carry transmissions back and forth between principals who are unable or unwilling to communicate directly; consider here the 1979–80 crisis between Iran and the United States during which a number of individuals—including former Attorney-General Ramsey Clark, an emissary of Pope John Paul II, leaders of the PLO, and the secretary-general of the United Nations—offered to serve as a conduit for bilateral communication.

Regardless of the particular function the informal third party is asked, or volunteers, to provide (be it communication, the arrangement of a meeting place or meeting time, and so forth), the role carries with it little or no presumption of legitimacy of impartiality. Because informal roles typically emerge out of unilateral considerations on the part of one of the disputants, the other is likely (often accurately) to regard the third party as a spokesperson for the interests of the first. Occupants of informal third party roles therefore tend to be viewed with greater suspicion than more formal third parties.

Both formal and informal third party roles have existed for thousands of years, as can be readily seen in the Bible. For example, as described in Deuteronomy 17:8–13, Old Testament law established the scribes (Levites) as formal third parties with binding decision-making power. The scribes often sat by the gates of the city and were available to resolve the many and varied controversies and arguments that might arise. Or consider the role of kings such as Solomon and Ahasuerus vis-à-vis dispute resolution. When Haman, the prime minister of King Ahasuerus, argued that Mordecai and the Jews were not law abiding and should therefore be destroyed, it was the king who was required to adjudicate the conflict.

Less obvious and less frequent, although no less interesting, are the biblical illustrations of more informal third party roles. Consider here the impromptu, time-limited role of Naomi, who served as something of a marriage broker between Boaz and her daughter-in-law, Ruth (Ruth 4:1–9). There also were situations in which Jesus or one of the Apostles either assumed or was asked to assume a dispute resolution role, as when Jesus intervened in the conflict between the two sisters, Mary and Martha (Luke 10:38–42), when Jesus intervened on behalf of the sinful woman (John 8:1–12), and when Paul wrote to Philemon about the latter's former slave, Onesimus (Philemon 10–19).

Individual versus Representative and Collective Roles

Although it is typically the case that a third party is a single individual, this person is often the spokesperson or representative of some group, organization, or other collectivity. As such, the third party might be expected to have far greater legitimacy and power than would occur were the party to function without this constituency. Consider the example of a mediator for the Federal Mediation and Conciliation Service (FMCS) who intervenes in a labor-management dispute not only as an individual but also as the spokesperson for the interests of the U.S. federal government; it is surely no accident that FMCS conference rooms often have the seal of the United States of America prominently displayed on the wall behind the federat mediator. Similarly, the secretary-general speaks for the United Nations and its member governments, the Pope speaks for the Vatican and world Catholicism, and the U.S. secretary of state represents the interests, power, and authority of the United States government.

Aye, and there's the rub! The third party's legitimacy is likely to be enhanced by the role of spokesperson for a constituency only so long as this constituency is regarded by the principals as reasonably impartial. To the extent that the collectivity represented has, or is believed to have, a vested interest in a particular dispute outcome, the third party's legitimacy may be adversely affected, and may actually be less than would occur were the party to intervene as a private citizen. As a third party spokesman for the United States government in international affairs, the Secretary of State may be hamstrung by the disputants' suspicion of U.S. foreign policy and its underlying motives.

In short, the presence of a third party constituency functions as a two-edged sword, amplifying the disputants' interest, and concern about, the impartiality, legitimacy, and clout of the collectivity of which the third party is representative. In addition, whereas the unencumbered, individual third party is responsible only to the disputants and a personal sense of wise and appropriate behavior, the third party as representative is accountable to a constituency. As such, the third party is subjected to constituency pressure to behave in particular ways vis-à-vis the principals; even if not so pressured, the disputents may suspect the third party of vulnerability in this regard, either now or in the future.

Occasionally a third party is not an individual at all, but rather some sort of social conglomerate. Umpires and referees at sporting events sometimes assume this collective role, as do the members of a military tribunal or judicial board. In general, as one moves from individual to collective third party roles, it appears that third party functioning is both more interesting and far more complex. Functioning in unison, a collective third party can be far more effective than a single individual; a unanimous decision by the members of the United States Supreme Court or the World Court in The Hague carries far more collective weight than the combined sum of its individual component judgments.

On the other hand, a collectively functioning third party is also more vulnerable to division, rupture, and the accessibility of individual members of the third party to differential pressure and social influence. Even this has its merits, as when the disputants trust different third party members who are able, in turn, to forge an acceptable agreement that would otherwise have been far more difficult to achieve. On the whole, however, the presence of third party members with divergent points of view is likely to have a deleterious effect on dispute resolution, primarily because the principals may develop an illusory sense of their own bargaining strength and distance from agreement.

Consider the 1971 takeover by the inmates of Attica prison in upstate New York, an event that ended in the tragic death of 43 people. A collective third party became involved in this dispute, consisting of more than two dozen people, some of whom were invited to come to Attica while others simply showed up; some of whom saw themselves as partial to the prisoners while others clearly favored the guards (and the penal system they represented). Abetted by those third party members who appeared partial to their cause, the inmates developed an illusory sense of their chances of being granted amnesty by Governor Rockefeller and being given a plane that would fly them to freedom in Africa. For their part, those third party members who were partial to the prison system tended to add fuel to the belief of Commissioner Oswald and Governor Rockefeller that the lives of the hostages were in danger and that the dispute was a long way from settlement.

Invited versus Noninvited Roles

It is often the case that third parties are sought out for assistance by one or both of the disputants in an effort to forestall or reduce conflict. The third party is invited to enter the fray, perhaps to assist in identifying the issues in dispute and to recommend or impose a settlement. Implicit in such an invited third party role are two assumptions: first, the disputants are sufficiently motivated to address their conflict that one or both of them are willing to enlist the services of a third party; and second, the third party is regarded as sufficiently attractive by one or both disputants that this party is invited to intervene rather than some other individual.

From the third party's vantage point, an invited role is desirable both because it suggests that the disputants are ready to work and because the third party is placed in a unique position to exercise influence. Consider in this regard the example of a married couple in a troubled relationship that seeks the services of a couple therapist. The very act of seeking or being referred to a particular therapist indicates that at least one member of the pair is motivated to work on the marriage (while the other is at least willing to oblige this concern), and that the therapist can begin to work from a position of relative strength.

It should be kept in mind in this example that one or both members of the couple may seek the services of a therapist not out of a genuine desire to resolve conflict, but for a tactical reason, such as to "prove" to one's partner that one is the more hard working, sincere, and committed marriage partner, thereby attempting to gain points in the ongoing marital struggle. More generally, the possibility of an asymmetrical invited third party role—in which one disputant wishes the third party to intervene for one reason or another, while the other disputant does not—raises the spectre of a third party caught up in the principals' conflictual web, and being used in ways that render effective intervention rather unlikely. Thus, one can envisage the circumstances under which one or more of the principals in the Middle East have occasionally sought

American intervention not out of genuine motivation to advance the prospects of peace, but primarily in order to cause the other nation(s) to lose face. The trick for the United States, in such a situation, is to exploit the show of commitment to conflict resolution by converting it into actual movement toward settlement.

In contrast with invited third party roles are those roles in which a third party's intervention is compulsory or is the result of the third party's own initiative. The Taft-Hartley Law, for example, requires that the parties to labor-management disputes affecting national welfare agree to submit to third party intervention if the dispute in question is not resolved after a certain period of time. Although a third party that intervenes under such circumstances does not necessarily do so with the blessing of the disputants, the party is likely to bring to bear much of the power and legitimacy associated with formal third party roles.

Third parties that elect to intervene of their own initiative comprise the other major sort of noninvited role. A bystander attempting to break up a schoolyard fight, a prominent citizen offering to intervene in a labor-management dispute, and the head of one nation offering to help break a conflictual impasse between two other nations are all of intervention as the result of third party initiative. To the extent that the disputants believe the third party's initiative is well intended, impartial, and genuine, and that the third party is capable of facilitating the identification of issues and conflict resolution, such third party initiative will probably be effective. On the other hand, to the extent that the third party's initiative is distrusted or is regarded as an unwanted, meddlesome intrusion (consider here the plight of the would be Good Samaritan attempting to intervene in a lovers' quarrel), such initiative may actually backfire, possibly leading the principals to remain in conflict longer and with greater intensity than would have occurred in the absence of any third party intervention at all.

Impartial versus Partial Roles

It is generally assumed that a third party will be impartial. Indeed, such evenhandedness is typically regarded as a cardinal third party virtue, and the great preponderance of third party roles are relatively impartial. There are also, however, important (if less frequent) instances of more partial roles, as when a parent intervenes in a sibling quarrel in favor of the smaller child, or when it is known that a mediator or arbitrator has a longer history and stronger ties with one side than with the other.

One of the ways in which a third party can attempt to offset an obvious discrepancy in the relative power of the principals to a conflict is by (at least temporarily) favoring the weaker party, thereby providing the underdog with greater counterpower than before. The effect of doing this is to force the more powerful disputant to wage the conflict through means other than coercion; for example, by siding with the smaller child in a dispute between two siblings, the parent serves notice on the stronger that alternatives to the exercise of brute strength will have to be found.

At another level it is also clear that partial third party roles may emerge when the third party wishes to give each side the impression of being partial to it, thereby forging an agreement that the disputants might otherwise prefer to avoid. To wit, the third party could go to principal A, attempt to convince A of its partiality to A over party B, that the third party has A's interests at heart, and therefore recommends that A make a concession on the grounds that it would lead to the most favorable agreement possible under the circumstances. The third party could then attempt to persuade B of the same thing (namely, of being partial to B over A),and use this leverage to exact a similar concession from B. As a result of such duplicity, the chances of reaching a bilateral agreement may well be increased.* This sort of third party ploy is likely to work only so long as the disputants trust the third party and remain largely incommunicado. Should the principals begin to talk directly with each other, they might discover they had been duped by the third party, and the latter's reputation would be sorely tarnished. The disputants might also be bound together, at least for a while, by their shared contempt for the third party.

Advisory versus Directive Roles

Most third party roles are advisory only, entailing a set of recommendations that may (but need not) be adhered to by the principals. A mediator has precisely this role, as does a conciliator provided by a court in order to intercede in a dispute between employers and employees, or a fact finder who has been selected to advise the principals about the issues in dispute. At the other end of the continuum are directive roles, in which the third party has the power to impose a particular binding agreement. An arbitrator—regardless of whether this person functions as a baseball umpire, a courtroom judge, or a conventional arbitrator in a labor-management problem—has precisely this sort of directive role in the intervention process. Lying somewhere between the extremes of mediation and arbitration are a number of other arrangements, including the procedure of "med arb," by which a third party first attempts to mediate a dispute and, if unsuccessful, goes on to impose a binding settlement.

Advisory roles clearly lack the "teeth" of enforcement, hence one

---

* It has been said, perhaps unjustly, that Kissinger attempted to employ this very strategy in his dealings with Israel, Egypt, and Syria during the 1973-75 disengagement talks.

might expect such roles to be less effective than those that are more directive. To some extent this is precisely the case; directive third parties are indeed better able to elicit the concessions and impose the agreements they prefer. The issue is less clear-cut when one considers the effect of directive and advisory roles in the long run, when the heat of the dispute has passed and the third party is no longer on the scene. Here it may actually be those agreements that were reached under advisory, rather than more directive, intervention circumstances that are more likely to endure. Why? Because it may be that when disputants make concessions and reach agreement in the presence of a mediator or some other advisory third party role, they tend to attribute their agreement not to third party coercion but to their own willingness and motivation to settle the dispute. Since the disputants are likely to feel that they reached agreement not because they had to, but because they chose to, they are likely to adhere to and believe in their agreement even when the third party no longer maintains surveillance over them. Ironically, then, although directive third party roles may elicit speedier, more complete agreement between the principals in the short run, in the long run it may be the advisory roles that yield greater internalization of attitude change and greater endurance of any agreement reached. The most effective third party role may thus be one in which the least necessary force and direction is applied in order to move the disputants to resolve their conflict.

Interindividual versus Intragroup and Intergroup Roles

Although third parties are typically thought of as intervening in conflicts between individuals, there are also important instances of intervention within and between groups and other more complex social arrangements such as organizations and nations. Moreover, it is often the case that what appears at first glance to be simple third party intervention in a dispute between individuals is actually interposition between the respective groups to which each of the principals is accountable. Only a foolhardy labor-management mediator would assume that a strike can be resolved simply by meeting with the representatives of each side, without taking into account the constituency pressures to which each side has been subjected. Suffice it to say that interindividual third party roles are far more likely to be associated with successful intervention than those roles in which the third party must juggle the competing preferences and intentions of group members.

During the mid- and late-1970s, the bilateral negotiations between Israel and Egypt—with the financial and other assistance of the United States—were characterized by the presence of very different social units with very different accountability arrangements. On the one hand,

President Anwar Sadat of Egypt appeared to sit unfettered at the pinnacle of the Egyptian power structure. He was accountable to virtually no individual or group within the Egyptian government (although he did appear to feel accountable to the other nations of the Arab world). As a result, he was repeatedly able and willing to make a series of expansive and dramatic moves and concessions in an effort to secure both an agreement with Israel and U.S. military, economic, and political support. The situation in Israel stood in stark contrast. Israeli Prime Minister Menachem Begin, although the most powerful figure in the country, was nevertheless accountable both to his cabinet and to the Israeli parliament (Knesset). This accountability was far from token, as evidenced by the fact that Begin could only agree to a particular concession or settlement with the Knesset's explicit approval. As a result, Prime Minister Begin tended to make a number of small concessions, to do so with considerable reluctance, and almost always in the expectation of some quid pro quo in return.*

The role of the United States during this period was enormously complicated by the fact that the spokespersons in the negotiations between Egypt and Israel were strikingly different in decision-making autonomy, and in the number and kinds of audiences and constituencies to which they were accountable. How much easier the U.S. third party role might have been had the principals really been able to act as if they were in an interindividual dispute. Indeed, how much easier the situation might have been had there been social structural symmetry among the parties; even if both principals had been encumbered by elaborate bureaucracies that slowed the pace of concessions (instead of only the Israeli prime minister), it might have been possible for the United States to help coordinate the role and degree of movement by the parties in a way that would have generated less distrust and mutual suspicion.

In summary, when a third party intervenes between individuals it is possible, in principle, for each party's preferences, intentions, and expectations to be evaluated, accepted at face value, and used by the third party to coordinate agreement. In contrast, when a third party is interposed within or between more complex social structures, it may be dramatically more difficult for each side's multiple, occasionally competing, viewpoints to be evaluated and integrated, and it may be far more

---

*To this simple and abbreviated analysis of the bargaining styles of President Sadat and Prime Minister Begin must be added at least two other considerations. First, the two men appear to have had very different personal styles, Sadat tending to be expansive, outgoing, and willing to take risks, while Begin tended to be more taciturn and cautious. Second, one should not lose sight of the nontrivial fact that the major issues in dispute concerned the return of territory by Israel (a tangible issue) in exchange for intangible Egyptian recognition and promises of nonbelligerency. It is not surprising that the party with tangible control (Israel) was more reluctant to make concessions than the party in control of the most important intangible resources.

difficult to execute an agreement that is mutually satisfactory—let alone acceptable—for all concerned.

Content-Oriented versus Process-Oriented Roles

A third party is typically regarded as a person who helps the principals to resolve a conflict by identifying the issues in dispute and then proposing a particular solution. The focus of the third party's activity is thus the content of a settlement that may result from the third party's intervention. Examples of such content-oriented third party roles are abundant and readily apparent, including most instances of traditional labor mediation and arbitration, many forms of intervention in international diplomacy, decision making by a trial judge, and so forth.

If content-oriented third party roles are primarily focused on moving the disputants toward the goal of a settlement, more process-oriented roles are focused instead on the ways in which the principals go about waging conflict. How do the parties in conflict communicate with each other, and how may this communication be improved? How may the disputants' willingness to trust each other, as well as the third party, be increased? Are the parties angry? If so, how may this anger be discharged in such a way that they can begin to move toward resolution of their conflict? These are the sorts of questions and kinds of issues that the occupant of a process-oriented third party role is likely to address.

Consider here the example of a conciliator such as a couple therapist. It is not typically the therapist's job, nor the therapist's objective, to preserve the relationship between the two people in question; indeed, there may even be circumstances in which the couple is more likely to dissolve its relationship after having been in therapy than it was before. A more typical therapist role entails helping each member of a couple to understand better: the way in which he or she talks and listens to the other, and how related communication skill can be improved; the degree to which the relationship is characterized by anger and mutual suspicion, some of the underlying reasons for this negative sentiment, and some techniques for managing and reducing it; and, most generally, some of the ways in which the members of the couple can learn to help themselves.

It is this last point that constitutes perhaps the most fundamental distinction between content- and process-oriented roles. Whereas a content-oriented third party is likely to take charge of the conflict in question and do whatever is necessary to facilitate its resolution, a more process-oriented third party is likely to do whatever is necessary in order to help the principals to take charge of their own conflict and take care of themselves. As was suggested in the earlier discussion of directive and advisory roles, although a content orientation is likely to generate a more immediate conflict settlement than a process orientation, it is also likely to lead to less attitude change and internalization than occurs when the disputants are helped to resolve a conflict of their own accord. Agreement may thus be less likely under the auspices of a process-oriented third party; but if reached, such an agreement is likely to be far more durable.

Conflict-Preventing versus Conflict-Managing versus Conflict-Escalating Roles

Although we think of most third parties as occupying conflict management roles—in which intervention occurs in order to help the disputants to work on an already existing conflict—there are also important instances where the third party's presence or intervention helps to prevent a conflagration from erupting in the first place. When a third party has an ongoing, relatively permanent role vis-à-vis the principals, it is often the case that the third party occupies both conflict prevention and conflict management roles.

As an illustration, consider the role of the baseball umpire. By virtue of his very presence behind home plate, calling balls and strikes for each batter, the umpire serves notice on the two opposing teams that all judgment calls are strictly within his purview. The not unreasonable assumption here is that were there to be no consensually agreed upon third party umpire, arguments would continually flare up between the catcher of one team and the opposing batter whenever a close pitch was thrown. The umpire, and indeed the very idea that an umpire will be working the game, thus has an important deterrent effect: only the umpire can prevent forest fires. On the other hand, despite the umpire's presence throughout the game, rhubarbs do occasionally erupt for various reasons, either between one of the teams and the umpire (as when a baserunner is called safe or out on a close call) or between the two opposing teams (as when a pitcher brushes back a batter and nearly hits him). Here the umpire is called upon to display a conflict management role, either by enacting or reversing a decision he has previously reached or by intervening between the two opposing teams in an effort to restore order.

Far less common than either conflict management or preventive roles is the occasional role by which a third party's intervention actually leads an existing conflict to escalate further. To pursue the fire metaphor one step further, it is clearly possible for third parties to not only prevent fires and get them under control, but also to add fuel to them. Given their unique position of credibility, trust, and at least some control, third parties are quite capable of upping the conflictual ante if they so choose. But why would third parties ever wish to do this? First, out of the third party's conviction that the disputants are not yet sufficiently motivated to take their problem seriously, and the belief that they can only be made to do so if the gravity of their situation is made more apparent; second, because the third party believes that the conflict over the underlying issues in dispute is so grave that the only resolution possible is through termination of the disputants' relationship; and third, because the third party has a stake in protecting the importance of his or her own role, and therefore pushes the conflict in an escalatory direction in order to justify the necessity of continued, active involvement.*

Permanent versus Temporary Roles

As illustrated by the role of baseball umpire, some third parties exist in an ongoing, semipermanent relationship with (potential) disputants. This individual may have a history of intervention in particular disputes between particular individuals, and may be expected to continue to serve indefinitely in this capacity. The *Boston Globe*, for example, has an individual who occupies the role of ombudsman, mediating between the newspaper and a changing clientele of individual petitioners. Although the identity of the individual complainants may change, the ombudsman's role remains the same and has a permanence that is often absent in many third party roles. Similarly, a member of the Federal Mediation and Conciliation Service, an official of the United Nations Secretariat, or the members of a watchdog committee or board of overseers may have a history of intervening in particular disputes and may exist in an ongoing, permanent working relationship with the principals or the interest group they represent.

In contrast are the many third party roles whose emergence is dictated by exigencies of the moment, and whose necessity ceases to exist once the dispute has been resolved. Such third parties, like bystanders who intervene in a playground spat or a lovers' quarrel, intervene temporarily because their assistance appears necessary. Their intervention is time bounded, often limited in scope, and occasionally of limited value.

The great virtue of permanent third party roles is that they imply the existence of a corps of trained professionals whose job it is to help disputants resolve conflict. The cost of permanent third party roles, however, may be in the emergence of vested interests. Apart from managing conflict, professional third parties may wish to preserve their own special and important role as intervenors. In contrast, although temporary third party roles are characterized by the presence of off-the-

---

*It has been said of Secretary of State Kissinger, perhaps unfairly, that he occasionally misrepresented or only partially presented the views of one side to the other during the 1973–75 Middle East disengagement talks, in order to protect his own instrumental importance as a mediator and the centrality of the United States.

cuff, spontaneous, well-intentioned plans for intervention that are often lacking in adequate forethought and professionalism, they have an important redeeming feature: the objective of these third party roles is to render themselves irrelevant and obsolete. What these temporary roles should continually remind us of is the distinct possibility that the most effective third party is the one whose eventual obsolescence is a planned and foregone conclusion.

Relationship-Facilitating versus Relationship Inhibitory Roles

Some third parties are in the business of bringing the disputants together, of reconciling differences between them, improving communication, and leaving the principals in a stronger, more durable working relationship than existed prior to the third party's intervention. Examples of such relationship-facilitating roles include those of conciliator, process-oriented mediator, and couple therapist. In general, third parties are typically presumed to occupy these sorts of facilitating roles.

On the other hand, there are also third parties whose very raison d'etre is the separation of the principals, rendering unnecessary their direct interaction. By inhibiting or dampening the possibility of direct contact between the principals, these third parties have an effect similar to the conflict preventive role described previously. A real estate broker or marriage broker, for example, by separating the principals until it has become time to conclude a contractual agreement, prevents the sort of conflict and misunderstanding that might arise were the parties to talk directly with each other. The realtor typically separates the seller from the prospective buyer, works closely with each person in an effort to convey a sense of understanding of each party's position and thereby engenders trust, bringing the parties together only after a contractual settlement (a deal) has been reached.°

At another level entirely, relationship-dampening third party roles may arise when the disputants are in the midst of an intense, protracted conflict that can only be managed by separating the parties and doing whatever is possible to terminate their direct relationship. An arbitrator in a chronic labor-management dispute, for example, accomplishes this end by removing (or accepting) control over the allocation of resources between the principals and unilaterally imposing a final settlement.

°Apart from keeping the principals separated in order to minimize conflict and disruption, it should be added that such third parties occasionally may do so because of a vested interest in preserving their own instrumental role. Many buyers and sellers, for example, could no doubt be successfully brought together without the intercession of a realtor; to do so, however, would deprive the realtor of a broker's fee.

SOME THIRD PARTY FUNCTIONS

Having briefly listed and commented upon some of the many roles that third parties occupy in a wide range of situations, should now be directed to third party functions, per se. Two caveats should be borne in mind in the following listing of third party functions. First, the primary focus of concern here is the function of mediation, *per se*, rather than arbitration, fact finding, or any other form of intervention. This is so, both because mediation is probably the most ubiquitous form of third party intervention, and therefore requires the lion's share of attention, and also because the case history that comprises the book's focus describes the intervention of a mediator. Second, although it has been seen that third parties may not only serve in conflict resolution roles, but may also help to prevent conflict in the first place, or alternatively to prod the disputants in such a way that conflict escalates and leads eventually to rupture of their relationship, the primary focus of the analysis here is conflict management.

Given that conflict exists between two or more principals, what can a mediator do to modify the conflict in such a way that the disputants move, or are moved, toward agreement? How can a mediator go about creating what Walton (1969) describes as a "constructive confrontation" between the principals? The following listing of functions will suggest a threefold answer to this query: the mediator can attempt to modify the physical and social structure within which the conflict is waged; the mediator can assist in the structuring of issues; and the mediator can attempt to modify the disputants' motivation to address their conflict.

Modification of Physical and Social Structure

Even though asked to serve in an advisory capacity only, the third party is nevertheless likely to retain considerable control over various aspects of the physical and social structure within which conflict is waged. As the following discussion will indicate, these areas of control include communication structure, site openness, site neutrality, time limits, and resources.

Communication Structure

It is widely believed that if one can only get the principals in conflict to communicate with one another, thereby giving their mutual grievances a full airing, their conflict will surely resolve itself. Although it is true that communication between disputants expedites conflict resolution under many circumstances, such may not be the case in conflict-intensified relationships. Here the availability of communication channels may not only fail to generate pressures toward agreement, but may actually escalate the conflict. An effectively functioning third party must know when to encourage communication between the principals, and when such communication should be curtailed.

The effect of introducing communication into a deteriorating relationship was demonstrated some years ago in a classic series of laboratory studies by Morton Deutsch and Robert Krauss (1962; 1966). Pairs of participants were asked to play a laboratory bargaining game known as the Acme-Bolt Trucking paradigm, the details of which need not concern us here. The ability to coerce one's bargaining adversary through the use of threat was made available to neither, to one, or to both members of a pair. The researchers discovered early in the experiment that the presence of bilateral threat potential led to the escalation of conflict, to the predominance of competitive motivation, and to poor bargaining outcomes.

Having succeeded in creating the conditions of intense conflict, Deutsch and Krauss set out to study the circumstances under which the resolution of such conflict could be facilitated through the introduction of communication channels. First, the researchers provided the bargainers with an intercom and allowed them to communicate at will about any topic they chose or, if they so wished, to say nothing at all. It was found that the introduction of such permissible communication had no effect on the bargainers' ability to reach agreement; they continued to achieve poor bargaining outcomes and failed to use the opportunity to communicate. In a subsequent experiment, Deutsch and Krauss therefore introduced compulsory communication, requiring the bargainers to say something to each other at the beginning of each turn in the game. As before, it was found that communication did little to reduce the conflict to more manageable porportions or to increase bargaining effectiveness. Interestingly, when required to communicate, the participants used the communication channel to heap abuse on each other, hurling insults, threats, and lies. Rather than facilitating the reduction of intense conflict, the introduction of compulsory communication exacerbated it.

In a third study, Krauss and Deutsch introduced an intervention that helped communication to work in the way that we would like to believe it is supposed to work. Bargainers were tutored by the experimenter in the effective use of communication; they were urged to put themselves in their adversary's shoes, to be fair, to make proposals that they believed were reasonable and acceptable for the other as well as for themselves. It was found that participants who were provided with this sort of intervention bargained more effectively and obtained higher outcomes than those who were not. So it was only when a third-party experimenter reminded the disputants how to communicate, and in effect explicitly urged them to cooperate, that they were able to use their communication channel effectively; the more introduction of permissive or compulsory communication was not sufficient.

To summarize: A third party may be able to regulate the communication between the principals. In order for the introduction of communication to have a facilitating effect on dispute resolution, it must be paced in relation to the intensity of conflict. Whereas the introduction of full and open communication between the principals may help them to resolve a relatively low level conflict—by allowing the parties to coordinate better the solution to a relatively easy problem—when conflict is intense or protracted, the third party may be best able to help by introducing a temporary cooling-off period. During this time the third party may choose to serve as a go-between, funneling (and occasionally filtering) information back and forth until the disputants are able and willing to address the issues in dispute through direct exchange.* Such a go-between function may prove extremely tempting to a third party who, for personal reasons, wishes to be placed and to remain in a pivotal position. It is therefore in the disputants' interest to ascertain for themselves the point at which they consider themselves ready to communicate directly with each other.

Lying between the extremes of full and open communication and drastically restricted or severed communication among the principals, are several additional alternatives that a third party may wish to encourage. One of these, already mentioned in the description of Deutsch and Krauss' bargaining research, entails teaching disputants those skills that are necessary to communicate more effectively. For example, the parties may be encouraged to make proposals that both sides would consider fair were they standing in the other's shoes. Or the parties may be asked to make proposals without judging the other, as in Jesus' response to the Pharisees' query regarding the stoning of an adulterous woman: "He that is without sin among you, let him cast the first stone" (John 8:1-12). As Walton (1969) has pointed out, the disputants may be invited to work on the reliability of their communication by having the third party continually translate and restate the communication between the principals until both sides agree on the meaning of a particular statement.

Apart from teaching the disputants basic communication skills, the third party may wish to allow communication, but only in limited, highly controlled ways. Thus the principals may be given a particular pace at which offers and counteroffers are to be made, or they may be told that

---

*Pruitt (1981) has recently pointed out that the cooling-off period has a number of other functions, enabling the third party: to encourage the disputants to vent their anger; to teach them communication and bargaining skills; to improve their attitudes toward each other; to increase their motivation to reach agreement; and to encourage the informal exploration of proposals.

the only communication to be allowed consists of offers to concede; threats, bluffs, and other rhetoric are not permitted.

Site Openness

Apart from influencing the process of communication between the disputants, a third party may be able to modify the exchange between the disputants and their respective constituencies, as well as a number of other audiences, by regulating the openness of the conflict site. Such variations in site openness are likely to affect the pressure experienced by the disputants to behave in particular ways. By selectively exposing or shielding the principals from various publics, the effective third party may be able to increase the chances of settlement.

Although they do not always have precisely this effect, constituencies typically apply pressure on their respective spokespersons to adopt a tough bargaining stance; indeed, this stance is often expected to be tougher than the spokespersons might adopt themselves were they left to their own devices. Given that disputants are in the midst of a conflict-intensified exchange, a third party may wish to isolate them from access to their respective constituencies, much as President Carter did to Prime Minister Begin and President Sadat during the 1978 meetings at the Camp David retreat. On the other hand, to the extent that the third party happens to regard the constituencies as a source of pressure toward agreement, it may be wise to selectively invite them to observe the proceedings in the conflictual arena and/or to communicate directly with the principals.

Although constituencies are apt to be the audience of greatest salience to the disputants, there are often other interested audiences whose presence and active involvement may be skillfully managed by a third party. These audiences include neutral figures, would-be allies or adversaries, and occasionally the media. As Rubin and Brown (1975) and others have documented, the effect of introducing such interested audiences is typically to increase the bargainers' need to appear competent or effective, and to avoid looking weak or foolish—in short, to save face by behaving in the "right" way.

Social psychologists have experimentally demonstrated that the presence of other people has the effect of strengthening an individual's "dominant response." Thus, if you are the sort of person who gets nervous when taking an exam, the presence of other people in the room should increase your test anxiety even further; conversely, if you are a person who likes to work under pressure, the presence of others should really get your adrenaline going and please you all the more. In like fashion, one might expect disputants' tendencies either toward intransigence or conciliation to be amplified in the presence of an interested audience. A skillful third party intuitively understands this principle and knows how to apply it to advantage.

In the early stages of a conflictual impasse, a third party may have to be extremely cautious about the introduction of observing audiences, lest these audiences render a bad situation even worse; at this point the third party may be well advised to shield the disputants from public view. At a later time, after the principals have embarked upon the concession-making process and may even have reached a tentative agreement, the third party may wish to deliberately throw open the gates of public and media visibility in an effort to solidify the disputants' commitment to this course of action. Consider the example of the 1978 Camp David talks among Egypt, Israel, and the United States, during which the principals were housed at a secluded retreat and protected from public access. Post-hoc accounts of the proceedings suggest that such protection was absolutely essential, since the negotiations were constantly in danger of irreparable rupture. It was only at the conclusion of the talks, when an agreement between Israel and Egypt had been reached in principle, that the media was allowed access. The ritualistic signing of the Camp David accords on the White House lawn, in full view of the eyes of the world, may be regarded as a vehicle for solidifying the agreement through an irrevocable public commitment.°

Site Neutrality

Apart from regulating the access of the disputants' exchange to various audiences, the third party can often make recommendations about the site chosen for the negotiations. It is often in the third party's (and therefore the disputants') interest to encourage the selection of a neutral site, rather than a location comprising the home turf of one principal or the other. By selecting a neutral site, the third party can maximize control over the various constituencies and other audiences that may wish to gain access to the proceedings. A neutral site, moreover, may help assure the principals that neither side has a tactical advantage nor a home territory that must be defended. It surely is no accident that the SALT talks between the United States and the Soviet Union took place in Finland, the four-way Vietnam peace talks were held in Paris, and the

---

°Another example of the use of audiences to solidify pressure for agreement can be seen in the biblical account of Paul's efforts on behalf of Onesimus. Onesimus was formerly a slave of Philemon before escaping to freedom in Rome. The apostle Paul promises to return Onesimus to his former owner if Philemon promises not to harm Onesimus and to treat him as he would treat Paul himself (Philemon 17). In order to help constrain Philemon to this commitment, Paul sends a letter to the neighboring town of Colosse, in which he informs the Colossians of his high regard for Onesimus and urges them to read Paul's letter before the entire congregation (Colossians 4:7–16)!

Camp David meetings between Egypt and Israel were conducted in the Catoctin Mountains of Maryland.

There may well be occasions in which it is in a third party's interest to schedule meetings on the third part's home terrain. By doing so, the third party's legitimacy and credibility as an intervenor may be increased. This is particularly so when the site itself contains symbolic paraphernalia (flags, logos, insignia, special seminar tables and chairs) that are likely to enhance the third party's perceived virtues. As mentioned earlier, it is not uncommon for federal mediators to conduct labor-management negotiations in a seminar room provided by the federal government, complete with a special armchair for the mediator at one end of the table, and the seal of the Federal Mediation and Conciliation Service of the United States of America conspicuously displayed on the wall behind the mediator's head.

Finally, although site neutrality is more often the rule than not, the third party may occasionally recommend a site that favors one principal over the other. This may be a particularly important consideration when the two sides are bargaining from positions of differential strength, and the third party wishes partially to offset this asymmetry by conducting the negotiations on the home terrain of the weaker party. Although such a structural modification of power discrepancy may be more illusory than real, it nevertheless permits the third party to inform the disputants about certain assumptions regarding the balance of power and the kind of agreement that the third party is apt to find acceptable.

Time Limits

Time limits can be tricky, with effects on conflict that are not always obvious. On the one hand, the existence of a deadline for negotiations, after which talks break off and an impasse is declared, should have the effect of pressuring the disputants to make meaningful concessions in an effort to reach agreement before time runs out. On the other hand, it is often true that the symmetry of this time pressure—the fact that both principals are under pressure to concede—leads each to hope that the other will give in first and foremost. This is the basis of the eleventh-hour phenomenon in labor-management negotiations, by which each side refuses to make concessions until the clock has nearly struck twelve, thereby hoping to force the other to yield.

Given the complexity of time limits and the tactical advantage to which they may be used by the disputants, a third party must attempt to modify deadlines with some care. This caution notwithstanding, several generalizations are possible. First, if a deadline for exchange does exist, and the principals appear to be using this time limit in order to justify intransigence and to wage a "game of chicken," it may be appropriate for the third party to delay the time limit if possible, or eliminate it altogether. Nations negotiating in the shadow of a treaty that is about to expire may be reluctant to make concessions lest the other side conclude that a precedent of weakness has been set, inviting exploitation in the future. By recommending that the deadline be changed to give the disputants more time, the third party may be able to open the way for concessions without pressure—and without the symbolic significance that concession making under pressure may imply.

On the other hand, there are occasions when a third party may wish to impose time limits where none currently exists. This is likely to make particular sense when a third party is already on the scene and senses that the disputants are either not taking their conflict very seriously or are extremely reluctant to move toward agreement. Under these circumstances, assuming the third party is a valued participant in the proceedings, the third party's imposition of a deadline beyond which the interchange will end (along with the involvement of the third party), may have the effect of generating greater conciliatory movement. During the Camp David talks, President Carter threatened to terminate the meetings and his own participation as mediator if an agreement were not reached by a particular time. Whether this threat was instrumental in generating a settlement is not entirely clear, although it no doubt had the effect of upping the ante for agreement.°

Resources

A third party may be able to exercise control over at least three types of resources, the modification of which may generate pressure toward agreement. One of these resources, the third party's willingness to continue participating in the discussions, has already been examined. By threatening to discontinue services, or by making these services contingent upon some significant movement by the principals, the third party may be able to generate pressure to make concessions.

A second resource to which the third party may have access is the domain of public sentiment. By restraining or threatening to unleash the "mad dogs of the media," for example, the third party may be able to

---

° Note that a third party threat of this kind, and indeed any third party threat, is likely to succeed only as long as it is credible. If a third party threat fails to elicit compliance, and the threat is not subsequently carried out, the third party's credibility is likely to diminish rapidly along with the success of such threats in the future. Consider here the example of the Camp David accords, which specified a set of dates by which avrious subsequent agreements would be reached in the Middle East—and which implicitly hinted at a weakening of U.S. economic and military support for Egypt and Israel if these target dates were not met. Although many of the promised later agreements between Israel and Egypt were not reached, let alone by the dates proposed, the U.S. government evidenced no clear weakening of its support for the principals. One wonders whether these unenforced threats will not have the effect of tempting Egypt and Israel to renege in the future.

couple intransigence among the disputants with the threat of public opprobrium, and genuine conciliatory movement with the promise of public approval (Kerr 1954). Although intangibles such as the possibility of public praise or public scorn may appear to be insignificant resources with which to work, a skillful third party is able to use them to considerable advantage. Labor mediators, for example, well know the power of a timely press release both to generate movement where none existed before and to consecrate a settlement once it has been reached. Conversely, the inept or untimely exploitation of public sentiment by a third party may have disastrous consequences, as when some of the third parties involved in the Attica prison takeover made statements to the media about the legitimacy of the prisoners' grievances and the high probability that these grievances would be redressed. Such public statements fueled an illusory sense of bargaining strength and control among the prisoners, helped blind them to their adversary's intransigent bargaining posture, and led the prisoners to misjudge the state's determination to regain control of the prison at any cost.

Finally, a third party may be able to modify the size of the pie over which the conflict is being waged. As Kerr (1954) has pointed out, third parties may be able to identify and promote the use of additional resources that are not immediately apparent to the principals. By soliciting additional money, land, or other tangible resources from parties that are external to the conflict, or by directly providing such resources themselves, third parties can attempt to transform a constant-sum dispute (characterized by outcomes that are acceptable to one party at the exclusion of the other) into a nonconstant-sum exchange (in which mutually acceptable outcomes are possible). During Kissinger's step-by-step diplomacy in the Middle East, it was not uncommon for an apparently intractable conflict between Israel and Egypt, or Israel and Syria, to be resolved through the promised infusion of U.S. economic and military resources. More recently, Carter was able to "sweeten the kitty" during the Camp David talks by promising to build the Israelis a new airfield in the Negev Desert in return for their evacuation of the Sinai, and by promising enormous economic and military assistance to Egypt in exchange for its agreement with Israel. In some sense it can be argued that the 1978 Camp David agreement was made possible by the involuntary generosity of the American taxpayer.*

A third party may thus be able to increase the likelihood of settlement by helping to increase the size of the conflictual pie. In addition, there may be circumstances in which movement toward agree-

---

*The lesson to be learned here is not that third parties should refrain from introducing additional resources; rather, they should be cautious lest they lead the disputants to expect such infusions of generosity in the future, and lest they convert a dyadic conflict into a triadic one—making themselves into more of a participant than is sensible.

ment can be facilitated by actually shrinking the pie or, more likely, by pointing to the fact that resources are diminishing over time. For example, a labor mediator may be able to encourage bilateral concession making by repeatedly observing that the longer labor and management remain without a contractual agreement, the more money each side is losing. The general point is that by modifying the resources that the disputants have to work with, or by increasing the disputants' awareness of the ways in which these resources may change, a third party can generate significant pressure for agreement.

Modification of Issue Structure

It has been seen that one of the functions of a third party is to modify the physical and social environment in ways that facilitate movement toward dispute resolution. At another level, a third party can help the principals identify the issues in dispute, order these issues in terms of importance, make recommendations concerning their packaging and the order in which they should be addressed, introduce new issues if necessary, and identify alternative solutions to the conflict. On those occasions when the principals are too close to the issues in dispute, a third party may be able to structure the issues so as to bring about a necessary increase in distance. Conversely, there may be occasions where the disputants are either insufficiently hooked into the available issues or unable to identify those issues that are most central or workable. In these cases, the third party may be able to move the disputants closer to the issues at hand. In general, a skilled third party can use the structuring of issues to modify the principals' perspective, thereby facilitating the resolution of conflict.

Identification of Existing Issues and Alternatives

One of the most useful things a third party can do during conflict is help the principals identify the issues in dispute. By directing their attention to the several points of agreement and disagreement, the third party can provide the disputants with accurate information about each other's preferences, expectations, and intentions with regard to the issues. Such information should help the disputants understand better which issues require considerable further work and which are close to resolution, which issues are particularly central to the conflict and which are more superficial and remote. By identifying the issues in dispute and developing an importance ordering among these issues, a third party can help the principals accurately evaluate the size and scope of their conflict.

Is it always helpful for a third party to encourage accurate evaluation of conflict intensity by the disputants? The answer, it appears, is no.

Just as the introduction of communication between adversaries in a conflict-intensified relationship encourages the exchange of hostility—and may actually escalate the conflict even further than would have occurred in the absence of communication—the effectiveness of issue identification also tends to be integrally related to the amount of conflict in the disputants' relationship. Bonnie Erickson and her colleagues (1974) have found that issue identification by a third party results in more frequent settlement and in higher joint profit only when conflict is low. Under conditions of high conflict, the exact reverse is found: issue identification leads people to reach fewer agreements than they do in the absence of this procedure. When conflict is relatively small in intensity, issue identification helps the parties to zero in on the few problems that require their serious attention, while reminding them of the several points on which they already are in, or are close to, agreement. Under conditions of high conflict, issue identification by the third party serves to remind the disputants that they are in serious disagreement regarding most points, are able to see eye to eye on only a small number of issues, and that their chances of reaching a settlement are therefore negligible.

In summary, the procedure of issue identification is extremely important and can be enormously helpful in facilitating dispute resolution, but it must be applied with caution. A skillful third party must attempt to reconcile the increased understanding and insight that result from issue identification with the possibility that such understanding may lead the principals to abandon hope or to wage the conflict with greater fervor than before. Couple therapists, labor mediators, and international diplomats know full well the cost of reminding protagonists of the enormity of their disagreement. It may make far more sense under these circumstances for the third party either to ignore the identification of issues temporarily or to help target the particular subset of issues that is likely to prove relatively tractable. On the other hand, it can also be argued that if the principals do indeed have a truly fundamental and irrevocable disagreement with regard to one or more underlying issues, all the third party issue management in the world will not suffice to change the situation one iota, and may only fuel an illusory sense of the conflict's solubility.

As a case in point, consider once again the 1978 Camp David talks. Although there were, and continue to be, multiple issues in dispute, only a small number of these issues were targeted for clear identification and exploration. Thus a decision was made, no doubt largely at the behest of Carter, to focus the discussions primarily on the fate of the Sinai Desert and its oil fields, as well as the establishment of normal diplomatic and economic relations between Israel and Egypt. The much more intractable and enduring issues in the Middle East—the fate of the West Bank and the Gaza Strip, Palestinian autonomy, and the fate of Jerusalem—appear to have been either ignored altogether or sidetracked for further discussion at a later time. Just as Kissinger elected to pursue a series of relatively workable bilateral disengagements during his step-by-step diplomacy by deferring the more difficult problems for a later time, so too did Carter, with consequences that will be explored a bit further in the next section.

Packaging and Sequencing of Issues

It is occasionally the case that a dispute revolves around a single issue, as when two people are exclusively concerned with the division between them of a single tangible resource. Under such circumstances, there is little that a third party can do to structure the issue in new or interesting ways. More often than not, however, disputes involve multiple issues that can be packaged and ordered in ways that are likely to have a powerful impact on the number and kinds of issues that are addressed.

Given that multiple issues exist, a third party can affect the dispute resolution process by advising the principals to adopt either a holistic set (in which the multiple issues at stake are considered as an integrated, unitary package) or a partitive set (in which the issues are addressed one at a time). All things considered, there is some reason to believe that a holistic approach is preferable. It has been found (Kelley 1966) that negotiators who treat multiple issues as a package tend to have greater latitude to make concessions and trade-offs at a later time, and are less likely to make the sort of premature commitments and take the premature last stands that prolong the life of the conflict. Similarly, other laboratory research (Froman and Cohen 1970) indicates that bargainers who are free to logroll multiple issues, by working on several at once, tend to reach more equitable agreements more rapidly than those who are required to settle the issues one at a time. The evidence from these studies and others suggests that a third party would be well advised to recommend the coupling of issues (Fisher 1964).

Actually, as Erickson and her colleagues have demonstrated (1974), the situation turns out to be more complex. While they found that the participants in their laboratory experiment reached settlement more frequently when they were urged by a third party to adopt a holistic rather than a partitive set, these results held only when the parties negotiated under conditions of low conflict. When the conflict was high, the presence of a holistic or partitive set made no difference: subjects reached only half as many settlements as they did under conditions of low conflict, and their ability to do so was unaffected by the set they were given.

The sense of these findings is that a third party should take conflict size into account in making a recommendation for dealing with multiple issues; the integrative set that proves so effective under conditions of low conflict may be useless when conflict is high. In fact, given that a conflict is particularly intense, it may make sense for a third party to induce the disputants to address multiple issues in sequence. Assuming that these issues are of differential importance, as is likely to be the case, what order of address should the third party recommend? Should the third party advise the disputants to tackle the central problems first before moving on to more peripheral issues? Or should the reverse sequence be encouraged? Reasonable arguments can be advanced for and against either arrangement.

On the one hand, it may be argued that a third party should encourage the disputants to address the most important issue or issues near the outset of their exchange. After all, if the disputants can successfully resolve these central problems, they should have little trouble managing the more tangential issues that are considered later. Consider the example of a labor-management dispute consisting of four issues: employee wages, retirement benefits, hospitalization insurance, and vacation days. If a mediator can structure the issues in such a way that the most central issue (employee wages) is addressed first, and if this issue is resolved successfully, there is every reason to believe that solutions can be readily found for the three remaining issues. On the other hand, since it is often the case that the most important issues are also the most difficult to address, early efforts to resolve the major problems may well result in failure. Early failure, in turn, may create a climate of resistance that spills over to the more peripheral issues, making them more difficult to resolve than would have been the case had they been addressed first.

The argument in support of a third party recommendation that less central issues be tackled first initially seems quite compelling. These lesser issues are more likely to be resolved successfully, and may help to establish the climate of goodwill, cooperativeness, and confidence that is necessary if more knotty problems are to be addressed effectively at a later time. Surely Carter was aware of this when he advised or encouraged the parties at Camp David to reach a bilateral agreement, and to defer the more central problems in the Middle East till later. Like Kissinger during the 1973-75 disengagement talks, Carter hoped to generate sufficient momentum at Camp David to keep a proliferating peace process in motion.

Unfortunately, the virtues of a third party addressing the easy issues first are offset by several potential difficulties. First, reaching agreement too early on tangential issues may reduce the possibility of later trade-offs on the more central and difficult problems. This is so because the less central issues tend to be easy to resolve, offering each side the possibility of making concessions at little cost to oneself, and making it possible to offer the other side the sweetener that may be necessary to reach a final, integrated settlement. Second, there is always the possibility that the disputants, for one reason or another, will fail to reach agreement on the peripheral issues, in which case there is very little hope for movement on the more central problems. Finally, and perhaps of greatest relevance to the Camp David illustration, it may be that in addition to generating momentum, the disputants' successful management of easy issues also tends to generate an illusory sense of control over the conflict, thereby making subsequent setbacks all the more disappointing and infuriating, and damaging the chances of an enduring settlement. The risk of Camp David is that the principals may have collectively generated the mirage of peace in the Middle East, only to discover that the really central issues—the fate of Jerusalem, the West Bank, and Gaza—not only failed to be addressed, but actually seemed more difficult to tackle than ever before.

Introducing New Issues and Alternatives

Apart from helping the disputants to identify issues, and recommending that these issues be packaged and ordered in particular ways, a third party can introduce new issues and alternative solutions. The effect of such interventions is to change the size of the conflictual pie, not by increasing the tangible resources at stake (as was seen earlier), but by modifying the disputants' perceptions of their conflict and the ways in which it can be managed. As a result of introducing new issues and alternative solutions, a third party can thus generate significant pressure to break a conflictual impasse and move toward agreement.

Although a third party can introduce new issues and alternatives in a great many ways, several of these methods are of particular importance and therefore deserve special comment. First of all, a third party may attempt to break a conflictual impasse by dividing large, all-encompassing issues into smaller, more manageable pieces that were not previously apparent to the disputants. This technique, known as conflict fractionation, has been described in detail by Roger Fisher (1964), and serves the important function of encouraging concession making without loss of face. The concessions that each side was unwilling to make with respect to a monolithic issue may now be made more readily in relation to a series of smaller issues in which the disputants are likely to have far less investment. The history of U.S. mediation in the Middle East is dotted with instances of conflict fractionation, as efforts have been repeatedly made to gain a toehold on the peace process by developing issues over which the parties can agree.

Yet another example of the role of fractionation in the resolution of conflict is the 1962 Cuban missile crisis, in which the United States and the Soviet Union were engaged in an eyeball-to-eyeball confrontation with very little hope of escape. The solution that eventually evolved, allowing both superpowers to end the conflict without loss of face, did so because the monolithic issue of Soviet-American supremacy was successfully transformed by the principals into subissues that included U.S. assurances against the invasion of Cuba, Soviet assurances to destroy and withdraw all nuclear missiles and sites in Cuba, as well as an important bargaining issue: a U.S. promise to withdraw archaic and outmoded missiles in Turkey that it planned to withdraw even before the crisis arose.

A second important third party technique involves the introduction of new goals and objectives that transcend the disputants' conflict, and are of shared concern to both sides. The effect of a third party's introduction of such superordinate goals is to transform, at least temporarily, a conflictual relationship into an exchange that requires cooperation if the shared objective is to be met. If only humanity were threatened by an invasion of aliens from another planet, it has been argued, the nations of the world would gather together to pool their resources in the face of this shared threat, and wars would presumably cease. The underlying principle, of course, is that disputants have both cooperative and competitive motives with regard to each other, and that the cooperative concern may be accentuated by introducing a transcendent objective that is impossible for either party to achieve alone (Sherif and Sherif 1969). As a mediator in the Middle East for over a decade, the United States government has no doubt repeatedly reminded the regional protagonists that they are bonded together not only by conflict, but also by a set of shared external concerns, including a harsh climate, economic woes, and a number of potentially hostile neighbors.

Third, it is often true that conflictual impasses are accompanied by statements of overcommitment by the principals to a belligerent or intransigent course of action; such commitments are likely to seriously impede subsequent efforts to reach agreement. Pruitt (1981) has pointed out that under these circumstances a third party may be able to move the disputants out of the commitment trap in one of two major ways: (1) By proposing a decommitting formula, a new definition of a situation that changes it in ways that supersede the commitment. As an example of a decommitting formula, Pruitt describes a conflict between two foreign students that was mediated by his wife, France. One of the students informed her that his roommate had refused to pay the rent, and that he was therefore bound by his religion to kill him. France asked the student not to do it, at which point he said that her request had created a new situation that invalidated his prior commitment. (2) By attempting to circumvent the commitment in one of several ways. One of the most important techniques for circumvention is the use of communication back channels, conduits for communication that exist behind the scenes, away from public view. Throughout the Cuban missile crisis, even during the moments of most heated public exchange and most vitriolic public commitment to conflict escalation, representatives for the United States and the Soviet Union continued to meet informally in the fine restaurants of Washington, D.C. in order to hammer out an acceptable agreement.

In summary, a third party can increase the chances of agreement by introducing alternatives and issues of which the principals may be unaware. Thus, by fractionating large issues into new and smaller pieces, by introducing superordinate goals that transcend the disputants' conflictual relationship, and by helping them to supersede or circumvent their commitment to intransigence, a third party can move the principals toward conciliation.

Increasing the Motivation to Reach Agreement

In order to function effectively, a third party must be able to do more than modify the disputants' physical and social environment and the structure of issues they are asked to address. The third party must also be able to modify the conflict's psychological climate in ways that enhance the disputants' mutual motivation to reach agreement.° As the following analysis will suggest, a third party must address four fundamental motivational concerns: concession making without loss of face, trust, irrationality, and autonomy.

Concession Making Without Loss of Face

Numerous theorists have observed that people in conflict tend to have accentuated concerns witht he image of strength, competence, honor, and wisdom that they convey to their adversary and to various constituents, as well as with the image they have of themselves.† Given the importance that disputants attach to saving face in the eyes of salient others and themselves, the presence or anticipated involvement of a third party provides a socially appropriate mechanism for managing such concerns. Thus, a concession that one was unwilling to make before lest it cast doubt on one's strength and resolve, may now be made in the belief that it was done at the behest of the third party. The disputants can reason that they, as well as their adversary, have agreed to make a concession not because they had to (that is, because their adversary forced them to do so), but rather because they chose to (that is, because the third party was seen as wanting or expecting such behavior). A concession that was taken

---

° In keeping with Walton's (1969) analysis, it is assumed here that there is an optimal level of motivation, such that the principals are neither indifferent about reaching agreement nor so energized that they are inclined to make concessions prematurely.

† See, for example, Douglas (1962), Dunlop and Chamberlain (1967), Kerr (1954), Peters (1955), Stevens (1963; 1966), and Walton and McKersie (1965) in the labor-management domain; Fisher (1978), Iklé (1964), Schelling (1960), Touval (1975), and Young (1967) in the international arena; Deutsch (1973) in the area of intrapsychic conflict; and Brown (1968; 1970), Deutsch and Krauss (1962), Pruitt (1971; 1981), Rubin (1980), and Rubin and Brown (1975) in the area of interpersonal bargaining.

as a sign of personal weakness before may now even be seen as a sign of personal strength, to the extent that it is viewed as a product of the moral determination to do the right thing, to bite the bullet, if necessary, and make a concession simply because the third party has asked one to do so. Moreover, if concession making subsequently leads to a mutually satisfactory agreement, the disputants can assume credit for their success; if it leads to exploitation at the hands of one's adversary, the disputants can blame the third party. In either case, concessions can now be made without loss of face.

It has been argued thus far that, almost by virtue of being a presence on the conflictual scene, a third party may reduce the disputants' concerns with loss of face and increase their motivation to work toward agreement. In addition, a third party may be able to deflect face maintenance concerns onto his or her shoulders by taking a more active intervention role. Thus, by serving as a go-between who conveys offers back and forth between the principals—as President Carter's subordinates allegedly did at Camp David—a third party can prevent a face-to-face confrontation and all that it implies. Similarly, a third party may be able to encourage the disputants to make concessions that are labeled exploratory. The effect of such feelers, made at the third party's behest, is to encourage the disputants to test the waters for possibilities of compromise without committing them to a course of action that may invite exploitation. Finally, a third party can partially defuse the disputants' face maintenance concerns by proposing that any agreement reached be limited in its duration and be subject to renewal and re-evaluation at a later time. In this way the principals can make concessions and reach agreements in the knowledge that, even under the worst of circumstances—a concession or agreement that invites exploitation—they need not be concerned about setting a dangerous precedent. Many of the agreements reached in the Middle East have followed precisely this pattern.

Trust

In order for the principals to be mutually motivated to reach agreement, they must be willing to trust both the third party and each other. The third party can engender trust by behaving in clearly trustworthy ways; that is, by personifying norms of fairness and impartiality and by never making commitments to the disputants unless they can be honored. Kenneth Kressel (1971) has reported that labor mediators list gaining the trust and confidence of the disputants as their single most important task.

The situation with respect to the disputants' trust of each other is considerably more complex. After all, the principals are in the midst of conflict, and the services of a third party have been deemed necessary at least partially because the parties are unable or unwilling to trust each other. A skilled third party must therefore be able to move the disputants away from a position of shared suspicion and hostility, in the direction of increased goodwill, tolerance, and understanding.

One of the things a third party can do in this regard is to teach the disputants to attend to those areas and issues for which their interests are convergent rather than divergent. For example, by requiring that any communication between the principals be prefaced with a statement regarding actual or potential areas of overlap, or insisting that points of disagreement be cast in as positive a light as possible, a third party may be able to encourage the disputants to focus on some of the desirable facets of their relationship. At another level, a third party can attempt to engender trust and trustworthiness by asking each side to make several concessions and commitments, no mater how small or apparently insignificant, with the understanding that the concessions are irreversible and the commitments irrevocable. In this way the disputants may be encouraged to regard each other and themselves as people who can be trusted to do what they say. Finally, if all else fails, a third party can temporarily bypass the issue of trust by offering to serve as a guarantor of any agreement reached. Assuming that the third party has tangible resources and is willing to use them in order to protect a settlement between the disputants, the third party can promise to uphold the terms of any agreement reached. Assuming the disputants can trust the third party's word, their trust of each other is now quite irrelevant.

Irrationality

The disputants will not be motivated to reach agreement so long as they harbor irrational feelings, particularly anger, toward each other. One of the things a third party can do to address this problem is to encourage the principals to vent their feelings, preferably not in the presence of the other person (Kerr 1954). A second, related possibility is for the third party to volunteer to be the target for the disputants' angry displays, thereby deflecting this anger away from the adversary. Pruitt (1981) points out that a third party in such a role may have a function analogous to a psychotherapist dealing with negative transference; the therapist serves as a substitute target for the client's anger and emotion, allowing the client to experience catharsis and to adopt a more realistic outlook. In his contribution to this volume, Pruitt points out that Kissinger performed this function in his dealings with the principals in the Middle East, particularly Israeli Prime Minister Golda Meir. A final technique for reducing irrationality, also used rather extensively and well by Kissinger, involves the timely injection of humor. A third party may be able to engender greater trust and greater distance from the negative climate of the dispute by poking gentle fun at the conflict, at the seriousness with which it is taken by all concerned, and at the third party's own role and input.

Autonomy

In order for the disputants to be genuinely motivated to reach agreement, a third party must acknowledge, and must help the principals to understand, the importance of their autonomy: it is their set of decisions to make and their dispute to revolve. All too often, scholars and researchers interested in the intervention process have made the assumption that disputants welcome outside intervention, that they view themselves as victims awaiting rescue by a white knight on a speeding charger. Perhaps they do not. Perhaps people in conflict very much want to find the solution to their shared problems without the intrusion of an outsider. If so, then it becomes increasingly important that an engaged third party be sensitive to the autonomy needs of the disputants and have sufficient insight to understand that the interests of the parties may best be served with the help of a catalyst rather than a messiah. To this end it is essential that a third party be able to judge when and for how long to intervene in a dispute, and when to withdraw. As was stated earlier, the best third party may be the one who is rendered obsolete and unnecessary by the quality of his or her intervention.

SOME UNANSWERED QUESTIONS ABOUT THIRD PARTY EFFECTIVENESS

Throughout this chapter, comments have been repeatedly made in passing about the hallmarks of intervention effectiveness. The time has come to admit that far less is actually known about the characteristics of effective third party intervention than may appear. It is only fitting, therefore, that this chapter close by listing some of the many questions that remain, along with occasional suggestions for possible answers.

Third Party Timing

Granted that a third party plans to intervene in a conflict, when should this occur? More generally, is it reasonable to think of there being an optimal point of intervention? If so, what is this point? By intervening rather early in the conflict, the third party may be able to assist the disputants in their effort to identify and differentiate among the issues in dispute. Moreover, the third party may be able to nip problems in the bud, facilitating a settlement that might prove more difficult at a later time. On the other hand, early intervention may prove premature. Perhaps the parties have not yet experienced sufficient tension to truly motivate them to work on their problem. Perhaps for third party intervention to prove maximally effective, the disputants need to have achieved a state of readiness that may be delayed or otherwise hindered through premature third party action. If so, then it stands to reason that the third party should wait before intervening.

Waiting, however, may also prove to be a risky course of action. If the third party waits too long before intervening, the conflict may have already escalated to such a point that opinions are polarized and bargaining positions are now frozen in intransigence. Interventions that may have proved useful at an earlier time are likely to prove ineffective in the midst of intense conflict. In summary, then, the issue of intervention timing is a tricky one. The third party must decide precisely where to intervene along the slippery slope of an escalating conflict. Too great a deviation from this optimal point of intervention is likely to result in slippage either in the direction of having acted before the parties were truly ready to work on their conflict, or in the direction of having moved too late—after the parties had already generated so much heat that they were no longer particularly interested in the light.*

Existence of an Ongoing Relationship among the Disputants

When is a third party's job likely to prove easier, and the resulting intervention more effective: when the disputants are members of a short-term relationship with little prior history or basis for future interaction, or when their relationship is an ongoing one? On the one hand, one might expect the disputants in an ongoing relationship to have far greater interest and investment in preserving this relationship. They should therefore be more motivated to cooperate in an effort to resolve their conflict, making the third party's job easier and intervention more effective. On the other hand, the very fact that the members of an ongoing relationship have a history and a future together, the fact that they have a vested interest in their relationship, may make it all the more important that matters of precedent be taken into account. If the disputants have reason to believe that they will need to negotiate with each other on various occasions in the future, then the substance of any settlement reached in the present may become a matter of some concern. Too generous a concession or too great a willingness to negotiate in the first place may be construed as a sign of personal weakness, setting a dangerous precedent. To the extent that the disputants in an ongoing relationship adhere to the view that "if you give 'em an inch, they'll take a mile," they are likely to be reluctant to make concessions, and a third party may find it particularly difficult to intervene effectively.

---

*Of the two possible errors of third party timing, it is the error of too late an intervention that is probably the more costly. If so, then a third party may prefer the risk of premature action, especially since one can return at a later time or do things to enhance a state of readiness among the disputants.

Prior Experience with the Third Party

Will the effectiveness of outside intervention be affected by a third party's prior acquanitance and experience with the disputants? More specifically, will a third party be able to intervene more effectively in the present if that party has worked with the disputants in the past? The answer would appear to depend on the nature and extent of this prior third party involvement. If the disputants' experience with the third party has been negative, they will probably resist subsequent intervention efforts. Indeed, intervention by a disliked or distrusted third party may even prove to the less effective than no intervention at all.* On the other hand, if the disputants' experience has been a favorable one, if third party intervention has led to speedier and more satisfactory conflict resolution than might otherwise have occurred, then one might expect the disputants to have greater trust and confidence in the third party and to be increasingly receptive to any subsequent overtures. However, even under these conditions where prior third party experience with the disputants would seem to be an asset, it may also be something of a liability. Perhaps the prior intervention of a third party, regardless of the favorability with which it was received, will lead the disputants to view the third party as too close to the problems at hand, too much a part of the system, somehow not sufficiently detached to give the relationship the fully impartial hearing it deserves.

Third Party Power

How much of the possible power to impose agreement should a third party exercise in order that intervention prove maximally effective? At an intuitive level, the answer to this question might appear to be that the greater a third party's ability to impose agreement, the more effective the intervention. Indeed, Frei (1976) reports that international mediation is more effective when the disputants are dependent on some external agency for help. The effects of third party power, however, are probably more complex than at first appears, and may depend both on the degree of conflict in the disputants' relationship as well as the third party's intervention goals. As Walton (1969) has pointed out, if the third party's objective is to facilitate a long lasting agreement characterized by the internalization of changed attitudes, then the less power the third party has to exercise in order to bring about a settlement, the better. In other

---

*An important exception should be noted here. If the result of a third party's intervention is to provide the disputants with a common enemy against whom they can work more cooperatively than might otherwise be possible, then the presence of a distrusted or disliked third party may actually facilitate agreement.

words, the less powerful the third party appears to be, the more likely the disputants are to reach agreement of their own accord.

Unfortunately this rule may hold only when the conflict is relatively small in scope. When conflict is intense, it may be unreasonable for the third party to entertain any immediate objective other than bringing about a cessation of overt hostilities between the disputants. Before the third party can move the disputants to the bargaining table and get them to work together on the issues that underlie the conflict, it may first be necessary to get them to lay down their literal or figurative weapons. To do so, the third party may have to exercise all available power. Under circumstances such as these, the greater the third party's power, the greater the likelihood that the conflict can be managed, if not truly resolved. In summary, a third party who wishes to facilitate immediate (if short-term) resolution of conflict should probably exercise as much power to impose agreement as possible; a third party who wishes to pave the way for a more long lasting agreement should probably make use of as little power as is absolutely necessary in order to induce the disputants to resolve their conflict.

Third Party Attributes

What are the attributes of an ideal third party? The behavior of an effective third party must of necessity vary in relation to such things as the particular situation being addressed, the character of the disputants and their interaction, the intensity of conflict, the existence of time and constituency pressures, and so forth. Nevertheless, are there certain third party attributes that transcend such considerations and are clearly related to effectiveness? The answer is probably yes, although it may be necessary to distinguish between two rather different classes of third party attributes: those that are linear and those that are curvilinear in nature.

The greater the degree of possession of a linear attribute, the more effective a third party ought to be. Just as there is no such thing as too much good, truth, or beauty in the world, so does it make little sense to think of a third party who is somehow too trustworthy; the greater a third party's trustworthiness, the more effective the intervention is apt to be. In addition to trustworthiness, examples of other linear third party attributes include credibility, empathy, impartiality, and rapport.

On the other hand, the greater the degree of possession of a curvilinear attribute, the more effective a third party is apt to be—up to a point. Beyond this optimal point, however, the greater the presence of the attribute in question, the less effective the third party is likely to become. Within limits, their party assertiveness is probably desirable. The more assertive the third party, the more actively that party will take control of an escalating conflict, help the disputants to identify the issues in conflict, and make known his or her own, often sound advice. Beyond some point, however, the disputants may begin to feel that the third party is domineering, more interested in making his or her own ideas and opinions known than in listening to what the disputants have to say. Similarly, third party competence and expertise are clearly desirable traits, although as a third party's perceived competence and expertise continue to increase beyond a certain point, that party may be viewed by the disputants as too capable or expert—as so professional that the third party can no longer view the issues and the disputants with the care and empathy that the disputants feel they deserve. Thus, to be too smart or capable (indeed, to be too much in possession of any third party virtue) is to run the risk of being seen by others as disimilar, aloof, and somehow lacking in the compassion and insight that come from being fundamentally similar to oneself.

Examples of other curvilinear attributes include inquisitiveness and similarity. Up to some point, one wants a third party to be curious and interested enough in the disputants to make the effort necessary to find out about their background, interests, and so forth, thereby acquiring information that may put the conflict in broader perspective and facilitate its resolution. Beyond this point, however, continued inquisitiveness may be construed as an invasion of the disputants' privacy, as constituting a demand that the third party be provided with more personal information than that party has a right or need to know. Analogously, perceived similarity between the disputants and the third party is a desirable attribute. The more similar the parties are in background, interests, and values, the better able the third party should be to identify with the disputants and do an effective job of adjudicating the conflict. However, beyond some point of optimal similarity, the third party may be seen as too close to the disputants, as having a vested interest that may hinder the ability to intervene with impartiality and detachment.

The general point with respect to curvilinear attributes is that it is possible for there to be too much of a good thing. An effective third party must know not only when to display curvilinear attributes to their best advantage, but also when to hold back and let the disputants' own abilities come to the fore.

CONCLUSION

It is only fitting to conclude this chapter with some indication of the many areas of inquiry that remain. Although people have been engaged productively in the practice of third party intervention for thousands of years, the formal study of the intervention process is a recent phenomenon. Moreover, although their party practitioners and theorists have begun to systematize their understanding of the process in such far-flung arenas as international relations, labor-management affairs, couple counseling, and interpersonal bargaining, we know of no effort to organize this understanding across interdisciplinary lines rather than within them. This book hopes to move our collective understanding of third party intervention in this general direction by inviting experts from different persuasions to analyze a case that is of common interest.

REFERENCES

Brown, B. R. "The Effects of Need to Maintain Face on Interpersonal Bargaining." *Journal of Experimental Social Psychology*, 1968, 4, 107–22.
———. "Face-saving Following Experimentally Induced Embarrassment." *Journal of Experimental Social Psychology*, 1970, 6, 255–71.
Chertkoff, J., and Esser, J. "A Review of Experiments in Explicit Bargaining." *Journal of Experimental Social Psychology*, 1976, 12, 464–86.
Deutsch, M. *The Resolution of Conflict*. New Haven, Conn.: Yale University Press, 1973.
Deutsch M., and Krauss, R. M. "Studies of Interpersonal Bargaining." *Journal of Conflict Resolution*, 1962, 6, 52–76.
Douglas, A. *Industrial Peacemaking*. New York: Columbia University Press, 1962.
Druckman, D., *Negotiations: Social-Psychological Perspectives*. Beverly Hills, Calif.: Sage, 1977.
Dunlop, J. T., and Chamberlain, N. W., eds. *Frontiers of Collective Bargaining*. *New York: Harper and Row, 1967.*
Erickson, B.; Holmes, J. G.; Frey, R.; Walker, L.; and Thibaut, J. "Functions of a Third Party in the Resolution of Conflict: The Role of a Judge in Pretrial Conferences." *Journal of Personality and Social Psychology*, 1974, 30, 293–306.
Fisher, R. "Fractionating Conflict." In R. Fisher, ed., *International Conflict and Behavioral Science: The Craigville Papers*. New York: Basic Books, 1964.
———. *International Mediation: A Working Guide*. New York: International Peace Academy, 1978.
Frei, D. "Conditions Affecting the Effectiveness of International Mediation." *Peace Science Society (International)*, 1976, 26, 67–84.
Froman, L. A., Jr., and Cohen, M. D. "Compromise and Logroll: Comparing the Efficiency of Two Bargaining Processes. *Behavioral Science*, 1970, 15, 180–83.
Iklé, F. C. *How Nations Negotiate*. New York: Harper and Row, 1964.
Kelley, H. H. "A Classroom Study of the Dilemmas in Interpersonal Negotiations." In K. Archibald, ed., *Strategic Interaction and Conflict: Original Papers and Discussion*. Berkeley, Calif.: Institute of International Studies, 1966.
Kerr, C. "Industrial Conflict and Its Mediation. *American Journal of Sociology*, 1954, 60, 230–45.
Krauss, R. M., and Deutsch, M. "Communication in Interpersonal Bargaining." *Journal of Personality and Social Psychology*, 1966, 4, 572–77.

Kressel, K. "Labor Mediation: An Exploratory Survey." Unpublished manuscript, Teachers College, Columbia University, 1971.

Morley, I. E., and Stephenson, G. M. *The Social Psychology of Bargaining.* London: Allen and Unwin, 1977.

Nemeth, C. "A Critical Analysis of Research Utilizing the Prisoner's Dilemma Paradigm for the Study of Bargaining." In L. Berkowitz, ed., *Advances in Experimental Social Psychology,* Vol. 6. New York: Academic Press, 1972.

Peters, E. *Strategy and Tactics in Labor Negotiations.* New London, Conn.: National Foremen's Institute, 1955.

Pruitt, D. G. "Indirect Communication and the Search for Agreement in Negotiation." *Journal of Applied Social Psychology,* 1971, 1, 205–39.

———. *Negotiation Behavior.* New York: Academic Press, 1981.

Pruitt, D. G., and Kimmel, M. J. Twenty Years of Experimental Gaming: Critique, Synthesis, and Suggestions for the Future." *Annual Review of Psychology,* 1977, 28, 363–92.

Rubin, J. Z. "Experimental Research on Third-Party Intervention in Conflict: Toward Some Generalizations. *Psychological Bulletin,* 1980, 87, 379–91.

Rubin J. Z., and Brown, B. R. *The Social Psychology of Bargaining and Negotiation.* New York: Academic Press, 1975.

Sartre, J. P. *No Exit and Three Other Plays.* New York: Random House, 1955.

Schelling, T. C. *The Strategy of Conflict.* Cambridge, Mass.: Harvard University Press, 1960.

Sherif, M., and Sherif, C. W. *Social Psychology.* New York: Harper and Row, 1969.

Simmel, G. "The Number of Members as Determining the Sociological Form of the Group. *American Journal of Sociology,* 1902, 8, 158–96.

Stevens, C. M. *Strategy and Collective Bargaining Negotiation.* New York: McGraw-Hill, 1960.

———. "Is Compulsory Arbitration Compatible with Bargaining?" *Industrial Relations,* 1966, 5, 38–52.

Touval, S. "Biased Intermediaries: Theoretical and Historical Considerations." *Jerusalem Journal of International Relations,* 1975, 1, 51–69.

Walton, R. E. *Interpersonal Peacemaking: Confrontations and Third-Party Consultation.* Reading, Mass.: Addison-Wesley, 1969.

Walton, R. E., and McKersie, R. B. *A Behavioral Theory of Labor Negotiations: An Analysis of a Social Interaction System.* New York: McGraw-Hill, 1965.

Young, O. R. *The Intermediaries: Third Parties in International Crises.* Princeton, N.J.: Princeton University Press, 1967.

Zartman, I. W., ed. *The Negotiation Process.* Beverly Hills, Calif.: Sage, 1978.

2

HOW KISSINGER DID IT:
STEP BY STEP IN THE MIDDLE EAST

Edward R. F. Sheehan

For over two years, newspapers and newscasts around the world have been filled with the chronicle of Henry Kissinger's comings and goings in the Middle East, his seemingly ceaseless shuttling between Cairo, Jerusalem, Damascus, Riyadh, Amman, and other capitals to find partial agreements between the Arabs and the Israelis.

It has been, at best, a difficult saga to follow, full of sound and some fury—but signifying what? Even the expert will be excused for having on occasion failed to follow the course of the negotiations, or having lost interest in them.

But their importance is clear. They have established, in the words of one of America's leading Middle East experts, Edward R. F. Sheehan, our first postwar "Arab policy." Beyond that fact lie further questions, about the long-term value of the accomplishment, and about the future of U.S.-Israeli relations. Whatever lies ahead, however, a specific phase in the tortured history of Mideast diplomacy is now over, although it is too early to pass definitive judgment on it.

In the lengthy article that follows, Sheehan presents the first comprehensive account of that phase and of Kissinger's efforts. Based on extensive talks with American, Arab, and Israeli officials on three continents, Sheehan's article continues the effort of this magazine to present major investigative diplomatic reporting to our readers. An expansion of this article will appear as a book to be published next autumn by Reader's Digest Press.

The direct quotations of dialogue in the article are verbatim, condensed from the actual conversations between participants only when necessary for space reasons.—The Editors.

Since the Arab-Israeli war of October 1973, Secretary of State Henry A. Kissinger has devoted more of his time and craft to the consequences of that conflict than to any other issue of foreign policy. Never has American diplomacy—or the man who conducts it—been so visibly committed to the solution of a problem. Throughout a dozen missions to the Middle East, throughout thousands of hours of negotiations there and in Washington, throughout three hundred thousand miles or more of flying to and fro, Kissinger has summoned all the power of his prodigious intellect to the fashioning of a new equation between the greatest of the Semitic peoples, aspiring to prevent another war that might overwhelm the world beyond. Today, nearly two and a half years after he began, we must assess his achievements, his failures, and his method—step-by-step diplomacy.

The most crucial of Kissinger's labors occurred in moments of great tension: between October 6, 1973, when the war broke out, and late December of that year, when the Geneva conference was convened; during January 1974, when he separated the Israeli and Egyptian armies and asserted the necessity of his personal intervention to achieve interim solutions; during May 1974, when he separated the Israeli and Syrian armies whilst the Syrians were waging a war of attrition; during March 1975, when his endeavor to negotiate a new agreement in the Sinai collapsed amidst recriminations with the government of Israel; and in August 1975, when he finally achieved that agreement at a high cost to the United States—though much lower, he insisted, than its alternative, another war.

Some significant features of Kissinger's diplomacy emerge from the multitude of his decisions:

In the aftermath of the October war, he created a coherent Arab policy for the United States—the first secretary of state to do so. The policy was based on a quasi-alliance between Washington and Cairo—or more particularly, upon friendship between Kissinger and Egyptian President Anwar el-Sadat. Kissinger assumed that with Sadat in hand the other Arabs would follow, but today that assumption is cast in doubt.

Simultaneously with his effort to diminish the Arab-Israeli conflict, Kissinger has pursued a parallel policy in the Arab world— promotion of American technology—as a means of increasing American influence throughout the Arab nations.

From the morrow of the war until late last year, Kissinger tenaciously avoided the Palestinian problem, though it is crucial to the Arab-Israeli conflict.

Relations between the United States and Israel, which began to erode during the October war, have deteriorated to a condition of chronic crisis—dramatized by Kissinger's recurring clashes with Israeli leaders and Israel's American constituency.

Kissinger had deep misgivings about stationing American technicians in the Sinai desert, and about his own policy of supplying vast quantities of arms to Israel.

Kissinger consistently refused to promise the Arabs that the United States would push Israel back to its 1967 borders, but in June 1974 and June 1975, Presidents Nixon and Ford secretly assured the Arab leaders that the United States favored substantial restoration of the 1967 frontiers—a position Washington has so far declined to make public.

A DANGEROUS TEST

"I never treat crises when they're cold," Kissinger once told a friend, "only when they're hot. This enables me to weigh the protagonists one against the other, not in terms of ten or two thousand years ago but in terms of what each of them merits at this moment." His principle was put to a dangerous test on the morrow of the October war. Both Israelis and Egyptians expected Kissinger to rescue them from the impasse he had helped to contrive as the conclusion of that contest.

The armies of Israel and Egypt were chaotically intertwined; the Egyptians still held fast in the northern sector of the Suez Canal's eastern bank, but in the south their Third Army was surrounded; on the western bank, the Israelis had thrust to within 60 miles of Cairo and had encircled the city of Suez. Sadat was demanding an immediate Israeli retreat to the cease-fire lines of October 22 (as required by U.N. Security Council Resolution 338), and a peace conference to arrange total Israeli withdrawal from all of the Arab territories. Prime Minister Golda Meir, claiming that the October 22 lines were impossible to establish, demanded an immediate return to the lines of October 5, and a swift exchange of prisoners. The cease-fire threatened to collapse.

At the end of October, President Nixon invited Golda Meir to Washington; Sadat sent Ismail Fahmy, his irrepressible new foreign minister, without waiting for an invitation. As it happened, this enabled Kissinger to try his hand at instant mediation; he shuttled indefatigably between Fahmy at the State Department and Golda Meir at Blair House, though without palpable result. Fahmy insisted on the October 22 lines, Golda Meir upon her prisoners. Kissinger drew up a working draft of six points, providing in part for relief of the Third Army and an exchange of prisoners, and then, on November 5, 1973, flew off to the Middle East to deal with the belligerents *sur scène.*

He paused, en route, in Morocco and Tunisia to render his respects to Hassan II and Habib ben Ali Bourguiba, but Cairo was the focus of his quest. Sadat, whose acquaintance he was about to make, he had long considered a bombastic clown. He could be pardoned for that assumption, for it corresponded—until the war—with the assessment of numerous Egyptians. Gamal Abdel Nasser, whose own pigment was only faintly lighter, was reputed once to have called Sadat "that black donkey." Little in Sadat's previous career appeared to have prepared him for the presidency of Egypt or for the sublime ordeal of matching wits with Kissinger. He was a peasant of the Nile Delta, who told me 20 years ago that "the West hates the Arabs because they think we're Negroes."

More naturally sly than Nasser, more preternaturally Egyptian, Sadat had learned in the shadow of his master that in politics patience can be as sharp a tool as cunning. When he succeeded Nasser in 1970, his enemies assumed he was a half-wit. This seemed to serve his purpose. For seven months after his accession, real power in Egypt was wielded not by Sadat but by the intelligence services, headed by a clique of goons posing as Nasser's authentic heirs. Sadat built an alternative power base centered upon the army. Then, provoked by plots amongst the goons, he *pounced*—turning the government on its head, packing his rivals off to jail.

This was, as I wrote then, "a marvel of political craftsmanship, a masterly lesson of how to proceed, step by modest step, from impotence to supreme power." But it did not solve any of Sadat's external problems. By the time of Nasser's death it had become obvious to any lucid Egyptian that the two pillars of Nasserist policy—Arab socialism and dependence on the Soviet Union—had failed. Sadat knew that Egypt needed a new policy, but in struggling to concoct it he could not get anyone outside of Egypt—particularly the United States—to take him seriously. Kissinger, in practice, ignored Sadat's dramatic cries for help and clung to a cozy theory that the only strategic ally he needed in the Middle East was Israel. But now the war had shattered that supposition, and as his aircraft turned from the Mediterranean to descend upon the Nile Delta, Kissinger—no less than Sadat himself—was in search of a new policy.

For Kissinger had seemed indifferent to the Middle East until the October war. He had been cynical from the beginning about the plan launched in 1969 by William Rogers, his predecessor as secretary of state, when Rogers publicly endorsed substantial Israeli withdrawal from conquered territory in exchange for contractual peace from the Arabs. Privately he was contemptuous of Rogers, and he contributed to Nixon's decision that Rogers' endeavors should collapse quietly of exhaustion in the autumn of 1971. That eventually, after he replaced Rogers as secretary of state. Kissinger should adopt Rogers' policy of pursuing peace in the Middle East through interim agreements is not the least irony of his subsequent diplomacy.

"HOW ABOUT IT, DEAR HENRY . . . ?"

Perceptive Arab diplomats recognized early during the Nixon years that real power in the administration reposed with Kissinger, not Rogers; a few urged Kissinger to undertake an active role in seeking a settlement. Ashraf Ghorbal, then chief of the Egyptian Interests Section in Washington (now ambassador), perhaps despairing of conventional diplomacy, tried his hand at doggerel, which he dispatched to Kissinger on the morrow of his first visit to Peking: "On one of my recent excavations/ I ran across an old exclamation/ It was in Amenhotep's tomb/ The god of medicine of ancient gloom/ It said, 'Come and visit my Nile'/ And you do not have to stand in file/ For your stomachaches I have a cure/ And for your headaches for sure/ How about it, dear Henry/ Shall we make the Middle East a double entry?" To an Arab statesman whose plea, though more prosaic, was essentially similar, Kissinger retorted, "I will never get involved in anything unless I'm sure of success. And if I do get involved it means I'm going to succeed. I hate failure," The Middle East, he mused to friends, "isn't ready for me."

Furthermore, Kissinger accepted and in fact helped to promote the conventional strategic wisdom of the first Nixon administration—that in the absence of fruitful negotiations, a strong Israel, militarily much superior to its Arab foes, would prevent war and serve as the surest sentinel of American interests in the Middle East. When Kissinger glanced at the map of the Middle East, he saw the Soviet Union and the United States. He was distressed by the flow of Soviet weapons and military technicians into Egypt, and he had no mind to permit American munitions in Israel to be vanquished by Russian logistics to Cairo. Kissinger indeed became very much a "hard-liner" in the Middle East. Israeli Ambassador Yitzhak Rabin was his close friend, and privately, for a period, he favored Israel's aspiration to retain significant portions of Arab territory. He shared Assistant Secretary of State Joseph Sisco's argument that the Israelis would never make concessions until they had confidence, and they could not have confidence until they achieved invincibility.

Sadat, meanwhile, was thrashing about in quest of a new policy. His "year of decision" (1971) had ended ignominiously, and—deprived of the Soviet offensive arms he needed to match Israel's—he was going nowhere with the Russians. Rogers had suggested to Sadat in Cairo that Nixon might be more forthcoming were Sadat to diminish the enormous Soviet presence in Egypt; in a famous indiscretion, Kissinger had already announced that the American purpose was to "expel" the Russians. Provoked also by the contradiction of Soviet policy—the Russians' preference for improved relations with the United States vs. their inadequate posture as Egypt's arsenal against Israel—and by internal pressure from his own army, Sadat in the summer of 1972 expelled nearly all of his 20,000 Soviet technicians.

Kissinger was astounded. "Why has Sadat done me this favor?" he asked his aides. "Why didn't he get in touch with me? Why didn't he demand of me all kinds of concessions first?" For in a curious intelligence failure, Kissinger learned of the expulsion from news dispatches. Sadat, in desperation, had decided upon a *coup de théâtre*, a colossal thrust to buy more time, whilst he groped to elude his demon of "no war, no peace." Whatever his immediate motivations, he must have known that the expulsion would be perceived as another cry for American help. Publicly, Nixon all but ignored Sadat's epochal decision, though privately he responded—without committing himself. Kissinger drafted several secret messages for Nixon's signature which were then dispatched by intelligence channels directly to Sadat through Hafez Ismail, his national security adviser. In these, Nixon acknowledged the expulsion as an important act, and pledged that the administration would concentrate on the Middle East as soon as the presidential elections and the Vietnam negotiations were concluded.

At the end of February 1973, Ismail came to Washington. Kissinger spent a weekend in secret talks with that tall and taciturn Egyptian, expounding to him his notion of seeking a formula that would reconcile Egypt's sovereignty in the Sinai with Israel's insistence on security. Ismail left Washington prepared to advise Sadat that finally the Americans seemed serious about promoting negotiations. In Paris, en route home, Ismail read a *New York Times* report that Nixon had decided to furnish Israel with 36 new Skyhawks and 48 Phantoms. Through his secret channel, Kissinger hastened to assure Sadat that the report was false, that the Israeli request (long since pending) was still "under study." Kissinger was furious at the leak because it undermined his conversations with Ismail. The report, however, was not false, only premature; Nixon confirmed it in the spring.

The abortive Ismail mission was the turning point on the path to war. As the spring proceeded, Kissinger brooded on the Middle East and became progressively more uneasy. Secretly (without even informing Rogers) he met Ismail once more in Paris, where he sought to penetrate Egyptian suspicion with pleas for confidence. Sadat allowed the meeting chiefly as a cover, for he had taken his decision to wage war. From Riyadh, King Faisal began to warn that he might wield his "oil weapon" if Washington did not move the Israelis and very soon. Nevertheless,

Kissinger thought he had time—and besides, Watergate was inching in on Nixon, shrinking his domestic power base, crippling his will to make decisions.

Whilst in New York in late September for the General Assembly of the United Nations. Kissinger (now secretary of state) invited the Arab foreign ministers to luncheon. Kissinger hitherto had avoided Arabs as best he could, and on this occasion was ill at ease because he fancied that his Jewishness might prejudice the dialogue. He decided to dissolve the barrier with a joke. "I recognize," he told his guests, "that many of you view me with suspicion. This reminds me of a story which corresponds to our situation. The Communists called a rally, and the police infiltrated it with an informer. Then the police broke in and beat everybody up. The informer protested and said, 'I'm the anti-Communist.' The police said, 'We don't care what kind of a Communist you are—you're under arrest.'"

Half the Arabs understood this as Kissinger's subtle way of poking fun at his own Jewishness, of assuring them he was not a Zionist, and they laughed. The other half had no idea of what he was talking about. "The problem of the Middle East is a complex one," he continued. "The United States recognizes that it involves a legitimate concern for security on one side and for justice on the other. Resolution 242° has many elements, but it is difficult and not practical to impose theoretical and comprehensive formulas on the Middle East. The problem should be approached gradually, piece by piece." He concluded by offering his friendship to the Arab world. "We recognize that the present situation is intolerable to the Arabs." Kissinger's style impressed the foreign ministers; no Anglo-Saxon secretary of state had displayed such warmth—*Semitic* warmth. Understandably pleased with his performance, Kissinger left the luncheon confident that he had several months to come up with something.

The fourth Arab-Israeli war began less than a fortnight later. That was on October 6; Kissinger believed the CIA and assumed the Israelis would win quickly. Perplexed and angry, for several days he complained constantly to his aides of "irrational Arabs," "demented Arabs," and of the Arabs' "romanticism which leads them to impossible expectations." Certain that Israel would crush Egypt, he feared that the Soviet Union would intervene, forcing the United States to intervene on the side of Israel and risking a war of the great powers.

On October 8 and 9, however, Kissinger's views began to change. After initial success on the Golan Heights, the Syrians were beginning to falter, but the Egyptians had crossed the Suez Canal, destroyed the Bar-Lev line, and now were entrenched several miles deep inside the Sinai desert. The Israelis had lost numerous tanks and aircraft; Kissinger

---

°United Nations Security Council Resolution 242 of November 22, 1967 calls for Israeli withdrawal from Arab territory in return for secure and recognized frontiers.

was amongst the first to sense that the strategic balance was shifting away from them. He had no mind to restore it straight-away, because he recognized instinctively that the new balance tendered him an exquisite chance to use the war as an extension of diplomacy. If he allowed neither side to win decisively, then he might manipulate the result to launch negotiations, and—ultimately—to compose the Arab-Israeli quarrel. All of Kissinger's ensuing moves must be understood in this perspective.

Much has been written about Kissinger's role in the resupply of arms to Israel during the October war; he has been variously portrayed as a hero, valiantly struggling to overcome the obstructions of the Pentagon, and as a villain, malevolently playing games with Israel's fate. The evidence disavows such extreme interpretations. In keeping with his early perception that the war must be used to promote a settlement, Kissinger decided to wihhold major deliveries to Israel so long as the Russians exercised restraint and so long as he hoped that Sadat would accept a cease-fire. Not only did he perceive an important opening to Egypt, he wished to prevent an oil embargo and a torrent of violent anti-American reprisals throughout the Arab world. Therefore, early during the war, Kissinger and Nixon devised a stratagem that became the source of many subsequent polemics. Nixon told the Pentagon to "play tough," to appear to impede major deliveries to Israel until such time as he and Kissinger determined otherwise. Neither Nixon nor Kissinger intended to be rushed by the Israelis, and both of them coveted the credit amongst American Jews should later circumstance constrain them to unleash an airlift.

The crisis with the Israelis intensified on October 10, when it became obvious that the war might drag on for weeks, but Kissinger persisted in blaming the Pentagon for obstructing major deliveries—the better to prevent Simcha Dinitz, the Israeli ambassador, from mobilizing American Jews against the administration. Dinitz swallowed Kissinger's protestations that the Pentagon bureaucracy was at fault, and withheld his "shock troops" (Kissinger's description). Kissinger was trying now to achieve a cease-fire in place; the Israelis angrily accepted it on October 12, and were rewarded with a slight crescendo of supplies. Sadat's refusal the next day, coupled with an enlargement of the Soviet airlift to Egypt and Syria, provoked Kissinger to cast aside the stratagem and release immense quantities of arms to Israel so as to end the war quickly and prove to the world that the conflict could not be decided by Russian guns.

Kissinger thereupon flew to Moscow, where he negotiated with the Russians the terms of Security Council Resolution 338, which called for an immediate cease-fire in place, the implementation of Resolution 242 in all of its parts, and immediate negotiations between the parties to establish "a just and durable peace in the Middle East." The resolution was adopted on October 22, though the hostilities raged for several days more as the Israelis maneuvered to destroy the Third Army. Supported by Nixon, Kissinger applied intense pressure upon Israel to desist, and the war ended in deadlock—just as he had planned—with neither victor nor vanquished.

The October war revealed Kissinger at the apogee of his skill. Propelled by the vehemence of events, he recognized very early the paradoxical opportunities for peace, and he pursued peace without bending to the Russians, abandoning Israel, or irrevocably alienating the Arabs. For 10 days he was deeply anxious, but by the eleventh day he had snatched control of events. With Nixon enmeshed in scandal (Vice President Spiro Agnew's resignation and the Watergate "Saturday Night Massacre" took place at this time), Kissinger was in real measure running the world.

True, the airlift, when it came—then Nixon's request to Congress for $2.2 billion in aid to Israel—provoked the Arab oil embargo. True, the airlift and the subsequent (perhaps unnecessary) American nuclear alert imposed severe strain upon the Atlantic Alliance. But the airlift did not burn Kissinger's bridges to Sadat; hardly a fortnight after it began, Sadat announced to the world press that American policy was "constructive." This statement, so much at variance with Nasser's vindictive accusations in 1967, was the psychological breakthrough that Kissinger sought; a clear signal from Cairo that Sadat was aching to strike a bargain with the United States. In fact, throughout the war, even with American weapons flooding into Israel and the Sinai, Kissinger marveled at the mildness of the Arab reaction—save for the embargo, no confiscations, no riots, no reprisals against American interests of any sort. Sadat had concluded before the war was done that though America remained the arsenal of his enemy it wished also to be his friend; that the Russians could deliver arms but not peace; that for peace he needed the United States. Indeed, by waging war, Sadat finally seized Kissinger's fascinated attention.

KISSINGER MEETS SADAT

Their first encounter, on November 7, 1973—simply because it happened—was the food of history. Kissinger was apprehensive, for he was as dissimilar to Sadat as Talleyrand was to Wellington. Indeed, what greater contrast can we fancy than this plump Jewish professor in rumpled blue and the lean, brown, erstwhile terrorist in khaki who welcomed him amongst the gilded armchairs of Tahra Palace? Kissinger had brought Sisco and several other senior aides, but only to confer in the garden with Sadat's subordinates. Sadat he saved for himself; without even a note-taker, the two of them retired to talk tête-à-tête.

Kissinger was touched at once by Sadat's urbanity and charm; Sadat liked Kissinger's incisiveness, so refreshing after the naiveté of Rogers. However, the reports of their instant romance (soon to be dramatized by their public kissing) have been exaggerated. Essentially, we glimpse a pair of foxes, exchanging oaths of confidence, each of them intent on wielding the other for his own purpose. Sadat evoked his hostility to the Soviet Union, and urged that the United States and Egypt pursue a "common strategy" in the Middle East. They spoke of the peace conference, under joint Soviet and American auspices, envisioned by Resolution 338. Sadat urged a role for the Palestinians; Kissinger replied he would try to arrange some form of Palestinian participation—a significant departure from previous American indifference to the central role of the Palestinians in the Arab-Israeli conflict. The swiftest way to peace, Sadat went on, was a swift implementation of Resolution 242, meaning a swift Israeli withdrawal from all of the Sinai. This was, of course, a maximum position, but Sadat imagined then that Kissinger could accomplish it, if not at once, in six months or a year at most.

Kissinger replied, "Look, I am a serious person. I shall keep what I can promise, but I shan't promise what I can't keep. If you expect from me broad and sweeping declarations, then I'm not your man." If Sadat persisted in voicing his demands in the ultimate language of Resolution 242, Kissinger continued, then the Israelis would not move an inch. Hinting that he sympathized with Sadat's objective of reclaiming all of the Sinai, just as he sympathized with Israel's insistence on security, he defined the ultimate goal as "mutually agreed borders"—a concept that eventually could accommodate Egypt's demand for sovereignty and Israel's for security. The ways and means to reconcile the two would be worked out in the peace conference, but there would never be a conference if Egypt insisted on a commitment from Israel for total withdrawal before negotiations started. "We must put aside irreconcilables for the moment," Kissinger said. "We must build confidence; conceive a negotiating dynamic. We must set in motion small agreements. We must proceed step by step."

But how was that possible, Sadat wondered when the Israelis wouldn't even return to the lines of October 22? "Nobody knows where the lines of October 22 are," Kissinger retorted. "If I spend my capital with Israel on every point of the cease-fire, there won't be any left for the peace conference. Look, instead of wasting time on the October 22 lines, why don't we try for something bigger?" If Sadat would give him a few more weeks, Kissinger would try to negotiate a "disengagement" of the armies along the Suez Canal. He would try to move the Israelis off the western bank, then away from the canal and deeper into Sinai.

Sadat puffed at his pipe, and brooded. He was under intense pressure in his own camp to rescue Suez and the Third Army; each hour counted. Fahmy had been adamant, but now Sadat overruled Fahmy and himself—and accepted Kissinger's proposition. This decision was crucial. It became the basis of their friendship, and the foundation of future American policy; it was at that moment that Kissinger decided he was dealing not with a clown but with a statesman. Moreover, Sadat accepted Kissinger's draft of six points, providing for a relief corridor to Suez and the Third Army, to be followed by a full exchange of prisoners. The modalities were to be determined by direct military talks between Israelis and Egyptians at Kilometer 101, the point on the Suez road where the Israelis sat entrenched, an hour's drive from Cairo's gates. Sisco would leave forthwith for Israel, to win Golda Meir's acquiescence. Finally, they agreed to re-establish full diplomatic relations, suspended during the Six-Day War.

The conversation was very cordial, and very tough. The Egyptians claim that weaving through the dialogue, like a barely visible thread, was Kissinger's implied threat that he would unleash the Israelis on the Third Army if Sadat did not defer to his suggestions.

When Kissinger emerged from Tahra Palace, it was with something the United States had never really possessed before—an Arab policy. Its essence was a commitment to the Arabs that, so long as they understood the United States would not abandon Israel, Washington would truly wield its power to regain Arab rights. Henceforth, Sadat was to serve as the keystone of that policy, the first recipient of whatever political, territorial, and financial favors Kissinger had the capacity to bestow. Henceforth, Kissinger would undertake no initiative in the Middle East without first consulting the president of Egypt. "The enemy of my enemy is my friend," the Arab proverb says. In a single meeting Sadat had rewritten it to read, "The friend of my enemy is my friend, too." Where this new friendship was to lead Egypt and America had yet to be perceived, but the hopes of both were gleaming as Kissinger's blue and white Boeing flew away from Cairo to the east.

MORE HAGGLING

Kissinger proceeded to Amman, thence to Riyadh; he was bombarded in both places by messages from Sisco. Golda Meir was balking at Kissinger's six points, in particular at the provisions for supplying Suez and the Third Army. She wanted to be certain that no weapons slipped through. Her protestations foreshadowed the haggling that was to feature all of Kissinger's future negotiations with the government of Israel. Words in the document were changed and rearranged, but no sooner was that accomplished than new messages descended from Israel and Egypt, each accusing the other of violating the six points Kissinger had imposed upon them. Sleepless and exhausted, Kissinger drove to the Royal Palace for a dramatic audience with Faisal ibn Abdel-Aziz ibn Abdel-Rahman al-Faisal al-Saud, King of Saudi Arabia.

Faisal received him in the royal study, sitting on an overstuffed armchair amongst his robed entourage, beside a table with a white telephone. Kissinger had asked Sadat what to expect from this master of much of the world's oil and the mightiest Arab of a millenium. "Well, Dr. Henry," Sadat replied, "he'll probably preach to you about Communism and the Jews."

> *Kissinger:* I recall Your Majesty's visit to the United States early during President Nixon's administration, when Your Majesty pointed out to the president some of the dangers in the Middle East. Many of Your Majesty's prophecies have come true. I wish to explain our actions in the war of last month. Your Majesty may not approve, but he must know why we acted as we did. We were motivated by a desire to prevent an increase of Communist influence, and when the Soviets began to send in arms we had to react.

As Kissinger spoke, the king hunched in his chair, his hooded head surmounted by a band of woven gold, his remarkable mouth frozen with distaste, his long, speckled fingers plucking at lint on his cloak. Kissinger was the Western secularist par excellence: Faisal was the incarnation of Wahhabism—that puritanical movement which preached a revival of Islamic simplicity and a fundamentalist fidelity to the precepts of the Koran forbidding all terrestrial pleasures save those of the marriage bed. When the king answered Kissinger, his voice was high-pitched, like a lamentation.

> *Faisal:* Thank you for your explanation. I wish to remind you of what I said to President Nixon and to Secretary Rogers. It is essential to press Israel to withdraw from occupied territory. As you know, the Communists want the situation to remain critical. The United States used to stand up against aggression—you did that in World War II and in 1956 during the Suez war. If the United States had done the same after 1967, we would not have witnessed this deterioration. I speak as a friend, and I want you to know how painful it is for me to take steps which injure our friendship. . . . Israel is advancing Communist objectives. It is unfortunate that amongst those of the Jewish faith there are those who embrace Zionism. Before the Jewish state was established, there existed nothing to harm good relations between Arabs and Jews. There were many Jews in Arab countries. When the Jews were persecuted in Spain, Arabs protected them. When the Romans drove the Jews out, Arabs protected them. At Yalta, it was Stalin who said there had to be a Jewish state. It is necessary to establish in Palestine a mixed Jewish-Moslem state. Most of the immigration to Israel is from the Soviet Union, and they want to establish a Communist base right in the Middle East. Communists have no faith. They don't believe in God.
>
> *Kissinger:* Your Majesty, our problem now is how to proceed from the present situation—which we know is intolerable—to genuine peace.

Faisal: That's easy. Make Israel withdraw.

Kissinger: I agree that there must be Israeli withdrawals, but this is a complicated problem for the United States—and not just a foreign policy problem. We have decided to make a major effort to achieve a settlement. We've made a beginning in Egypt, and we've agreed with President Sadat to convene a peace conference. We wish to establish good relations with all Arab countries that desire them with us. I mentioned Syria to Your Majesty at the dinner table.

Faisal: I asked a Syrian friend if Syria would object to a visit by Your Excellency. The Syrian said Syria would welcome him.

Kissinger: . . . Your Majesty will see that in the coming months we'll make a major effort to achieve progress.

Faisal: I hope it will only take weeks.

Kissinger: Well, that raises the question of Your Majesty's oil embargo. We understand the emotions that led to the embargo.

Faisal: That is why you must move as quickly as possible—so that we can rescind the embargo. It was very painful for me to have been forced to take this action against our American friends.

Kissinger: Your Majesty's decision had a serious effect, coming as it did from an old friend.

Faisal: That's why I've suffered even more than you have.

Kissinger: But now we face a new situation. Those who oppose peace seek to portray the Arabs as hostile to the United States. They are trying to turn opinion against our peace efforts. It will be difficult for us to go ahead if we face a continuing oil embargo. We can absorb the economic impact of the embargo, but the psychological impact worries me. I'd like to suggest that Your Majesty take steps to limit the application of the embargo.

Faisal: I should like to rescind it immediately. I, too, am in a difficult position. It would be easier if the United States would announce that Israel must withdraw and permit the Palestinians to return to their homes.

Kissinger: Such a dramatic announcement would produce very strong reactions. We must move step by step. I should like to urge Your Majesty to reflect. . . .

Faisal: Our predicament is the other side of the coin. The Communists are accusing some Arabs of bowing to American pressure. To those who accuse you of bowing to Arab pressure, you can reply that the only reason the Arabs are doing this is because you support the enemy of the Arabs.

Kissinger: Your Majesty, it doesn't work that way in the United States.

Our best argument is not to say that we're anti-Israeli or pro-Arab, but that we want peace in the Middle East and that we're pursuing the interests of the United States. If we try to put it on the basis of the merits of the Arab-Israeli dispute, there will always be more people defending Israel than the Arab side. So we have to put it in terms of American national interests.

Faisal: I appreciate your reasoning, but I hope that you can appreciate ours. The embargo was a common decision of the Arab family. To urge an end of the embargo, I must be able to go to the other Arab governments with an argument. Therefore I need swift action from you. You need to announce your position.

Kissinger: If we announce this before negotiations, we will undermine our effectiveness in the negotiations. I don't want to promise anything I can't deliver.

An exchange of courtesies, and the conversation ended there—at an impasse. During the royal pronouncement on the Jews, Kissinger remained serene. Earlier, at dinner, it had been a bit more difficult to digest. The American ambassador to Riyadh, James Akins, sat separated from Kissinger by several senior princes; through the veil of robes and the click of coffee cups Akins caught snatches of the princes' discourse. " . . . Israel . . . Zionism . . . Jewish Communist conspiracy. . . ." On the way out, Kissinger whispered to Akins, in his deepest Teutonic accent, "That was your idea of light dinner conversation?"

And yet, whilst half of Faisal's head was filled with primitive rage against Jews and simplistic notions that with a wave of the hand Kissinger could dismiss the Israelis from Arab territory, the other half was exquisitely subtle. For all of its intransigence, his first audience with Kissinger contained the seeds of a remarkably compliant policy. The king's allusion to Syria was crucial. After the audience, Omar Saqqaf, the minister of state for foreign affairs, urged Kissinger to visit Damascus, revealing Faisal's conviction that Syria was the key to peace. In subsequent missions to Riyadh for more than a year thereafter, Kissinger practiced every persuasion to soften the Wahhabite pope. True, Faisal went on protesting about the Jews, and did not rescind the embargo until the spring, but in mid-December he promised Kissinger to do all he could to promote negotiations—particularly in Syria. Crucial. In fact, as time passed and it became clear to the king that he could not hope for total Israeli withdrawal quickly, he became the financier of Kissinger's interim diplomacy throughout the Middle East. He subsidized Sadat, seduced the Syrians, bribed the Beirut press. His horror of radicalization prevailed over his hatred of Zionism.

Besides, Faisal needed the United States to modernize his kingdom. Kissinger knew this, and he played the card shrewdly. On December 15, at the height of the oil embargo, he had a revealing conversation in Riyadh with Hisham Nazer, the minister of state for planning, and several important princes.

> *Nazer:* When I was in Washington, I talked to Bill Simon about an American development mission to Saudi Arabia.
>
> *Kissinger:* What kind of industries are you planning? How much of your population is rural and Bedouin?
>
> *Nazer:* There is more of a shift to settlement and urban living.
>
> *Kissinger:* I assume that the shift has political implications, since urban populations tend to be less traditional. How can the United States relate to the Saudi development process?
>
> *Nazer:* There are two conditions. First, peace, and second, help in organizing our industrial sector. You can provide technology. Specifically, you have the technology of desert agriculture which we could use.
>
> *Kissinger:* Are the present mechanisms for cooperation adequate?
>
> *Nazer:* We've never had trouble going directly to the American private sector, but we need help in tapping the resources and technology of the United States government.

We glimpse here the essence of Kissinger's parallel Middle East policy; for, in fact, his diplomacy has always proceeded on two levels. The first level is the containment of the Arab-Israeli conflict, which he considers almost intractable. The second level is the promotion of American technology, which all of the Arabs (including the radicals) crave and which helps him to buy time whilst he copes with the first problem. In effect, he is saying to the Arabs, "I know what you want— your territory—and I'm working on it. Meanwhile I'll give you *everything else* you want to compete in the twentieth century." For the Saudis, this has meant a vast commitment by the U.S. government to play a major part in fashioning their infrastructure, and to sell them, over the years, arms worth many billions of dollars. Whole cantonments and towns have been and will be constructed for the Saudis by the U.S. Army corps of engineers (this began before Kissinger); today there are nearly 20,000 Americans in the kingdom; tomorrow there may be twice that. For the Egyptians, the parallel policy has meant American diplomatic support, American money, and encouragement of American investors and of the oil princes to rescue Cairo's economy—not to mention encouragement of the West Europeans to sell arms to Sadat, since it is also Kissinger's long-range plan to pre-empt the Soviet Union as the chief source of weaponry amongst the Arabs. The parallel policy has even succeeded to an extent in such militant states as Syria and Iraq, which still depend on the Russians for their guns but are as covetous of American technology as the Saudis and the Egyptians.

MORE TALKS

Kissinger flew from Riyadh on November 9 to Peking to see Premier Chou En-lai and Chairman Mao Tse-tung. Whilst he was en route, Israel accepted his amended six points. The exchange of prisoners was consummated, but the military talks between Israelis and Egyptians at Kilometer 101 soon reached deadlock on the issue of Israeli withdrawals. The Israelis persisted in proposing a return to the lines of October 5, though now with the provision that the United Nations fill the vacuum of the retreating armies; the Egyptians demanded that Israel withdraw to the Mitla and Giddi passes. Kissinger returned to Washington only to conclude that he was needed urgently again in the Middle East.

On the eve of his departure, December 7, General Moshe Dayan, the Israeli minister of defense, called at the State Department. Dayan sought more weaponry—tanks, aircraft, armored personnel carriers—than Israel was already receiving. Kissinger put him off.

> *Dayan:* Another thing bothers me. Israel's best card is our continuing occupation of the pocket west of the canal. If we have to pull our forces back from the canal, then we must receive something of real value—such as assurances of no more war.

> *Kissinger:* You'll never get that in this phase. You're asking for the impossible.

Ambassador Dinitz spoke of the Israeli elections, now scheduled for late December—and of the Palestinians.

> *Dinitz:* I have Golda's instructions to get an understanding between the United States and Israel on Geneva.

> *Kissinger:* I'll be in touch with you, especially on the problem of Palestinian participation.

> *Dinitz:* Golda cannot go into the elections if there's any doubt on the Palestinians at Geneva.

Kissinger repulsed the Israeli demand for immediate Egyptian nonbelligerency—it would bedevil him again and again—but he capitulated straight-away on the issue of the Palestinians. Faced with Israel's refusal to go to Geneva if the Palestinians were present, he instructed his ambassador in Cairo to inform Sadat that now he did not favor Palestinian participation at the convening of the peace conference. Israel would permit "safe" Palestinians of King Hussein's regime to sit on the Jordanian delegation, but would not tolerate a separate delegation dominated by the Palestine Liberation Organization (PLO). In late November, the Arab summit meeting at Algiers had endorsed negotiations with Israel and designated the PLO as the "sole representative" of the Palestinians at Geneva. Yasir Arafat had arrived at Algiers from Moscow, where the Russians had prevailed upon him to accept the original United Nations plan of 1947 which partitioned Palestine into Jewish and Arab states. To demand the 1947 U.N. borders could only have been a negotiating position; but that Arafat was willing to advance it meant a de facto recognition of Israel's right to exist—as would his very presence at a peace conference with Israel. True, an invitation to Arafat to participate at Geneva would have provoked a violent debate within the PLO, and he might have demurred in the end; true, the Jordanians as well as the Israelis opposed the PLO. Nevertheless, in excluding the PLO from the start, Kissinger excluded from the process of peacemaking the very essence of the Arab-Israeli quarrel. This lost opportunity was lamentable, for as difficult as it may have been to confront the Palestinian dilemma in late 1973—on the morrow of the war when Arab confidence was high, when old rigidities were less inflexible and possibilities more fluid—it has become more difficult today.

In Cairo on December 13 and 14, Kissinger found Sadat distressed by his failure to arrange a role for the Palestinians at Geneva, but acquiescent. "We look upon you as the principal Arab leader," Kissinger reassured him, "and our purpose is to strengthen your position—in Egypt and throughout the Arab world." They agreed that the first goal at Geneva would be to "disengage" the Egyptian and Israeli armies. Kissinger wished to convene the conference on December 18, but now he had to convince the Syrians to attend. He proceeded, on December 15, to Damascus at last.

Save for Iraq, no nation in Araby had so tempestuous a past as Syria; the Syrians seemed to be ungovernable. Their president, Hafez al-Assad, was a mountain boy of the north, the head of the Socialist Ba'ath, an Alawite who appointed other Alawites to key commands to maintain himself in power. Curious, since the Alawites number hardly more than a tenth of Syria's populace. Nominally they are a sect of Shi'a Islam, but in practice they may not even be monotheistic. Publicly they revere Ali, the husband of the Prophet's favorite daughter, Fatima; privately they worship him as the godhead. When praying, Alawites turn not to Mecca but to the sun, in whose eye Ali lives. The cult is clouded in secrecy and clandestine rites; Alawites will do anything to conceal their true convictions from Christians and orthodox Moslems alike. Persecuted for centuries, cunning became their armor.

Assad has ruled Syria longer than any of his predecessors, and ruled it rather well. Self-reliant and shrewd, humorous, stubborn, unforgiving, not very cultured, a night worker who never seemed to sleep, he learned much from his own mistakes. He balanced a precarious coalition of Sunni and Shi'a Moslems, Alawites and Christians, Nasserists, Communists, urban entrepreneurs, rural conservatives, extremist Ba'athi ideologues within and without the army. The militants amongst these constrained Assad almost as much as he constrained them, and on Israel they were implacable. Hatred of Israel was far more fierce in Syria than in Egypt. During the October war, the Syrians snatched back much of the Golan Heights, but then the Israelis counterattacked and marched beyond the Golan almost to the suburbs of Damascus.

Assad was prepared to accept the reality of Israel; he accepted U.N. Resolution 338 following Soviet assurances that Israel would withdraw from all occupied territory and recognize the rights of the Palestinians. But he was wary of Kissinger, whose gradualist diplomacy appeared to him as just another stratagem to strengthen Israel. Suspicion is perhaps the predominant Syrian trait. It hovered in the halls of the presidential palace on that evening of December when—beneath an oil painting of Saladin's victory over the Crusaders—Assad welcomed Kissinger and his party.

Typically, Kissinger began by being funny. Through the interpreter he said, "I should teach you English, Mr. President. You'll be the first Arab leader to speak English with a German accent. Did you meet Mr. Sisco? I had to bring him with me—if I left him in Washington he might mount a coup d'état." Assad laughed. Kissinger assumed that the Syrians, like other Arabs, were intrigued by his success with women, so he talked about women and repeated some lecherous pleasantries. There ensued a seminar on world affairs, Kissinger reverting to his role of Harvard professor—analyzing China, the Soviet Union, American domestic politics—the president of Syria his attentive pupil.

Kissinger: It's not our policy to divide the Arabs. I'll always tell everyone I talk to the same thing. We must have confidence in each other. We must get a peace conference started to establish a legal framework for negotiations. With that, we'll work for a disengagement agreement, first on the Egyptian front, then seek to do the same on the Syrian front. The immediate problem is the letter of invitation to the conference. What are your views?

Assad: They depend upon our talk today.

Kissinger: We have no peace plan of our own. It's easy to make specific proposals—the important thing is to take practical steps. We and the Soviets agreed only that there should be a peace conference. Eventually it will have to deal with all of the questions—withdrawals, security, borders, Jerusalem, and the Palestinians.

Kissinger produced his draft letter of invitation to the conference, to be sent simultaneously by the United States and the Soviet Union to the United Nations secretary-general. He pointed to the crucial sentence: "The parties have also agreed that the question of other participants from the Middle East area will be discussed during the first stage of the conference"—i.e., the Palestinians were to be excluded from the initial phase of negotiations.

> *Kissinger:* Israel didn't want a reference to the Palestinians at this point. We recognize that you will not solve this problem without taking Palestinian interests into account, but we think it would be a mistake to take up the Palestinian question at the beginning of the conference.

> *Assad:* I understood that an earlier text had referred to "the question of the Palestinians."

Assad was alluding to his exchanges with Sadat. Through interminable cups of Turkish coffee and sweet tea, the conversation dragged on; two and a half hours had been scheduled but after six hours they were still talking. Rattling his amber worry beads, Assad began a long exposition of Syrian policy, assailing the United States for its support of Israel.

> *Kissinger:* I think we should talk now of the practical problems of convening the Geneva conference.

> *Assad:* Does the United States agree, first, that Syria cannot surrender territory in a settlement; second, that there can be no settlement without a solution for the Arab people of Palestine; and third, is the purpose of the peace conference to carry out these two objectives, or to use up time without achieving a solution?

> *Kissinger:* We're prepared to discuss with you the withdrawal of Israeli forces in the first stage, and we recognize that there would have to be further withdrawals in later stages. It's evident there won't be any settlement that you don't agree to. Now we must move into the disengagement phase.

> *Assad:* Any disengagement must involve all of the Golan Heights.

> *Kissinger:* That's out of the question. The first problem is the territory occupied in the October war—and whether Israel will withdraw from *that*.

> *Assad:* Before Geneva convenes there ought to be a disengagement agreement.

> *Kissinger:* For Israel, it's important that Syria provide a list of Israeli prisoners of war, permit the Red Cross to visit them, and release wounded prisoners.

Assad: Why should I give up this card? What am I getting for it? Brezhnev never mentioned that to me. The disengagement ought to involve the whole of Golan because Golan is very small.

Kissinger: Look, it took me four years to settle the whole Vietnamese war. You're asking for the impossible. I thought we were going to discuss the date for convening Geneva. What about the language regarding "other participants"?

Assad: Anything in that letter that you and President Sadat agree upon is agreeable to me.

Kissinger: But how will you answer the letter?

Assad: There should be disengagement before the conference convenes. The text of the letter is not accurate. It says Syria has agreed to attend the conference. I have not agreed.

BUT KISSINGER PREVAILS . . .

Nor had Israel agreed. In Jerusalem the next evening and the day after, Kissinger debated Golda Meir and her senior advisers (Dayan, Abba Eban, Yigal Allon, Pinhas Sapir, Dinitz et al.) over the Syrian refusal to produce a list of prisoners of war (without it, Israel "would not go to Geneva"), the role of the United Nations at the conference (Israel insisted it be minimal), and the concessions Israel would need to make to Egypt to achieve a disengagement. The Israelis were unsatisfied with Kissinger's letter of invitation to the conference, and they dissected every phrase. Finally, Kissinger fell back upon a favorite device. "Accept the letter as it is," he told them, "and then explain your own interpretation in a statement to the Knesset."

Kissinger: If Sadat gets disengagement, he'll start economic reconstruction and reopen the canal—but he wants to keep some forces on the East Bank.

Meir: Why—if he wants peace?

Kissinger: His view is that he can't afford to withdraw from his own territory which he has reconquered. We have to relieve the oil embargo, the threat of renewed hostilities. Time is critical. Sadat will thin out his forces on the East Bank, limit arms in that area, and accept a buffer zone under the U.N. . . . Look, Sadat has already changed his position. Initially he demanded El Arish, then the evacuation of the Sinai passes.

Meir (sharply): What you call disengagement is really just a withdrawal of Israeli forces, and there's nothing reciprocal about *that*.

Kissinger: He will restore the civil populace to the canal zone—a guarantee against hostilities.

Meir (passionately): What does Sadat say about peace? This is just the first step back to 1967. After this agreement everything will be the same—except the world will have its oil.

Kissinger (mischievously): That would make a big difference.

Kissinger prevailed. Nightmarish eleventh-hour complications followed, but the peace conference opened at Geneva on December 21. Israel was there, with Egypt and Jordan—but not the Syrians or the PLO. Officially, the conference was convened by Kurt Waldheim, the United Nations secretary-general, but—as the Israelis wished—he was but a decorous bystander. Nominally the co-chairmanship was shared by the United States and the Soviet Union, but the Russians were surprisingly serviceable and Kissinger stage-managed everything. Some foresaw the conference as a kind of Arab-Israeli Congress of Vienna, but in retrospect it amounted to little more than an international cartoon. Kissinger recognized the obstacles but voiced ambitious hopes: "Our final objective is the implementation in all its parts of Resolution 242. This goal has the full support of the United States. . . . The agony of three decades must be overcome . . . to put an end to the conflict between peoples who have so often ennobled mankind." There was a squabble about seating arrangements, a predictable exchange of polemics between Ismail Fahmy and Abba Eban, but otherwise Kissinger's scenario was observed: after the ceremonial overture, an Egyptian-Israeli working committee embarked upon discussions of disengagement, and the conference adjourned— supposedly to come alive again soon after the Israeli elections. It has yet to reconvene.

"It was the most peculiar conference I ever attended," Zaid al-Rifai, the prime minister of Jordan, lamented to me recently. "I expected it would be based on Resolutions 242 and 338. But it had no terms of reference, no rules of procedure, and no agenda." Rifai requested a disengagement on the Jordan-Israeli front, but the conference broke up without considering that or the concerns of the Palestinians. In fact, on December 20, the day before the conference, Kissinger passed to the Israelis a secret and very significant "Memorandum of Understanding" promising that no other parties would be invited to future meetings at Geneva "without the agreement of the initial participants"—which meant an Israeli veto on participation by the PLO.

Rifai was not the first to suggest that Kissinger staged the conference mainly as pomp and circumstance, a public-relations drumroll for a mouse-sized marvel—the first Egyptian-Israeli disengagement. In justice to Kissinger, however, it should be remembered that *at the time* he considered Geneva might subsequently serve a useful purpose as the site for negotiations.

Golda Meir's government was returned to power with a reduced majority; in early January 1974, Dayan returned to Washington. Though a "hawk," Dayan was the most creative of the Israeli leaders; implicitly he conceded an Israeli withdrawal into the Sinai, and now he produced his "five-zone" concept. The area of disengagement should cover five zones, he said—a U.N. buffer (zone one) between the Israeli and Egyptian armies, whose forces in those zones (two and three, respectively) would be severely limited. Beyond zones two and three there should extend on either side of the Suez Canal zones four and five, respectively, each 30 kilometers deep, where surface-to-air missiles would likewise be forbidden.

This became the conceptual foundation of the accord that was soon to follow. The idea was Dayan's, not Kissinger's. Dayan invited Kissinger to return to the Middle East; Kissinger contacted Sadat, who urged him to come at once. On January 12, in Aswan, where he was recovering from bronchitis, Sadat exhorted Kissinger to undertake an immediate "shuttle" and to conclude the disengagement forthwith. Kissinger had hitherto planned to mediate the principles, then defer to the Egyptian-Israeli military committee to resolve the particulars at Geneva. "Why Geneva?" Sadat asked. "You can do it all here."

Kissinger returned to Aswan the next day from Jerusalem; Sadat accepted Dayan's conceptual framework and added, "I won't quibble over details." In Washington and Jerusalem, Kissinger had already determined the scope of the Israeli withdrawal; now the problem focused on limitations of force. "It's difficult for me," Sadat said, "to sign a document which limits the forces in my own territory."

That afternoon, Kissinger proposed to enshrine the disengagement in two documents—a formal agreement to be signed by Israel and Egypt, and a separate letter from the United States, to each government stating its understanding of the limitation of forces. The formal agreement would only allude to the limitations; the American letter would define them. With this sophistry, Sadat could claim that Israel had not *imposed* the limitations upon Egypt.

By evening, the American team had produced the two draft documents. The Egyptians refined them, then Kissinger flew to Israel. He negotiated mostly with Allon, Eban, and Dayan, because Golda Meir was ill with shingles. The Egyptians, exceedingly sensitive to force limitations, had asked Kissinger to camouflage Dayan's five-zone framework. They agreed to specify five zones in the agreement, but only three on the map—for Egypt, Israel, and the United Nations respectively. "All right," Dayan told Kissinger, "there will be three zones. We'll produce a new map you can take back to Aswan." The Israelis further dissected Kissinger's drafts, and with remarkable virtuosity Kissinger managed to accommodate their fixation on legalisms. We glimpse him scratching out, interpolating, scribbling all over the drafts: "Paragraph one could be divided into two paragraphs. The next three paragraphs—no problem. Paragraph five probably won't survive in this form. . . ."

By the fourth day of the shuttle, the agreement was assured. Some technicalities remained to be negotiated, but Kissinger was already quibbling with Dayan about the timing of the announcement: Dayan wanted to brief the Knesset first; Kissinger had a horror of leaks and wished to unveil his victory as a bombshell for the evening telecasts in the United States. The agreement was announced by Nixon at the White House on January 17, 1974 and signed by the Egyptians and Israelis at Kilometer 101 the next day—less than a week after Kissinger's appearance at Aswan.

It contained all of Dayan's essentials—indeed, Dayan can be called its secret father. The Israelis were to withdraw into the Sinai to a line roughly 15 miles from the Suez Canal, protected by a U.N. buffer, leaving the Egyptians a thin ribbon of territory on the East Bank, where reciprocally they would diminish their army from 60,000 to 7,000 men; symmetrically beyond either line, no missiles for 30 kilometers. Sadat gave no promise of nonbelligerency, but neither did he get a timetable for further Israeli withdrawals, and secretly he promised the United States to permit nonmilitary Israeli cargoes to transit the canal as soon as it was cleared. Additionally, Kissinger gave the Israelis a secret "Memorandum of Understanding" in which the United States conveyed Egypt's promise to clear the canal, rebuild its cities, and resume peacetime activities in that region. Egypt and Israel had accepted American aerial reconnaissance of the disengagement area; the memorandum concluded that "the United States will make every effort to be fully responsive on a continuing and long-term basis to Israel's military equipment requirements."

Kissinger's predominant emotion in this shuttle should be obvious—*it was easy.* He applied minimal pressure on either party, since both Israel and Egypt needed the agreement badly. Israel had to demobilize or face bankruptcy. Sadat had to save the Third Army and prove that the war had won him territory. Not that Sadat's subordinates were satisfied—Fahmy felt that Kissinger could have delivered more of the Sinai; General Mohammed el-Gamasy, the chief of staff, considered the agreement militarily unsound. But then, like Kissinger's subordinates, they were treated as mere technicians, and entrusted only with details. In Israel, the agreement required approval by the cabinet; but Sadat made every crucial decision alone with Kissinger.

THE SYRIAN DISENGAGEMENT

The swift success of the Israeli-Egyptian disengagement confirmed Kissinger's belief that step-by-step diplomacy was the best—indeed the only—method for containing the Arab-Israeli conflict. By now, Egyptians and Jews were well schooled in the dynamics of that method. Kissinger avoided essence—viz., the Palestinian problem—and clung to the periphery; for in his view, rearrangement of the periphery alone was possible. On the periphery he encouraged the belligerents themselves to provide the points of reference; that done, he identified the components, then skillfully composed them. His great function—he has said so many times—was to explain persuasively to either party the constraints upon the other.

The disengagement also helped to kill the Geneva conference. Sadat was loath to negotiate with Israel alone; he could not risk returning to Geneva until Syria, like Egypt, had regained some territory in disengagement. Moreover Israel—tormented by a cabinet crisis—was in no mood to negotiate affairs of substance. En route home from Aswan, at Sadat's behest, Kissinger called again at Damascus, where he found Assad furious at Sadat for accepting disengagement but more willing now to consider disengagement for himself. Assad reduced his demands, and asked for only half of Golan. This gave Kissinger a point of reference; he passed it to the Israelis, who refused to negotiate until Assad produced his list of Israeli prisoners. Kissinger returned to Damascus in February, then delivered the list to Golda Meir. Israel and Syria dispatched negotiators to Washington, where Kissinger found their positions still far apart.

Meanwhile, Kissinger was grappling with the oil embargo. As part of his bargain with Kissinger for the Sinai disengagement, Sadat endeavored to persuade the oil princes to end the boycott, but his good offices were not enough. During December and January, Nixon and Kissinger played "impeachment politics" with the Saudis, warning that the embargo would weaken the embattled president and diminish his power to promote peace. The warning was buttressed by murky hints of American military intervention in the Persian Gulf. When neither ploy worked, Kissinger threatened to publish previous correspondence with the Saudis which might embarrass them before the other Arabs. At Riyadh, Ambassador Akins had already clashed with Kissinger in November, threatening to resign should Kissinger exclude him from the audience with Faisal; Kissinger had relented. Now Akins refused to convey Kissinger's message to the king, and sought out Omar Saqqaf, the minister of state, instead. Saqqaf warned against informing the king; Saudi Arabia, he suggested, could also publish correspondence which might embarrass the United States. Kissinger reconsidered, and the message Akins transmitted to Faisal was more gracious.

But Kissinger sustained his pressure. Though the Arabs had vowed to lift the embargo only when Israel withdrew completely, by February they were alarmed by Europe's penury and plagued with doubt. Syria urged a prolongation, but the oil princes sent Saqqaf and Fahmy to Washington to strike a bargain: Do something for Syria, they told Nixon and Kissinger, and the embargo will stop. Kissinger promised to try; in

March the embargo was suspended. Kissinger subsequently denied the "linkage," but, in fact, his Syrian shuttle was the price he paid to end the embargo.

Kissinger returned to the Middle East on the last day of April, calling first at Alexandria to see Sadat, by now his chief adviser on Arab affairs. Throughout the negotiations that followed, Sadat urged Assad to accept "Dr. Henry's" definition of the possible. In Jerusalem, on May 2, the Israelis were ready only to divide the salient they had captured in October, retaining half of it for themselves and the whole of Golan, too. Moreover, the matter was vexed by internal Israeli politics—Mrs. Meir would remain in office only long enough to negotiate the disengagement, to be succeeded by Yitzhak Rabin as prime minister. General Mordechai Gur, the new chief of staff, began with a military briefing that stressed Israel's strategic need to maintain positions on Mount Hermon, which abutted the Heights on the north and overlooked Damascus, and the hills near Kuneitra, which dominated the rest of Golan.

> *Kissinger:* This problem cannot be dealt with in military terms alone. This is a geopolitical problem, and you must weigh the alternatives you'll face if we fail to get a disengagement.
>
> *Gur:* But the Israeli settlements are almost against the prewar line.
>
> *Kissinger:* This isn't an argument that will carry weight with world opinion. Those settlements are in occupied territory.

Privately, Kissinger has described the Golan settlements as "the worst mistake the Jews have made in 2,500 years."

> *Kissinger:* The minimum essential for the Syrians is to get back Kuneitra.
>
> *Meir:* None of our neighbors—certainly not Syria—is prepared to negotiate real peace. All the Syrians want to talk about after two wars in six years is the disengagement of forces—so we can't just brush aside the military arguments of our chief of staff. Besides, regimes change in the Arab world. Suppose something happens to Sadat and someone more anti-Israeli and pro-Soviet comes to power? What happens then to all these agreements?
>
> *Kissinger:* In that case a great deal would depend on how reasonable Israel has been in negotiations. The extent to which the United States could help you would depend on the nature of the crisis and how it came about.

This is one of the basic arguments Kissinger has constantly wielded with the Israelis—the scope of future American commitments to Israel will be determined by Israel's readiness to rise above narrow military advantage and take risks for political reasons. But in this conversation, he could not even get them to propose a line closer to Kuneitra, the old capital of the Golan Heights near the cease-fire line of 1967. With no more than an agenda from the Israelis—prisoner exchange, nature of the U.N. buffer zone, etc.—Kissinger saw Assad in Damascus the next day. He explained Israel's unstable internal situation, then asked about Soviet Foreign Minister Andrei Gromyko, who was expected soon in Damascus:

> *Kissinger:* I can see the scenario. The foreign minister will meet Gromyko at the airport, then take him to lunch. Then they will make a statement condemning the United States and "partial solutions." Then Syria will get some more MIG-23s.

Assad was amused. Kissinger's eyes came to rest on Abdel Halim Khaddam, Assad's radical and rather handsome young foreign minister. "Such pretty blue eyes," he said. "Won't you come back with me to Israel? I want to fix you up with Golda." Presently he produced the Israeli map, with its proposed line dividing the salient. "It does not seem," Assad replied angrily, "that Israel wants peace. Unacceptable."

Kissinger returned to Jerusalem, and urged the Israelis to be realistic. For weeks the Syrians had been waging a war of attrition across their lines with Israel; the cease-fire, Kissinger's diplomacy itself, were at stake.

> *Kissinger:* It's necessary to give back Kuneitra, plus a bit of the areas west of the pre-October line. We need a line that's negotiable, or the negotiations will collapse very soon. Israel should understand the Syrians' perception. You're sitting on their territory.
>
> *Meir* (angrily): We didn't just get up one day in 1967 after all the shelling from the Heights and decide to take Golan away from them. In October we had 800 killed and 2,000 wounded in Golan alone—in a war *they* started. They say this is *their* territory. Eight hundred boys gave their lives for an attack the Syrians started. Assad lost the war— and now we have to pay for it because Assad says it's *his* territory!
>
> *Kissinger:* Each side has its own definition of justice. Remember what this is all about—to keep the negotiating process alive, to prevent another round of hostilities which would benefit the Soviet Union and increase pressure on you, on us, and on Sadat to rejoin the battle. . . .
>
> *Dayan.* Maybe we could divide Kuneitra.
>
> *Kissinger:* It won't work.
>
> *Meir:* There's a cabinet meeting tomorrow—we must ask for authority to propose a new line. We'll have a big fight in the Knesset and with our people who live in Golan.

Kissinger encountered some of the Golan settlers outside his hotel, screaming "Jew boy go home!"—a reference, apparently, to Nixon's reputed remark describing Kissinger in that idiom. The cabinet relented, and Golda Meir proposed a new line. The concept, of course, came from Dayan, soon to relinquish his defense portfolio. Now the government agreed to give back the salient and a slice of Kuneitra, proposing to divide that city into three zones—for Israel, the United Nations, and Syria respectively. In Damascus, Assad rejected this proposal. For the next three weeks, Kissinger shuttled back and forth struggling to reconcile the contradictions. By May 12, he was so exasperated with the Israelis he said, "Assad is no longer demanding half of Golan—we're negotiating on your line, and you're arguing about a few kilometers or a few hundred yards here and there. If we didn't have this negotiation, there'd be an international forum for the 1967 frontiers." The Israelis improved their map slightly, but not enough to satisfy Assad—"he must have some breathing space around Kuneitra," Kissinger told them. Israel insisted on retaining the hills outside Kuneitra; this outraged the Syrians. On May 13, Kissinger warned the Israelis the negotiation might collapse.

The next day, to Assad and his chief aides, Kissinger tried to put the best face upon the Israeli proposal. "There are demonstrators in the streets," he said, "crying 'Don't give up an inch of Golan!' Look, the Israelis have made considerable concessions—no salient, back to the pre-October line, and now they'll get out of all of Kuneitra and draw the line at the edge of the town. There will be Syrian civilians inside Kuneitra." Assad protested, "They're making Kuneitra a pocket surrounded by Israelis north, south, and west. Unacceptable."

On May 15, Palestinian guerrillas attacked Maalot, killing 16 Israeli adolescents; this hardened the cabinet. Next morning, to the Israeli negotiators, Kissinger expressed his sorrow, and presently—perhaps to relieve the tension—told a story about his masseur at the King David Hotel.

> *Masseur:* We support your efforts. We must have peace.
>
> *Kissinger:* What are you willing to give up for peace?
>
> *Masseur:* Nothing. Not an inch.
>
> *Kissinger.* Shall I break off the negotiations?
>
> *Masseur:* Absolutely not. I would give up 10 years of my life for peace.
>
> *Kissinger:* How many kilometers would you give up?
>
> *Masseur:* Not a kilometer.

This exchange, Kissinger mused, echoed the attitude of the Israeli government. In desperation, throwing out an idea that had emerged from discussions with his staff, he suggested that perhaps Israel could continue cultivating the fields around Kuneitra—so long as they were demilitarized and placed within the U.N. zone.

Allon and Rabin picked this up, promising to discuss it with the cabinet. Kissinger's idea revived the negotiations, for it became the basis of the crucial Israeli concession. But for another fortnight, the haggling did not cease. On May 23, in conference with the Israelis, Kissinger contrasted Sadat and Assad: "Sadat has a fixed determination to overcome obstacles and move toward peace. He makes big moves and breaks impasses. With Assad, each issue when you get to it becomes major, and you have to bargain over every point. It's so time-consuming! Sadat makes command decisions. Assad had his lieutenants there, and I had to convince them, too." In describing Assad, Kissinger was also describing the Israelis to themselves.

So the haggling went on—and with it the war of attrition. In Damascus, recently, Assad told me that during the negotiation "the Israelis were exploiting Dr. Kissinger's aircraft when he took off from Tel Aviv toward the sea. Their warplanes flew in the shadow of his wings, and at a certain point they parted—then struck at targets in our territory." The haggling went on—about the location of the line, the cultivation of the fields, a village here, a crossroads there, the width of the buffer zone, the limitation of forces and artillery (another American letter to resolve that!), the length of the U.N. mandate, the exchange of prisoners wounded and unwounded, the quantity of Syrian police to be permitted in Kuneitra. The Syrians wished only observers in the buffer zone; the Israelis insisted on an armed force; the issue was resolved by calling them both—the United Nations Disengagement Observer Force (UNDOF). The talks nearly collapsed again at least twice, and Kissinger kept threatening to go home. Nixon—who needed the agreement as much as anybody—told him to stay, and started calling up Golda Meir. An audacious poker-player, constantly bluffing to improve the pot, Assad retracted his previous assent to the Israeli line. On May 27, Assad and Kissinger composed a communiqué announcing the collapse of the negotiations. On the way to the door, Assad touched Kissinger's hand and said, "What a pity. We've come so far and we've not succeeded. Can't anything be done about the line? Go back to Jerusalem—and try again."

Two days later, the agreement was achieved. It was modeled on the Israeli-Egyptian disengagement—in effect, five zones, embracing the U.N. buffer; two zones of 10 kilometer depth for Israel and Syria each where troops, artillery, and tanks were severely limited; symmetrical zones 20 kilometers deep where missiles were proscribed. The new Israeli line roughly corresponded to the cease-fire demarcation of 1967, except that Syria regained Kuneitra, which was placed inside the buffer zone. Just beyond the town's periphery, the Israelis could continue to cultivate the fields within the buffer, and they retained their settlements and the strategic hills. American memoranda were conveyed to both sides; Syria had refused to agree in writing to prohibit "paramilitary" (Palestinian) operations from its soil, so the letter to Israel sanctioned—in the event of such incursions—Israeli retaliation.

In the euphoria of the achievement—hailed then as the diplomatic miracle of our time—the torment of the experience almost seemed to be forgotten. Kissinger had spent nearly five weeks away from Washington, struggling as well during sleepless days and nights to run the entire State Department from his Boeing or the King David Hotel. Privately, Kissinger described the Syrians and Israelis as "the only peoples in the Middle East who deserve each other"—but in fact he did not feel quite that way about Hafez Assad or Golda Meir. He admired Sadat, and respected Faisal, but he grew fond of Assad. This Syrian fascinated Kissinger as the embodiment of that Arab romanticism he used to curse, as a sometimes too simplistic man of steel who could compete with him on his own terrain of humor and dissimulation, as a despot of high principle who in fundamentals—for all his Alawite cunning—said what he meant and meant what he said.

As for Golda Meir, Assad observed to me that "one of the weaknesses I discovered in Dr. Kissinger was his special love of that woman. It struck me as strange that this university professor and secretary of state was unable to conceal such a furious affection. And for your information he used to describe her as 'Miss Israel.'" Golda Meir's tantrums, her volcanic obstinacy, drove Kissinger crazy—but there was no doubt of his deep affection. She was a woman of steel, and she alone in Israel, once her word was given, could enforce discipline and deliver the cabinet. Now she was stepping down, but in the year to come Kissinger would yearn for Miss Israel.

The Israeli-Syrian disengagement marked the high noon of Kissinger's gradualist diplomacy in the Middle East. Thereafter we begin to observe lengthening shadows, faltering steps, frustration, recrimination, paralysis, and doubt.

SIGNIFICANT PROMISES

In mid-June, Kissinger returned to the Middle East—with Nixon. Nixon's tour was largely ceremonial, undertaken not only to dramatize the American commitment to peace but to portray the president in his statesman's toga as he struggled to elude impeachment. Nevertheless, during his peregrination, Nixon made significant promises to the Arab chiefs of state.

They involved the American interpretation of Security Council

Resolution 242. On the territorial dimension of 242, Kissinger has commonly been accused of making contradictory promises to Arabs and Israelis, but, in fact, such duplicity is difficult to establish. He had stated often that the United States would labor for the fulfillment in all its clauses of that ambiguous resolution, but he was evasive when anyone asked him to define it. On May 18, 1974, when pressed by President Assad, Kissinger replied, "My predecessor once stated publicly his interpretation of 242, and for four years he was beaten over the head. Obviously, for a settlement you have to agree, but for us to take a position on final borders would destroy our capacity to conduct negotiations." He said essentially the same to Sadat and to the Saudis. Certainly Kissinger *allowed* the Arabs to think he favored complete or substantial Israeli withdrawal. In January 1974, Sadat told me, "I have assurances from Kissinger" on total withdrawal, but this may have been Sadat's wishful exegesis of "Dr. Henry's" conundrum.

Kissinger's replies to the Israelis resembled his opacity with the Arabs. On May 2, 1974, Rabin and Eban probed him for his views on final borders. "I can't predict how it will all come out," he answered. "What's important is the process itself—to keep negotiations going, to prevent them from freezing." Kissinger was more explicit in a meeting on December 6, 1973 with American Jewish intellectuals. Then, according to an Israeli journal which published the notes of participants, he said Israel would not have to withdraw to her 1967 borders; he believed that more favorable borders would be agreed upon in the negotiations. But even on that occasion, he stressed that Israel would be obliged to return "substantial territories."

Perhaps preoccupied by presentiments of doom, Nixon was uncomfortable in Cairo. Before the mob, he was convivial with Sadat, but that was mostly theater. Privately, the two presidents groped for words; their silences were long and awkward. But Nixon did tell Sadat that the American objective in the Sinai was to restore the old Egyptian international border. Kissinger was sitting there when Nixon said it. Afterward, also in Kissinger's presence, the president informed President Assad and King Hussein respectively that the United States favored the substantial restitution of the 1967 frontiers on the Golan Heights and on the West Bank of the Jordan within the framework of a general peace.

President Ford reaffirmed Nixon's position on the 1967 frontiers to Sadat last June in Salzburg. Of course the Arabs want all of this in writing, but that is the sort of memorandum Nixon and Ford and Kissinger have—so far—refused to render up to them. Anyway, why this change of tactics? As the clock continued to tick after the conclusion of the war, and Israel stood firm upon most of her conquests, the Americans evidently sought to sustain their credibility with the Arabs by restoring once again to verbal reassurances.

ACROSS THE JORDAN

Are words worth anything—to Jordan, for example? The Hashemite Kingdom, and the Palestinians who resided there and in parts beyond, assumed a critical importance during the final summer of Nixon's presidency—though curiously Kissinger did not seem to notice.

Kissinger, like Nixon and President Johnson before him, took Hussein for granted. Jordan, after all, was nearly an American protectorate; but unlike Israel it possessed no American constituency and thus had to be content with whatever scraps Washington might care to cast its way. In 1967, Hussein had lobbied amongst the other Arabs for their acceptance of Resolution 242, in return for which he received hollow promises from Johnson (then Nixon) that the United States would persuade Israel to disgorge its conquests.

Of the Arab leaders, Hussein alone knew Kissinger before the October war, for he visited Washington regularly; Kissinger liked him, and flattered him, each time they met, for his fortitude in the crisis with the Palestinian *fedayin* in 1970. Though not a belligerent in the October conflict, Hussein expected his old friend to redeem Nixon's promises and to include Jordan in his new diplomacy. Kissinger's original scheme for Geneva, once Israel and Egypt were disengaged, was to disengage the Syrian and Jordanian fronts, then assemble all of the parties to fashion a final settlement. This scenario was undone by the delays of the Syrian disengagement, by rivalry amongst the Arabs, Israeli obstruction, and Kissinger's own miscalculations.

In January 1974, Hussein and Rifai presented Kissinger with a map proposing an Israeli withdrawal from the Jordan River eight to ten kilometers into the West Bank; the king was prepared for a phased retreat, demilitarization of the zone, inspection by the United Nations. Kissinger passed the map to the Israelis, who rejected it. In late spring, Israel proposed, instead, not military disengagement, but a final political settlement with Jordan. The proposition was humiliating, not even serious. Israel would retain Arab Jerusalem, important portions of the West Bank, a defensive frontier along the river—and return the remaining balloons, sausages, and corridors to Jordan, intermeshing them with the Israeli army, creating an Arab Lesotho. Hussein refused.

Following the Syrian disengagement, the Jordanians warned Kissinger that either they rapidly regain the West Bank or the PLO would pre-empt their claim. Distracted by the dénouement of Watergate, Kissinger was dithered—with Nixon paralyzed, he was unable to press Israel. Shortly after Nixon's resignation in August, Hussein visited Washington, where Kissinger and Ford assured him that disengagement in the Jordan valley shared equal priority with another disengagement in the Sinai. The king was elated, but from past experience he should have known better; moreover, he did not reckon upon the intrigues of his Egyptian cousins. Ismail Fahmy was in Washington, too. The Egyptians, coveting a second Israeli withdrawal soon, pleaded their preeminence over the Hashemites.

By October, the growing international prominence of the PLO aroused Kissinger's alarm. He was not innately hostile to Palestinian aspirations, but he considered the PLO a pot of contradictions; its moderates immobilized by radicals, it policies the hostage of rhetoric and illusion. Its leader, Yasir Arafat, was like a cyclist atop a tightrope, yearning perhaps to descend to earth but urged by his disciples to pedal up to heaven—to the unattainable secular Palestine. Granted, in negotiations Arafat might accept a smaller part of paradise—Gaza and the West Bank—but until he put his house in order why should Kissinger do him favors? Besides, even supposing a rump Palestine was possible, the notion did not enchant Kissinger. His history books had taught him that such miniature principalities breed irredentist passions, cause subsequent explosions, provoke dangerous quarrels between great powers. The Palestinians might have their state, but only as part of Jordan—the very goal that Kissinger had failed to advance.

Kissinger flew to Cairo on October 9, not only to discuss new Sinai negotiations with Sadat, but to solicit his support for Jordan at the imminent Arab summit conference. Sadat promised to try, but in the event he did not try hard. At Rabat, a fortnight later, the Arab kings and presidents asked Hussein about commitments from Kissinger and prospects of Israeli withdrawal from the River Jordan. Hussein held up his empty hands. With that admission, his case collapsed. Led by Syria, the other Arab governments anointed the PLO as the new sovereign of the West Bank, conferring upon the Palestinians the metaphysical right to resolve their own future. In fact, this suited Egypt, for it protected Sadat on his Palestinian flank as he pursued his own national interests and maneuvered to negotiate again with Israel. Secretly, the summit approved a resolution recommending a Palestinian state in Gaza and the West Bank, along the borders of 1967; the PLO acquiesced. But with Jordan out of the running, and with no prospect in the near future of Israel sitting with the PLO, Kissinger perforce would favor the Sinai as the site of his next negotiation.

Rabat was the first major defeat for Kissinger since the October war—and a major brake on interim diplomacy. During subsequent visits to Amman, he has lamented to the king and to Rifai his own failure, whilst there was still time, to restore the West Bank to Jordan.

"So you made a mistake," Rifai said.

"We miscalculated," Kissinger replied, "our manipulative capabilities." (That is the Jordanian version. In the American version Kissinger tells Rifai, "*You* miscalculated our manipulative capabilities.")

On the morrow of Rabat, Kissinger returned to Cairo. Sadat was ill with influenza, and received his guest clad in a dressing gown in the bedroom of his residence at Giza. Gone was the bonhomie of previous visitations, the gracious exchange of flattery ("We could never have come this far, Mr. President, without your statesmanship . . ." "Dr. Henry, you are my favorite magician") for now both men were embarrassed. Sadat had failed to repulse the PLO's claim to the West Bank; Kissinger's diplomacy was bogged down and his credibility was beginning to vanish. At Rabat the other Arabs, in Cairo some of his own advisers, kept warning Sadat that "Kissinger is playing games with you." Increasingly, Sadat was gnawed by doubt, by suspicion of Kissinger's intentions. Kissinger had no mind to lose the anchor of his Arab policy, and after ritual pleas for confidence he promised to pursue another Israeli retreat in the Sinai. Sadat sought the Mitla and Giddi passes, his oil fields on the Red Sea, and he would accept nothing less.

NONBELLIGERENCY

That, Kissinger knew, would not be easy to achieve. Rabat and its repercussions—Arafat at the United Nations, for example—outraged the Israelis. For another withdrawal, Rabin required a pact of nonbelligerency from Sadat; Israeli strategists talked openly of separating Egypt from Syria and of removing Egypt from the Arab-Israeli conflict. Even for nonbelligerency, Rabin seemed to be in no hurry. Kissinger and his aides suspected now that tactically the paramount Israeli purpose was to delay and prolong whatever negotiation he might favor. In a revealing interview with *Haaretz* on December 3, 1974 Rabin stated that "the central aim of Israel should be to gain time"—up to seven years, the period essential to Europe and the United States to free themselves from dependency on Arab oil. During that interval Israel would continue to seek partial agreements, but he implied it would avoid a total settlement until the United States was no longer constrained by the need for oil to impose conditions that Israel found unpalatable. In this interview, Rabin did not insist on Egyptian nonbelligerency; as the winter progressed, however, right-wing pressure intensified in the Knesset and nonbelligerency became his sine qua non.

In February 1975, Kissinger returned to the Mideast, where he found the Egyptian and Israeli positions still irreconcilable. In Jerusalem, and in Washington for the next three weeks, he exhorted the Israelis again and again to recognize the constraints upon Sadat—that Sadat could not risk a rupture with the other Arabs, that nonbelligerency could only come with final peace and was unattainable at this stage. The Israelis were either unconvinced or prepared, for the purpose of gaining time, to hazard an abortive negotiation. An eminent Israeli official told me that shortly before the March shuttle he took Kissinger aside and said, "Henry, you must be under no illusions. Israel will never withdraw from the Sinai passes for anything less than full nonbelligerency from Egypt." Kissinger assumed this was a negotiating position; subsequently he said that the Israelis softened on nonbelligerency then hardened again when he reached Jerusalem—that they brought him back to the Middle East with premeditated deception.

In Jerusalem on March 9, Rabin began the new negotiation by outlining to Kissinger seven points as the basis of the Israeli position— briefly, Egypt must agree to practical steps toward peace, to terminate the use of force, to resolve the "dilemma of vagueness about duration." Israel would refuse to discuss a new line in the Sinai until Egypt had replied positively.

Kissinger was dismayed, for it was obvious that the Israelis were demanding nonbelligerency. Under point two—practical steps toward peace—they sought Egypt's disavowal of the Arab boycott, and the free movement of peoples between the two nations. Under point three—the "non-use of force"—they sought a formal "renunciation of belligerency clearly and in its appropriate legal wording." They required many features of a final peace, though after their withdrawal they would remain in possession of most of the Sinai.

In the ensuing days, at Aswan, Kissinger persuaded Sadat to offer Israel the "functional equivalent" of nonbelligerency in the military sense—no resort to force until the agreement, renewable annually, was superseded by another. On the political level, Sadat agreed to diminish the boycott and hostile propaganda, and to permit a limited communion of peoples—though this dimension would be de facto, not a promise he could commit to paper. But the Israelis continued to demand formal nonbelligerency, and they refused to draw a new line in the Sinai. "The Israelis," Sadat told Kissinger, "should be under no illusions that they will remain in the passes." That—and Sadat's insistence on free access to the oil fields at Abu Rudeis and its environs—was Egypt's final word. At the end, in exchange for Sadat's "nonrecourse to force," the Israelis offered to withdraw halfway into the Mitla and Giddi passes and to restore the oil fields in an enclave reachable by a U.N. road. Sadat refused.

During the negotiation, Kissinger complained bitterly to Sadat, and to Assad and Hussein in side trips to their capitals, about the intransigence of the Israelis. "You can't believe what I'm going through," he said. Perhaps in speaking thus Kissinger sought also to ingratiate himself with the Arabs, but his aides insist he was at his wit's end. At that moment Indochina was collapsing; détente was tenuous; American power was waning in Turkey, in Portugal, and elsewhere in the West. Now the Israelis, vexed with his pressure to make concessions, were taking aim at Kissinger himself. "They're trying," he told the Arab leaders, "to bring me down." At the eleventh hour, Ford wrote to Rabin, warning were he not more flexible American policy toward Israel would be drastically reassessed—but it was too late.

On Saturday, March 22, after sunset of that sabbath, Kissinger conferred with the Israelis in two final, dramatic meetings—from 6:30 PM to 8:15 PM and from 10:35 PM to 12:05 AM. Rabin, Allon, Gur, Dinitz, and Minister of Defense Shimon Peres faced Kissinger, Sisco, Assistant Secretary Alfred L. Atherton, Jr. Deputy Assistant Secretary Harold H. Saunders, and Ambassador Kenneth Keating.

Allon: We'd still like to negotiate an interim or overall agreement, but not on the basis of an ultimatum from the other side.

Kissinger: There was no ultimatum. In the absence of new Israeli ideas, we received no new Egyptian ideas. We have no illusions. The Arab leaders who banked on the United States will be discredited. Step-by-step has been throttled, first for Jordan, then for Egypt. We're losing control. We'll now see the Arabs working on a united front. There will be more emphasis on the Palestinians, and there will be a linkage between moves in the Sinai and on Golan. The Soviets will step back onto the stage. The United States is losing control over events, and we'd all better adjust ourselves to that reality. The Europeans will have to accelerate their relations with the Arabs. If the interim agreement in 1971 had succeeded there would have been no war in October 1973. The same process is at work here. We just don't have a strategy for the situation ahead. Our past strategy was worked out carefully, and now we don't know what to do. There will be pressures to drive a wedge between Israel and the United States, not because we want that but because it will be the dynamic of the situation. Let's not kid ourselves. We've failed.

Allon: Why not start it up again in a few weeks?

Kissinger: Things aren't going to be the same again. The Arabs won't trust us as they have in the past. We look weak—in Vietnam, Turkey, Portugal, in a whole range of things. Don't misunderstand me. I'm analyzing this situation with friends. One reason I and my colleagues are so exasperated is that we see a friend damaging himself for reasons which will seem trivial five years from now—like 700 Egyptian soldiers across the canal in 1971. I don't see how there can be another American initiative in the near future. We may have to go to Geneva for a multilateral effort with the Soviets—something which for five years we've felt did not offer the best hope for success. I had assumed that when Geneva reconvened everybody would look to us to propose the way of success. But that won't be so now.

Allon: The Egyptians really didn't give very much.

Kissinger. An agreement would have enabled the United States to remain in control of the diplomatic process. Compared to that, the location of the line eight kilometers one way or the other frankly does not seem very important. And you got all the military elements of nonbelligerency. You got the "non-use of force." The elements you didn't get—movement of peoples, ending of the boycott—are *unrelated* to your line. What you didn't get has nothing to do with where your line is. . . .

Peres: It is a question not just of the passes, but of our military [intelligence] installations that have no offensive purpose and are necessary. The previous government couldn't overcome the psychological blow—that the Syrians and Egyptians launched a surprise attack. We need an early warning system. We need 12 hours of warning. Under the proposed arrangement, we'd only have six. If there had been any Egyptian concessions regarding the duration of the agreement and the warning system, then what you've said would be very touching. But then we would have faced new negotiations with Syria. . . .

Kissinger: This is a real tragedy. We've attempted to reconcile our support for you with our other interests in the Middle East, so that you wouldn't have to make your decisions all at once. Our strategy was to save you from dealing with all those pressures all at once. If we wanted the 1967 borders we could do it with all of world opinion and considerable domestic opinion behind us. The strategy was designed to protect you from this. We've avoided drawing up an overall plan for a global settlement. I see pressure building up to force you back to the 1967 borders—compared to that, 10 kilometers is trivial. I'm not angry at you, and I'm not asking you to change your position. It's tragic to see people dooming themselves to a course of unbelievable peril.

Rabin (wryly): This is the day you visited Masada.

Other Americans at the Meeting described the atmosphere as "eerie." The Israelis were passive as Kissinger spoke; now they did not quibble. It was almost as though, from the very first, they wanted no agreement; as though they had determined to demolish—for a time—step-by-step diplomacy. The Israelis were distraught by the Arabs' riches and by their rising power. The United States was weak; Ford was weak; so was Kissinger. In its weakness, America might even sacrifice Israel to satisfy the Arabs. American weakness was one thing, Israeli resolution quite another, and now Israel intended to be strong.

Israel's perception was one thing, Kissinger's quite another. Rabin was not strong, he was clumsy and indecisive. Before the negotiation he had discarded nonbelligerency, but then the Likud challenged him in the Knesset, and he embraced it again. Perhaps Rabin agreed with Kissinger, but it was Peres who dominated this negotiation. Ambitious, dogmatic, rather superficial, he was the strong man, ready to risk the disasters Kissinger conjured up. Peres was vastly more popular in Israel than Rabin and Allon together, and beneath his shadow their misgivings could not prevail. Kissinger longed for Golda Meir; for had he convinced her, the cabinet would have bowed. He missed Dayan, too, for his imagination might have found a way.

Afterward, to an acquaintance, Kissinger ruminated on his defeat. "Israel has no foreign policy," he said, "only domestic politics. . . . The Jews in history are generally intellectuals, cosmopolitans, people of long vision. But in Israel the ideal is that of the soldier-peasant. Generally the soldier is not intellectual, and few soldiers have vision. The peasant is known for his recalcitrance and excessive caution. It is the recalcitrance, excessive caution, lack of vision, that have caused the Israelis to refuse this agreement. . . . They're so legalistic, so Talmudic."

REASSESSMENT

Shortly before the collapse of the negotiation Kissinger visited Faisal at Riyadh. Their rapport had never been easy, but now Kissinger's travail with the Israelis provoked the king's compassion and his pledge to persevere in support of Kissinger's diplomacy; it was of their encounters the warmest and most satisfactory. A week later, Faisal was murdered by a mad nephew. The conjunction of that event with the failure in Sinai appeared to render the more probable all of the disasters Kissinger prophesied in Jerusalem. He was furious with the Israelis, and he took their refusal very personally—as directed not only at the United States but, above all, at himself.

For weeks after his return to Washington, Kissinger sulked and raged, castigating Israeli blindness to aides and visitors alike, compulsively telephoning distinguished Jews all over the country to complain of Israel's intransigence. His much-trumpeted "reassessment" of American policy in the Middle East was his revenge on Israeli behavior, a euphemism for the selective embargo of military equipment that he imposed forthwith upon Jerusalem. He summoned Dean Rusk, George Ball, David Rockefeller, Robert McNamara, and other dignitaries of the foreign policy establishment—the Israelis considered them a "stacked deck"— plus all of the important American ambassadors in the Middle East, to participate in this elaborate enterprise. He conferred as well with congressmen, Jewish leaders, and eminent academicians. The prospect of reassessment made marvelous theater, but what did it produce?

There options soon emerged:

1. The United States should announce its conception of a final settlement in the Middle East, based on the 1967 frontiers of Israel with

minor modifications, and containing strong guarantees for Israel's security. The Geneva conference should be reconvened; the Soviet Union should be encouraged to cooperate in this quest to resolve all outstanding questions (including the status of Jerusalem) which should be defined in appropriate components and addressed in separate subcommittees.

2. Failing the first option, the United States should seek a quasi-total settlement, for the near future, with Egypt the beneficiary. Israel should withdraw from most of the Sinai in return for political nonbelligerency; her final frontiers with Egypt to be determined at a later stage.

3. Failing the first and second options, the United States should endeavor to revive step-by-step diplomacy.

In the beginning, from April till early May, practically everyone Kissinger consulted favored the first option. His key ambassadors— Hermann Eilts (Egypt), Richard Murphy (Syria), and Thomas Pickering (Jordan)—all contributed to a long position paper urging this course; Kenneth Keating, his ambassador to Israel, concurred with reservations, then died shortly after his return to Tel Aviv. Oddly, though resolution of the Palestinian problem was implied in the first option, the question was otherwise deferred in the secret position paper and in the numerous discussions Kissinger undertook. That the United States should abandon Kissingerian ambiguity and publicly proclaim its concept of a global settlement based upon total or near-total Israeli withdrawal was the supreme Arab wish, just as to the Israelis it had always been the supreme abomination. Non-Zionists such as former senator William Fulbright had been urging it on Kissinger and Ford as the best means to achieve a settlement, but till now both had demurred for fear of the repercussions amongst supporters of Israel. In any event despite his apocalyptic warnings to the Israelis on March 22, Kissinger never really refined the first option. For as the weeks passed, his emotions cooled, his capacity for cold analysis prevailed, and his plunge into the metaphysics of reassessment was negated by other forces.

The Arabs had no common strategy nor consensus about the concessions they should render Israel should Geneva be revived. The Russians had hesitations about Geneva without a common strategy and with no Arab consensus; they were in no hurry to sponsor a fiasco. Sadat coveted territory quickly, but he feared further Israeli procrastination at Geneva, and he could not risk the second option—a quasi-total settlement—because without similar progress on all fronts he would become a leper to his brother Arabs. Kissinger's peroration to the Israelis on March 22 was brilliantly contrived, but their flair for realpolitik is as keen as his, and he did not deceive them. Sadat possessed no serious war option—American deliveries of guns and aircraft to Israel had seen to that—and the Israelis knew it. Sadat's relations with the Russians could hardly have been worse; he had chosen the Americans exclusively and now he was stuck with them. The radicals of Araby roared with impotence; Sadat reaffirmed his faith in Kissinger, renewed the United Nations Emergency Force (UNEF) mandate in the Sinai, and, in early June, reopened the Suez Canal. All of these factors coalesced to belie Kissinger's apocalypse—or at least to postpone it—but it was the Israeli lobby that dealt reassessment its coup de grâce.

Kissinger's interaction with American Jews has played a crucial and tempestuous part in the fashioning of his Middle East policy. If he could not convince American Jews, how could he move Israel? From the morrow of the October war he has conferred regularly with Jewish leaders and intellectuals, explaining the motives of his diplomacy and appealing for their support. His basic message has never changed—the war created new realities; the moderate Arabs are ready for peace; Israel, for its own survival, must respond whilst America can influence the Arabs; peace can never come unless Israel makes concessions. For a time Kissinger seemed to make some impression with this argument, but by the end of 1974 he was regarded by many American Jews as a foe of Israel and by some as a traitor to his race. It became a truism in the State Department that Kissinger's Jewishness helped him with the Arabs, harmed him with the Israelis. Last summer, a luminary of the lobby echoed a sentiment I had already heard: "Kissinger is a self-hating Jew."

I cannot penetrate Kissinger's heart, but his closest aides observe that nothing has caused him greater anguish than accusations such as that. "He's objective about Israel," says one, "but not detached. How could he be? He has a strong sense of 'these are my people.' He's immensely proud to be a Jew. When he pleads for changes in Israeli policy it's precisely because he wants Israel and Jewry to prosper. It tears his guts out to be accused of treachery to his own." During those impassioned weeks following the abortive negotiation, Kissinger asked several of his Jewish visitors, "How could I, as a Jew, do anything to betray my people?" More than once, he came close to tears.

During April, the corridors of the State Department resounded with brave resolve for the pursuit of the first option. "We've got to save the Israelis from themselves. . . . Congress is fed up, too, and whatever we decide, Congress will go along. . . ." There was indeed much general speculation last spring about erosion of pro-Israeli sentiment in Congress; the lobby recognized that if Kissinger was to be stopped, he would have to be stopped on Capitol Hill. The American Israel Public Affairs Committee (AIPAC), the vanguard of the lobby in Washington, was intensely active during this period, assailing not only Kissinger's person but his policies in the Middle East, Turkey, and far beyond; militants of the lobby canvassed the House and Senate, exhorting the members to ever greater moral and military support of Israel. Simultaneously, Israeli "truth squads"—composed of such as Eban, Allon, and Dayan—dispersed throughout the nation, rebutting Kissinger's version of the March negotiation and struggling to sustain the image of Israel as a beleaguered democracy still ardent in the quest of peace.

Whatever resentment many congressmen may inwardly entertain about the pressures of the lobby, the American system itself predestines them to yield. Israel possesses a powerful American constituency; the Arabs do not, and despite their wealth, the oil companies as well as unequal to the impact of ethnic politics. In formulating the first option, Kissinger's advisers envisioned Ford going to the American people, explaining lucidly and at length on television the issues of war and peace in the Middle East, pleading the necessity of Israeli withdrawal in exchange for the strongest guarantees. The president, too, was angry at Israel, and for a time he toyed with this notion of appealing over the heads of the lobby and of Congress directly to the people. He hesitated. "How will it play in Peoria?" he asked. "You'll never know until you do it," Fulbright urged him. "Do it first—then Peoria will follow." But Ford was afraid of the political repercussions, and so was Kissinger. A senior diplomat who visited Washington frequently during this period told me. "Each time that I returned, I remarked the further erosion of the first option."

On May 21, 76 U.S. senators wrote collectively to the president to endorse Israel's demand for "defensible" frontiers and massive economic and military assistance. The letter was a stunning triumph for the lobby, a capital rebuke for Kissinger in Congress. (The lobby reaffirmed its strength in summer, humiliating Kissinger and Hussein by obstructing in the Senate the sale of defensive Hawk missiles to Jordan.) The senatorial epistle was Israel's riposte to reassessment; it helped to kill the reassessment, notwithstanding later pretenses that the corpse lived on. At about this time, Sisco, Atherton, and Saunders unanimously advised Kissinger that the first option had no hope of surviving the counterattacks of the lobby—that now the administration had no choice but to resume step-by-step diplomacy. Kissinger concurred, and reserved a new option—that at some future date, when the president was stronger, when his prospects were more auspicious, he might go to the people with a plan for peace based upon the first option.

Thus, when Ford met Sadat at Salzburg in early June, he repulsed Sadat's plea for a public commitment to the 1967 borders, and soothed him instead with a restatement of Nixon's secret promise. Sadat agreed to resume interim negotiations, but stood on his insistence that Israel disgorge the passes and the oil fields. When Rabin visited Washington a week later, Kissinger and Ford were extremely stern. Again they endorsed the Egyptian demands, stressing that Israel could not count on substantial American aid until it negotiated a new settlement in the Sinai. With unwonted adroitness, Ford dangled the first option before Rabin's wary eye. If Israel did not negotiate more generously, the president warned, then he would revive Geneva. There, he implied, the United States would favor substantial restitution of the 1967 frontiers. Kissinger, in fact, protested the continuing entrenchment of Israeli settlements in occupied Arab territory, and bluntly told Rabin that eventually Israel must abandon the settlements and retreat substantially to the 1967 boundaries.

Rabin got the message. Nevertheless, he knew that to sustain its Arab policy the United States needed the agreement desperately, and for that he intended to extract a very high price. Thus, the Israelis resumed their tested posture—playing for time— whilst the price was worked out. At Jerusalem, cabinet meetings were postponed, "clarifications" were requested, and "elucidations" were demanded of Kissinger and Sadat. The Israelis aspired to retain at least a foothold in the passes; the rest of June, all of July, much of August was consumed as they haggled with Kissinger over the locus of the new line. Kissinger promised about $1.8 billion in new arms and economic aid. An Israeli request for $2.5 billion was pending, but by mid-August the demand had mounted to nearly $3.5 billion. At that point, Mordechai Gazit, the director general of Rabin's office, arrived in Washington with the Israeli drafts of the secret "Memoranda of Understanding" that Israel expected the United States to append to the new agreement. The drafts, says one of Kissinger's senior aides, "were simply incredible. They amounted to a formal political and military alliance between Israel and the United States. They would have granted Israel an outright veto over future American policy in the Middle East."

Kissinger, meanwhile, was distressed by the Israeli maps. He had to be certain the Israelis would leave the passes, so he sent a senior CIA official to authenticate their line *sur place*. On August 11, the official strolled through Giddi with Mordechai Gur and said, "General, you're still inside the pass." Nevertheless, Kissinger resumed his shuttle on August 20—his twelfth major mission to the Middle East.

The particulars of that negotiation—defining the "non-use of force," the buffer zone for the oil fields, the limitation of troops and weaponry et cetera—we need not dissect anew. For the Israeli right, it was all perfidious. At Jerusalem, on the first night, after a dinner with the cabinet, Kissinger was trapped in the Knesset for over an hour by thousands of angry youths. When he regained the King David Hotel, they gave him no repose. My room was situated a few floors below his, and toward 4:00 AM I was awakened by a chorus of loudspeakers. "Kissinger go home! Kiss-in-ger go! Kiss-in-ger go go! Kiss-in-ger go go home home! Jew boy! Jew boy go home!" I got up from bed and opened the shutters. The youths were concealed in the darkness of the old no man's land; beyond them the walls of the Old City and the Mount of Olives loomed in a soft light. "Jew boy go home!" They were the Gush Emunim—Front of the Faithful—and every time the police suppressed one loudspeaker, another erupted somewhere else. In the morning. Kissinger was beside himself. "We're moving to the Hilton," he told his entourage. But the King David was a transplanted State Department—a warren of typists, staff aides, Telex installations—and could not be abandoned.

Later, at Rabin's residence, Kissinger discussed monitoring stations in the Sinai—to be manned separately by Israelis, Egyptians, and Americans.

> *Kissinger:* I don't think an American presence is a good idea. I think it's a mistake.

> *Peres:* It has a logic and a purpose. The aerial reconnaissance the United States provided after the first disengagement—mere American involvement—reduced tension and helped stabilize a nervous situation. We're now adding an American land reconnaissance role in the most sensitive part of the Sinai. The presence of even a symbolical group of American technicians would serve as a [deterrent] for either side. . . . I know that Americans might say, "This is the way things began in Vietnam." I see no comparison. A buffer zone is a buffer zone. It's extraterritorial.

> *Kissinger:* It's a mistake. There will be a reaction in the United States to this kind of thing. How will it appear to the American people—Americans there against a surprise attack?

At Alexandria, Sadat seemed strangely resigned to whatever "Dr. Henry" might do for him. Sadat could not accept less than the passes and the oil fields, but otherwise he accommodated most Israeli conditions. Kissinger spent comparatively little time in Egypt. Sadat was simply not a quibbler; he guided the negotiation, but left the details to Fahmy and Gamasy. Whilst Sadat napped in the afternoons, Kissinger repaired to Fahmy's beach house on the Mediterranean, in the shadow of Montaza Palace, Farouk's old fantasy of Kubla Khan. There, sometimes as they waded in the sea, Kissinger resolved with the two ministers such complexities as U.N. checkpoints, early warning systems, and the limitation of SCUD missiles. Once, Sadat joined them for luncheon and a swim. Again, during this negotiation, Kissinger complained to the Egyptians of Israeli excess. "It's unbelievable what they're demanding," he said. "Rabin, Peres, Allon—they're not negotiating as a team, they're each pursuing personal ambitions." Or were they, he asked, deliberately acting thus to destroy the negotiation and to bring him down?

The great issue was still the passes. The Israelis claimed their line took them out, but Kissinger examined aerial photographs and told them it did not. By August 26, the Egyptians had agreed to Israeli and American monitoring stations, but the Israeli line was still in doubt. At the eleventh hour, the Israelis capitulated—though not completely. In the Mitla, it was difficult to define where the eastern entrance was, but basically they were out of that pass. In the Giddi, they relinquished the road, but clung to some high ground on the northern perimeter, and bent their line west-ward slightly between the passes to retain some hills. Sadat was bemused that Kissinger could not push them further, but acquiesced.

Whilst Kissinger was resolving the line, Atherton remained in Jerusalem negotiating American commitments to Israel—a task equally tortuous. The Israeli drafts, which they had insisted be renamed "Memo-randa of Agreement" to render them more binding, were phrased in absolute language which Atherton kept watering down. When Kissinger returned each night to Jerusalem, he diluted them further still. For example, the Israelis wanted an absolute American commitment to intervene if the Soviet Union threatened to attack Israel. Kissinger promised only to consult Israel. At the end of the negotiation, Atherton went two nights without sleep as the Israelis kept demanding word changes in the main agreement and military annex. Peres did not wish the Egyptians to renew the UNEF mandate "annually" but "for a year every year." The quibbling continued till the moment Kissinger took his last leave for Alexandria on September 1. "What you must understand," an Israeli leader told me, "is that we're not negotiating with the Americans. We're negotiating with the Arabs."

Even as modified by Kissinger, the final American-Israeli Memo-randa of Agreement was—as his own aides admitted—"mind-boggling." For example:

> The [U.S.] Government . . . will seek to prevent . . . proposals which it and Israel agree are detrimental to the interests of Israel. . . . The United States is resolved . . . to maintain Israel's defensive strength through the supply of advanced types of equipment, such as the F-16 aircraft [and] to undertake a joint study of high technology and sophisticated weapons, including the Pershing ground-to-ground missiles with conventional warheads, with the view to giving a positive response. . . . The United States . . . will not recognize or negotiate with the Palestine Liberation Organization so long as the [PLO] does not recognize Israel's right to exist and does not accept Security Council Resolutions 242 and 338. The [U.S.] Government will consult fully and seek to concert its position and strategy at the Geneva peace conference with the Government of Israel.

In the shadow of such promises, Kissinger's commitment of 200 techni-cians in the Sinai seemed suddenly inconsequential.

The memoranda, however qualified, and despite Kissinger's and Ford's denials, amounted almost to a marriage contract. If America must pay a dowry so large for a small fraction of the Sinai, what must it pay for real peace? Such were the alarums of the Congress, whose letter of the 76 had helped to kill Kissinger's first option, and whose members were themselves at fault. I have no evidence of this, but I suspect that lurking in Kissinger's Medicean mind was at least half the wish that the Israelis would overreach their American constituency and impair their power base in Congress. If that was his trap, the Israelis stepped into it. Demanding the Pershing missile—with its capacity to carry atomic warheads from Tel Aviv to Aswan—was a terrible mistake, and it is not astonishing that later the Israelis demurred.

Nevertheless, the second Sinai agreement was a major tactical triumph for Israel. She relinquished little (by the admission of several Israeli generals) of strategic value in the passes, and wrested from the United States a moral, monetary, and military cornucopia unattained by any other foreign power. Above all, the agreement partially fulfilled Rabin's central purpose. As a senior Israeli official told *Time* magazine:

> Given nonacceptance of Israel by the Arabs, we have been maneuvering since 1967 to gain time and to return as little as possible. The predominant government view has been that stalemates are to our advantage. Our great threat has been the Rogers plan—and American policy to move us back to the [1967] lines. The . . . agreement with Egypt is another nail in the coffin of that policy. We realize that the entire world is against us on the issue of borders and that we are terribly dependent on one nation for sophisticated arms. Nevertheless, we have been successful for the past . . . eight years, and we may have to go on maneuvering for another ten. If the . . . interim agreement [gave] us only six months rather than three years, we would buy it because the alternative is Geneva and . . . more pressure to go back to the 1967 borders. The . . . agreement has delayed Geneva, while . . . assuring us arms, money, a coordinated policy with Washington and quiet in Sinai. . . . We gave up a little for a lot.

Moreover, even though the agreement may not assure Israel a stalemate of several years, it is doubtful she will move an inch before the American elections. The pause should be more than ample to enable Israel to pursue the second level of her policy—entrenchment in the territories. In Gaza and all over Golan; at Yamit and Sharm el Sheikh in the Sinai; at Jerusalem and near Jericho, Hebron, Nablus, Bethlehem, and Ramallah on the West Bank—thousands of acres have been expropriated, thousands of Israelis have taken root in farms, industries, and apartment complexes. The entrenchment continues with deliberate speed. "I don't see those installations," Kissinger has said. "They're transparent. I look right through them. When the time comes for me to open my dossiers on Golan and the West Bank, I shan't let them impede a settlement. When the time comes, the president will prevail on the Israelis to withdraw." I wonder.

As for Egypt, Sadat gave Israel nonbelligerency in all but name. Secretly, he promised Kissinger not to participate in battle should Syria attack Israel. Kissinger briefed him on the American-Israeli memoranda, but not about the superweapons. Sadat disliked the agreement, but he had no choice. Egypt's economy was desperate; it would collapse without foreign investment. The army, bereft of weapons to match Israel's, could not resume war for several years. No choice? Nonsense, says Mohammed Hassanein Haikal, the celebrated editor who once was Nasser's (and Sadat's) gray eminence. "Kissinger is destroying his own investment in Sadat," Haikal told me on the morrow of the agreement. "He's isolated him from the rest of the Arab world, and in that isolation Sadat will fail to find the oil money he needs for Egypt. Kissinger has no strategy, except to reduce the Arab-Israeli conflict into fragments. Egypt alone will not be worth much to the United States, and powerless to cope with its own poverty."

Kissinger received similar reproaches from Assad and King Hussein when he visited them in early September. Assad accused him of dividing the "Arab nation," a foreshadowing of his furious attacks upon Sadat. During an angry meeting at Amman, Rifai assailed the agreement and refused to support it publicly; the king was more cordial, though equally distressed. When I saw Assad and Hussein in late September, they complained bitterly of the weapons for Israel. Assad all but described Kissinger as Israel's foreign minister; Hussein warned me of "new disasters not far away."

Assad and Hussein were no more vexed about the Israeli weapons than were many officials of the U.S. government. Led by Secretary of Defense James Schlesinger, most of the Pentagon, the CIA, the Treasury, the Office of Management and Budget, many officials of the State Department, strongly opposed substantial quantities of new arms for Israel. If Kissinger's current commitment is sustained for the next four years, Israel will receive $5 billion or more in arms by 1980, many of them outright gifts. Does Israel truly require hundreds of F-15 and F-16 aircraft, Hawk missiles, Lance missiles, M60 A3 tanks, and laser-guided "smart" bombs to maintain an effective deterrent against the Arabs? "Israel wants 1,000 per cent security," says a Pentagon official, "and she's getting it."

Since the October war, the United States has provided Israel with at least $3 billion worth of precision-guided munitions, cluster bomb units, tanks, armored personnel carriers, self-propelled artillery, cargo trucks, cargo aircraft, rifles, helicopters, antitank guided rockets, electronic counterradar boxes, Phantoms, and Skyhawks. Before October 1973, the Israelis relied excessively upon their air force, but now the United States has rectified their failings in infantry and artillery and instilled in them the science of coordinated warfare. "In quality, and even quantitatively in some respects," says the Pentagon official, "Egypt, Syria, and Jordan together cannot match the force of Israel nor shall they for the next decade. Their MIGs cannot compare with the F-15s and F-16s, and besides, their pilots lack skill. Their SCUDs? If they fired a dozen at Tel Aviv, half might hit Beirut."

Several ministers in Rabin's own government dissent from his and Peres' arms policy, protesting that if Israel continues thus she may perish from insolvency. Early last year, Kissinger complained to friends that "When I ask Rabin to make concessions he says he can't because Israel is weak. So I give him more arms, and he says he doesn't need to make concessions because Israel is strong." During the abortive negotiation of March, Kissinger lamented his failure to extract concessions first; immense arms shipments to Israel "was naive—my biggest mistake." Following the second Sinai agreement, Kissinger argued that the new arms would encourage Israeli flexibility. He had said the same five years ago, when he assumed concessions would result once Israel was invincible. Kissinger had come full circle.

"WHAT ARE THE ALTERNATIVES?"

We have witnessed in Kissinger's journeys through Israel and Araby a diplomatic odyssey unequaled in our time. But the works of peace that he so hopefully embarked upon two years ago seem suspended now in a winter of doubt and discontent. In late October, I confronted Kissinger in Washington with some of the reservations about his policies that I have recorded here. He appeared harassed and exhausted, but his answer gave me pause. "What are the alternatives?" he asked. "The conflict in the Middle East has a history of decades. Only during the last two years have we produced progress. It's easy to say that what we've done is not enough, but the steps we've taken are the biggest steps so far. They were *the attainable*—given our prevailing domestic situation."

His response impressed me because it pleaded what is, not what might have been. His maxim, "Israel has no foreign policy, only domestic estic politics," he might have uttered of the United States—especially as it involves the Middle East. When I observed once to an aide of Kissinger's that Israel's American constituency is the greatest constraint upon our policy, he replied, "Of course. And the constraint becomes the determinant." Within and sometimes against those constraints, despite his errors, Kissinger has often behaved heroically.

Moreover, the second level of his policy—promoting American technology amongst the Arabs whilst he copes with the Arab-Israeli conflict—has proven a considerable success. For this, Kissinger must share his laurels with several agencies of the government and with American technology at large; but he has encouraged the phenomenon and helped it prosper. Paradoxically, despite her tactical victory in the second Sinai agreement, Israel may ultimately suffer the most from Kissinger's parallel policy if she does not conclude a final peace before the Arabs master all the marvels of American technology.

Kissinger's Arab policy—still anchored on Sadat—remains intact, though it is buffeted by angry winds. Kissinger erred in supposing that Sadat could control the rest of Araby; Assad's acrimonious rupture with Egypt over the second Sinai agreement may emasculate Kissinger's credibility as an arbiter between Israel and the Arabs. Beyond this, Egypt's chaotic internal condition is scarcely Kissinger's fault; Sadat may be a world statesman, but he knows little of managing an economy, and parts of his government are dank with corruption. Even on the world stage, Sadat has stumbled. Had Sadat been less ardent in pressing Kissinger to favor the Egyptian interest and more loyal to the Arab unity he achieved for the October war, the Arab world might be more confident today to make concessions and closer to peace with Israel.

A questionable hypothesis, perhaps—but strategy is based upon hypothesis and we must wonder about Kissinger's. Did Kissinger ever conceive a coherent strategy for concluding the Arab-Israeli conflict? Assad, had he eavesdropped on that dramatic meeting at Jerusalem on March 22, 1975, might have confirmed his fear that Kissinger's strategy was simply to protect Israel from having to retreat to her old borders. I feel that Kissinger planned to nudge the Israelis back toward those very boundaries, and much more quickly, but was obstructed by circumstances he himself helped to bring about. I agree with professor Stanley Hoffmann of Harvard, who remarked to me that Kissinger has been caught in the dilemma of "playing several roles at once. He's a conceptualist, a negotiator, and a day-to-day manager. The conceptualist begins by defining his goal, then recognizes obstacles en route, and tries to reduce them. The negotiator is caught up in the complications of the day, no longer defines the goal for its own sake, and makes the goal whatever remains after allowing for all the obstacles. Henry has done this in Vietnam, and in the Middle East. He favors the short run over the long run. Curious, because he's equally gifted in either direction. He'll produce a brilliant conceptual analysis of a problem, then a set of almost completely tactical proposals."

Thus tactical success becomes a goal in itself. If Arafat is like a cyclist atop a tightrope, Kissinger is like a lumberjack leaping from log to log, wishing that the river will lead him somewhere else. He suffers, by his own admission, from the syndrome of success; though his tactics have been brilliant and his techniques, too, strategically he has sinned on the side of caution. Perhaps his greatest achievement is to have bought time, prevented war, and erected the foundation for the pursuit of real peace. But can Kissinger himself consummate that wish? His method seems simply too slow, and if clung to may imperil peace for the great future. Interim diplomacy could conceivably conclude another minor Israeli withdrawal on the Golan, but it cannot address the central issues of the Arab-Israeli conflict such as the future of the Palestinian people, and those issues cannot be postponed much longer.

There are signs that Kissinger—eager to revive the confidence of Assad—is softening his attitude toward the Palestinians; for example, the declaration of former Deputy Assistant Secretary Saunders defining the Palestinian dimension as the "heart" of the Arab-Israeli conflict, and Kissinger's acquiescense to the participation of the PLO in the Security Council debate in January. Contacts between the United States and the PLO have existed sporadically for several years, but so far no negotiations of substance have resulted. Privately, Arafat agrees to recognize Israel, but he will not publicly deal this, his most potent card, until he is confident of a Palestinian state. That state, confined to Gaza and the West Bank, demilitarized, totally autonomous or confederated with Hashemite Jordan, is—despite immense obstacles—imaginable of creation; but it cannot be created unless the United States endorses the goal and then pursues it.

The endorsement may not come this election year, but the next administration will be unable to avoid the urgency of a general peace. That peace will perforce be based upon the 1967 boundaries, butressed by guarantees for Israel that can include a defense treaty with the United States should Israel require further assurance of her security. Israel might not be asked to withdraw at once, simply to accept the principle then negotiate a timetable tied to concessions from the Arabs which would ultimately include formal recognition of her legitimacy. This is, of course, the first option, favored last spring by most American officials involved with the Middle East. If Kissinger—his capital and credibility spent with Israelis, Arabs, and Congress alike—cannot accomplish it, perhaps his successor could.

An illusion? Ironically this sort of settlement might have been possible on the morrow of the October war had Kissinger truly seized the opportunities of that period. But he feared then that to seek so much so soon was doomed to fail. We shall never know. What he did accomplish, and it was not small, resembles the reconciliation between T. S. Eliot's Archbishop and the King—"Peace, but not the kiss of peace/A patched-up affair, if you ask my opinion." Hopefully, Kissinger or his successor will make an act of faith in failure, and in the end help Arabs and Jews to fashion something more substantial than interim solutions.

PART II

ANALYSIS OF KISSINGER
THE ACTOR

3

PLAYING THE WRONG GAME?
Roger Fisher

INTRODUCTION

Sound advice for dealing with an international conflict is to start by trying to understand how the other side sees things. That advice is probably equally sound for an academic who has been asked to criticize the performance of an operator in the field of international affairs. This chapter will begin by trying to understand, from Kissinger's point of view, what he was doing from 1973 to 1976. What was his perception of the problem? What was his approach for dealing with it? What game was he playing? This will be followed by an analysis of some risks and costs of playing that game the way Kissinger played it. In conclusion, the author will suggest better games to play.

The conduct of international affairs can usefully be compared with a game because of the similarities of structure. Whether implicit or explicit, "rules of the game" goals are pursued by players who have a repertoire of standard moves. These three basic elements—the goals, the participants or players, and the methods or standard moves—will serve both to help one understand what Kissinger was doing and then as a basis for criticism.

THE GOALS

Kissinger's highest priority was the maintenance of a global political balance. He recently expressed this view to the Senate Foreign Relations Committee:

The geopolitical equilibrium must be maintained lest radical forces
hostile to the West gain such momentum that they appear the
irresistible wave of the future (*NYT*, August 1, 1979, p. A6).

Whatever happened to Palestinian refugees, Israeli settlers, or Egyptian
farmers was insignificant compared to the necessity of avoiding a nuclear
war between the Soviet Union and the United States. "When Kissinger
glanced at the map of the Middle East, he did not see Israel, Egypt,
Jordan, Syria; he saw the Soviet Union and the United States" (Sheehan,
1976, p. 18).

Limiting Soviet military and political influence and reducing the risk
of nuclear war were Kissinger's fundamental concerns. In the Middle East
his goals were subordinated to his concern with the Soviet Union.
Kissinger was therefore less interested in producing a settlement of the
Arab-Israeli conflict than he was in avoiding open warfare between Israel
and its neighbors—warfare that could trigger a military confrontation
with the Soviet Union. Conflict between the superpowers would be the
single largest disaster for the national interest of the United States.
Consequently, Kissinger saw little point in worrying about peace between
Israel and its neighbors in the long term unless peace between the Soviet
Union and the United States in the immediate future could be maintained
day by day.

Quandt (1977) explains Kissinger's theory of how to reduce the risk
of war:

> ... the status quo must be stabilized through a combination of
> diplomacy and arms shipments. A political process must begin that
> would offer the Arabs an alternative to war, but it must be carried on
> at a pace that the Israelies could accept" (p. 251).

Matti Golan (1976) emphasizes the larger context in which Kissinger was
negotiating individual agreements:

> Kissinger, of course, viewed all the problems concerning the disen-
> gagement of forces in a global context. For him disengagement was
> one more link in the policy of detente, (p. 172).

Kissinger's substantive goal was to win the Middle East by excluding
the Soviet Union. This he saw as clearly in the national interest of the
United States, both because a large Soviet role there could adversely
affect political stability in the area, U.S. oil supplies, and Israel, and
because any apparent Soviet success there might adversely affect the
world balance. "One of Kissinger's primary goals was to weaken the
Soviet influence in the Middle East, especially in Egypt" (Quandt 1977,
pp. 261, 285).

The third immediate objective of Kissinger's Middle East diplomacy was power. If the United States was to maintain and increase its ability to influence world events, it needed to be seen as an effective government that accomplished what it set out to do. Diplomatic success would enhance U.S. power. The image of success is what Kissinger sought. A Secretary of State who was widely perceived as successful would be better able to keep other conflicts under control and to shape the world more to the United States' liking than one who was not.

Kissinger thus saw himself less as an impartial mediator between Israel and Arab states than as someone dedicated to advancing the national interests of the United States. This was to be accomplished by launching a diplomatic process that would avoid an Arab-Israeli war, at least for the time being; by excluding the Soviet Union from that process; and by having the U.S. Secretary of State attain a series of diplomatic successes.

THE PLAYERS

The methods used by Kissinger in his Middle East diplomacy are in part a product of the assumptions he made about the participants and their roles. For Kissinger, the role of the United States was not that of a neutral, but rather that of an active negotiator in its own right. Nor were the participants seen as governments or nations, but as a handful of individuals.

The United States as an Involved Negotiator

In conventional thinking about mediation, the third party should be someone with no interest in the conflict. An ideal mediator is seen as a kind of eunuch from Mars who happens to be temporarily available. Kissinger appreciated that such disinterested parties do not exist and are not needed. Third parties can be judged on their respective merits, which include their ability, their interest in promoting a peaceful accommodation of the conflict, and their acceptability to the parties.

Kissinger recognized that his ability to play a constructive third party role did not require the United States to be disinterested (Quandt 1977, p. 285). On the contrary, the support the United States had long been giving Israel was seen by Arabs as providing a special basis for exerting influence upon it. Arabs often believe that the United States has more influence over Israel than it has, which can lead to disappointment. But Kissinger correctly appreciated that his special relationship with Israel, as a United States official and as a Jew, enhanced rather than weakened the ability of the United States to act as a third party.

Kissinger also recognized that as an involved party the United States was free to plunge actively into the negotiating process. He saw his role as that of a hard-bargaining negotiator, committed to achieving an agreement not because it was in the interests of both sides (though he would try to convince them that it was), but because any agreement, however limited, served the national interest of the United States.

This active role gave full scope to Kissinger's intelligence, initiative, drive, and diplomatic skill. He freed himself in an admirable fashion from bureaucratic constraints on his role. He did not shirk the hard work of acquiring detailed knowledge. By the time the Mitla and Giddi passes had become a major source of controversy in the second Sinai disengagement talks, Kissinger had been over the maps and photographs in great detail and in some respects knew more about them than those with whom he was negotiating (Sheehan 1976, p. 188).

Personal Diplomacy

Kissinger's second working assumption was that the parties involved were not governments or states but individual people. Kissinger did not see the U.S. player as being the government of the United States, but rather the Secretary of State as an individual human being. Kissinger was not a team player; the United States was not fielding a team. The Kalbs point out that "Kissinger wanted to be in personal charge of the negotiations from the very beginning" (Kalb and Kalb 1974, p. 482). Starting during the October 1973 War if not before, "he took care to insure that he alone was kept informed of all aspects of the conflict and that he alone was in communication with all of the parties" (Sheehan 1976, p. 38). Kissinger was apparently able to use staff well and to work them hard. Sheehan reports that he "assimilates the best of their ideas for his own purposes, then comes to his decision—alone. When the policy succeeds, *he* receives the acclamation—alone (p. 172).

Kissinger saw foreign players in the ongoing game very much the way he saw the United States. Instead of Israel as a player, he saw Golda Meir or Itzhak Rabin; instead of Jordan, he saw King Hussein; instead of Syria, he saw Assad.

Treating individuals rather than countries as the players in the game of nations has great advantages. It reduces the risk of becoming locked in by abstractions. It is far easier to develop understanding and empathy for the concerns of an individual than for the positions of a state. It is also easier to appreciate the constraints under which a government is operating when one sees how they impinge upon the choice of a particular human being.

For Kissinger, personalizing the international actors had the further advantage of allowing full rein for his techniques of personalized diplomacy. Before going to Damascus he prepared himself on Arab customs and ways of thinking so that he would spend an appropriate amount of time on coffee and small talk before turning to matters of substance (Sheehan 1976, pp. 120–21). Beyond appreciating cultural differences, Kissinger was a student of a common weakness of all men, and adept at dealing with it: "It has always been Kissinger's special style to flatter and charm an adversary" (Kalb and Kalb 1974, p. 511). Flattery may not be admirable, but it can be effective. "Kissinger believed that he could get Waldheim to do anything for him by flattering him till he was 'breathless'" (Golan 1976, p. 167).

The secretary's concern with the individual went far beyond paying compliments. His well-known self-deprecating humor was used to ingratiate himself with those with whom he dealt. He could also make the person he was speaking with feel that he had a special and preferred relationship with Kissinger because Kissinger was telling him candid and indiscreet things about others.

STANDARD MOVES

The now famous shuttle diplomacy entailed a great deal more than air travel. Indeed, the specific methods Kissinger employed largely determined the structure of the negotiating process. Kissinger regarded negotiation as a contest of will in which each party tried to induce the other to change its position.

In choosing his issues, Kissinger sought to break them down into manageable pieces and to avoid seeking agreement on long-term goals so as to maximize his chance for success. He sought to educate each party to the other's concerns and then exchange proposals from each side, successively asking each party for a concession to take to the other. To move negotiations along, Kissinger used U.S. aid and political commitments as carrots, and he used linkage, leverage, and threats to pressure the parties to agree.

Breaking the Issues into Manageable Pieces

One feature of Kissinger's method was to seek agreement on a manageable piece of the puzzle, not to postpone progress until it might be possible to reach agreement on everything. The logic in favor of a step-by-step approach is persuasive. One may argue about the steps, but even a comprehensive settlement needs to be built step-by-step. Whether the steps are on-the-ground measures to be implemented one at a time or procedural steps to be agreed upon and implemented, disagreement on some issues should not be allowed to hold up progress on others. (See

Fisher 1972, especially the section entitled "Break up the Problem" at pp. 12 et seq.; and Fisher 1964.)

One particular aspect of Kissinger's strategy of fractionating conflict was to avoid arguments over where everybody was going to end up. The technique was to seek agreement where agreement was most likely; not to argue over points that did not have to be settled now. As a standard move, biting off some aspect of a conflict on which to work is not always congenial to others, but it is a highly useful technique. By taking on only those situations that the secretary thought were "sure things" he often "sinned on the side of caution" (Sheehan 1976, p. 204), but the concept is powerful and should be used more regularly.

Educating Each Party on the Other's Concerns

In any conflict it is highly likely that each adversary has a one-sided view of the problem. In his own mind, Kissinger's "great function—he has said so many times—was to explain persuasively to each party the constraints upon the other" (Sheehan 1976, p. 113). "Look, you guys, my greatest contribution is to explain clearly to each party the position of the other" (Sheehan 1976, p. 7). Presumably Kissinger did not limit himself to clarifying the official position of the other side and restraints on what it might do, but also conveyed their perceptions, illuminated their choices as they saw them, and effectively transmitted some feeling of what they cared about. Effective communication of an opposing side's interests and ideas is one of the most useful functions a third party can perform. Adversaries, even face to face, rarely find the words that are most persuasive to each other.

Requesting Proposals from the Parties

Quandt reports that when Kissinger's technique for arranging limited agreements was well developed it "began by eliciting proposals from each side" (Quandt 1977, p. 260). Such a request has the advantage of helping a mediator frame a problem. An exchange of proposals also allowed Kissinger to refrain from advancing any substantive suggestions from the United States. For a third party to put forward its own ideas at an early stage is likely to result in three rejected plans lying on the table. Only after the parties' proposals had been exchanged would Kissinger come up with an American plan (Kalb and Kalb 1974, pp. 534–35).

Pressing for Concessions

The heart of Kissinger's method was to seek concessions from each party to take to the other. The flavor of this basic move in the secretary's game is conveyed in his reported statement to Golda Meir: "You are not giving me anything to go to Cairo with. I have nothing to offer them" (Golan 1976, p. 109).

It is clear through the history of his Middle East shuttle diplomacy that the secretary and those with whom he was dealing were following a model of negotiation well illustrated by that of a buyer and seller haggling over the price of an old rug. The sequence of events is often as well structured as the steps of a minuet: the seller names a high price; the buyer expresses disbelief and makes a modest offer; after talk, the seller makes a slight concession on his asking price; the buyer points out defects in the rug, refers to his limited resources, and raises his offer. And so it goes until either a price is agreed upon or there is no sale.

Threatening Linkage, Leverage, and Pressure

Presumably the secretary sometimes tried to persuade one person or another by reasoned argument addressed to the objective merits of a problem. It is striking, however, the extent to which he is reported to have relied on means of persuasion unrelated to the merits. He not only emphasized "the dire consequences internationally of a failure to reach agreement," but also marshalled "forces that might influence the parties, such as other Arab countries or the United States Congress" (Quandt 1977, p. 260). Sheehan states that the secretary's step-by-step diplomacy "presupposed a strong and popular president fully prepared to impose his will upon the obstinacy of either party—particularly the Israelis" (p. 151).

The secretary demonstrated his willingness to inflict hardship as a means of persuasion during the United States "reassessment" in the spring of 1975 following Israel's failure to be as forthcoming as he desired in the Sinai II disengagement talks. He suspended negotiations of new F-15 fighter planes for Israel, imposed a selective embargo on military equipment for Israel, delayed delivery of some already committed missiles, and told Israeli cabinet officers not to make scheduled visits to Washington (Sheehan 1976, p. 165). Another example of the secretary's use of threats was against Saudi Arabia in an attempt to end the boycott (Sheehan 1976, p. 116).

Offering Aid and Political Promises

A final tactic in the secretary's repertoire of standard moves was to buy the decision he wanted by promising economic or military aid, or by entering into a political commitment purporting to tie his hands for the future. This technique was employed widely and at substantial economic and political cost to the United States.

The foregoing attempts a sympathetic if brief summary of the

Middle East game being played by the Secretary of State from 1973 to 1976. By his own criteria, it worked; he accomplished his objectives. He bought time, he excluded the Soviet Union from most Middle East diplomacy, and he attained widely hailed diplomatic successes. But that diplomatic record needs to be judged more rigorously.

The temptation in judging a performance so personal is to judge the person. However, we are not here concerned with what kind of human being Henry Kissinger was, but rather how best to conduct international affairs. The question is not what was wrong with Henry Kissinger, but what, if anything, was wrong with his conduct of U.S. diplomacy? Would one advise someone else to behave as he did?

RISKS AND COSTS IN PLAYING KISSINGER'S GAME

Problems with His Formulation of Goals

Preoccupation with Power

Secretary Kissinger regarded power as the single most significant element in international relations. He saw the ability of the United States to affect future hands in the game of nations as far more important than the substantive outcome of any one hand. Although writing about Kissinger's assessment of conditions during a crisis, Heikal's statement about Kissinger applies far more broadly: "In his estimate, the facts of power take precedence over all other factors" (quoted in Sheehan 1976, p. 59).

To focus on power is to give less attention to what is to be done. Power is like money in the bank: it gives one an ability to affect the future. But to see power as an end in itself is to become like a miser, scrounging resources rather than using them wisely. To maximize his chance of success, the secretary set narrow limits on what he tried to accomplish. His priority goal was not to bring justice or a durable peace to the Middle East, but to produce a personal success so that, in theory, at some later time he could do something more important. To be so concerned with the power that comes from success is to be too little concerned with making the world a better place, as two of the cases on which the contributors to this volume were asked to comment particularly indicate.

First, in November 1973 Kissinger discouraged Israel from going forward with direct bilateral disengagement talks (which appeared promising) between General Yariv and General Gamasy of Egypt. Kissinger wanted "to demonstrate that a United States role was essential for sustained diplomatic progress" (Quandt 1977, p. 220). A more important role was the development of improved relations between Egypt and Israel. Further, it would have been desirable to have those countries recognize that their basic task was to reach agreement with each other, not to strike bargains with the United States. Other considerations cited by Quandt (1977, p. 220) are unpersuasive. It is an instance of the United States' being too concerned with itself and with how it appeared. Based on the available record, the secretary should have been advised to have encouraged the talks to go forward and to have offered, should either side desire, the presence of a United States official to facilitate progress.

In the second case, on December 7, 1973, Kissinger again discouraged the Israelis from moving so quickly in negotiations, and urged them to be less forthcoming so that "Israel should not look weak" (Quandt 1977, p. 221). Again, the apparent purpose was to promote the illusion of power in the United States government at the cost of possible progress on the ground. The secretary wanted the Arabs to see Israel as responding only to pressure from the United States. In retrospect, the supposed danger that Israel would look too forthcoming is hardly plausible. The secretary should not have discouraged the substance of the Dayan disengagement proposal. Procedurally, it might have been wise to have converted the Dayan suggestion into a United States discussion draft, which could have been shown to both Egyptians and Israelis for comment. Such a move would have capitalized on Israeli willingness without either weakening their hand or labeling the plan as one "made in Israel." The secretary's concern for keeping himself and the United States in the driver's seat appears to have distorted both his priorities and his judgment.

Overemphasis on the Power of Success

Not only did the secretary's conduct overemphasize the importance of power, he overemphasized the power that comes from having an image of success.

At the outset one must recognize that Kissinger's ability to acquire power through reputation and appearances was astounding. He arrived in Washington in 1969 as an academic who had been appointed National Security Adviser to the newly elected President Nixon. Within a short time he had turned himself into one of the most powerful, if not the most powerful, man in the world. To enhance the power of the office, Kissinger wanted the Secretary of State to look important. This was partly a matter of world press coverage and partly a matter of having the trappings of power with which to impress those he encountered. Kissinger's cultivation of the media was masterful. Nearly a score of correspondents accompanied Kissinger on his Middle East travels and were assured of things to write about by frequent briefings, witty quotations, and off-the-record conversations with "a high State Department official." Looking important was also achieved by the way in which Kissinger traveled. On one Middle East trip, for example, he had an entourage of some 134 people, two bulletproof limousines flown ahead in special Air Force planes (to assure that one was available at each end of every flight), helicopters, 35 Secret Service agents, and other conspicuous features sufficient to convince anyone of his importance (Sheehan 1976, pp. 2–3).

One must also concede that political opponents and the press tend to treat without mercy anything that can be called a failure. The brutal media treatment of President Carter for not "looking effective" demonstrates the risk of concentrating on the merits at the expense of concern with appearances. Yet little effective power is gained by being perceived as being concerned with one's appearance by a reputation for being worried only about one's reputation. To look for the power that comes from appearing to be successful is to pay too little attention to the power that comes from being a person of integrity, of being concerned with others, and of adhering to principle.

There is also a risk that any public official who puts such emphasis on power will confuse power for himself with power for the government, and will concentrate his efforts on ingratiating himself with the press and on building an international image. Such concentration may result in his leaving office as a famous millionaire while his government is left indebted by billions of dollars and hobbled by political commitments that he personally may never have intended to keep.

Negativity of Substantive Goals

Kissinger's prime substantive goal was to remove Soviet influence from the Middle East. There is a risk that by focusing so acutely on the Soviet Union one ignores the very problems, such as those of the Palestinians, that drive otherwise moderate people to seek solutions through violence and Soviet support. To have a negative goal as the primary concern of one's foreign policy gives Arabs and others reason to look elsewhere for inspiration and leadership.

Kissinger's extreme concern with the Soviet Union sharply limited the ability of the United States to promote a peaceful settlement of the Arab-Israeli conflict. His anti-Soviet goal tended to restrict his interests and therefore his comprehension of what was going on. Quandt reports: "The net effect was to keep the focus on the U.S.-Soviet dimension of the crisis at the expense of understanding developments in Israel, in the Arab world, and in the region as a whole" (Quandt 1977, p. 298).

Also, the very goal of precluding the Soviet Union from the peace-making process almost certainly precluded the possibility of peace. Sheehan reports that during the spring 1975 reassessment of United States policy toward the Middle East, many of those called in for advice were critical of the U.S. approach "because in practice it excluded the Soviet Union and the European powers; without Soviet participation particularly, a final Arab-Israeli settlement could never be accomplished" (1976, pp. 165–66). Sheehan also records his own concern: "If the Russians and the Palestinians were to be excluded from the American plan for peace, what, I wondered, was the point in having one?" (p. 167).

The Soviet Union almost certainly had the capacity to disrupt any Middle East peace agreement if it wished to do so. Choosing to pursue the goal of excluding the Soviet Union from the peace-making process made it impossible to attain real peace.

Short-Term Versus Long-Term

A question can be raised as to whether the secretary's goal of peace was sufficiently long term. He saw his objective as holding his thumb in the dike. Aware of the long-term desirability of cooperation with the Soviet Union, he apparently made no effort to move in that direction. Faced with a crying need for genuine peace between Israel and its Arab neighbors, he limited himself to seeking short-term pacifiers.

In connection with the ratification of SALT II, Kissinger stated:

> The great powers, having learned that they cannot dominate each other, must practice moderation and *ultimately* cooperation (*New York Times*, August 1, 1979 page A6, emphasis added).

The wise long-term goal of cooperation with the Soviet Union was ignored and progress toward it set back by the secretary's short-term, anti-Soviet goal of exclusion and noncooperation.

Problems with Kissinger's Personal View of the Players

There are many risks and costs in treating the human beings with whom one deals as *the* players in the international game to the exclusion of governments and other institutions. Some of these risks and costs were evident during the United States' diplomatic efforts in the Middle East.

There is a risk of undue emotional involvement; a statement made to a government is likely to be treated as a personal attack: "He was furious with the Israelis, and he took their refusal very personally—as directed not only at the United States but, above all, at himself" (Sheehan 1976, p. 164).

Failure to delegate to others exacts a high price in terms of human resources. The secretary had to spend enormous amounts of time on detailed issues of tactics, leaving him less time for larger issues of purpose and approach. He admired Sadat for concentrating on important issues of principle, but found himself "the prisoner of his own method" (Sheehan 1976, p. 115).

A highly conspicuous personalized style of diplomacy also runs the risk of undercutting the status and hence the usefulness of every ambassador and foreign service officer. If the top official is the only one who knows what is going on and no one else counts, the ability of the entire government to deal with international affairs is reduced to the ability of one man: a man who is immersed in details and exhausted from flying. A period of one-man rule, even by a benevolent dictator, inflicts lasting damage on the ability of institutions to cope effectively and creatively with all the problems that he does not handle and all those problems that will come up after he has gone. A period of one-man rule in international affairs runs the risk of sabotaging not only national institutions like the State Department, the Foreign Service, and the National Security Staff, but also the United Nations and its affiliated agencies. The United States, like other countries, has a vital interest in the United Nations becoming increasingly respected and effective.

Personalized diplomacy is antidemocratic. The more personalized the decision-making on the U.S. side, the less opportunity there is for participation and contribution from others. Further, it tends to cause the United States to prefer to deal with one-man rulers abroad, rather than with broadly based governments. The secretary found that from his point of view Sadat was a better nogotiating partner than either the Israelis or the Syrians. When Sadat said something, it happened. There was no nonsense about discussing with a cabinet or with the Knesset. "In Israel, Kissinger seemed at times to be negotiating with a whole country" (Kalb and Kalb 1974, p. 537). When dealing with Rabin on the Sinai disengagement, "Kissinger longed for Golda Meir; for, had he convinced her, the cabinet would have bowed" (Sheehan 1976, p. 162). The secretary found that even Damascus was too democratic for his personal style of diplomacy: "Sadat makes command decisions. Assad had his lieutenants there, and I had to convince them, too" (Sheehan 1976, p. 126).

Personalized diplomacy tends to cause one to ignore those one does not meet and know. The secretary's failure to deal with the Palestinian problem may well be the consequence of his treating the individuals he met as the only players in the game. Having never met Arafat or other Palestinian leaders, it was possible for him to ignore the Palestinians and to think of them in ideological terms as terrorists with whom it would, in any event, be useless to negotiate.

Finally, personalizing the players in the international game increases the risk of confusing one's own interests with those of the government. The more one consider's oneself rather than one's government as the international player, the greater the danger that personal considerations will affect governmental decisions. It is easy to assume that there is no conflict of interest. (What's good for General Motors is good for the U.S.A.) An ongoing personal relationship with a foreign leader, such as King Hussein or the Shah of Iran, may blind the government to political realities.

Problems with Kissinger's Concession-Hunting Strategy

A critical problem with Kissinger's style of negotiation was his method of seeking proposals and then concessions from each side. This process tends to cause the parties to develop extreme opening positions so that they will have more room within which to make concessions. Making concessionary or "backing-down" decisions, however, is difficult and time-consuming. This is particularly true for governments that depend on collective decision making. The concession-hunting process also tends to encourage obstinacy by rewarding it, as demonstrated by the Israeli negotiations over the disengagement on the Golan Heights:

> The affair of the city of El Quneitra is illustrative. The decision to give it up, all of it, had already been taken by Mrs. Meir and Dayan early in the negotiations. But it was decided to surrender it street by street—a strategy that proved its efficacy. For every street in El Quneitra, Assad was forced to pay something (Golan 1976, p. 211).

Progress becomes bogged down when parties are taught that the less they give the more they will get. The third case on which the contributors to this volume were asked to comment illustrates the dilemma. On May 8, 1974, Kissinger kept some of Israel's concessions in his pocket rather than reveal them to Assad. He appeared to be making a modest tactical decision. But Israeli officials could only conclude (as they apparently did) that they had been too forthcoming with concessions if even Kissinger thought they had gone too far too fast. Kissinger's holding back of Israeli concessions may well have been responsible for the degree to which Israel held back concessions during the rest of May.

A more fundamental flaw with the concession-hunting minuet is that it directs attention to the comparative concessions made by each side and away from the best means of reconciling their basic interests. The process suggests that interests are simply arguments to be used in support of positions, rather than the central concern with which the negotiators should deal. Kissinger's method tends to assume that the optimal agreement is to be found at some hypothetical midpoint between the opening positions of the two sides.

An Alternative: The Single-Negotiating-Text Strategy

It is more likely that a workable and durable settlement will be reached by generating an objectively good solution to the problems that divide the parties involved. Getting parties to agree to such a settlement is more likely if a single-negotiating-text strategy is used.°

Consider the way an architect might mediate a dispute between a husband and wife who wanted to build a house. One way would be to have each draw up a separate plan, and then to ask for concessions until a common plan could be reached. "You give up the bay window and maybe he will give up the garage." A better way would be for the architect to listen to the parties, try to understand their basic interests, and then make a preliminary sketch. Each party then criticizes the sketch and the architect prepares a revised draft. After a series of drafts have each been subjected to criticism by the parties, the architect finally says "this is the best I can do."

It is much easier for a party to criticize a draft than it is to make a concession. The differences between the two strategies can be seen as follows:

Kissinger's Concession-Hunting Minuet	*The Single-Negotiating-Text Strategy*
Ask the parties for their positions and proposals.	Ask the parties for their interests and concerns.
Focus discussion on each party's position.	Focus discussion on a single text aimed at reconciling their conflicting interests.
In turn, ask each party for a concession.	In turn, ask each party to criticize the text wherever it fails to meet their legitimate interests.
Communicate the concessions you obtain.	Prepare a revised single text in light of criticism.
Repeat the process of pressing first one and then the other for concessions.	Repeat the process of preparing revised drafts in light of criticism until you have the best draft you can prepare.
Press one party or the other for a final concession to produce agreement.	Ask each party to accept the final draft if the other will.

The single-negotiating-text strategy was used by President Carter and Secretary Vance at the first Camp David meeting with President Sadat and Prime Minister Begin. They did not ask Begin and Sadat for

---

° In *International Mediation: A Working Guide*, William Ury and I develop this and a number of other suggestions for an international mediator. The April 1978 draft edition is available from the International Peace Academy, 777 UN Plaza, New York.

concessions from their opening proposals. Instead, they listened to both sides and then drew up a draft that they presented to each party for criticism. Twenty-three successive drafts were prepared, each incorporating or responding to some criticism made by a party. On the thirteenth day, Carter decided that that was the best he could do and asked each party to agree.

Kissinger's concession-hunting diplomacy was conducted over a three-year period and at great cost to the United States; it produced modest disengagement agreements on the Golan Heights and in the Sinai. Conducted over a period of seven months, beginning at Camp David, the efforts of Carter and Vance produced far more significant agreements at less cost to the United States.

The single-negotiating-text strategy is not a panacea for all problems involved in negotiations. In particular, it requires a mediator. But it does resolve many of the problems that handicap Kissinger's style of diplomacy. Its advantages can be seen in Table 3.1.

TABLE 3.1

Which Game Should a Mediator Play?

The Concession-Hunting Game	*The Single-Negotiating-Text Game*
+ It is the game most parties expect a mediator to play.	− The process is contrary to the expectations of most parties.
+ It maximizes participation by the parties.	− It may reduce the parties' sense of participation.
+ It avoids premature concern with the shape of a final agreement.	− It risks focusing too early on the details of a final text.
+ It requires less skill on the part of a mediator.	− It is difficult to know how much to include within the single negotiating text.
	− The process is difficult to terminate without an ultimatum of some sort.
But	*But*
− It rewards taking extreme negotiating positions.	+ It makes extreme negotiating positions irrelevant.
− It requires each party to make many decisions.	+ It requires each party to make only one decision at the end of the process.
− Making decisions to back down is painful and slow.	+ Making criticism is easy.

TABLE 3.1 (continued)

Which Game Should a Mediator Play?

– The process encourages hard bargaining.	+ The process encourages principled problem solving.
– It rewards obstinacy.	+ It rewards concentrating on important interests.
– It focuses discussion on attacking and defending extreme positions.	+ It focuses discussion on possible middle-ground solutions and how they might be improved.
– The process depends on pressure.	+ The process depends on reason.
– The process tends to exacerbate relations.	+ The process is consistent with improving relations.
– Each decision to make a concession runs the risk of whetting an adversary's appetite for more.	+ The one affirmative decision asked of each party will lead either to agreement or to freedom from blame if there is no agreement.
– At no time is either party faced with a clear-cut choice; each can easily blame the other for deadlock.	+ At any time the mediator can, if necessary, focus public opinion on a noncooperating party by confronting it with a draft agreement recommended by him and accepted by the other party.
– Any agreement is likely to be a mechanical compromise between opening positions.	+ Any agreement is the product of impartial inventing of the best means for reconciling conflicting interests.

The Cost of Commitment to Success

It is one thing for a diplomat to adopt the goal of success; it is quite another for him to pursue the strategy of publicly committing himself to attain that goal. To do so where success requires reaching an agreement is to put himself at the mercy of those whose agreement he needs. Whether as a negotiator or a mediator, one who insists that an agreement must be reached runs the risk of being taken to the cleaners.

The secretary widely and publicly committed himself to producing an agreement. Although Kissinger denied the authenticity of Heikal's full account of their conversation in November 1973, there is no reason to doubt his report of Kissinger's commitment to succeed: "I hate failure. I

have a credit balance of success and I do not want to throw it away—
. . . I hate failure and do not want to fail." (Sheehan 1976, p. 54). Sheehan
quotes Kissinger as telling an Arab statesman:

> I will never get involved in anything unless I am sure of success. And
> if I do get involved, it means I am going to succeed. I hate failure
> (Sheehan 1976, p. 18).

And again, in his first audience with King Faisal, Kissinger is reported to
have told him in effect: "I hate failure. I have not failed. I shall not fail"
(Sheehan 1976, p. 203).

The secretary's highly conspicuous role, his widely advertised
commitment to succeed in reaching agreement, combined with the
economic and military assets of the United States, put the United States
government in a highly vulnerable position. Quandt tersely summarizes
the Israeli response: "If the Americans wanted an agreement so badly,
they could pay for it" (Quandt 1977, p. 272).

Israel quickly turned to its benefit the fact that the United States was
negotiating, not mediating. Hard bargaining is a game two can play. The
negotiations shifted so that predominantly they were not between Israel
and Egypt or between Israel and Syria, but between Israel and the United
States. The pattern became one in which Israel would make a concession
to Egypt or Syria only in exchange for military, political, or economic
commitments from the United States.

When negotiations are seen as an unprincipled contest of will, the
party that wishes to change the status quo is in the weaker position. This is
particularly true if that side is in a hurry. The United States assumed a role
where it was in a hurry to reach an agreement that would change things in
the Middle East. Israel (in particular) was in no hurry, and in fact
preferred a continuation of the status quo.

Israel and Egypt were better off moving toward peace with each
other, whether or not they received special economic aid, nuclear
reactors, military hardware, and political commitments from the United
States. But when the United States put itself in a position where it was
willing to pay Israel and Egypt whatever it had to in order to produce
agreements, the price went up. It is fair to say that the United States has
never given to any other government—even to military allies in time of
war—commitments comparable to those Kissinger promised Israel. In an
unprecedented fashion, the United States entered into secret agreements
tying its hands in dozens of ways with respect to future policy decisions.
(For the text of some of these commitments, see Sheehan 1976, pp.
251-57.) The U.S. government committed itself to more than $3 billion in
aid to the Middle East for fiscal year 1976 alone (Quandt 1977, p. 279). In
Sheehan's words:

the second Sinai agreement was a major tactical triumph for Israel. She relinquished little (by the admission of several Israeli generals) of strategic value in the passes and wrested from the United States a moral, monetary, and military cornucopia unattained by any other foreign power (1976, p. 192).

As mediators define their roles in future conflicts, they will want to be fully aware of the high cost of promising to produce an agreement. Selecting the goal of looking successful runs the risk of diverting one from substance to appearances; publicly committing oneself to reach an agreement turns that risk into reality.

Breaking the conflict into manageable pieces is admirable, but it is something else to let one's need for success divert one from the heart of a problem. This is apparently what happened in the fourth case on which special comment was requested.

In August 1974 Kissinger chose to seek a second disengagement agreement for the Sinai rather than to try for an agreement between Israel and Jordan over the West Bank. It was the fact that the secretary's primary goal was power and that power required success that caused him to avoid the Palestinian problem (Sheehan 1976, pp. 85, 113). It also caused him to avoid the West Bank issue even as between Jordan and Israel. "He needed another success. It could not be on the Jordan front, so it would have to be in Sinai" (Quandt 1977, p. 258). Given the goal of success, the secretary's choice of an easier agreement was sound. But he should have been less concerned with U.S. prestige and somewhat more concerned with the human beings caught up in the Arab-Israeli conflict. Even if he had been unsuccessful, a reputation for caring might have been more beneficial to the United States than a reputation for ignoring the heart of a problem and dealing with the fringes.

In August 1974 it might still have been possible to involve Palestinian leadership in talks with Jordan, Israel, and the United States. It was two months later, at Rabat, that an empty-handed King Hussein had to agree that the PLO should represent the Palestinians.

One may also question whether the United States had to choose between a second Sinai disengagement agreement and one covering the West Bank. On a basis that was somewhat less hectic and less personal to the Secretary of State, the United States might well have moved forward concurrently on both fronts.

The Risks of Reliance on Pressure

The essence of the secretary's view of international affairs is that it is a dog-eat-dog world in which principles, law, morality, and ethical standards do not count. It is a contest of will to be determined by force, threats of force, hard bargaining, linkage, and pressure of all kinds. One prevails by exerting more pressure, having the courage to take great risks, and the guts to use brutal force as in the bombing of Cambodia and the Christmas bombing of North Vietnam.

To operate on those working assumptions involves high costs as well as high risks. First, it is the wrong game for a civilized country to play. On purely technical grounds, the more a society depends on complex equipment, telephones, electric-generating and distribution systems, city water supplies, elevators, gasoline, credit, banking, aviation, automobiles, and so forth, the more vulnerable it is to illegitimate force and pressure. Those who live in glass houses should not encourage a contest in stone throwing.

The strongest weapons are ideas: ideas like democracy, liberty, rule of law, human rights, freedom from arbitrary governmental action, and a decent respect for the opinions of mankind. To abandon these powerful resources for unprincipled naked pressure is not only to abandon those qualities that distinguish us from our most dangerous adversaries (and justify our very right to believe that we ought to prevail), but also to remove the foundations from our physical power itself. Physical might without legitimacy turns out to be a hollow shell. The heaviest bombardment in history inflicted against the small country of Vietnam was counterproductive when both we and they doubted the legitimacy of what we were doing. All the jets and tanks the United States sold to the Shah of Iran left him powerless when it appeared that he was pursuing power, not principle.

On July 31, 1979, former Secretary of State Kissinger, in an opening statement to the Senate Foreign Relations Committee, acknowledged the interest this country has in having the world not play the kind of pressure game that he played: "we have a stake in the principle that political or economic pressure . . . not become the arbiter of the world's political disputes" (*New York Times*, August 1, 1979 p. A6). It is to be hoped that future diplomats will be guided more by Kissinger's thoughtful words than by his earlier deeds.

Agreements produced by pressure or by side payments set bad precedents. As with the paying of blackmail, the true cost of obtaining an agreement by giving to Egypt a nuclear reactor and to Israel long lasting and unrelated political commitments is not the immediate cost. Every such payment makes the United States vulnerable to future payments.

The cost of making payments that work may be exceeded by the cost of making threats that work. In October 1973 the United States put its armed forces on a nuclear alert as a means of warning the Soviet Union not to put troops back into Egypt. No one thought that the issue justified nuclear war, yet one might conclude that the threat was successful. For a few million dollars worth of military exercises we reduced whatever likelihood there was that Soviet troops would return to Egypt. A future Secretary of State, however, is likely to appreciate that any short-term benefits that were achieved by crying wolf in that fashion were bought at a high cost indeed. One of the few margins the world had between a real crisis and a nuclear war has now been seriously eroded. Any future use of such tactics will create even greater risks.

Time and again, those who have looked at the record have concluded that Kissinger used not only deliberate ambiguity but also conscious deception and outright lies to advance his purposes. Sheehan (1976), who stated his belief that the secretary was not guilty of duplicity regarding final frontiers, finds the accusation of duplicity "closer to the truth" when looking at his assurances to Arab leaders regarding a role for the Palestinians (p. 212). Sheehan also points out that although the secretary denied to Israeli Ambassador Dinitz that he had anything to do with Saunders testimony of November 12, 1975 regarding the Palestinians, he had in fact "carefully edited the declaration, investing it with his co-authorship" (p. 213). Golan (1976), in his book based primarily on Israeli sources, goes further: "The record of the discussions reveals a pattern of deception and broken promises that would have made even Kissinger's heroes, Metternich and Castlereagh, blush" (p. 253). There is substantial cost to any public official who acquires such a reputation. His statements and his promises are worth less. Such costs fall on the entire nation.

LOOKING FOR BETTER GAMES TO PLAY

Any Secretary of State, consciously or unconsciously, operates on the basis of an assumed negotiating strategy. The more consciously he selects the strategy the better his performance is likely to be. A common assumption about negotiation is that it is a process of bargaining.

Friendly Bargaining

A negotiator operating on the assumptions of friendly bargaining considers the ongoing relationship more important than the merits of any one substantive issue. Although substance is at risk, the commitment is to reach agreement. This is a perfectly fine strategy to use—so long as both parties are playing the same game (see Table 3.2).

Friendly bargaining confronts each party with a tactical dilemma: although both will be better off if both play "soft," if one party plays "soft" the other can gain an advantage by playing "hard."

Hard Bargaining

When a party to a dispute puts less value on the long-term relationship, the immediate victories that can be obtained by hard bargaining will be perceived as outweighing the long-term costs of doing so (see Table 3.2). Hard Bargaining is a dominant strategy over friendly bargaining. It is

TABLE 3.2

Standard Moves of Two Negotiating Strategies

Friendly Bargaining	*Hard Bargaining*
Make a strong commitment to reach agreement no matter what.	Make a strong commitment to your position.
Put personal relationships above the merits of a case.	Identify people with their case.
Trust your adversary.	Distrust your adversary.
Be easygoing.	Be ruthless.
See negotiations as an opportunity to acquire friends (if necessary by giving them expensive presents).	See negotiations as a contest of will (cf. arm-wrestling).
Disclose your minimum position.	Mislead as to your minimum position.
Demonstrate a willingness to compromise your position.	Demonstrate an unwillingness to compromise your position.
Cultivate friendship through making substantive concessions.	Make your friendship depend upon receiving substantive concessions.
Treat substantive differences as personally embarrassing.	Treat substantive differences as a personal challenge.
Be passive.	Attack your adversaries.
React amicably; turn the other cheek.	React strongly; strike back.
Ask them to be friendly.	Press them to make concessions.
Insist that we agree.	Insist that they back down to you.
Offer friendship and goodwill.	Threaten linkage, leverage, and pressure.
Yield points as needed to avoid a confrontation.	Yield to pressure slowly as a last resort.

TABLE 3.3

Illustrative Standard Moves of Three Negotiating Games

Friendly Bargaining	*Hard Bargaining*	*Principled Problem Solving*
Make a strong commitment to reach agreement no matter what.	Make a strong commitment to your position.	Commit yourself to seek a principled solution.
Put personal relationships above the merits of a case.	Identify people with their case.	Separate people from their case.
Trust your adversary.	Distrust your adversary.	Proceed independently of trust.
Be easy going.	Be ruthless.	Adhere to principle.
See negotiations as an opportunity to acquire friends (if necessary by giving expensive presents).	See negotiations as a contest of will (cf. arm-wrestling).	See negotiations as a joint search for a principled solution (cf. two judges seeking a basis for a joint decision).
Disclose your minimum position.	Mislead as to your minimum position.	Avoid fixing a minimum position.
Demonstrate a willingness to compromise your position.	Demonstrate an unwillingness to compromise your position.	Demonstrate a willingness to respond to reason and principle.

Cultivate friendship through making substantive concessions.	Make your friendship depend upon receiving substantive concessions.	Treat personal friendship as independent of substantive differences.
Treat substantive differences as personally embarrassing.	Treat substantive differences as a personal challenge.	Treat substantive differences as an objective problem to be dealt with.
Be passive.	Attack your adversaries.	Attack the problem.
React amicably; turn the other cheek.	React strongly; strike back.	Do not react; act purposively only.
Ask them to be friendly.	Press them to make concessions.	Press them to invent wise ways of reconciling our interests.
Insist that we agree.	Insist that they back down to us.	Insist on objective criteria that both can accept.
Offer friendship and good will.	Threaten linkage, leverage and pressure.	Direct reasoned argument at the merits of the problem.
Yield points as needed to avoid a confrontation.	Yield to pressure slowly as a last resort.	Never yield to pressure; respond to principle and to sound arguments on the merits.

also a game-changing strategy. If negotiators have been playing soft, and one starts to play hard, the game will become hard.

Kissinger apparently saw his strategic choice as being between friendly bargaining and hard bargaining. He convinced himself and most everyone else that he was a great, hard-bargaining diplomat. His early commitment to reach agreement, a standard move for the friendly bargainer, contradicts such a characterization. In hard-bargaining terms, Kissinger's commitment to reach agreement was a disaster since it enabled Egypt and Israel to exact a high price for the agreement Kissinger had publicly committed himself to produce.

The costs of hard bargaining are well recognized and have been suggested above as the risks involved in Kissinger's approach. Hard bargaining encourages one's opposite number in the negotiation to bargain even harder. Conflicts tend to escalate, as does the value of the time and resources devoted to them. The process becomes more dangerous as each side tries to press the other to the brink.

When attention is focused on positions and pressures, the content of any agreement that is reached is also likely to suffer. This can be illustrated by a hypothetical negotiation over the specifications of a building. Here, the unwisdom of bargaining one issue against another or of using pressure tactics is apparent. Suppose the contractor said, "Go along with me on putting less cement in the foundations because I went along with you on stronger girders in the roof." No owner in his right mind would yield. Neither would he yield on the necessary strength of the foundations if the contractor threatened to have the owner's brother-in-law lose his job, or offered the owner a special favor. Such tactics all increase the risk that the building, if agreed upon, would be unsound and in danger of collapse. The same holds true for an international treaty.

It is certainly no easier to build a stable international peace than it is a building. In each case, clauses that are agreed upon as a consequence of hard bargaining, pressure tactics, threats, and offers run the risk of being poorly designed and the product of inappropriate considerations.

The example suggests the answer to hard bargaining: don't play that game. Don't bargain at all. When the contractor suggests changing the amount of cement in the foundations, the owner remains open to reason, but not to bargaining tactics and not to pressure. He will listen to arguments based on engineering facts, on professional opinion, on precedent, on community practice, or on other sound principles. He will perceive their differences not as a contest of will, but rather as a problem to be solved. "Negotiating positions," as such, are to be given no weight. The reference points are not the will of the parties but facts and reasons: objective criteria in the real world such as strength factors, costs, and appropriate margins of safety.

Principled Problem Solving

To insist on objective criteria is itself a negotiating strategy—and a good one. The commitment is to principle and the necessity of a solution based on the merits of the matter at issue. It is a strategy that has been used by diplomats and negotiators like Benjamin Franklin, Daniel Webster, and Dr. Martin Luther King, Jr. Some standard moves of the principled problem solver, or principled negotiator, are compared in Table 3.3.

Principled problem solving is not without its own risks and costs. It does not guarantee that an agreement will be reached, and it involves its own forms of brinksmanship. Commitment to principle serves as the hard-hearted partner that protects one from yielding to unprincipled threats and pressures.

Just as hard bargaining is a dominant strategy over friendly bargaining, principled problem solving tends to be dominant over hard bargaining. When the hard bargainer discovers that pressure does not produce results but that the principled negotiator is flexible and willing to respond to good arguments on the merits, then he, too, begins to emphasize objective arguments on the merits. Comparative merits and demerits of hard bargaining and principled negotiation are shown on Table 3.4.

TABLE 3.4

Which Negotiating Game Should One Play?

Hard Bargaining	*Principled Problem Solving*
+ It is the game everyone expects.	− It is not the game people expect.
+ We apparently minimize the risk of agreeing to a bad deal.	− It is often difficult to play.
+ Constitutents understand and support our adversarial style.	− It requires flexibility of position.
+ We may win a short-term victory.	− It requires insistence on principle.
	− It requires a solution on the merits.
	− Applicable principles are often difficult to find and difficult to agree upon.
	− It deprives constituents of victory.

TABLE 3.4 (continued)

Which Negotiating Game Should One Play?

But	*But*
– It tends to escalate each conflict.	+ It tends to keep conflicts small and on their respective merits.
– It subjects us to counter pressure.	+ It provides a basis for resisting pressure.
– It exacerbates our relations with those whom we pressure.	+ It rewards the inventing of solutions.
– It exacerbates our relations with those over whom we win.	+ It encourages candor and co-operation.
– There can be no agreement without someone giving up his position.	+ The process builds better international relations.
– We cannot expect others to play a game in which we win every time.	+ The results set good precedents.
– The game rewards obstinacy, encouraging more obstinacy.	+ We maintain a reputation for integrity.
– It exacerbates the process of conducting international affairs.	+ We gain the power of principled behavior.
– Both the process and the results set bad precedents.	+ When we agree we have accepted principled argument, not yielded to pressure.
– Effective tactics damage our reputation for integrity.	+ We can maintain good relations with people despite the existence of difficult and un-resolved problems.

That comparison suggests how much this country lost by having a Secretary of State who paid little attention to principle, law, and objective criteria. Principled problem solving is a far better game to play than ad-hoc bargaining, whether played hard or soft; it is better for the world and better for each player who plays that way, whatever the others do.

CONCLUSION

In his Middle East diplomacy, Kissinger's insistence on the appearance of success precluded the possibility that his efforts would lead to a real settlement of the region's problems. Not wanting to bite off more than he could chew, he nibbled at the edges of the Arab-Israeli conflict. Not wanting to fail, he so conducted his diplomatic operations that they, like many in medical history, were more successful for the doctor than for the patients. Not wanting to be weak, he accumulated the indicia of power at the cost of not using for good ends the power he had.

Principled conduct is not simply a good strategy; it goes to the heart of what international relations are about. If the United States is to be a leader of the free world, there must be a greater difference between it and totalitarian regimes than the size of its arsenals or the toughness and shrewdness of its negotiators. There needs to be a qualitative difference— a difference in the way it conducts its internal affairs and the way it conducts its foreign affairs. The difference lies in adherence to principle. In the Middle East, as in Chile and Vietnam, Kissinger lost sight of that difference.

REFERENCES

Fisher, R. "Fractionating Conflict." In R. Fisher, ed., *International Conflict and Behavioral Science*. New York: Basic Books, 1964.
———. *Dear Israelis, Dear Arabs: A Working Approach to Peace*. New York: Harper and Row, 1972.
———. *International Mediation: A Working Guide*. New York: International Peace Academy, 1978.
Golan, M. *The Secret Conversations of Henry Kissinger*. New York: Quadrangle, 1976.
Kalb, M., and Kalb, B. *Kissinger*. Boston: Little, Brown, 1974.
Quandt, W. B. *Decade of Decisions: American Policy toward the Arab-Israeli Conflict, 1967–1976*. Berkeley, Calif.: University of California Press, 1977.
Sheehan, E. R. F. *The Arabs, Israelis, and Kissinger: A Secret History of American Diplomacy in the Middle East*. New York: Reader's Digest Press, 1976.

4

STEP-BY-STEP IN THE MIDDLE EAST FROM THE PERSPECTIVE OF THE LABOR MEDIATION PROCESS

Thomas A. Kochan

The purpose of this chapter is to examine the step-by-step diplomacy of Henry Kissinger from the perspective of mediation in labor negotiations. At present there is no single, well-accepted theory of the labor mediation process. In fact, mediation has often been described as the form of third party intervention in labor negotiations about which the least is known. Even so, recent research on the labor mediation process has yielded findings that can be used to help interpret the dynamics of Kissinger's step-by-step intervention in the Middle East. The first section of the chapter will briefly outline the major assumptions and propositions underlying a model of the labor mediation process. This model will then be used to interpret and analyze Kissinger's intervention.

COLLECTIVE BARGAINING AND INDUSTRIAL RELATIONS

Since labor mediation takes place within the context of the collective bargaining process, one should first note some of the fundamental assumptions underlying the models of collective bargaining and industrial relations. The starting point for most collective bargaining models is an assumption that the relationship between labor and management in industrial relations is characterized by a partial conflict of interests. Such conflict arises from the fundamental differences in the economic goals of workers and employers in an industrial society (Barbash 1964) and from the structure of authority relations found in organizations (Dahrendorf 1959; Fox 1971). This conflict of interests is limited, however, by the long-term interdependence of the parties. Each needs the other to achieve its goals; therefore each has a stake in the survival and minimal satisfaction of the other. Furthermore, the industrial relations system is structured to provide unions with a legitimate role as the officially designated representatives of an employer's workers. Thus unions are recognized by employers and by the public as legitimate participants in the negotiation process, albeit often grudgingly and only after considerable conflict and/or government pressure. In return, U.S. labor unions accept the role of employers and the legitimate representatives of the efficiency interests of the organization and society.

It is these key features—an inherent yet limited conflict of interests, shared interdependence, mutual recognition of the other party's legitimacy in the negotiation process, and motivation to insure the survival of the other party—that give rise to periodic negotiations and agreement making in collective bargaining. It is these same characteristics that provide a context in which the mediation process comes to play an important role in collective bargaining.

THE LABOR MEDIATION MODEL

The Objectives of the Mediation Process

The ultimate measure of mediation effectiveness is whether the process brings about a settlement. Even so, there is more to mediation than the final step that closes the contract. Mediation is also a continuous narrowing process in which the third party constantly attempts to whittle away at the number of unresolved issues. Consequently, mediation is partially successful if it reduces the number of issues that remain unresolved. It is also possible to move toward a settlement without completely resolving any of the issues if the parties can narrow their differences on the open issues. Similarly, mediation can also help the parties to "come clean without prejudice," to explore informally what would happen if they were to move to their final positions or "resistance points" (Walton and McKersie 1965; Stevens 1963; 1967). Such an exploratory effort is designed to avoid a strike without formally jeopardizing the bargaining position that a negotiator would take if a strike or continued impasse were to become inevitable. One major function of mediation is to facilitate this form of tacit bargaining and information sharing by having both parties share confidential bargaining information with the third party. Although the ultimate measure of the effectiveness of mediation is its ability to achieve a settlement, these intermediate indicators should also be considered as partial measures of success since not every dispute is amenable at any given point in time to resolution via the mediation process.

The mediator's primary goal should be to resolve the conflict. While this assertion may sound rather obvious, it is sometimes the case that third party intervenors have goals that compete with this singular objective. To the extent, for example, that the mediator prefers a particular outcome of the conflict, the mediator becomes another interested party to the negotiations. The more the attainment of this preferred outcome dominates the mediator's strategy, the less apt the parties will be to treat the mediator as a neutral resource. Another aspect of this problem stems from mediators' concern for their public reputation. The more mediators use a dispute as a means of furthering their reputation and choose options and strategies that are designed to protect their image or reputation, the less effective their intervention is likely to be.

Determinants of the Effectiveness of Mediation

Mediator Characteristics

Perhaps the most generally accepted principle of the mediation process is that mediators must be mutually acceptable to the parties if the process is to succeed (Simkin 1971; Kerr 1954). Because of the voluntary nature of this form of intervention, no mediator can function without the trust and cooperation of the parties. Acceptability can be achieved by prior reputation; however, most experienced negotiators tend to be hesitant to trust mediators based on reputation alone. Thus, in the early stages of an intervention, when mediators are not personally known to the parties, the mediators must establish their credibility and gain the trust and confidence of the parties. If mediators fail to gain, or at some point in the process lose, acceptability, their effectiveness in the later stages of the negotiating cycle may be jeopardized.

Studies have also shown that the personal attributes associated with success in other occupations are also important to the success of the mediation process (Landsberger 1955). In fact the litany of desirable mediator attributes often reads like a modified Boy Scout oath. A good mediator is trustworthy, helpful, friendly, intelligent, knowledgeable about the substantive issues of collective bargaining, has a sense of humor, and so forth. Undoubtedly these personal characteristics are as important in mediation as they are in other walks of life.

Type of Impasse

A central proposition underlying this model of the mediation process is that mediation is best suited for dealing with certain types of conflict. The results of a study by Kochan and Jick (1978) showed that mediation is most effective in conflicts that reflect a breakdown in the negotiation process, because one party has become overcommitted to a bargaining position, the negotiators lack experience, and so forth. Mediation encounters the greatest difficulty in coping with conflicts arising out of the economic context of the dispute—for example, the problem of inability to pay, major differences in the expectations for settlement, and so forth. Thus the mediation process is best suited to helping the parties move up to, or perhaps marginally beyond, their bottom line positions. Only in conjunction with some external source of pressure can mediation succeed in getting the parties to adjust their bottom lines and reach agreements when a real gap between them exists.

Mediation also has difficulty in impasses that involve intragroup conflict. In this type of dispute the mediator must deal with negotiators who lack the political power or authority to make concessions because doing so may threaten their internal political position. Yet for a mediator to either intervene in these internal conflicts or to bypass the formal negotiators is at best risky, since the mediator must maintain sufficient credibility and acceptability to all potential victors of internal power struggles.

Situational Factors

The major situational factor influencing the success of mediation is the degree of pressure or motivation to settle that the parties perceive. Normally, the threat of a strike is the major inducement to settlement in the negotiation and mediation process. It is therefore generally believed that mediation works best when operating under a real and immediate strike threat, namely at the final stages of the contract negotiations process or at the point during a strike where both parties are under the greatest pressure to settle. The importance of pressure on the parties to settle illustrates why the timing of mediation is so critical to its success. Unless the pressure for settlement is ripe, little progress can be made via the mediation process alone.

Mediator Strategies

While the success of mediation clearly depends upon the quality of the mediator, personal characteristics are not the only factors that influence the outcomes of intervention. Perhaps the most difficult determinant of the effectiveness of the mediation process to study, and yet the heart of the process itself, is the set of strategies a mediator uses to help produce a settlement (Kressel 1972).

Mediator strategy and behavior vary at different stages of the intervention process. During the initial stages the mediator is primarily concerned with such objectives as achieving acceptability; identifying the issues in dispute; understanding the underlying obstacles to a settlement (that is, diagnosing the sources or type of conflict involved); assessing the attitudinal and political climate between the parties; and identifying the distribution of power and degree of internal conflict within each negotiating team.

During the intermediate stage of negotiations, the mediator seeks to get the parties to exchange proposals and counterproposals and begins probing for potential areas of compromise. During this stage the mediator continues to probe to identify the relative priorities and bottom line positions of the parties, and keeps listening and questioning to find possible acceptable solutions to the outstanding issues. Once these proposals and counterproposals begin to be exchanged and discussed, the mediator attempts to determine whether the parties' bottom line positions overlap or are close enough to try to press for a modification that would produce an agreement. If the bottom line positions are judged to be close enough to push toward a settlement, the mediator may begin to take a more active, assertive, or aggressive role in suggesting actual compromises by pushing the parties to make compromises they resisted earlier, and in general by trying very hard to close the gap between the parties.

Engaging in such active or aggressive tactics prematurely, however—as when the parties are really too far apart, when the pressure to settle does not exist, or when some other political constraint stands in the way of a settlement—may ruin the mediator's credibility and acceptability. Thus when conditions are not ripe for settlement, the mediator must refrain from these aggressive tactics; when the conditions are ripe, a settlement may not occur unless the mediator engages in them. Moreover, even as the mediator actively suggests compromise solutions, care should be taken to avoid getting overly identified with a specific compromise or settlement point. Overidentification with a solution that one or both parties reject also implies rejection of the mediator and limits the mediator's continued usefulness to the parties.

APPLICATION OF THE MODEL TO KISSINGER'S STEP-BY-STEP DIPLOMACY

What types of insights does this model of labor mediation within the collective bargaining process afford for an understanding of Kissinger's step-by-step intervention strategy in the Middle East? The central thesis developed here is that a number of contradictions exist between the assumptions underlying the use of mediation in collective bargaining and the particular intervention that Kissinger chose.

Kissinger's Competing Objectives

Kissinger's intervention went far beyond the conception of the mediator's function in labor negotiations, namely, to help the parties reach agreement. Instead Kissinger consistently balanced this objective against a number of other concerns on his personal and diplomatic agenda. Quandt (1977) notes that in addition to seeking a settlement, Kissinger wished both to demonstrate that the U.S. role in the negotiations was essential for progress, and to use the U.S. role in the Middle East negotiations to strengthen its position vis-à-vis the Russians.

Perhaps the most controversial point of Kissinger's intervention came when he reportedly foiled Israel's General Yariv and Egypt's General Gamasy in their effort to negotiate directly at Kilometer 101 in November 1973. Did Kissinger discard a chance for a major breakthrough by discouraging progress through direct negotiations? Although it is impossible to definitively answer this question, failure to allow the parties to go as far as possible on their own is usually viewed as a cardinal sin in mediation. A mediator normally seeks to intervene only when failure to do so means that a breakdown is imminent, or when the parties ask for assistance. In this case, however, Kissinger feared that progress between the Egyptians and Israelis might reduce both the influence of the United States over the parties in the Middle East as well as the ability of Kissinger and the United States to bring the Syrians and other Arabs into the negotiations. His decision to discourage direct negotiations again reflects Kissinger's multiple objectives for intervention in the Middle East. The more Kissinger tried to balance his other objectives off against the objective of simply facilitating a peace agreement, the more his effectiveness as a mediator was compromised. Thus Kissinger traded off the potential for progress in his own step-by-step plan (that is, potential narrowing of the differences or perhaps even an agreement between Egypt and Israel) for a stronger U.S. diplomatic position vis-à-vis the Syrians, the Soviets, and the suppliers of oil to the United States.

Another example of a Kissinger decision to slow the pace of negotiations came in his advice to Dayan to go slow in proposing Israeli return of the Mitla and Giddi passes in exchange for Egyptian reopening of the Suez Canal. Quandt (1977) argues that Kissinger believed Israel was moving too quickly, and by doing so would raise the expectations of the Egyptians for further concessions. In this instance, and later when he chose to convey only some of the concessions Israel was ready to make to Assad, Kissinger displayed both his desire to control the pace of the negotiations and his sensitivity to the personalities with whom he was dealing.

This is a common strategy a mediator uses when trying to build credibility with one party whom the mediator knows will have to be pressed hard to get a quid pro quo later in the negotiations. The more the mediator is seen as an effective advocate of this party's interests, and as responsible for obtaining whatever concessions were wrung out of an opponent, the greater leverage the mediator will have in extracting concessions from that party when the crucial time comes. On the other hand, the more concessions appear to flow voluntarily from an opponent without requiring the heavy hand of the mediator, the more the party in question will expect the mediator to continue to be able to extract concessions when the final hour of the negotiation process is at hand. One can only surmise that Kissinger understood this, and had this motive in mind when he chose to slow the pace of Israeli concessions. The major risk of this type of strategy is that by not taking advantage of concessions when they are offered, one risks losing them for good as events unfold and circumstances change.

Quandt (1977) notes that "Kissinger's main objective at the outset was to avoid another war but he didn't have a clear idea of what positive goals might be attainable at this time" (p. 251). This observation illustrates the importance of not judging the effectiveness of mediation intervention solely on the basis of the single or ultimate criterion of achieving a comprehensive settlement. Achieving a cease-fire, negotiating the disengagement agreements, and initiating dialogue among the Israelis, Egyptians, and some other key Arab leaders must be viewed as partial indicators of the success of step-by-step diplomacy. Viewed in this way, therefore, the initial strategic decision to embark on the step-by-step approach appears to have been based on a realistic appraisal of what was possible, which is the mark of an effective mediator.

Another example of Kissinger's strategy of pursuing limited objectives can be seen in what some may view as his failure to seek a solution to the West Bank problem, or more generally, to the Palestinian issue. While finding a solution to this issue would have been (and continues to be) a necessary precondition to a comprehensive settlement, the Israelis were clearly not ready to address this problem when Kissinger intervened. For him to push this issue before achieving successful resolution of other, less sensitive issues would have risked suffering a premature breakdown in the negotiations. As a strategy for achieving partial success, avoiding the Palestinian issue until a number of the other issues were resolved made sense. This is a common tactic of mediators: tackling less controversial issues first and saving the issues where conflicts are greatest for later in the process in order to benefit from the momentum gained from the earlier progress.

Legitimacy and Interdependence

One of the consequences of Kissinger's inclination to tackle the "easy issues" first is that insufficient attention was directed to the parties' satisfaction of a fundamental assumption. Recall that collective bargaining assumes that the parties accept the legitimacy of each other and recognize their long term interdependence. This assumption was lacking in two respects when Kissinger first attempted to intervene in the Middle East after the October 1973 War. The Arab states were not ready to recognize the legitimacy of Israel as a permanent, sovereign government in the Middle East. Conversely, the Israelis were unwilling to recognize the legitimacy of the Palestinians. Without these two preconditions for a permanent peace, a comprehensive settlement of the Middle East conflict was impossible.

Nature of the Impasse

Other characteristics of this dispute also reduced the possibility of total success through mediation. This was a case in which a negative contract zone existed between the resistance points of the parties. The Arabs insisted on a return to the 1967 boundaries and the establishment of a Palestinian state. The Israelis, in turn, were completely opposed to a Palestinian state, demanded recognition of Israel's right to exist (recognition Arabs were unwilling to grant), and were not prepared to retreat to the 1967 boundaries.

Significant internal conflicts were also major sources of impasse that needed to be overcome in order to achieve a mediated settlement. Sadat did not, and would not, have the support of the Syrians, the Palestine Liberation Organization, or the Saudis unless he could wrest major concessions from the Israelis. Economic differences and differences in the benefits and costs associated with the Arab oil embargo and rising oil prices further split the Arab states. After Prime Minister Meir was replaced by Rabin, conflict within the Israeli government and society presented another serious obstacle to a comprehensive settlement. Rabin was constrained from making significant concessions both by the pressure of the right-wing rivals to the Labor Party and by the jockeying of other leaders within his own party such as Allon, Dayan, and Peres. The result was that Israel's positions hardened as compromises became politically hazardous.

Analysis of the conflicts involved in this dispute suggests that it was the type of dispute that mediation is least able to resolve effectively. The differences separating the parties on the substantive issues were large; key assumptions underlying the bargaining process regarding legitimacy and interdependence were missing; and unresolved conflicts within each party made it nearly impossible for the negotiators to make major concessions. Any effort to judge the effectiveness of Kissinger as a mediator, therefore, should begin with a full understanding of the difficulties he faced upon entering this dispute.

Situational Factors

Two fundamental propositions presented in the mediation model are that mediation requires the parties to be motivated to reach an agreement, and that efforts to move toward agreement through mediation are most likely to succed when the parties are under the greatest pressure to resolve their differences. Neither of these conditions was present during the step-by-step intervention processes. Sheehan (1976) notes that Israel had little incentive to reach a comprehensive settlement once the initial disengagement agreement was signed. Instead, Israeli leaders felt that the United States was under too much pressure to adopt a pro-Arab policy in response to the pressures of the oil embargo. Once the immediate threat of war had subsided, the Israelis perceived the costs of reaching agreement to be higher than the costs of continued stalemate and disagreement.

This raises an interesting contradiction between the labor mediation model and the mediation of international disputes. In labor mediation, intervention often starts rather slowly and passively. The mediator is most aggressive and assertive in the final hour when the pressure on the parties is at its peak. Indeed, the mediator often does not enter a dispute until the parties are well into the final stages of negotiation and the pressure to settle is mounting. In step-by-step intervention, the pressure on the parties was greatest prior to, or at the beginning of, the intervention process (namely, during the October 1973 War and before the disengagement of forces in the Sinai). Kissinger reserved his most intense pressure on the Israelis, however, for the Syrian disengagement negotiations and the second Sinai disengagement. Thus he tried to pressure the parties the most at the time when the objective pressures to make concessions were weakest. The harder he pressed Israel, the more his credibility declined. In this way, his strategy was completely opposite that of labor mediation. It is not surprising that he encountered stiff opposition from the Israelis.

This aspect of Kissinger's intervention illustrates the interdependence among the timing of entry, the situational pressures on the parties, and the mediator's credibility. A mediator who is dealing with sophisticated negotiators cannot pressure them to do something they firmly believe is against their self-interests, especially when the costs of not changing their position are declining over time.

Kissinger's Personal Characteristics

Examination of Kissinger's characteristics as a mediator points to some positive and negative features. The positive features all reflect Kissinger's superb personal qualities. It is not necessary to dwell here on his interpersonal skill, reputation, experience, technical knowledge of negotiation, or substantive expertise in Middle East diplomacy. These can be taken as given. Kissinger also enjoyed considerable credibility and acceptability with the Israelis prior to his intervention. On the other hand, as Sheehan (1976) points out, he was relatively unknown to the major Arab leaders. In addition, Kissinger's Jewish heritage and his identification with a pro-Israeli U.S. policy made it essential to establish his credibility with the Arab leaders early in his intervention. Kissinger clearly was not only aware of this but also successfully overcame the suspicions of Sadat and Assad. As the negotiations moved from the first Israeli-Egyptian disengagement, an ironic twist occurred: Kissinger's acceptability and credibility with the Israelis began fading even as it was growing with the Arabs.

Kissinger's negative characteristics as a mediator were a function of the multiple objectives he carried with him throughout his intervention: he wished to shore up the U.S. interests in the Middle East, especially as the pressure of the Arab oil embargo mounted; he used his role to enhance his personal prestige; and he hoped to shore up the faltering domestic status of President Nixon. These multiple objectives acted to weaken his role as a mediator because he lacked the power to compel the parties to place any significant weight on any one of them. In a sense he was trying to mediate (or in this case negotiate) the dispute toward outcomes that he valued, but he lacked the bargaining power to steer the course of events in this direction. This was most evident during the negotiation of the first disengagement agreement between Egypt and Israel.

OVERALL ASSESSMENT OF KISSINGER'S INTERVENTION STRATEGY

Let us now turn to the general questions that analysis of any intervention effort must seek to answer. First, what were the distinguishing features of Kissinger's style of intervention? Here we will rely on a modification of Kressel's (1972) distinction between mediator strategies that are passive or nondirective and those that are highly aggressive or directive.

It is clear from the accounts of authors who have traced Kissinger's intervention that he was a highly directive and aggressive mediator. He clearly tried to control events and to direct the strategies of the parties. He pressed hard for substantive compromises when he felt he needed them in order to keep the process moving. He used the full force of his office, the power of U.S. foreign policy, the power of information control that came with the presence of reporters who shuttled with him throughout the Middle East, and the full power of his personal reputation and ability to charm, cajole, coerce, and convince the parties to make concessions. At no time was Kissinger satisfied with the nondirective style of intervention.

A nondirective style was incompatible not only with his personality but also with the role he sought for himself and for U.S. influence in the Middle East.

Kissinger's intervention transcends the Kressel description, however, in that it was clearly calculated to protect and enhance the image of Henry Kissinger, the statesman, peacemaker, and controller of world events. One cannot understand the behavior of Kissinger, the mediator, without also taking account of Kissinger's tremendous ego and his perception of himself as indispensable. The downfall of President Nixon and President Ford's dependence on Kissinger in the early days of his administration served to feed into and enhance Kissinger's view of himself as the sole person able to piece together a Middle East settlement. Every successful mediator has a tendency to develop this same self-image. The more successful the mediator, the stronger the temptation to harbor such a self-perception. Ultimately reality catches up with the illusion. During the height of one's involvement in the mediation process, however, it is difficult to maintain perspective.

To counter the development of this illusion, a mediator must have strong advisors and counselors, or alternatively, strong superiors who can keep rein on such misperceptions. Neither Kissinger's style of management of the State Department nor his style of mediation provided for this type of strong advice. He controlled foreign policy and the diplomatic process without check from anyone of equivalent stature. Only the president could exert a countervailing force. Preoccupation with the events of Watergate and his ultimate loss of control precluded President Nixon from exerting this type of control. President Ford's lack of familiarity with the issues likewise precluded him from playing a strong supervisory role.

Should Kissinger's mediation be characterized as a success? The answer ultimately depends on one's criteria of mediation effectiveness. Although his step-by-step diplomacy did not produce a comprehensive peace, it did end one war and deterred the outbreak of another. In addition, the disengagement agreements did help resolve immediate military problems and allowed the parties to eventually turn their attention to more basic political dilemmas. Without these preliminary agreements, it is hard to see how Sadat could have subsequently embarked on his historic trip to Jerusalem, a trip that set in motion the negotiations that ended with the 1979 Egyptian-Israeli peace agreement. Even Kissinger's harshest critics must regard his intervention as a partial success, a necessary step on the road to a permanent peace.

Could the result have been achieved without third party intervention? Would similar results have been achieved by anyone other than Kissinger? There simply is no way of definitively answering these questions. It is clear, however, that no agreement had been reached for thirty years by the numerous parties who sought to bring peace to the Middle East before Kissinger embarked on his step-by-step diplomacy. In addition, the major breakthroughs in the Middle East have come about largely through the exercise of bold steps by individuals. Kissinger's shuttle diplomacy is an example of this. So is Sadat's trip to Jerusalem. So is President Carter's personal involvement in the Camp David meeting of 1978 and his historic trip to the Middle East in March 1979. So is the strong leadership exercised by Prime Minister Begin when he led the Israeli government in the negotiation of a peace treaty. Henry Kissinger did not bring lasting and total peace to the area, and neither has anyone else to date. He did, however, move the peace process forward in a more significant way than any of his predecessors, and in doing so he set the stage for the remarkable achievement of the Sadat-Begin-Carter agreement. Whatever else history may say of Kissinger, one should not lose sight of this mark of personal success.

IMPLICATIONS FOR THE LABOR MEDIATION MODEL

Comparison of third party intervention in this case with the traditional labor mediation model suggests a number of insights worthy of further thought. In labor mediation the third party is usually assumed to be neutral with respect to the substantive outcomes of the dispute. A mediator is expected to facilitate the negotiating process but is assumed to not have the power to impose a solution on the parties. In the case analyzed here, the third party had his own motives, as well as power that he wielded as it served his interests. Students of labor mediation should examine the implications of this type of role carefully since it may become increasingly common as a form of third party intervention in collective bargaining. When the federal government intervenes in negotiations under the guise of a voluntary incomes policy and attempts to jawbone a settlement, the process resembles Kissinger's intervention more than it does traditional labor mediation. A similar type of intervention occurs in the tripartite negotiation of consent decrees in equal employment opportunity disputes, or where the government attempts to use joint labor-management committees to improve the delivery and enforcement of occupational safety and health standards. A process known as "med-arb" (in which the mediator arbitrates a settlement if mediation fails) is now being used in collective bargaining in some public sector jurisdictions. Again, this process is one in which the mediator has an independent base of power to use in the negotiations.

The dynamics of mediation when the negotiating cycle is reversed (that is, when pressure is greatest at the start of the process rather than at the end) also has important implications for the mediation of labor disputes. As bargaining issues grow in complexity, there is an increasing need to engage in continuous negotiation and/or problem solving rather than trying to resolve all issues in the heat of a formal contract negotiation process that is under the pressure of a strike deadline. Yet the record of continuous bargaining in the United States has not been very favorable, largely because the parties are used to relying on the pressure of a strike deadline to motivate compromise. Perhaps a lesson to be drawn from the Kissinger intervention in the Middle East is that for continuous bargaining to work in the absence of immediate pressures, the third party must possess sufficient power to keep the parties motivated to negotiate.

Finally, there is an implication that students of all forms of negotiation, conflict, and conflict resolution can draw from the analysis of this case: while the specific terms and concepts used to explain human and organizational behavior under conflict vary across institutional settings, the underlying processes do have much in common. One can learn a great deal indeed by comparing the dynamics of these processes in different institutional settings.

REFERENCES

Barbash, J. "The Elements of Industrial Relations." *British Journal of Industrial Relations*, 1964, 2, 66–78.

Dahrendorf, R. *Class and Class Conflict in Industrial Society*. Stanford: Stanford University Press, 1959.

Fox, A. *A Sociology of Work in Industry*. London: Collier Macmillan, 1971.

Golan, M. *The Secret Conversations of Henry Kissinger*. New York: Quadrangle, 1976.

Kerr, C. "Industrial Conflict and Its Mediation." *American Journal of Sociology*, 1954, 60, 230–45.

Kochan, T. A., and Jick, T. "A Theory of the Public Sector Mediation Process." *Journal of Conflict Resolution*, 1978, 22, 209–40.

Kressel, K. *Labor Mediation: An Exploratory Survey*. Albany, N.Y.: Association of Labor Mediation Agencies, 1972.

Landsberger, H. A. "Interaction Process Analysis of the Mediation of Labor-Management Disputes." *Journal of Abnormal Social-Psychology*, 1955, 51, 522–58.

Quandt, W. B. *Decade of Decisions: American Policy toward the Arab-Israeli Conflict, 1967–1976*. Berkeley: University of California Press, 1977.

Schelling, T. C. *The Strategy of Conflict*. Cambridge: Harvard University Press, 1960.

Sheehan, E. R. F. "How Kissinger Did It: Step by Step in the Middle East." *Foreign Policy*, 1976, 22, 3–70.

Simkin, W. E. *Mediation and the Dynamics of Collective Bargaining*. Washington, D.C.: Bureau of National Affairs, 1971.

Stevens, C. M. "Mediation and the Role of the Neutral." In J. T. Dunlop and N. Chamberlain, eds., *Frontiers of Collective Bargaining*. New York: Harper and Row, 1967, 271–90.

————. *Strategy and Collective Bargaining Negotiations*. New York: McGraw-Hill, 1963.

Walton, R. E., and McKersie, R. B. *A Behavioral Theory of Labor Negotiations*. New York: McGraw-Hill, 1965.

5

KISSINGER AS A TRADITIONAL
MEDIATOR WITH POWER

Dean G. Pruitt

Although it was sometimes considered the work of a miracle man, Kissinger's performance in the Middle East between 1973 and 1975 was mainly the result of the sort of traditional mediation found in industrial relations. Hence his success can be largely understood within the framework of standard mediation theory, with its origins in case studies of industrial mediation. However, Kissinger did differ from an industrial mediator in two ways: he was able to wield considerable power over the two parties, particularly Israel, and he represented a country with its own strong interests in the area. These special features of his situation both contributed to and detracted from his success as a mediator. Standard mediation theory therefore needs to be amended, in this case to include the variables of mediator power and mediator interests.

The traditional elements of Kissinger's effort, the strategies he used and the conditions underlying their success, will be described first. The analysis will then turn to more novel elements of Kissinger's intervention, deriving from his status as the primary representative of one of the most powerful countries on earth. Finally, attention will be directed to the theoretical assumptions made in the prior analysis.

TRADITIONAL MEDIATION STRATEGIES

The theory of mediation has its origins in the writings of such industrial relations specialists as Peters (1955) and Stevens (1963). It has

Preparation of this manuscript was made possible by a fellowship from the John Simon Guggenheim Memorial Foundation and grant number BNS-76-10963 from the National Science Foundation.

been further developed in recent years by scholars in the same field (Kochan 1979) and in social psychology (Kressel 1972; Pruitt 1971; Rubin and Brown 1975). Seven strategies that Kissinger employed are identified in these writings.

First, Kissinger separated the bargainers and shuttled back and forth between them. This procedure enhances negotiator flexibility in two ways: it reduces the likelihood of angry displays, which are encouraged by face-to-face interaction and can lead to a hardening of negotiating positions (Kressel 1972); and it prevents nonverbal dominance struggles, in which the bargainers trade efforts to stare one another down or engage in other dominance displays. Such struggles, which are especially common when bargainers have a competitive orientation toward one another, also lead to a hardening of positions (Carnevale, Pruitt, and Seilheimer 1979; Lewis and Fry 1977). In addition, shuttle diplomacy gives the mediator total control over the communication between the two bargainers. This facilitates the use of several of the other strategies described below.

Second, Kissinger spent much of his time trying to persuade both parties to make concessions. When dealing with each other directly, bargainers also try to persuade one another to make concessions. But mediators are more often successful in this enterprise because they are not as likely to be suspected of concocting phony arguments to advance their interests. Kissinger used three typical arguments in an effort to elicit concessions. (1) "Making a concession is in your interest." For instance, Kissinger urged Israel to retreat from the Suez Canal on the grounds that the oil embargo would be lifted, ending Israel's isolation from Western European states and Japan (Golan 1976). (2) "Concessions are necessary because the other party cannot be expected to concede." For example, Kissinger persuaded Sadat to withdraw his demand for control of the resupply corridor to the Third Army on the grounds that Meir's government would fall if she conceded on this matter (Golan 1976). (3) "The other party is interested in peace and will be conciliatory if you concede." Thus he often told Israel that Sadat was seeking a relaxation of tensions and would be willing to be flexible if Israel were flexible too (Golan 1976).

Third, Kissinger allowed himself to become the target of angry displays, thus deflecting them from the other bargainer. For example, at one point he listened to a long, angry lecture from Meir about the suffering of Israel and the unjustness of its world position (Golan 1976). At the end of this diatribe, he agreed with her but pointed out the realistic need for concessions. A mediator who takes such a role acts like a psychotherapist dealing with transference. The mediator serves as a surrogate target for emotion, allows catharsis, and then leads the client to a more realistic interpretation of the situation.

The shuttle format permitted use of a fourth common strategy: Kissinger coordinated concession exchanges without weakening the bargainers' negotiating positions. The way this strategy works is that the mediator elicits a concession from one side and then presents it to the other side as the mediator's own proposal. This shields the first side from being seen as soft by the other side prior to the development of an agreement (Pruitt 1971). Support for the assumption underlying this strategy can be seen in an experiment by Podell and Knapp (1969), in which expectations of further concessions from the adversay were found to be larger if the adversary conceded than if the mediator suggested the same concession. Rubin (1980) calls this the "tar baby" function of the mediator, absorbing responsibility for a concession until the party who has made it is ready to assume credit for it. An example would be Kissinger's mediation of the issue of who would control the access road to the Third Army during the initial cease-fire talks between Egypt and Israel. Having achieved Sadat's approval of United Nations checkpoints on an Israeli controlled road, Kissinger presented this formula to Israel as his own idea (Sheehan 1976a).

Fifth, and related to the preceding strategy, Kissinger allowed the bargainers to save face by making their concessions to him rather than to the other party. Theorists (Kressel 1972; Stevens 1963) have argued that this shields the conceder from looking soft both to constituents and to the other party. In addition, Pruitt and Johnson (1970) have shown experimentally that a bargainer who concedes in response to a mediator's suggestion sees himself as stronger than one who concedes spontaneously. Use of this strategy was facilitated by the shuttle format, with Kissinger arguing vigorously in both capitals for concessions he felt were necessary to achieve agreement. Sometimes this strategy helped structure the actual form of a treaty. For example, in the Israeli-Egyptian disengagement agreement negotiated at Kilometer 101, the details of force reductions and arms restrictions were spelled out in a private letter from Nixon to Sadat and Meir.

Sixth, Kissinger occasionally developed novel alternatives that would integrate both parties' requirements. An example can be seen in the negotiation of the disengagement agreement between Israel and Syria. Israel wanted protection for settlers on farms near Kuneitra, but Syria was unwilling to have Israeli troops so close to the city. Kissinger suggested that these settlements should come within a zone of disengagement that would be protected by United Nations troops (Sheehan 1976b). Mediators are often better than bargainers at devising such integrative alternatives because they usually have a more balanced perspective and frequently have received valid information about both parties' requirements (Pruitt 1976).

Finally, Kissinger maintained momentum in the negotiations. This amounts to sustaining the belief, on both sides, that future agreement is possible. In the absence of such a belief, one or both sides may turn to other means of achieving what they want, such as military attack, the development of alliances, and so forth. Momentum has the effect of strengthening the moderates or doves on both sides in their internal struggles with the hawks. In Kissinger's view, Sadat was clearly a dove who needed support in his battle with the hawks in his own and other Arab governments.

ENGINEERING MOMENTUM

Momentum is best maintained by a steady diet of concessions and agreements. Hence one can argue that the shuttle format contributed to momentum, since each party apparently felt constrained to make at least a small concession during the visit of the U.S. Secretary of State. Another method for maintaining momentum is to place less controversial issues early on the agenda, so that the parties can develop some faith in the negotiation process before trying to solve more controversial issues (Kressel 1972). Kissinger's entire philosophy of step-by-step diplomacy can be seen as an exemplification of this method, beginning as it did with simple cease-fire agreements and moving forward into ever more difficult territory. Janis and Mann (1977) describe Kissinger's technique:

> [Step-by-step diplomacy had] the advantage of preventing the representatives of the contending parties from feeling hopeless about arriving at a solution . . . thus [reducing] the likelihood that any of the negotiators [would] bolster an unviable partisan stance or display closed-minded rejection of all compromise proposals. It is easy for a negotiator to justify his intransigence when he is offered a total package of unsliced salami that contains numerous objectionable ingredients; when one slice at a time is served, each discrete proposal is more likely to be dealt with on its merits rather than disputed by bolstering the original belligerent stance with jingoistic slogans and facile rationalizations (pp. 289–90).

It can be argued that the momentum generated by Kissinger's successes between 1973 and 1975 bore fruit in Sadat's dramatic visit to Jerusalem in November 1977. During this visit, Sadat exuded confidence that agreement could be reached by negotiation. Such confidence can be reasonably traced to the fact that four prior agreements had been reached under Kissinger's tutelage.

Kissinger's decision in fall 1974 to push for a further withdrawal of Israeli forces on the Egyptian front rather than an Israeli-Jordanian treaty dealing with the West Bank and Palestinian sovereignty can be viewed as an effort to maintain momentum. In making this decision, Kissinger was simply bowing to political reality in Israel and the Arab world. He and

President Ford had tried repeatedly to persuade Rabin to open a dialogue with Jordan but to no avail. Then came the Rabat declaration of October 26, 1974, denying King Hussein the right to negotiate for the Palestinians of the West Bank. At this point the prospects for a treaty between Israel and Jordan presumably became so remote that Kissinger felt the need to turn to the Egyptian front to maintain the momentum of his overall program.

The assumption that Kissinger was trying to maintain momentum throughout this period might seem to be contradicted by the fact that he tried to slow down Israeli concessions at two points in the negotiation. According to Quandt (1977), on December 7, 1973, Kissinger advised against a dramatic Israeli proposal to set up a new line of disengagement in exchange for an Egyptian reopening of the Suez Canal. On May 8, 1974, he failed to disclose to Assad some of the concessions Israel had recently made. However, the contradiction between these moves and Kissinger's other policies is more apparent than real. Momentum requires that there be steady progress. Such progress can be disrupted if a party moves too rapidly as well as if it moves too slowly. There are two interlocking reasons for this. First, the party that receives early large concessions is likely to view them as a sign of weakness and respond by slowing down its concession making. This effect has been shown experimentally (Benton et al. 1972; Komorita and Brenner 1968). Second, having failed to receive an adequate response, the party who makes the early large concessions is likely to avoid further concessions. For both reasons, the ultimate result is likely to be a disruption of momentum.

CONDITIONS CONTRIBUTING TO THE SUCCESS OF TRADITIONAL MEDIATION

This section will review a number of conditions that prevailed during this period of mediation and that can account for its success. Kissinger himself was responsible for the development of some of these conditions.

Kochan and Jick (1978) have shown that mediation works best when both parties are highly motivated to settle their controversy. While national motivation is tricky to measure, it seems clear that both Egypt and Israel were weary of war and had strong economic motives for peace. Furthermore, Egypt did not have as pressing a need as before to prove its military potency against Israel. Sadat could claim that his army had fought successfully when it crossed the Suez Canal and drove the enemy back.

It has also been argued that mediation is especially successful when there is a stalemate in which neither party can hope to force concessions out of the other (Pruitt 1971). To persuade the other party to move in such a stalemate, it is necessary to make concessions in return, and a mediator can be helpful in coordinating the two parts of the exchange. Stalemates develop out of a situation of relative equality in power. Accordinig to Sheehan (1976b), Kissinger was aware of this fact, being "convinced that, until the Arabs saw that Soviet guns could not regain their territory [and] until the Israelis understood that massive American support could not of itself bestow security for the future . . . his own or any American intervention was doomed to be abortive" (p. 18). This probably explains why Kissinger was unwilling to allow Israel to destroy the Egyptian Third Army at the close of the 1973 War. Had Israel done so, the power imbalance would have been so great that a negotiated agreement would not have been possible.

Certain personal characteristics also make a mediator more successful at promoting an agreement. It helps if the mediator, is viewed as an expert in the matter at hand and is seen by both sides as concerned about their welfare (Kressel 1972). Kissinger appears to have been strong on each of these dimensions. He put a great deal of effort into making both sides feel that he understood and appreciated their perspectives by frequently articulating their biases and interests as his own, as well as by occasionally voicing mildly disparaging remarks about the other party.

Rapport with the other party will often enhance a mediator's effectiveness, because the mediator is seen as having influence over that party. There is no point in making concessions to, or even in dealing with, a mediator who cannot elicit reciprocal concessions from the other side. Hence Kissinger's close relationship with each party probably helped him with the other.

It can be argued that Kissinger was, at least at first, closer to Israel than to Egypt, and that this violates the canon of mediator impartiality that has so often been stressed in discussions of effective mediation (for example, Stevens 1963). However, recent research suggests that impartiality has been overemphasized. A substantial minority of mediators interviewed by Kressel (1972) argued that the effective mediator should have particularly strong ties to the party with greater control over the outcome. Whatever partiality may result from these ties is presumably balanced by the mediator's greater capacity to influence that party. In the case under consideration, Israel was the party with greater outcome control because agreement depended on its willingness to withdraw from conquered territory. Hence it was appropriate that mediation should be conducted by the United States, with its close ties to Israel, and that Kissinger, a Jew, should act as mediator. Whatever Kissinger may have lacked in neutrality was presumably more than compensated, in Sadat's eyes, by his capacity to elicit concessions from Israel.

Kissinger's frequent flashes of humor may also have contributed to his effectiveness. Kressel (1972) argues that humor contributes to rapport

In addition, humor undoubtedly creates a good mood, and research suggests that people are more persuasible (Janis, Kaye, and Kirschner 1965) and more generous (Isen and Levin 1972) when in a good mood.

NONTRADITIONAL ASPECTS OF KISSINGER'S ROLE

While Kissinger's behavior was largely that of a traditional mediator, his intervention involved several nonstandard elements. He was a strong man, representing a powerful country. He was particularly powerful with respect to Israel, which needed the United States for political and military support. Moreover, his power over Egypt surely grew as Sadat became increasingly committed to a solution by negotiation. Unlike the traditional disinterested mediator, the United States had some interests of its own in the Middle East, especially in maintaining the security of Israel and the flow of oil.

Unfortunately mediation theory has not dealt with the powerful, nondisinterested mediator. Yet third party functions are often played by such individuals in the role of parent, government official, industrial executive, judge, and so forth. Furthermore, a theory of this sort of mediation is essential for understanding multilateral bargaining, where one full-fledged participant will often mediate a controversy between two others.

It can be argued that Kissinger's power was partly consonant and partly dissonant with his role as mediator. On the consonant side, by preventing Israel from destroying the Egyptian Third Army at the end of the war, he was able to produce conditions that encouraged both parties to negotiate. In addition, it was probably easier for the bargainers to make concessions to him, a powerful mediator, because such concessions were less likely to be viewed as signs of inherent weakness. Being powerful enabled Kissinger to guarantee each side's adherence to certain agreements, as when he gave Israel a letter indicating that Sadat would open the Suez Canal and rebuild its cities (Golan 1976). As Schelling (1960) points out, the possibility of a third party guarantee gives a bargainer greater capacity to make a personal commitment and hence to enter into a contract. Finally, U.S. power facilitated Kissinger's efforts to persuade both parties to make concessions. This was especially true for Israel, which received much military hardware in exchange for its concessions and was often the target of U.S. threats. One suspects that there would have been no agreements in the absence of U.S. pressure. Traditional mediation without muscle is a weak reed when issues are as deeply felt, and the two parties are as far apart, as was the case in this exacerbated situation.

However, Kissinger's exercise of power appears to have sometimes been dissonant with his mediation effort. As time went on, Israel became increasingly resentful of his threats. Sensing this problem, Kissinger often tried to pawn responsibility for these threats onto others in the U.S. government such as Schlesinger, Nixon, and Ford. These efforts were not credible because he was obviously the chief architect of U.S. foreign policy. A sign of Kissinger's diminished rapport with Israel occurred when Rabin openly accused him of lying during the last negotiation (Golan 1976).

The fact that the United States has vested interests in the Middle East also had its pluses and minuses. On the plus side, the U.S. desire to protect Israel, while maintaining access to Arab oil, made Kissinger especially interested in producing a peace settlement in the region. On the minus side, the Israelis tended to distrust his argument that settlement with the Arabs was of crucial importance for their welfare, because this argument was attributed to a U.S. desire for Arab oil. A disinterested mediator might have been more successful in changing attitudes on this matter.

ASSUMPTIONS MADE IN THE PRIOR ANALYSIS

A number of assumptions about bargaining and mediation underlying the prior analysis of Kissinger's performance will now be examined.

Separating the two bargainers, and shuttling back and forth between them, can contribute to the success of negotiation in a number of ways. It reduces the incidence of angry displays and deflects them away from the other bargainer. It prevents nonverbal dominance struggles between the bargainers. It places the job of persuading bargainers to concede in the hands of a party who is likely to be more sympathetic and credible than the representatives of the opposing side. It allows a bargainer to save face by conceding to the mediator rather than to the other negotiator. It allows the mediator to take credit for a proposal actually made by a bargainer, thus shielding that bargainer from the necessity of revealing how far he or she was willing to go until an exchange of concessions has been agreed upon. It allows the mediator to gather privileged information about the two bargainers' priorities, making the mediator better able than the bargainers to devise integrative options that satisfy both parties' requirements.

In addition to these functions, mediators often take responsibility for maintaining momentum in negotiations, in the sense of supporting the belief that agreement is around the corner. Momentum is best maintained by a steady stream of concessions and agreements. One way to encourage such a stream is to place less controversial items earlier on the agenda. Another is to solicit concessions from the bargainers after a period in which none has been made. A third is to advise against concessions that are so early, so frequent, or so large that they may signal weakness to the other party, causing the other to inhibit its concession making.

Mediation is most successful when bargainers are highly motivated to settle their controversy, and are in a stalemate in which neither hopes to persuade the other to make unilateral concessions. The latter point can be derived from a broader "strategic choice" theory being developed by the author. A bargainer wishing to settle a controversy faces a choice among three approaches: making unilateral concessions, trying to persuade the other to make unilateral concessions, and coordination—that is, collaborating with the other party in the search for a mutually acceptable solution. Cooperating with a mediator is one form of coordination. Others include asking for mediation, signalling a willingness to concede if the other concedes, reciprocating the other's concession, using back channels to discuss common interests with the other party, and so forth (Magenau and Pruitt 1978). Assuming that a choice must be made among these three approaches, it stands to reason that one choice will increase in likelihood as the viability of the others decreases. Hence, as postulated, bargainers will cooperate more with a mediator to the extent that they have little hope of persuading one another to concede.

Certain personal characteristics of mediators also contribute to their likelihood of success in achieving agreement. Attitude change theory (Hovland, Janis, and Kelley 1953) suggests that they will be more persuasive to the extent that they are viewed as expert in the matter under discussion and as concerned about both parties' welfare. Rapport with the other party can also be a source of influence for mediators, because they then seem capable of persuading the other party to concede. It follows that the most effective mediators are likely to have an especially close relationship with either the more obstinate party or the party who must make the larger concessions if agreement is to be reached. This principle of unequal rapport is probably more important than the principle of strict neutrality that was advocated in the early days of mediation theory (though a grossly biased mediator is, of course, likely to be unsuccessful). Another mediator asset is the capacity to put people into a good mood, for example, with humor.

The traditional industrial mediator was a powerless figure, without the capacity to reward or punish the bargainers. Yet it is clear that many mediators are quite powerful. Hence, a theory must be built about the importance of mediator power. Mediator power has both pluses and minuses with respect to mediator success. On the positive side, having power allows the mediator to press or compensate the bargainers for concessions and to guarantee each party that the other will fulfill its side of a contemplated agreement. It may also be especially easy for a bargainer to make concessions to a powerful mediator while saving face, because such concessions are unlikely to be seen as a sign of weakness. On the negative side, efforts to push the bargainers around have a necessary cost in rapport, and hence may adversely affect a mediator's capacity to be persuasive except by using threats.

On balance, the points just made suggest that a mediator is more likely to produce an agreement, the greater his·or her power over the bargainers. However, it must also be acknowledged that a mediator who exercises too much power may induce an agreement that will crumble when the mediator departs from the scene.

Mediator disinterest in the issues under discussion is also a mixed bag. On the one hand, disinterest should enhance the credibility of the mediator's arguments for concession making, because the mediator is seen as having no particular axe to grind. On the other hand, disinterest can contribute to mediator inactivity. A mediator who has a vital interest in achieving peace between the two parties is likely to be especially effective by virtue of being willing to work hard to achieve agreement.

POSTSCRIPT: SOME LONGER RUN IMPLICATIONS OF MEDIATOR POWER

The ideas presented above were put on paper in early 1979. Looking back at them from the perspective of the Fall 1980 election season, I realize that I now have a gloomier view of the impact of mediation by a powerful third party. Problems are likely to develop in the *later* relationship between the negotiating principals if the mediator uses his/her resources to compensate the principals for making concessions, as Kissinger and later Carter apparently did by the provision of economic and military aid. The longer run implications of such a practice appear to be (a) dependence on the mediator for further compensation in later negotiations and (b) development of a tripartite negotiation system in which much of the bargaining takes place between the mediator and the two principals with the aim of establishing a price to be paid by the mediator for each concession.

Such a system deflects responsibility for initiating and sustaining further negotiation onto the mediator, because the principals are likely to feel that they can get greater compensation from the mediator to the extent that they appear reluctant to concede and uninterested in settlement. It also requires that the mediator, like any negotiator, put continuing pressure on the negotiators to encourage them to concede. If the mediator later backs off from this role and tries to take the more typical passive, neutral stance, there will be no progress.

Such a system is basically unhealthy because it puts responsibility for negotiation progress into the hands of a third party rather than into those of the principals whose welfare is most at stake. The principals can sit back, without a policy vis-à-vis one another, "waiting for George to do it." The problem becomes particularly acute if the third party is ambivalent about putting pressure on one or both parties, as is true of the United States regarding Israel, especially in an election season. Such ambivalence, in combination with the lack of a sense of responsibility for progress on the part of the principals, is bound to lead to periodic loss of momentum.

I am not implying that Kissinger was mistaken in offering compensation for concessions, without which there probably would have been no agreements. What I am saying is that this produced new problems that now need to be solved.

REFERENCES

Benton, A. A.; Kelley, H. H.; and Liebling, B. "Effects of Extremity of Offers and Concession Rate on the Outcomes of Bargaining." *Journal of Personality and Social Psychology*, 1972, 24, 73–83.

Carnevale, P. J. D.; Pruitt, D. G.; and Seilheimer, S. D. "Negotiator Accountability and Nonverbal Communication as Determinants of Bargaining Outcome." Presented at the annual meeting of the Eastern Psychological Association, 1979.

Golan, M. *The Secret Conversations of Henry Kissinger.* New York: Quadrangle, 1976.

Hovland, C. I.; Janis, I. L.; and Kelley, H. H. *Communication and Persuasion.* New Haven, Conn.: Yale University Press, 1953.

Isen, A. M. and Levin, P. F. "The Effect of Feeling Good on Helping: Cookies and Kindness." *Journal of Personality and Social Psychology*, 1972, 21, 384–88.

Janis, I. L.; Kaye, D.; and Kirschner, P. "Facilitating Effects of 'Eating While Reading' on Responsiveness to Persuasive Communications." *Journal of Personality and Social Psychology*, 1965, 1, 181–86.

Janis, I. L., and Mann, L. *Decision Making.* New York: Free Press, 1977.

Kochan, T. A. "Collective Bargaining and Organizational Behavior Research." In B. M. Staw and L. L. Cummings, eds., *Research in Organizational Behavior,* Vol. II. Greenwich, Conn.: JAI Press, 1979.

Kochan, T. A. and Jick, T. "The Public Sector Mediation Process: A Theory and Empirical Examination." *Journal of Conflict Resolution*, 1978, 22, 209–40.

Komorita, S. S., and Brenner, A. R. "Bargaining and Concession Making under Bilateral Monopoly." *Journal of Personality and Social Psychology*, 1968, 9, 15–20.

Kressel, K. *Labor Mediation: An Exploratory Survey.* Albany, N.Y.: Association of Labor Mediation Agencies, 1972.

Lewis, S. A., and Fry, W. R. "Effects of Visual Access and Orientation on the Discovery of Integrative Bargaining Alternatives." *Organizational Behavior and Human Performance*, 1977, 20, 75–92.

Magenau, J. M., and Pruitt, D. G. "The Social Psychology of Bargaining: A Theoretical Synthesis." In G. M. Stephenson and C. J. Brotherton, eds., *Industrial Relations: A Social Psychological Approach.* London: Wiley, 1978.

Peters, E. *Strategy and Tactics in Labor Negotiations.* New London, Conn.: National Foremen's Institute, 1955.

Podell, J. E., and Knapp, W. M. "The Effect of Mediation on the Perceived Firmness of the Opponent." *Journal of Conflict Resolution,* 1969, 13, 511–20.

Pruitt, D. G. "Indirect Communication and the Search for Agreement in Negotiation." *Journal of Applied Social Psychology,* 1971, 1, 205–39.

———. "Power and Bargaining." In B. Seidenberg and A. Snadowsky, eds., *Social Psychology: Art Introduction.* New York: Free Press, 1976.

Pruitt, D. G., and Johnson, D. F. "Mediation as an Aid to Face Saving in Negotiation." *Journal of Personality and Social Psychology,* 1970, 14, 239–46.

Quandt, W. B. *Decade of Decisions: American Policy toward the Arab-Israeli Conflict, 1967–1976.* Berkeley: University of California Press, 1977.

Rubin, J. Z. "Experimental Research on Third Party Intervention in Conflict: Toward Some Generalizations." *Psychological Bulletin,* 1980, 87, 379–91.

Rubin, J. Z., and Brown, B. R. *The Social Psychology of Bargaining and Negotiation.* New York: Academic Press, 1975.

Schelling, T. C. *The Strategy of Conflict.* Cambridge, Mass.: Harvard University Press, 1960.

Sheehan, E. R. F. "How Kissinger Did It: Step by Step in the Middle East." *Foreign Policy,* 1976a, 22, 3–70.

———. *The Arabs, Israelis, and Kissinger.* New York: Reader's Digest Press, 1976b.

Stevens, C. M. *Strategy and Collective Bargaining Negotiation.* New York: McGraw-Hill, 1963.

6

EXPLAINING DISENGAGEMENT
I. William Zartman

The author wishes to express his appreciation to the National Endowment for the Humanities and the American Research Center in Egypt for support for this project.

This chapter evaluates Kissinger's mediation in the disengagement process as a case of negotiation. The thesis is that Kissinger mediated effectively because he well understood the negotiation process as described by a number of key concepts. The argument proceeds along three lines: the disengagement rounds as examples of negotiation concepts; negotiation concepts as a guide for identifying limitations and shortcomings in the process; and new questions for analysts and practitioners raised by the disengagements. Specifically, the chapter argues that the disengagement process was successful because Kissinger: recognized and, in part, engineered a situation propitious for negotiation; encouraged and, in part, invented a formula for settlement of the important issues; and used elements of power, deadline, trust, and momentum first to bring a process to fruition and then to leave it in a situation propitious for a new cycle of negotiation. It also argues that in the end, the formula that allowed such success was worn out and needed replacement, and the types of power that brought about results led to overpayment in the final round. Finally, the chapter asks whether mediation and negotiation are best pursued as a process that determines (as in the disengagement cases), or is determined by, the outcome.

USING STALEMATE

Kissinger understood that conflict resolution through negotiation is a process of balancing power in order to reconcile goals, and that it involves specific elements or phases such as past and future stalemate,

148

formula and details, and deadline. In his role as an interested mediator, he sought to seize upon, encourage, and manipulate these items to produce both a creative context and a positive result.

The initial situation provided almost exemplary characteristics of stalemate. Negotiations take place when parties come to the realization that an intolerable situation needs a solution, and that their goals are unattainable by other means. More specifically, negotiation occurs when the parties hold each other in the stalemate grip of a double veto, preventing each other both from attaining its goals unilaterally and from attaining its goals bilaterally without the other's agreement. "Stalemate is the most propitious condition for settlement," Kissinger has said (*New York Times*, Oct. 12, 1974). "We recognize that the present situation is intolerable to the Arabs," he told Arab ambassadors to the United Nations just before the October War (Sheehan 1976, p. 12), and the outcome of that war rendered it intolerable to Israel as well. "What is needed is to find ways to turn what is presently unacceptable to you into a situation with which you can live" (*New York Times*, Oct. 26, 1974).

The stalemate existed on many levels at the end of the war. First, there was the double encirclement on the ground. While the Israeli thrust under General Sharon had encircled the Egyptian Third Army, the Israeli salient, by the same token, was also encircled by the Egyptians. The very instability of the military situation meant that a simple cease-fire in place, as practiced in the June 1967 War, was impossible; something else had to be invented, involving a new type of outcome. Return to the October 22 lines, when the encirclement of the Third Army had been less nearly complete, was also impossible. This was impossible both because the Israelis had penetrated beyond the October 22 positions and were unlikely to return to them except in return for something else, and also because those lines were hard to ascertain. "Nobody knows where the lines of October 22 are," Kissinger told Sadat. "Look, instead of wasting time on the October 22 lines, why don't we try for something bigger?" (Sheehan 1976, p. 16). The way was open for a new formula, as discussed below.

Second, the stalemate existed on a strategic as well as tactical military level. As a result of the 1973 round of the Thirty Years War in the Middle East, both sides saw that their goals were unattainable militarily. Israel could not be erased. The Egyptian offensive sought to reestablish Egypt's claim on the territory occupied in 1967, not to destroy Israel or even to reconquer all of this territory. Nor could Israel impose its acceptance on its neighbors. Its military successes to date had not been sufficient to make its neighbors sue for peace, and the more it conquered of their territory, the more it would be burdened with an unassimilable Arab population. Egypt and Syria could not take Tel Aviv, and Israel could not conquer Cairo and Damascus. As so often happens, Israel's bargaining chips—the conquered territories—had become an albatross.

Third, the dynamics as well as the statics of the moment favored stalemate. The whole timing of Kissinger's policy at the end of the October 1973 War was to maintain a tactical stalemate, thereby preventing the Israelis from pressing on to elimination of the interlocking positions with their neighbors. Beyond the actual positions on the ground that required resolution, however, there was also the dynamic of changing fortunes and power relations that favored negotiation. Negotiations typically take place when power is shifting toward equality, most notably when the stronger side weakens and the weaker side improves its position. The 1973 war showed that the Israelis did not always win, nor did the Egyptians always lose. It reversed the fickle play of images under which each side operated, so that even the resounding Israeli comeback and the short-lived quality of the Egyptian and Syrian advances could not destroy this new appreciation of capabilities and potentialities. Once before this shift in fortunes had favored negotiations: in 1970 when Egypt received a new arms injection from the Soviet Union and Israel underwent reverses in its ability to hold the occupied Sinai undisturbed. At that time, U.S. policy tried but was unable to capitalize on the moment of shifting power. In 1973 Kissinger acted more forcefully. Egypt now had reason to capitalize on its fleeting advance by seeking negotiations, and Israel had reason to capitalize on its present position through negotiation before this position eroded further.

Fourth, this dynamic feature of the regional power relations was reflected in new aspects of stalemate on the global level. In the military alert declared by President Nixon during the course of the war, the United States had symbolically stiff-armed the Soviet Union, declaring that Washington was in charge of working out the problems of the Middle East. At the same time, the United States attempted to make this gesture palatable by indicating that it would not fully exclude Moscow, but would associate with it as it saw useful. This global gesture was accompanied by the development of privileged relations between Washington and Cairo, paralleling those that had obtained previously between Washington and Tel Aviv exclusively. Clients of a single, same patron who refused to adjudicate between them, the two parties were now placed in a position from which they could be played off against each other, again in stalemate. The way out of the stalemate was to turn this similarity in the structure of relations to their common advantage, as a catalyst for conflict resolution. Such a view reflected the interest and the policy of Kissinger as well.

The Syrian stalemate, although composed of many of the same elements, was fundamentally quite different in nature. Here there was no mutual encirclement, and therefore no mutually intolerable situation. Other elements were needed for the stalemate, as Assad quickly understood. The Israelis had Assad's land, and he had their prisoners of war. Sheehan (1976) has written of Kissinger: "On the periphery he encouraged the belligerents themselves to provide the points of reference; that done, he identified the components, then skillfully composed them" (p. 35). With these elements in hand, Kissinger proposed an opening to disengagement negotiations: the list of prisoners in exchange for a disengagement map.

A second element that strengthened the Syrian stalemate was the oil embargo. Originally, the Arab embargo was to hold until Israel had withdrawn from its conquests. As time wore on, pressures to lift the embargo as well as concern over its effects on Europe wore down the initial resolve. Although Syria urged a continued embargo, as was clearly in its interest, a meeting of the presidents of Syria, Egypt, and Algeria and the king of Saudi Arabia in Algiers in mid-February 1974 led to an agreement to make the embargo dependent on progress in the Syrian disengagement. Another Kissinger shuttle to the parties involved ten days later led to the lifting of the oil embargo a month after the Algiers meeting. By then the embargo's contribution to stalemate had had its effect in starting the talks.

With the end of the embargo's contribution to stalemate, and with it the prisoner issue, Syria's tight bargaining position necessitated an ongoing element of stalemate after March 1974. This was found in the constant military activity across the cease-fire line from March through May, when the disengagement agreement was finally signed. Militarily unimportant in their effects on the cease-fire line or on the outcome of the negotiations, the constant shelling and dogfights were crucial in giving meat to Kissinger's constantly repeated message: "Failure to achieve an agreement now could lead to an all out war" (*New York Times*, May 5, 1974), or "the situation would blow up" in the view of all three parties if there were no agreement (*New York Times*, May 31, 1974). The disengagement talks stood between a past and a future precipice, each representing stalemates that made the negotiated disengagement look attractive by comparison.

The situations along the Jordan River and along the Sinai disengagement line are less clear as examples of stalemate. The Jordan boundary was stable and unthreatened by escalation. Not surprisingly, there were no disengagement talks to trouble its stability, although that alone is an insufficient explanation. The first Sinai disengagement boundary was quite the opposite as it was unstable in the sense of being neither natural nor salient, and it was expected by the parties to be followed by a second withdrawal as early as mid-1974. In the second Sinai disengagement, therefore, expected movement rather than stalemate is probably the clearest explanation. It should be noted in this light that one of the criticisms of Kissinger is weakened by this explanation. Had he accepted

Dayan's offer of a first Sinai disengagement based on withdrawal to a line near the Mitla and Giddi passes, the line would have been stable enough to destroy momentum, and would have made a second Sinai disengagement unlikely.

The final element of stalemate was its characteristic use by Kissinger as a method of problem solving. A number of commentators have noted this style, not always with admiration and not always out of deep understanding. "The Secretary's essential method is to leash the dogs of war which he himself has previously unleashed," wrote Joseph Kraft (*Washington Post*, May 5, 1974). "It is not nice but it works what looks like wonders." Similarly, according to Sheehan (1976): "His great function— he has said so many times—was to explain persuasively to either party the constraints upon the other" (p. 35). Each observer sees in a different way that Kissinger's tactic was to cultivate an awareness of stalemate on both sides by heightening each party's understanding of the other's inability to meet the first's terms, while at the same time cultivating a preference for a negotiated solution; Kissinger's proposal would then break the stalemate and embody the preferred solution. Heightening a perception of the stalemate was the beginning of the solution, but that alone would have only convinced the parties of the need to break the impasse by any means possible, most notably the force under their own control—since the stalemate meant that neither party could agree to the other's minimum demands. Even as Kissinger was fostering the perception of stalemate, his real tactical skill came from an ability simultaneously to convince the parties that compromise was theoretically possible and that, wherever it lay, such compromise was preferable to the dire alternatives of unilateral action and inaction.

THE SEARCH FOR A FORMULA

As much as stalemate, the importance of formula in negotiation is particularly well exemplified in Kissinger's disengagement mediation. A formula is a conceptual definition of the problem or of the solution, encompassing as much as possible, of both sides' concerns within a coherent notion, and providing referents for the subsequent resolution of detailed points in the conflict. Although it is possible to assemble an accord inductively, negotiation from formula to details allows for a more orderly, satisfactory, and coherent reconciliation of differences.

The process of developing a formula actually began in 1967 with Security Council Resolution 242 and its formula of "security for territory," neatly expressed in the first of the resolution's four articles:

> The Security Council . . . 1. Affirms that the fulfillment of Charter principles requires the establishment of a just and lasting peace in the

Middle East which should include the application of both of the following principles: (i) Withdrawal of Israeli armed forces from territories occupied in the recent conflict. (ii) Termination of all claims or states of belligerency and respect for acknowledgement of the sovereignty, territorial integrity, and political independence of every state in the area and their right to live in peace within secure and recognized boundaries free from threats or acts of force.

Although this formula provided clear guidelines for terms of trade or exchange of concessions, it left open the difficult question of how much security was worth how much territorial withdrawal.

A way of attenuating the question, and actually maximizing the amount of security per territorial concession, was incorporated in the next modification of the formula, which might be·called "boundary-in-depth toward settlement." It is not clear where the idea originated. The concept of a five-zoned boundary is said to have come from Dayan in January at the negotiations (Sheehan 1976, p. 32), but the first application of the idea came from Egyptian General Gamasy at the Kilometer 101 talks, and the idea was mentioned in the Sisco-Sadat conversations of May 1971. (Gamasy's first proposal provided for withdrawal in stages, and only his second proposal included the zoned boundary or boundary-in-depth [Golan 1976, p. 101].) Both ideas, which later came to be combined, were clear alternatives to the static and unsuccessful formula of the 1967 war, which was simply a cease-fire in place (Golan 1976, p. 149).

In contrast to the 1967 formula, the 1974 formula was going somewhere. (See also Quandt [1977] and Aronson [1978], pp. 110–29, on the formula of the Rogers interlude.) It was an answer to the intolerable stalemate of military forces, and it moved toward a final settlement of the Sinai issue. The formula's dynamic character was self-reinforcing. By incorporating the idea of movement (toward settlement), the temporary withdrawal line itself was intolerable and called for the next round. It therefore led to the second Sinai disengagement and beyond, through a series of steps.

In the Syrian salient the formula was the same (boundary-in-depth toward settlement), and was based on a slight improvement of the 1967 line. However, it resulted from the Egyptian precedent, not from any mutual intolerability of the military situation. To the Syrians the situation was indeed intolerable, both militarily and diplomatically; but the Israelis, who would have been quite content to hold onto their territory, were under no internal pressure to move. The pressure came from outside, from Kissinger and from the fact that movement and eventual peace in the Sinai depended on some movement in the Golan. The problem in the Golan was that the territorial withdrawal was not mutual, and the application of the formula therefore involved much harder bargaining between the two parties. Kissinger is criticized for making the process more difficult by not revealing all the concessions Israel was willing to make at the outset (Quandt 1976, p. 241). However, he was right to do so, in light of the actual negotiations, for Syria merely took what was offered and asked for more.

In the second Sinai disengagement, the dynamic element took over completely. The new boundary-in-depth was justified, not only by the disengagement that had been accomplished in the first agreement, but by movement toward settlement on or about the pre-1967 boundaries. Although there was general agreement that the new boundary-in-depth would be located in the Mitla and Giddi passes, there was no agreement on its precise location. Some way had to be found whereby each side could claim that it had forced the other to surrender the passes without admitting that it had given up the passes itself.

The challenge of such logical impossibilities is the stuff of which formulas are made. By allowing the parties to bring their troops up to each side of the bottom of the passes, while implanting the United Nations buffer zone on the top of each pass—in other words by enlarging the notion of "pass" to the point where it could be divided and distributed—Kissinger provided a further ramification of "security for territory." Then he pointed out to the parties that, beyond symbolic concerns, their interest was not in territorial possession per se but in the security that it provided through early warning and physical defense. On this basis it became possible to assemble a combination of U.S., United Nations, Israeli, and Egyptian installations that would provide security in exchange for Israeli withdrawal from the territory, without giving it to Egypt.

The disengagement negotiations therefore took place under the umbrella of an established but broad formula. Kissinger's useful role consisted of repeatedly finding, or helping the parties to find, narrower applications of the formula that were true to its original meaning and that resolved the issue at hand. It is not altogether clear from the scattered record whether this process was intuitive or explicit. It is known that Kissinger repeatedly went to his staff and discussed or demanded new ideas relevant to the negotiations in process. While his was not a style of relaxed brainstorming, the process of continually looking for new ways of assembling the puzzle to form a picture is typical of the ad hoc methods generally required to find and refine a formula. Sheehan (1976) recognizes boundary-in-depth as not merely a bit of technical artifice, but rather "the conceptual foundation of the accord that was soon to follow" (p. 32). He also "quotes" Kissinger as indicating to the Israelis that their detailed demands had to fall within the formula in order to maintain the justifying coherence of the negotiations.

Kissinger: An agreement would have enabled the United States to remain in control of the diplomatic process. Compared to that, the location of the line eight kilometers one way or the other frankly does not seem very important. And you got all the military elements of nonbelligerency. You got the "non-use of force." The elements you didn't get—movement of peoples, ending of the boycott—are *unrelated* to your line. What you didn't get has nothing to do with where your line is . . . (p. 52).

One of the many ideas expressed in this statement to Yigal Allon was that details and demands had to fit under the terms of trade defined by "security for territory" (that territory had to have security value to be haggled over), and other considerations such as normalcy were outside the formula. These terms of trade were referred to in an earlier exchange:

> *Meir:* What you call disengagement is really just withdrawal of Israeli forces, and there is nothing reciprocal about that.

> *Kissinger:* [Sadat] will restore the civilian population to the Canal Zone—a guarantee against hostilities (Sheehan 1976, p. 30).

That still other matters remained outside that formula will be seen below.

THE USE OF POWER

Social scientists are still looking for an operational definition of power, while all the while working under its paradigm. For the present analysis, power may be categorized into force (which leaves no choice or alternative), persuasion (which leaves alternatives that are open to some conjecture), and, in between, coercion (which tries to remove doubt about alternatives through the demonstrative use of force). Power through persuasion and some forms of coercion involves the use of contingent deprivation and gratification. These contingencies can be further subdivided into those that are volitional (depending for their credibility on the party's willingness and ability to deliver) and those that are nonvolitional (depending for their credibility on the reliability of some outside agent).

Volitional deprivations and gratifications have come to be known as threats and promises; nonvolitional ones are termed warnings and predictions. Nonvolitional contingencies are cheaper to deliver in general, since they do not involve outlay by the persuader. They are also "nicer" and arouse less hostility or gratitude (which frequently ends up as a source of annoyance anyway) since, by definition, they operate independently of the persuader's will. Contingent deprivations, whether volitional or nonvolitional, are more expensive if the other party is expected not to comply, since they only come into play in the event of noncompliance. Contingent gratifications, while more agreeable, are more expensive if the party is expected to comply.

Kissinger operated within the realm of persuasion, with a few exceptions that will be discussed below. This was natural so long as he was not a direct participant in the conflict but only a mediator; but by the end he had become a participant in the outcome as well as in the process of resolving the conflict. Kissinger also specialized in the use of deprivations, which he wielded with great skill and credibility by building, and building upon, his reputation at the same time. Given a choice between the two forms of deprivation, Kissinger's Spenglerian weltanschauung was ideally suited for warnings about the dire consequences of failure to follow his counsel. Such consequences appear more dire for Israel in the telling, since it is only on the basis of Kissinger's parlor talks with the Israeli cabinet that records have emerged. Although the other side of warning is prediction, the accounts (for whatever reason) generally describe Kissinger painting pictures for his hosts with a dark brush rather than a light one. "I'm not angry at you and I'm not asking you to change your position," Kissinger is said to have told the Israelis as the second Sinai disengagement talks broke down. "It's tragic to see people dooming themselves to a course of unbelievable peril." To which Rabin retorted, catching the mood, "This is the day you visited Masada" (Sheehan 1976, p. 52). Although this was one of the mediation's darker moments, Golan's (1976) account indicates that the tone was not limited to such times alone.

To the warnings were added Kissinger's personal type of threat: leaving. The credibility of this threat was reinforced by its actual implementation from time to time. Again, what is at issue here is more than just a technicality, a ploy, or a personality. One of the most crucial procedural elements of successful negotiation is the use of deadlines. The existence of a deadline is crucial to the success of negotiations. If there is no point at which things suddenly get worse in the absence of an agreement, negotiations tend to drag on interminably since there is no time by which the parties must agree. A deadline is merely a jointly set or commonly recognized ultimatum. Its joint setting presupposes the presence of more common interest and cooperation among the parties than is usual in negotiation, or than is required for common recognition of an involuntary contingency. In the case of mediated negotiations, one of the mediator's crucial tasks is to impose a deadline—although the very term "impose" should alert one to the considerable skill required. The other element of skill required is the ability to perceive the most propitious moment for the deadline: too late, and it prolongs negotiations and invites breakdown; too early, and it invites formal, superficial agreements and mistrust of the mediator.

For Kissinger, the threat of leaving was a most natural exercise. It was credible since, as Secretary of State, he understandably had to return to tend the store. It also reinforced a sense of trust and usefulness in the secretary's mission, since with him gone the negotiations would not continue on their own. Kissinger exercised the threat of leaving in an almost perfect progression. First it was waved about to both sides during the Syrian negotiations, then it was actually implemented, and finally it was recalled under Assad's insistence just before the end of the negotiations. During the second Sinai disengagement talks, leaving was first threatened, then it was tested for credibility, and once Kissinger showed that the threat was no bluff, it was again tested for effect—this time coupled with a further threat to reevaluate policy in Washington.

Finally, when threats, warnings, and predictions began to wear thin, the final element of persuasion was brought into play: promises. With it the United States became a full partner to the negotiations, as the other two parties bargained their signature against the size of U.S. promises. They got a lot. Money, arms, security guarantees, physical presence, and diplomatic veto were promised and given up by the United States, leading many to wonder what the price of the next round would be.

Commentators on Kissinger's diplomacy have delighted in the topic of power, dwelling on the arrogance of threats, the dismalness of warnings, occasionally on the self-serving quality of Kissinger's predictions and, less frequently, on the cost overrides of promises. Outside of Congress, the last has received little attention and deserves special discussion below. As for the others, it should be remembered that these were the only means that Kissinger the mediator had to shape the perceptions of hitherto unreconcilable parties. This is the core of the diplomatic exercise, the element that differentiates diplomacy from force, a subject about which very little is known analytically or humanly appreciated.

BUILDING TRUST

Negotiation necessarily requires a change in mentality. The parties must shift from a winning or zero-sum outlook to one that is composing or positive-sum. Without this change, negotiations are unlikely to begin at all and, even in those exceptional cases where they begin anyway for other reasons, the negotiations have a negligible chance of ending in agreement. Finally, even if such negotiations do end in agreement, that agreement will hold only if it has succeeded in changing the parties' mentality.

Given the categorical quality of the preceding assertions, they must be carefully qualified. Even though change in mentality is necessary, it is unlikely to be total; if it approaches totality it is likely to turn sour in disappointment. Too much has been written suggesting that negotiation is the path of peace and the end of conflict, requiring an end to enmity and therefore precluding any further dispute. Such woolly nonsense is a disservice to the very process it seeks to support. Negotiation is both nonviolent conflict and conflict resolution, based on persuasion instead of force, in which neither party dares to let down its guard, forget its interests, or fully trust its adversary.

Taken together, the preceding categorical judgments call both for partial trust and for a willingness to lose something in order to gain—that is, a conviction that it will be safe to lose something and that the something gained will be as real as the loss. Trust and other such convictions were absent in the Middle East before the 1973 war. Not only had the parties withheld recognition of the other's legitimacy and existence by refusing to negotiate directly, but also they were sure that any truce would be a trick. The parties were convinced that territory was necessary precisely because there was no security, and that each was right to think so because the other side thought so too. In this situation, an agreement was not enough; it had to be of such a nature as to build trust at the same time.

Trust is built on a paradox. It grows out of situations in which deception is possible but not practiced. (If bluff and deceit are impossible, then trust is impossible and unnecessary, since the given word cannot be broken.) The Arab states had to be given an opportunity to see that they could talk to the Israelis, and be given a word that could be broken but would be held. The Israelis, in turn, required an occasion to see that they could give up territory without the Arabs using their new forward positions to renew the attack. The formula that Kissinger pursued eased the problem of trust by creating a boundary in depth, so that each party did not have to give up quite so much in order to make its gains. The strains on trust were greater as the boundary moved toward Israel, and implementation of the formula therefore required additional measures such as American presence. The very step-by-step nature of the disengagement was a dynamic and living demonstration that Arabs could talk with Israelis and achieve results, while the Israelis could move back toward the 1967 boundaries without losing their security. Step-by-step was thus the beginning of increasing trust although never, it must be remembered, of total trust—and rightly so.

The step-by-step approach came out of Moshe Dayan's Defense Ministry in October 1970 (Aronson 1978, pp. 139ff.), and was in Sadat's mind when he came to power, as he indicated in an interview at the end of 1970 (*New York Times*, December 18, 1970). Whatever its source, like most significant ideas, step-by-step is impressively simple. It is the idea of eating bit by bit what cannot be swallowed all at once, and it is the idea of building both mutual concessions and mutual trust upon the previous partial agreement. The step-by-step approach is an ongoing learning process under tutelage by means of which the parties can learn to rectify the stereotypes that each has of the other. As Kissinger told the Twenty-ninth General Assembly session:

Each step forward modifies old perceptions and brings about a new situation that improves the chances of a comprehensive settlement. . . . They [agreements] were achieved because of the wisdom of the leaders of the Middle East who decided that there had been enough stalemate and war, that more might be gained by testing each other in negotiation than by testing each other on the battlefield (UNGA/PV2238.31, Sept. 23, 1974).

One element in the logic of this argument may raise questions. Although it has been suggested that direct negotiations raise trust, these negotiations were in fact not direct. Not only was Kissinger present as the go-between, but it also seems clear that he called off earlier direct negotiations that began to grow out of the Kilometer 101 talks precisely in order to preserve his intermediation. For this he has been accused of ego-tripping and megalomania, accusations that are doubtless true but may be irrelevant. Since social science cannot experiment with history, we cannot learn whether the outcome would have been the same, or better, with Kissinger as without him. We can only argue logically about whether his action was reasonable or not. Kissinger believed that his mediation, for many of the reasons analyzed in this chapter, was essential for the step-by-step process of disengagement and ultimate peace in the Middle East. Whether his approach was the only one that would have worked or not is a matter for evaluation at the end of this chapter. Given Kissinger's approach, however, there is no evidence that it could have been accomplished without mediation, and there is ample indication that it was not accomplished before him.

Mediation requires trust in the mediator, not only belief in his integrity but also the confidence that the mediator will act as the trustee of each party in relations with the other. Trust grew, and indeed has grown, remarkably fast in the Middle East. Kissinger, by dint of his personality and his effectiveness, was soon trusted by both Prime Minister Meir and President Sadat. He felt more confident that their trust was in good hands when it was in his own than when it was left to the parties themselves. One can argue that Kissinger may have been wrong, but not very convincingly and with no evidence. The fact that the two parties agreed enough with Kissinger's estimate of the situation not to take the matter of trust into their own hands is sufficient evidence that his estimate of the situation was correct.

Sadat has written:

No one else except the United States can play this role, namely that of mediator between two sides that harbor intense hate for one another—a gulf of blood, violence and massacres. The United States did not impose the first disengagement agreement: She intervened to achieve a breakthrough and overcame the apparent impasse. The

heading of the first disengagement document reads: American Proposal (Sadat 1977, p. 293).

The Israelis, in turn, were reportedly "convinced that Kissinger played
straight with them and fairly represented their views to the other side"
(*New York Times*, Jan. 18, 1974). Finally, it was Assad who sent Kissinger
back to Jerusalem, just one more time, as talks were about to break off—
two days before a final agreement was reached. Clearly, the parties
trusted the mediator before they came to trust each other.

KNOWING WHEN TO LEAVE

Kissinger was not known for retiring gracefully from the scene,
particularly a scene in which he was at the height of his success.
Nevertheless, the crucial decision was made by the U.S. public in the 1976
elections. Although the secretary left under a cloud, in the context of a
fickle electorate that was properly instructed by a cavilling press, and
although Kissinger was partly responsible for the outcome of those
elections, he got out just in time. The step-by-step process had not run
down, as has been claimed; rather, it had led full circle to a new
stalemate, one that could now only be broken by the parties themselves.
The new impasse lasted an appropriate time, as the complicated arrangements for a Geneva Conference showed how fruitless such a meeting
would be. Once the depth of the stalemate had made its impression, the
moment was ripe for Sadat's dramatic journey to Jerusalem. Just as there
could have been no Kissinger mediation without Sadat's stalemate in 1973,
so there would have been no Sadat initiative in 1977 without Kissinger's
stalemate.

The emergence of a new stalemate did not mean that things went
back to the starting point again, except in a procedural sense. The
stalemate on the Egyptian front, after the second Sinai disengagement,
was far improved from both parties' point of view, and was inscribed in a
dynamic process that clearly indicated the next step to go. As in many
negotiations, the problem was not one of determining the outcome but of
deciding how to get there. Although the Camp David negotiations that
followed in fall 1978 have sometimes been described as qualitatively
different from Kissinger's mediated step-by-step process, the difference
was at most one of degree, not of kind. To describe President Carter's
mediation at Camp David, and in the Middle East in 1979, as an extension
of Secretary Kissinger's tactic is not to diminish either man's skill and
individuality by any means. The step-by-step process was represented at
Camp David, not as discrete items to be renewed each time through
separate negotiation, but prearranged in one negotiation session as a series
of withdrawals that would continue the security-for-territory exchange

formula under an accelerated dynamic of trust and movement. The final indication of the value of Kissinger's mediation was that it paved the way for the final settlement and withdrawal on the Sinai front and the Israeli-Egyptian peace treaty.

The subject of this book is the 1973–75 disengagement negotiations, but this chapter has moved beyond that subject by making its evaluation dependent in part on a judgment of the subsequent Jerusalem and Camp David process. Although this is not the place to launch into a full-scale evaluation of these more recent events, a few comments are required.

It is astounding to listen to critical claims that the Sadat-Begin peace effort is misguided. For one thing, evident progress has been made in resolving conflict; for another, no suggestion has ever been made of a better alternative. Progress has been made much as the disengagement talks made their own contribution to peace: by resolving some conflicts and creating others. To claim otherwise is to believe the old myth that "peace is indivisible" (a slogan that was in use in World War II when the surrender of Italy and then the surrender of Germany were accepted before the final Axis surrender on V-J Day). If peace is indeed indivisible, then there is no progress toward a goal, only total conflict followed by sudden attainment of peace (if at all), an analytically untenable position.

Nor have the critics of the various Sadat rounds ever proposed a realistic alternative. A global (Geneva-type) solution is unprecedented in history, and the Arab states were evidently not ready to attend a peace conference in order to negotiate a final settlement. No Rejectionist Front spokesman, moderate Arab statesman, or Western diplomatic analyst has ever suggested how such a global settlement could actually have emerged from such a conference. The critics of step-by-step disengagement have not only failed to provide an alternative but, more central to this analysis, they have ignored the fact that the process elements present in the disengagement talks were totally absent in the global context. There was no chance to build trust; there was no room for mediation; a settlement of this magnitude would have required a deadline so distant as to be procedurally inoperative; the elements of power were inadequate for the outcome; and a formula for a global settlement was absent, a point to be discussed below. This analysis holds that the elements of process that characterized the disengagement negotiations were necessary for its outcome, and that Kissinger's mediation was successful because it exemplified the component concepts of negotiation.

A CRITICISM OF STEP-BY-STEP NEGOTIATION

If negotiation concepts help evaluate Kissinger's performance as a mediator by showing his strengths, they also bring out several weaknesses. As is often the case, the weaknesses apparent in the Mideast case stemmed from limitations inherent in the very conceptual elements of strength. It is a common characteristic of human behavior that the very elements permitting progress in an intended direction also prevent it from going further; this is because both the nature of the direction changes and some elements, like most tools, grow dull in use. Weaknesses occurred in connection with power, formula, mediation, and the dynamic of the process itself.

The criticism that the price paid for the second Sinai disengagement was too high is correct by almost any account. Only in the long run might the price be justified, in that $5 billion was not much to keep the process going. On a relative scale, however, compared either to the cost of the preceding agreements on Sinai or Golan, or to the presumed cost of a third round of withdrawals based on the incremental rate of the second Sinai agreement, the cost was out of proportion. To note this fact is not to suggest an alternative. The cost came about because Kissinger ran through his threats, warnings, and predictions, and was left only with promises, by their nature the most costly means of persuasion in the event of compliance. Furthermore, unlike the other three means of persuasion, promises constitute an ongoing commitment and cost to the relationship between promisor and promisee.

The United States brought Israeli acquiescence by saying: Agreement with Egypt is in your interest and we will make it so. However, the interest provided was no longer in the agreement per se, but in the aid for which agreement was a condition. The means of power that the United States intended for leverage became partly an end in itself for the Israelis. "We gave up a little for a lot," a senior Israeli official told *Time* magazine about the second Sinai disengagement, referring not to Egyptian concessions but to the "sweeteners" proffered by the United States (Sheehan 1976, p. 64).

The financial cost of the second Sinai agreement is the problem most often cited, but there were other problems as well. At least two political promises were given to Israel during the Golan and second Sinai negotiations that were to hamstring U.S. policy in the Middle East throughout the rest of the decade. One was the U.S. carte blanche permitting Israel to retaliate for Palestinian attacks across the cease-fire line; this move may well have had some bearing on the south Lebanon problem. The other was a promise to accept both an Israeli veto of U.S. contacts with the PLO as well as other measures of close policy coordination. Apparently such concessions by the mediator were the price of these disengagement agreements. Unfortunately, they left unaddressed the basic problem in any negotiation of the concession that is necessary for an otherwise attractive agreement, but that is itself unacceptable. As the disengagement steps continued, the mediator got the recalcitrant parties together, but he sold parts of his skin to do it.

No one can say whether Kissinger's concessions were unavoidable, or whether their cost outweighed the value of the agreements. One conclusion is clear, however: the means of persuasion should not become the ends of negotiation. In a series of negotiations that are above all part of a dynamic process, it is not sufficient for the component outcomes to move toward the final goal; the process itself, including the exercise of power within it, should focus on that goal as well.

Criticism has also been leveled on the grounds that the disengagement talks were flawed because they did nothing for the Palestinians. The reason for this, within the process itself, has never been clearly identified. Apart from the two Sinai disengagements and the one in the Golan Heights, there was an additional round of talks. After Golan, movement began toward a disengagement on the West Bank, but it quickly fell through. The apparent reason is that the Rabat Summit of the Arab League occurred first and blocked movement by handing West Bank responsibility to the PLO, with whom there could be no disengagement.

It is not clear whether Jordan was originally planned for inclusion in the negotiations as part of a general settlement conference that would follow Egyptian and Syrian disengagement agreements (Sheehan 1976, p. 45), or whether a West Bank disengagement was to be negotiated as one of the steps after Sinai and Golan. In any event, the West Bank was to ride on momentum, not on stalemate. Jordan proposed a six-mile disengagement from the Jordan River in January 1974, similar to the first Sinai agreement. Israel rejected this and answered with an entirely different concept in late spring: a final settlement proposal (not a first step) for a wiggly border running through the West Bank territory. According to this proposal, Israel was to get the security and the valuable territory. In July the United States proposed a symbolic disengagement around Jericho that would establish Jordanian title and fit the Allon plan at the same time, and also suggested balloons of territory that could be linked to Jordan by some means. But the new and unsteady government of Rabin rejected any West Bank disengagement on July 21, 1974, and King Hussein was uninterested in anything else than withdrawal along the Jordan. The United States simply did not lean on them heavily enough (Aronson 1978, pp. 250 ff., 423; Reich 1977, pp. 299, 329; interviews).

After the Golan agreement had been reached and the generally expected midsummer moment for attention to the West Bank had passed, the debate shifted referents and began to focus on the question of who should speak for the West Bank. Egypt tried to reinforce the Jordanian hand in July, and Washington gave its approval in August when King Hussein came to visit a newly installed President Ford. But Egypt had its relations with the PLO to worry about, and the United States had no way to make good on its intentions toward Jordan. Therefore when the Arab states met in October, Jordan's inability to show some progress in proposals for disengagement weakened its claim as spokesman for the Palestinians, and the PLO was endorsed instead.

The deeper reason in terms of the negotiation process is that the disengagement formula simply did not apply to the West Bank. "Security for territory" was applicable to a Jordanian West Bank if the Palestinian problem was to be considered a refugee question, as Resolution 242 indicated. But once the West Bank became the Palestinian problem, the very release of territory to Palestinians (in whatever form) meant insecurity in Israeli eyes. This brings out the difference between the two pairs of opening positions on the Golan and West Bank fronts. In both cases, one party offered a final settlement proposal (Syria and Israel, respectively) and the other a disengagement proposal (Israel and Jordan, respectively). But in the Golan, the elements of the bargaining concerned the line and the security arrangements around it, whereas in the West Bank, any line and its security arrangements would have still begged the question of the Palestinians. This does not mean that the question is insoluble, only that it is insoluble within the formula of Resolution 242, disengagement, and Camp David. Such apparent irreconcilability is the stuff of which formulas are made, but the appropriate formula has yet to be found. In regard to formula as to other concepts, the element that allowed the success of the Sinai and Golan disengagement talks also prevented their success on the West Bank.

Kissinger did propose another formula in his first discussions with the parties in January 1974 when he carried an Israeli notion of "administrative disengagement," whereby King Hussein would "assume gradual administrative responsibility on the West Bank without immediate Israeli withdrawal" (Quandt 1977, p. 230). The formula was something like "title in exchange for temporary use," and Hussein was uninterested. In the last analysis it may be that the moment for a West Bank formula had not yet come in the mid-1970s, nor for that matter by the end of the decade. There are many conceivable "solutions" to the Palestinian question, ranging from statehood to integration into one country or the other, and many conceivable ways of attaining it, from self-determination to mutual recognition. Any of these can contain the apparently irreconcilable elements and thus provide the basis for a negotiation formula; which is chosen, however, depends in part on good fortune and perceptions that have crystalized at the moment, and that in turn depends on a greater element of stalemate than has existed during the 1970s on the West Bank front. There is nothing yet intolerable to both sides about the situation, nor is there a "frozen crisis" of the sort provided by the mutual encirclement along the Suez Canal in 1973 whose resolution could start the process rolling toward a particular perception and the formula it contains.

The mediator himself can be cited to support this judgment, when he said, "I never treat crises when they're cold, only when they're hot.

This enables me to weigh the protagonists one against the other, not in terms of ten or two thousand years but in terms of what each of them merits at this moment" (Sheehan 1976, p. 5). This is not a hopeful view. While it refers to negotiation as a means of reflecting changes in power relations, the notion of "merit" also mirrors "might makes right," and the idea of heat precludes preventive diplomacy. It may be, as Sheehan notes, that "Kissinger avoided the essence—viz., the Palestine problem— and clung to the periphery" (p. 34). But this is to underestimate the Sinai and Golan problems in hindsight. It would be more useful to conclude that Kissinger misjudged—or was forced by the event of Nixon's resignation to neglect—the importance of momentum as a source of "heat." Thus, although it would have been different and more difficult than in the other disengagement mediations, the chance was there to start West Bank negotiations in the summer of 1974. This chance was lost. Privately, Kissinger is said to have admitted afterward that it was his biggest mistake.

Critics have also pointed to the mediation itself as a weakness, a habit-forming crutch that invalidated the reconciliation it was designed to obtain. The point has already been discussed, and the conclusion is similar to that regarding the means of persuasion. Mediation was key to the success of the disengagement talks; and as a key ingredient the mediator became an end to be preserved. The weakness of mediation was not so much in evidence where it has usually been identified, at the end of the Kilometer 101 talks; rather, it appeared as the process moved on. Mediation became more and more necessary as the talks moved away from the initial stalemate and toward the final goal, and the well-known phenomenon of approach-avoidance began to set in. Ideally, however, the mediation would have been self-eliminating, becoming less and less necessary as the talks between the interested parties proceeded on their own momentum. Indeed, this is what happened when Sadat took matters into his own hands and went to Jerusalem, and in that sense the criticism is unfounded. Unfortunately, both before and after this move, mediation was still required. The parties had learned to walk with a crutch, rather than without one.

CONCLUDING COMMENT: THE RELATIONSHIP BETWEEN PROCESS AND GOALS

The weaknesses indicated thus far have appeared as the obverse of the strengths, inherent and inseparable from the conceptual components that made the Kissinger mediation an example of effective negotiation. There is at least one other area, however, in which Kissinger's approach raises new questions of both analytical and practical interest. The question is one of the relationship between process and goals.

To all appearances, Kissinger was all process. He indicated neither a goal toward which he was aiming nor one that he thought likely. On earlier occasions regarding other negotiations, he expressed the view that the process was the determinant of the outcome. On May 2, 1974, in response to questions from Rabin and Eban, he said, "I can't predict how it will all come out. What's important is the process itself—to keep negotiations going, to prevent them from freezing" (Sheehan 1976, p. 43). Again, on December 15, 1974, he is reported by Sheehan to have said to Assad: "We have no peace plan of our own. It's easy to make specific proposals—the important thing is to take practical steps" (p. 27).

It is of course quite possible that he had a firm goal in mind and felt it tactically unwise to tell the participants about it. But there is no evidence of this, and accounts by collaborators such as Quandt indicate no such goal. In fact, a comment on Kissinger's character by his former colleague, Stanley Hoffmann, contrasts the goal-oriented role of the "conceptualist" with the process-oriented role of the "negotiator." While noting that Kissinger was "equally gifted in either direction," Hoffmann implies that as a practitioner Kissinger chose the latter, leaving the goal to a residual category. Theory, experimentation, and common sense suggest that statesmen must do precisely the opposite.

Cross's concession rate theory (1969; 1978) and Bartos's (1978) more elegant theory of negotiation based on Cross, indicate that the negotiation process is best understood by conceiving of parties as moving toward a point of which they are each aware. Moreover, the dynamics of the process are to be found not only in the parties' movement but also in the manipulations they effect on each other's concept of that point of convergence. The classic article by Leites and Iklé (1962) also adopts this position, although it considers two sets of points, one held by each party. Zartman's (1978) scenario interviews with United Nations diplomats strongly indicate that practitioners constantly look to a probable outcome, and reject the process entirely if this outcome is out of range. Common sense, a good but not infallible guide, also supports this view: parties are expected to look where they are going and to ask themselves if they really want to get there; statesmen are also expected to know what they are after. Is negotiation like baseball, a matter of how you play the game rather than whether you win or lose? Is it like dancing, where doing it well is all that matters? Or is it like duelling, where the outcome alone is crucial? Has social science, in its recent emphasis on the study of negotiation as a process, compared with earlier historical analysis of negotiation outcomes, led its practitioners wisely or led them astray? We know by now that analytical answers are usually not votes between alternatives, and that it is sound judgment to suggest that process and outcome are both important.

Kissinger had a goal during the disengagement negotiations but it was procedural, not substantive: maintaining momentum. Inherent in this goal was a substantive core, since the momentum was moving toward agreement on the pre-1967 boundaries. The absence of a goal, however, was crucial in the West Bank discussions. More accurately, different goals were inherent in different types of discussions with different parties. Only with a clear notion of a goal could the U.S. mediator have tackled the West Bank and at least gotten the process started.

The United States has seemed to indicate that it does not want a Palestinian state, and that it wants a solution to the Palestinian problem in Jordanian terms. It does not appear to have the means to such an end, however, nor does it appear to have made much of an effort to secure this outcome. One might argue that Kissinger had a goal of a Jordanian solution, but finding that the procedure would inherently lead to another outcome, he decided not to start the process moving. Discretion may be the better part of valor, but it provides neither the evidence on which to evalutate process nor the outcomes by which to measure success. It is important to learn from the success of Kissinger's mediation process, too, by applying the lessons to goals that are judged important. Autonomy is not a formula for the Palestinian problem: it is a procedural artifice for finding a formula. A formula is needed rapidly. Otherwise we may find ourselves dancing when the game is duelling.

REFERENCES

Aronson, S. *Conflict and Bargaining in the Middle East.* Baltimore: Johns Hopkins University Press, 1978.

Bartos, O. J. "Simple Model of Negotiation." In I. W. Zartman, ed., *The Negotiation Process.* Beverly Hills, Calif.: Sage, 1978.

Cross, J. G. *The Economics of Bargaining.* New York: Basic Books, 1969.

———. "Negotiation as a Learning Process." In I. W. Zartman, ed., *The Negotiation Process.* Beverly Hills, Calif.: Sage, 1978.

Golan, M. *The Secret Conversations of Henry Kissinger.* New York: Quadrangle, 1976.

Leites, N., and Iklé, F. "Political Negotiation as a Process of Modifying Utilities." *Journal of Conflict Resolution,* 1962, 6, 19–28.

Quandt, W. B. *Decade of Decisions: American Policy toward the Arab-Israeli Conflict, 1967–1976.* Berkeley, Calif.: University of California Press, 1977.

Reich, B. *Quest for Peace.* New Brunswick, N.J.: Transaction, 1977.

Sadat, A. *In Search of Identity.* New York: Harper and Row, 1977.

Sheehan, E. R. F. "How Kissinger Did It: Step by Step in the Middle East." *Foreign Policy,* 1976, 22, 3–70.

Zartman, I. W. "Negotiation as a Joint Decision-Making Process." In I. W. Zartman, ed., *The Negotiation Process.* Beverly Hills, Calif.: Sage, 1978.

PART III

CONTEXTUAL ANALYSES OF KISSINGER'S INTERVENTION

7

THE PERSPECTIVE OF GREAT POWER FOREIGN POLICY: STEPS IN CONTEXT

Davis B. Bobrow

Some months ago, late at night in a bus jouncing away from a gathering of Jews and Arabs in Israel, I was foolhardy enough to accept an invitation from the editor of this volume. I was invited to apply the perspective of a student of great power foreign policy and U.S. foreign policy decision making to Kissinger's activities, drawing on whatever theory international relations had to offer about third party interventions for conflict abatement and resolution. My exploration would involve no special expertise about the combatants or inside knowledge of Kissinger's operations. It would be informed primarily by the accounts of Kalb and Kalb (1974), Quandt (1977), Sheehan (1976), and Golan (1976). And I thought it was hard to see clearly in the bus!

In order to evaluate Kissinger's performance, one must stipulate his goals in some fashion as well as the information that formed the basis of his tactical choices. Conclusions about the difference that his actions did make, or could have made, necessarily involve some judgments about the goals, information, and tactics of other pertinent parties. With respect to the alternatives that one might advance about how he should have acted, it seems only fair to recognize that the boundaries of time, geography, issues, and participation operating at the time for Kissinger and the other participants need not be the same as those selected by analysts in their post-hoc accounts.

Complete, trustworthy information does not exist for many of the matters just mentioned. Even if it did, one should not assume neat hierarchies of utilities, systematic information processing, or deliberate collegial policy choice. Instead, high level foreign policy officials usually have numerous goals and values, whose importance and immediate urgency fluctuate according to unplanned events and idiosyncratic experiences. Their information is incomplete. Their exposure to available information may well be arbitrary or accidental, and may arise in reaction to events rather than in anticipation of theory. The process of final policy choice is a highly private one with varying degrees of ritual collegiality. Finally, we must recognize that choices once made may well be masked and changed before the mask is raised, if it ever is.

Obviously, the major accounts of Kissinger's intervention are seriously incomplete for my purposes if one accepts the previous points. In particular, they are at best sketchy about the:

Relationship between the United States and the Soviet Union involving non-Middle Eastern matters;

Ongoing United States policy concerns with the major members of NATO, Japan, and China;

Dealings of U.S. institutions (public and private sector), other than Kissinger, with the regional participants (also the role of the Shah of Iran);

Post-cease-fire intelligence information available to Kissinger about the intentions of the regional parties, and their side discussions and communication with one another;

Information available to the regional parties about one another's policy strategy and bargaining with Kissinger; and

Erosion of Kissinger's status at home in the context of charges of authorizing dirty tricks, deceiving Congress, failing to achieve a viable South Vietnam, and naivete about the Soviets.

Although the major accounts are limited in scope, and understandably so, these were certainly not the limits of Kissinger's concern or of the other parties to United States-Middle Eastern relations during the period under examination.

Accordingly, any imputations to Kissinger are open to serious question, as is post-hoc conjecture about alternative possible courses of history. Nevertheless, some general points are reasonably compelling with regard to the Kissinger interventions.* These points will be presented in the next section of this chapter, while the general reasoning that underlies them will be deferred until later.

---

* This chapter was basically completed before the appearance of the first volume of Kissinger's memoirs (1979). That volume does not deal with the events pertinent to this chapter, but its treatment of the Soviets clearly supports the argument presented here.

KISSINGER: MANIPULATOR AND DEPENDENT

Kissinger's goals and means in the Middle East and his relationships with the regional participants did not originate with the October War. Step-by-step diplomacy was in part a continuation of earlier themes and in part an attempt to recover from the record of the days before and during the October War. From these beginnings, it started to take on a life of its own, and created stake for Kissinger that he did not initially have to defend.

Let us provide some of the context of Kissinger's entry into step-by-step diplomacy. The detente policy for U.S.-Soviet relations was in trouble. Congressional leaders close to American Jewry were tying the trade and technology transfer carrots Kissinger had promised the Soviet government to the relaxation of Soviet immigration restrictions on Jews, who might in turn mostly go to Israel. Kissinger had suggested that if American Jewry wanted him to cooperate with their preferred Middle Eastern policy, they might be well advised to cooperate with his Soviet policy. A new Secretary of Defense, James Schlesinger, had a most jaundiced view of the Soviets, and President Nixon was increasingly embroiled in domestic problems. With detente losing momentum and Kissinger serving as its major defender, Kissinger found himself tacitly misled, if not explicitly deceived, by the Soviets. Soviet leaders clearly had known in advance of the Arab attacks on Israel and had aided and abetted them. This inference seemed unavoidable given the withdrawal of the families of Soviet advisers in Egypt and Syria, increased Soviet intelligence activities pertinent to the theater of war, and the smooth and rapid Soviet resupply operation that had ships leaving Black Sea ports in time to unload at Syrian ports on October 11. In retrospect, reports of a Brezhnev-Sadat meeting in Bulgaria in the third week of September would probably have also seemed significant to Kissinger (Herzog 1975, p. 287).

Under a Kissinger policy of detente, the Soviets had supported exactly the sort of proxy aggression in third world areas that the opponents of detente had said they would. Linkage had failed, and Kissinger had been outmaneuvered. Even more dangerously, unless he could gain control of events, he faced three unattractive possibilities. First, the United States might find itself embroiled in a most dangerous military confrontation with the Soviet Union, with the prospect of direct war. Second, the United States might have to accept an outcome with politically unacceptable domestic consequences: a Soviet occupation force in the Middle East. Even if these two unwelcome alternatives could be avoided, the third possibility Kissinger faced was a Soviet demonstration to third world countries of its ability to provide the leverage necessary to defeat nations that were friendly to the United States, and to make the military pursuit of regional claims pay off. The Israelis were in a position to affect which of these several possibilities would dominate, and to make others feasible or not. For a host of reasons, the United States required a demonstration of strength.

Ideally, such course of action would dissuade the Russians, bolster support for Kissinger and the administration in the United States, show the Israelis that they were asking the United States to run unacceptable risks, and demonstrate to the regional opponents of Israel that the United States was a formidable party to any effective change in the region. While the worldwide U.S. strategic forces alert may have served some of these purposes, it also demonstrated to Kissinger, and presumably to many foreign observers, how weak the U.S. hand was in terms of public and congressional support for military intervention. Accordingly, some other instrument had to be found to affect the region.°

Relations with the major industrialized democracies were also in trouble. Tensions exacerbated by Nixon's foreign economic policy had not lessened, nor had the strains with Europe over the Vietnam War healed. European demands for greater foreign policy autonomy from the United States had not been blunted by Kissinger's proclaimed priority for rebuilding the Atlantic relationship (his "Year of Europe" speech). The leave-me-out-of-it position of most NATO allies toward the U.S. military resupply of Israel, and Kissinger's lack of consultation with them during the crisis, further strained relations.

And then there was, and is, the matter of oil. European and Japanese officials had long been aware of both their dependence on Middle Eastern oil and, compared to the United States, their greater vulnerability to supply interruptions and price hikes. Indeed, influential Europeans saw price hikes as working to the advantage of the United States in terms of international trade. Initially, then, Kissinger's Middle Eastern activities must be seen in the context of seriously strained relations with the United States' major allies, allies who played a central role in Kissinger's conception of the international system and the role in it of the United States.

Yet unlike the previous supply interruption (1955–56), the United States was unable or unwilling to provide substantial supplies of its own to Europe. Some way had to be found to lessen obstacles to oil supply that would show the Europeans and the Japanese that cooperation with the United States need not harm their economies. Again, some instrument other than military intervention had to be found.

If detente and the Western trilateral framework required serious

---

° For now, suffice it to note that Kissinger's Middle Eastern activities must be seen in the context of a seriously endangered set of policy relationships with the Soviet Union. Kissinger's most central policy emphases were failing. Let us also note that organized Jewry and Israel were sources of perturbation and trouble for Kissinger's Soviet policy.

repair, the relationship with China needed nurture. Nurture required a steady stream of evidence to the Chinese that the United States was not in global decline, that conventional military aggression by the Soviets and their associates would be defeated, and that the United States was able to pursue foreign policy initiatives. That is, it was necessary to demonstrate to the Chinese that they were not becoming involved with a paper tiger. At the same time, it was important to demonstrate that the United States was committed to making new friends internationally and was not rigidly committed to its former associates. Improved U.S. relations with Egypt would be good evidence of this new commitment. So too would be actions conducive to the satisfaction of Egyptian claims, which would simultaneously demonstrate that positive relations with the United States need not require the abandonment of progressive causes.

Step-by-step began then at a time when Kissinger's greatest accomplishments and the main pillars of an acceptable international order, as he conceived it, were in danger of crumbling. The threat of nuclear war was dangerously high; NATO was in disarray. To a great power foreign policy grand strategist such as Kissinger, Middle Eastern activities constituted moves in a much more important game. To say that step-by-step began in a situation where what happened in the Middle East was strongly tied to Kissinger's grand foreign policy rationale and arrangements does not imply that these provided the sole impetus for his actions. However, the obvious sensitivity of core U.S. foreign policy to developments in the Middle East, a sensitivity certified by the very attention that Kissinger came to pay to the region, was surely not lost on the regional parties.

Of course the Middle East was also of interest and importance in and of itself. In the months before the October War, the growing U.S. dependence on imported oil began to be recognized in policy circles, with its attendant implications for relations with the major exporters in general, and the Saudis and Iran in particular. Kissinger found himself opening up channels to Sadat, including a backchannel arrangement that cut out other U.S. officials and institutions, and to other Arab elites. He mused on the Middle East and on the need for Israel to receive a few blows from the Arabs before peace would come. Whether this reflected an intent to try to work out war avoidance measures in the region, to ameliorate the oil problem, or simply to pressure American Jews on detente is unclear. Whatever his intent, it is reasonable to assume that these developments were known to the Israelis. In spite of Kissinger's pre-October War recognition of the link between the Arab-Israeli conflict and oil, and in spite of Egyptian exploratory missions and signals earlier in 1973, he had not pursued Middle Eastern problems with any sense of urgency. Now he would have to do so. He would now also glimpse the opportunity to demonstrate to major governments in the region that the United States could deliver results that the Soviets could not.

Kissinger also had motives of a more personal and political nature. First, he had a rescue operation to perform on his own tarnished image as a manager of crises. After all, he had not attached sufficient importance to the Egyptian signals prior to the October War, he had urged the Israeli government to absorb a first strike, and he had at least tacitly accepted Israeli pursuit of the war to a point that induced the U.S. nuclear alert (Herzog 1975; Safran 1978). Unless something good could emerge in the aftermath of the war, Kissinger and the U.S. foreign policy apparatus in general would look in competent at best, and at worst malevolent and foolhardy. He had sufficient understanding of his enemies in the government to know that without some diversion, the subsequent leaks and postmortems would focus heavily on him.

Second, personal diplomacy conducted far away from Washington had the several virtues of diverting attention from other policy areas, from Kissinger's management of crisis avoidance and limitation, and from his involvement with the Nixon White House. Personal diplomacy also guaranteed media visibility.

Third, Kissinger was feeling pressure from President Nixon to divert attention from Watergate by pulling off a foreign policy miracle that would redound to Nixon's domestic advantage. In fact, Kissinger might well have been highly vulnerable to pressure from Nixon in two respects. His special clout with Nixon was Kissinger's major asset with the national security and foreign policy bureaucracy in Washington, a family of bureaucracies he had tended to treat with almost universal suspicion and often outright contempt. Without the backing of a strong Nixon, old grievances might well be redressed against him, including grievances by officials who had their own reasonably direct channels of communication to the regional parties. Kissinger's reputation as a statesman and as a man concerned with big issues may also have been captive to Nixon. Both Kissinger and Nixon had a penchant for having their conversations transcribed, and some of the contents could have been, and were, embarrassing indeed.

Political personalities who reach and hold prominent positions for a number of years tend to pay attention both to would-be competitors for their positions and to their own historical reputations. Here then is another aspect of Kissinger to join with that of the grand strategist. He needed to make himself central to the U.S. handling of the international aspect of its oil import problems, otherwise he would lose his central role in formulating foreign policy toward the Middle East, and thus foreign policy toward the OECD states as well. Such a turn of events would reduce his leverage upon the grand strategic designs mentioned earlier. Kissinger also needed to achieve a state of affairs in the Middle East that was less war prone than the atmosphere that prevailed before the war. This would divert attention from previous mistakes of the foreign policy system and of his own. It may well have seemed desirable to arrange matters in ways that would require extended personal travel from Washington with his own press corps in order to achieve widely publicized steps toward war avoidance and oil supply stabilization. Such diplomacy would help buy Nixon time and give Nixon a continued stake in Kissinger's prestige.

Great power foreign policy personalities, who are simultaneously grand strategists and politicians, have their own bargaining theories. Kissinger's thinking about bargaining has been discussed at length elsewhere (Dickson 1978; Brenner 1973; Walker 1977), so a few particularly relevant points will suffice here. Kissinger's bargaining theory held that small powers, historically associated with the United States, are most responsive to U.S. third party intervention when they are keenly afraid of regional threats and somewhat uncertain about American support. A Kissinger premise for step-by-step negotiations would thus have been the desirability of Israeli fear of the threat from their neighbors and anxiety about U.S. guarantees. The degree of anxiety should not be excessive of course; it should involve the view that U.S. guarantees were in some measure contingent on Israeli cooperation with Kissinger.

Another Kissinger bargaining premise called for emphasis on "linkage," whereby desired behavior in one issue area would have implications for behavior in another. From this point of view, linking United States policy toward Israel to Arab-American oil relations was not necessarily undesirable. Indeed, it would seem attractive to add still another issue: technology transfer to the Arab states. After all, of the industrialized oil importers, the United States had the most leverage on Israel and thus the most to gain from linkage. It would be important to show that linkage could cut two ways: it could induce the United States to restrain or to unleash Israeli military power. At the same time, it was possible that remorse about pressure on the Israelis to accept a first strike attack would impel Kissinger both to make a major commitment of personal energy to the amelioration of the conflict and to seek a sufficiently manifest improvement of the status quo ante to justify his earlier actions. If such improvement came to seem impossible in the absence of the war and his own personal diplomacy, so much the better. More generally, Kissinger may have felt genuine concern about the future viability of Israel unless he could somehow relieve the pressures for abandonment by the OECD nations stemming from the oil situation.

The set of concerns of grand policy, bureaucratic and personal politics, bargaining premises, and self-image all impelled Kissinger to work on the situation in the Middle East, and to do so in a particular way. In blunter terms, these concerns made him needy in ways that could not be satisfied without the cooperation of the regional parties. Accordingly, the regional parties began with substantial leverage, leverage that grew with Kissinger's conduct of step-by-step diplomacy and his growing vulnerability to the possibility that it would end in manifest failure. However, Kissinger's needs in no way required the achievement of a general peace, and might not even have been especially well met by such an outcome. Note also that all of the needs that have been mentioned here were readily observable by the pertinent governments in the Middle East and the Soviets.

In order to assess the consequences of Kissinger's third party intervention, it is necessary to have some grasp of the pressures to which he was subjected. A valid assessment also requires some comprehension of the needs and concerns of the other key participants, in this case the governments of the Soviet Union, Israel, Egypt, Saudi Arabia, and Syria—as well as their principal personalities. Third party intervention takes place at the frontier of interaction among such needs and concerns. Thus the outcomes of U.S. policy in the Middle East and of Kissinger's intervention were necessarily a function of what the other parties sought and could do, and not only of what Kissinger sought and did. Ideally, well-informed appraisal of these "significant others" should span grand policy considerations, domestic bureaucratic and political matters, bargaining theories, and personal feelings. Although the information available hardly allows for such treatment, a small number of significant points do stand out for each of the parties.

VIEW FROM THE SOVIET UNION

Soviet aims with regard to the October War and expectations concerning a U.S. response are not particularly clear. It may simply be that, for a host of international and domestic reasons, attempts to prevent the war would have been unacceptably costly to the highest leadership. The course of least resistance may therefore have been to tolerate the staging of the October War, and even to seem helpful in important ways, while striving to insure that the Arab states would freeze hostilities before the Soviets had to make unattractive commitments. Brezhnev's detente policy may well have been under substantial attack because of both the lack of delivery of the U.S. credits and technology that were central to its rationale, as well as the rapprochement between the United States and China. The U.S. buildup of Iran as a regional guarantor against Soviet proxies and radicals may have seemed to require a response. In addition, the Soviets, who were then generally perceived as energy rich, were aware of the vulnerability of major NATO members and Japan to disruption of their oil imports. Finally, Kass (1978) provides substantial evidence that important factions in the Soviet elite were committed to a general pursuit of aggrandizement and projection of force in the Middle East. These same factions were committed to the Arab front-line states as a theater for demonstrating the prowess of conventional Soviet military technology and assistance (Soviet arms as superior to American arms).

These considerations may explain prewar Soviet behavior. They are compatible with Soviet activity in the early days of the October War, including the attempt to halt the war immediately after the initial Arab successes. They fit with the Soviet position that it was politically unacceptable to have the war end with a humiliating defeat of principal Arab belligerents. The United States' strategic alert was probably a more frightening and serious reaction than the Soviet leadership anticipated or wanted. With defeat avoided, the Soviets had made a show of strength, underlined their value to their allies, and exposed the energy vulnerability of the industrialized capitalist states.

In the aftermath of the October War, the primary Soviet concern was probably the rescue of detente, an arrangement in which Brezhnev had invested so much of his personal prestige, which would also mean the rescue of Kissinger and, it was hoped, Nixon. Other groupings in the Soviet elite had never been enthusiastic about major military or economic investments in "bourgeois," if not downright "feudal," Middle Eastern regimes. Modest setbacks, attributable to the structure of those regimes rather than to U.S. military prowess, were not in themselves necessarily unwelcome. Such setbacks were certainly not a prohibitive price to pay to rescue detente, to step back from a situation that might get out of control, and to curb the resources allocated to conventional military bureaucracies for dispersal to proxies. Obviously, the price would be more palatable if the United States and Kissinger did not style their accomplishments as a defeat for the Soviets and did not freeze the Soviets out of the region. While a heavy investment in Egypt might be lost, the "anti-socialist" Sadat had already shown himself to be untrustworthy; any rapprochement between him and the United States would therefore make other actors in the region (Syria, Iraq, Libya, the PLO) more anxious to secure Soviet support. In terms of perceptions of relative military prowess, enough had been accomplished for the time being.

In sum, so long as Kissinger's goals were modest vis-à-vis the region, the Soviets, on balance, may well have found it tolerable to have him succeed. They would not have to forgo options of particular importance in irrevocable fashion. Should Kissinger fail in his step-by-step diplomacy, the Soviets would not bear the cost. In contrast, a general peace settlement had little attractiveness.

VIEW FROM ISRAEL

For the Israelis, their priorities before and during the initial stages of the October War were clearly to insure the U.S. connection as: first, a constraint on Soviet activity; and second, a supply source of the military wherewithal to deter the front-line Arab states, and the economic wherewithal to maintain domestic viability under a massive burden of defense resource requirements. The Israelis probably were fully aware of the energy vulnerability of the United States and other members of OECD. They may well have been sensitive to Kissinger's willingness to reduce support for long-standing U.S. allies (South Vietnam and Formosa) in pursuit of geopolitical and domestic concerns. As the October War and its aftermath unfolded, these goals and sensitivities were heightened. However, they came to operate in a changed context—a context of pervasive security anxiety, of public rage against major officials, and of pronounced fears of abandonment by the Western nations, including the United States. Israel soon entered into a period of intense internal political competition both within the ruling party and between it and the opposition coalition. While it would be presumptuous to claim to know what the various Israeli strategies and agendas were in detail, some general inferences are almost inescapable.

First, the immediate problem was to create a military situation that would have several properties. Israel must regain a security position from which it could afford, in relative terms, to bide its time. Israel must secure a renewed supply of bargaining chips vis-à-vis the Arab front-line states, and vis-à-vis the United States in general and Kissinger in particular. That implied the need to make grand U.S. policies significantly dependent on Israel's cooperation and to reestablish the issue of Israeli security as a part of the U.S. containment of the Soviet Union. It also implied making Kissinger's stature dependent in part on at least tacit Israeli consent to his moves. These would be the best guarantees of the American contributions needed to bring Israeli military capability to a new level.

Second, for a host of reasons it became crucial to buy time. Time was needed for Israeli society to adjust to the blows of the war, for the West to lessen its energy vulnerability, for American-Soviet detente to flourish or wane, and for Arab euphoria to decline. Only with time could Israel effect the military buildup and adaptation needed to deal with the surprising capability of Soviet weapons and Arab forces.

Third, it became a domestic political necessity to involve the United States so heavily and visibly in the postwar bargaining process that any self-limitations and adjustments on the Israeli side could be attributed to U.S. pressure and not to the preferences of individual Israeli personalities or the ruling party. Ideally, U.S. involvement would be structured in a way that would make it more difficult for the United States to behave again as it had prior to the October War and in its early days. Finally, all of these preferences were combined with the long established desire to weaken Arab unity in general, and Egyptian commitment to the anti-Israeli struggle in particular.

As a set, these concerns need not necessarily suffer under a process of step-by-step diplomacy; indeed, that might be the best available way to serve them. After all, a period of military quiet for renewal was desirable, and modest adjustments were tolerable if they led to an intensification of the U.S. commitment. Of course, from a tactical point of view it was important to make even the most modest adjustment seem like a substantial concession based on U.S. pledges. The resulting dilemma was that although such an image might be useful in bargaining with the United States and even the Arabs, it would inevitably have politically dangerous implications within Israel itself.

VIEW FROM EGYPT

The goals and concerns of the Egyptians, and Sadat in particular, were perhaps the most intriguing of all, and are extremely difficult to separate from distortion based on subsequent developments. We do know that Sadat saw his military initiative as a way of unfreezing a political stalemate in the Middle East, rather than as a means of achieving a definitive military solution. His forces apparently were not prepared to go all the way. We also know that Sadat had moved to open up channels to Kissinger before the October War, and to demonstrate publicly to the United States and to his own society his lack of affection for and commitment to the Soviets. We also know that the crumbling Egyptian economy was imposing social and political stress that required Sadat to offer some dramatic prospect of relief. He too was aware of the latent power of the oil weapon, as well as the pressures on, and diplomatic proclivities of, Kissinger. As the war unfolded, he eventually recognized that his initial gains, in terms of bargaining chips with the United States and U.S. incentive to put pressure on Israel, were endangered. The transformation of the issue into an American-Soviet conflict could only weaken Sadat's position. Accordingly, it became increasingly crucial for a direct American-Soviet confrontation to be diluted, and for the U.S. involvement with Sadat to be strengthened while it could still be portrayed not as a result of his weakness and defeat but rather of his strength and victory.

Even if Sadat had not thought so before, the October War convincingly demonstrated that a military solution to the Israeli problem was beyond his reach. What the war could provide was an avenue to create the sort of interdependence with the United States, and more particularly between Kissinger and himself, that would drastically narrow the gap between the importance to the United States of Egypt and Israel. If these were his goals, step-by-step negotiation was not a bad route to take, quite possibly preferable to a quick general peace even if that had been attainable. Step-by-step negotiation offered a substantial opportunity for Sadat to establish an image of himself in the United States as a statesman of reason, warmth, and almost Western sophistication. It offered opportunities for him and other Egyptian officials to build ties with U.S. elites as equals rather than as aid supplicants. It demonstrated his international stature to his own population and other Arabs, and effectively barred Israeli military attack. While Sadat's ultimate territorial gains might be modest, Israeli recalcitrance would help him to portray these gains as major achievements and to elicit an American view of him as a sympathetic personality. Moreover, if Syria were to enter into a similar but more limited arrangement, he would be relatively safe from charges of selling out, while also having shown unique bargaining prowess. He could move to establish momentum in his relationship with the United States without abandoning his position in the Arab world, one source of his attractiveness to the United States.

VIEW FROM SYRIA

Syrian considerations are extremely underdeveloped in most accounts. Perhaps all that can be said is that Assad had no particular interest in developing strong bonds of an ongoing kind with the United States or Kissinger. Compared to Sadat, he had much less internal political latitude and fewer bargaining chips. He also had less reason to have any hope for Israeli adjustments that he could portray as major accomplishments. To him, step-by-step negotiation seemed to hold little promise not only in terms of an attractive general settlement, but also in terms of other major payoffs. It could perhaps provide marginal bargaining advantages for him vis-à-vis the Soviets and adjust the embarrassing territorial situation at the end of the October War. So long as Kissinger's step-by-step continued, the Israelis would be effectively prevented from a revenge attack exploiting their favorable front-line position.

VIEW FROM SAUDI ARABIA

As for the Saudis, it is clear from the accounts that their concerns and relationship with the United States were considerably more complex and developed than appears on the surface, judging, for example, by the conversations with U.S. officials that the Saudis threatened to release. Their commitment to eliminating Israel as a nation of any substantial importance in the region was clear, as was their desire to minimize Soviet influence in the region and that of radical governments that might pose a threat to the Saudi elite. So long as step-by-step negotiation seemed important for preserving the power of Sadat in Egypt and dampening initiatives by the Soviets and radicals, it was certainly not harmful. Moreover, a posture that would avoid panicking the United States into a military response to the oil weapon, while at the same time underlining its potency and extracting arms and development assistance, would have short-term advantages. In the absence of a general settlement, the forces that would erode the American-Israeli relationship could only acquire more strength. The linkage between oil and the treatment of Israel was established firmly in Western foreign ministries, and it was available as a source of renewed.pressure whenever it was needed.

In conclusion, none of the regional parties, nor the Soviets, had a general peace settlement as a primary goal. If Kissinger had given primacy to that goal, he would probably have been unsuccessful. However, he too had other primary aims, aims that he largely achieved at least in short-run terms. Israel and Egypt were also strikingly successful, but their aims were not in a zero-sum relationship to those of the United States. If they had been, it is unlikely that Kissinger would have accomplished what he did. Whether the outcomes, resting as they did on the interests of the principal direct conflict participants, would have been similar without Kissinger's intervention and the form it took is a far more difficult question. Here one has to look at different aspects of the outcomes. Finally, the implications of Kissinger's intervention modalities and specific behavior for a general peace settlement require consideration of several additional matters.

In my view, Kissinger rescued himself and his policies from what could easily have been massive setbacks. He blunted what could have been a deathblow to detente, alleviated at least temporarily the most severe stresses of the oil situation on the United States' major allies, and reassured the Chinese. To the extent that the broader international and U.S. domestic situation allowed, he bolstered for awhile his own bureaucratic and political personal stature. However, he did so in ways that in the long run would only increase the U.S. stake in conflict abatement in the region. Thus he increased the propensity of the regional parties to seek, and their ability to extract, assets from the United States. Trends toward such involvement as well as U.S. policy investment were exactly what the Egyptians wanted. For the Israelis, such trends had obvious positive aspects also. Finally, the Saudis could view these tendencies as important in helping them to curb the presence and influence of the Soviets. Considered as a whole, Kissinger's intervention showed creativity, determination, boldness, even courage in a situation where other personalities might have resorted to more routine bureaucratic options or passively waited for something to turn up.

One might argue that, according to the previously imputed strategies and concerns, the resulting outcomes would have been much the same without Kissinger's involvement. This seems questionable. Other

American diplomats in a similar situation might have made similar attempts, but there was no other American diplomat at the time with the combination of international standing and the necessary skill and experience. Indeed, given the turmoil of Watergate and the unknowns of the Ford presidency, it seems possible that there was no other U.S. official who could have operated effectively between the heads of state in the region. With respect to U.S. courses of action, given the domestic unacceptability of a military response, it is evident that diplomacy had to be the instrument of prime importance. In this regard, it is important to remember the congressional difficulties faced in securing approval for the civilian, unarmed, U.S. presence in the Sinai under the second disengagement agreement; this presence was obviously far short of what a military response would have required. Moreover, even if all the parties' interests did converge on the eventual outcomes, U.S. involvement was necessary in order to convince the parties that the United States government was indeed giving the matter high priority and that the American representative could deliver on his commitments. Kissinger's presence also added desirable prestige to the negotiations.

American involvement enabled the regional parties to pursue their respective primary interests in securing certain terms and relationships with the U.S. government. Also, it was much easier for the parties to bargain with the United States than with each other given the historical issue of face-to-face negotiations between Israel and its enemies. The United States had a great deal to offer in security and economic terms. Its involvement provided a relatively persuasive rationale for dealing with domestic opponents (a clear Israeli problem) and with potential regional critics (an Egyptian problem). Further, none of the regional parties favored unrestrained Soviet operations in the Middle East, and none of them could individually deny such opportunities to the Soviets.

If these were necessary reasons for U.S. involvement, there were, at least in the period through the January 18, 1974 disengagement of forces agreement, additional reasons why U.S. involvement would help the regional parties to adjust modestly to each other. Compared to the Israelis and the Egyptians, Kissinger was in a better position to provide some time pressure, to insure at least minimally clear communication, and to inject formulas into the negotiation. Such brokerage activities were probably particularly crucial in order to insure that the Soviets had, and would take, a graceful way to lower their profile in the situation. We do not know the channels for direct communication available to the parties and used by them subsequently. Accordingly, one cannot tell whether such facilitation continued to be particularly important in fact rather than as an image useful to all sides, albeit for different reasons.

While the Kissinger intervention was neither insignificant nor ineffective, given his purposes and concerns, the specific gambits he used were probably of little particular significance in enabling outcomes that would otherwise not have occurred. The regional leaders were not sitting passively by, devoid of their own sources of information, waiting for him to arrive. Nor is there any particular reason to believe that they viewed him as a high fidelity, unbiased, disinterested channel for communicating with their counterparts. Indeed, some prominent elements of Kissinger's style rather quickly made him substantially vulnerable to those with whom he negotiated. By investing himself and his media image in Middle East accomplishments, Kissinger surely increased his need to close the bargaining with an accomplishment. The appetites of his media entourage provided the regional negotiators with greater access to U.S. audiences than they might otherwise have had.

FOUR EXAMPLES OF INTERVENTION

An after-the-fact assessment of four particularly controversial illustrations of Kissinger's intervention must pay particular attention to the degree to which the pertinent goals are attributable to Kissinger and the other parties, or primarily to the momentum toward general peace in the region. The first two specifics concern Israel and Egypt and occurred prior to the December 1973 elections in Israel. They involve Kissinger's displeasure with the direct Yariv-Gamasy disengagement discussions and the Dayan proposal to exchange Mitla and Giddi pass disengagement for reopening of the Suez Canal. If a prime goal was to improve Egyptian-Israeli relations as much as possible before the election, those steps should have been encouraged. We do not know what estimate Kissinger made of the likely postelection composition of the Israeli cabinet, of the political factions' shares of the election results, or what he knew of Meir's health.

From the point of view of generating momentum toward peace before Israeli politics would impose a slowdown, the initiatives surely did not seem harmful. If successful, they would have lessened the importance of the United States and Kissinger. The record provides no prima facie reason to assume that Egyptian demands would have soared, although those of Syria might have. If the initiatives were fully authorized by the Israeli government, which is not clear, success might have affected the election outcome in a way conducive to subsequent accommodation. If they were pursued and stalled, it is difficult to see why Kissinger could not have reentered the situation. Yet before being too critical, it is important to note another possibility. The Yariv-Gamasy discussions and the Dayan proposal could have been staged in part to spur Kissinger on. If the parties could successfully bargain directly, Kissinger would have less incentive to pursue his broader objectives on their ground. Israel and Egypt would then have less ability to extract concessions from the United States. Perhaps it was the case that, having put Kissinger in the position of constraining their adjustments independent of him, Sadat and the Israelis expected to be in a better position to pursue their respective goals vis-à-vis the United States. In my view, Kissinger's actions on these specific matters were conducive to the goals discussed earlier in this chapter. These actions were not helpful, and may have had a substantial opportunity cost for movement toward conflict resolution in the region.

The third controversial specific, Kissinger's May 1974 withholding of some Israeli concessions in his discussions with Assad, seems of marginal importance and arguably reasonable. Assad might have sought more, but that is an imponderable given our lack of understanding of how he would decide that he had achieved as much as he could get. Perhaps a more interesting question is what the Israelis knew about and expected Kissinger to do, and what he expected them to know about, and conclude from, his tactic.

The fourth specific, and perhaps the most controversial, was Kissinger's August 1974 decision to work toward a second Israeli-Egyptian disengagement agreement rather than a Jordanian-Israeli settlement involving the West Bank and the issue of Palestinian sovereignty. Obviously, if the Dayan initiative mentioned earlier had achieved its ostensible goal, the choice would not have been presented, at least not in those terms. Here there seems to be the starkest conflict between the grand strategic and political concerns that this chapter has attributed to Kissinger and the requisites for general conflict resolution in the region. From the former perspective, Palestinians and Jordan were of secondary importance, and the absence of a conclusion to the Palestinian issue was hardly all bad. On the other hand, as far as the prospects for peace were concerned, the issue had to be addressed, preferably through a Jordanian strategy, and it had to be at least discussable by important elements in Israel. For someone as concerned as Kissinger claimed to be with the escalation of Arab demands and Israeli intransigence, the postponement of that aspect of the Arab-Israeli conflict clearly had no desirable consequences, leading matters to deteriorate in the subsequent months. It is reasonable to suggest that the delay entailed by Kissinger's choice meant that the issue was to become more intractable, while his own ability to take it on was to become less and less. This is not to argue that he would have been successful if he had turned first to the Jordanian-Palestinian-Israeli tangle. However, the costs within the region of failure at such a venture (as distinct from the costs to the United States and Kissinger) were probably not so great as to make the risk prohibitive.

In all four instances, some general elements of Kissinger's diplomatic style are visible. First, in situations of choice he preferred to opt for tactics that he felt would give him the greatest prominence and control over the bargaining. Second, his behavior is compatible with an assumption that although the other parties were in some sense incapable of arriving at agreements themselves—either because of greed or a lack of sophistication—Kissinger could maneuver them into agreements that were otherwise unlikely. Third, although he assumed that he must move to anticipate unwanted developments in the Western world and in U.S. domestic politics, Kissinger did not attach equal importance to staying ahead of developments in the internal politics of the Middle East or initiatives by smaller nations and liberation movements in the Arab world. These tendencies, combined with the concerns imputed to him in this chapter, led to a pattern of behavior that failed to generate substantial momentum toward a general settlement.

SOME MATTERS OF PERSPECTIVE AND ASSUMPTION

I turned to the accounts of Kissinger's step-by-step diplomacy with several ideas in mind from international relations theory and the study of foreign policy decision making in the United States. The appraisal of Kissinger's intense and personally grueling efforts does not follow in any neat, logical fashion from these preconceptions, but it was shaped by them. Two theoretical discussions of the role of third parties contain most of what international relations theory has to offer on the subject. I refer to the work of Oran Young (1967) on third parties as intermediaries in international crises, and to that of Saadia Touval (1975) on biased intermediaries (written after many of Kissinger's activities of interest here had already taken place).*

Oran Young's Analysis

Young considers third parties as intermediaries pursuing two classes of purposes. The first is to help regulate and terminate a crisis; the second is to establish a substantive settlement and limit its destabilizing impact. With special reference to the role of the United Nations in East-West crises, he considers possible third party contributions, tactics, and the

---

*Since the completion of this chapter, Touval (1980) has provided an analysis of the major intermediary ventures in the Arab-Israeli dispute. He does not deny that personal styles and diplomatic strategems matter. However, he concludes that two other factors are far more crucial to the success of third party intermediaries. First, and of the utmost importance, an agreement results when the regional parties themselves want the agreement, quite apart from the arguments presented by the intermediary. Second, the effectiveness of intermediaries waxes and wanes with the strength of their political base of support outside the region.

factors that determine to what degree the third party can in practice realize its potential contributions. In all of these respects, Young provides the important elements of a checklist that can be applied to Kissinger's activities in the Middle East.

In principle, third parties can contribute to crisis regulation and settlement in two ways. First, they can make a direct positive contribution. Familiar examples include focusing the parties on a particular termination agreement, devising a formula to avoid hard issues, providing an agenda, and manipulating timing. Second, third parties can work to weaken constraints on the primary parties; that is, they can make it easier for the primary parties to do what they would in some sense like to do anyway. Third parties do this by lowering the net costs associated with a more flexible bargaining position, including the internal political penalties. In effect, third parties provide face-saving assistance for the primary conflict participants. They may do so by providing rationalizations for the disavowal of previous stands, by certifying the benefits of an agreement, and by providing insurance against the risks should an agreement fail.

Tactics available to third parties consist in general of mediation and conciliation, independent positive actions, and service activities. The persuasive focus of mediation and conciliation centers on helping the parties to identify compatible interests in the late stages of a crisis, providing a framework of issues and proposals, and applying pressure on the direct crisis participants. Independent actions and service activities primarily come into play after a crisis is terminated, and have strong implications for the implementation of agreements. Familiar emphases include provision of communications and information, physical interposition, compliance monitoring, agreement supervision, and arbitration.

The effectiveness of third party intermediaries depends on their own stakes, resources and capabilities, and the image they have in the eyes of the direct adversaries. Impartiality and independence matter, and they are present to the extent that two conditions are met: first, the intermediary stands to incur a roughly equal loss whichever direct adversary is responsible for continuing the crisis or for blocking or violating an agreement; and second, the stakes of the intermediary in crisis termination and settlement do not exceed those of the local parties.

The qualifications of third party personnel also matter. These include political-military knowledge, skills in timing and verbal facility, an unobtrusive ability to allow the primary parties to feel that their adjustments are their own idea, and a bureaucratic and political position that provides a relatively free hand to take initiatives. Positive actions and service activities require that the third party should possess pertinent resources and be able to mobilize them quickly. The perceptions that the primary parties hold of the third party are perhaps most important of all.

Perceptions conducive to third party effectiveness include respect for diplomatic skills, potential ability to bring pressure to bear (power), expectations of permanence and continuity, and empathy with the needs of the primary parties. Furthermore, any given degree of third party resources tends to gain in effectiveness when the primary parties view themselves as having rough parity of power. Effectiveness declines when the primary parties doubt the internal stability of the third party, see it as vulnerable to outside interference in its domestic affairs, and as inhibited from using its instruments for international assertion, no matter how physically formidable these may be (Liska 1962).

With respect to Kissinger's activities in the Middle East, available accounts provide numerous illustrations of his positive contributions and the ways in which his role and that of the United States weakened the constraints on the primary parties. The latter category of contribution is particularly marked, and it went well beyond Young's (1967) face-saving characterization. The United States and Kissinger, throughout the period under analysis, engaged in mediation and conciliation, and undertook several independent actions (such as military and economic transfers). While service activities were largely assigned to the United Nations, the aerial intelligence monitoring of the Sinai front was probably viewed as desirable by both parties, and was built into the second disengagement agreement between Israel and Egypt, together with a U.S. warning station in the Mitla and Giddi passes. Given the encompassing nature of these activities, it is difficult to see how any attempt at intermediary action would not have involved all of them.

Kissinger's personal involvement, Western oil vulnerability, and U.S. competition with the Soviets worked together to partially correct the imbalance in the historical U.S. stand toward the primary parties. Yet the United States continued to be the arsenal of Israel. This same American-Soviet-Israeli trio of forces made the satisfaction of Young's (1967) third party conditions of independence and impartiality highly debatable. At various points in time, the stakes of the United States and Kissinger were at least as great as those of the primary parties, and possibly greater. This reflects in part the simultaneous roles of the United States and Kissinger as Middle East intermediary and Soviet deterrent. While Kissinger had many of the skills and advantages of bureaucratic position that Young recommends, he was hardly unobtrusive. As for his image and that of the United States, he began with substantial respect for his own diplomatic skills and the ability of the United States to apply power to the problem. He worked hard at convincing the parties of his empathy with their problems. However, Kissinger's effectiveness would be eroded over time by political instability within the United States and limitations on the political willingness to use force. Clearly, third party activity in the Middle East was facilitated by the effect of the October War upon previously held perceptions of overwhelming Israeli military superiority.

Young's formulation is not inapplicable, only incomplete and partially unmet by the Kissinger case. One is left with the need to understand why Kissinger and the United States found themselves providing much more than face-saving assistance to the primary parties, the implications of the relative absence of impartiality and independence, and the reasons for and implications of Kissinger's obtrusive role. Touval offers help on all these counts.

Saadia Touval's Analysis

Touval is concerned with the phenomenon of a third party whom the primary parties find acceptable despite the absence of impartiality. The key here is the primary parties' calculation of the relative costs of accepting or rejecting the third party as intermediary. Acceptance of the third party must take the alternatives into account.

What are the ingredients that make a particular biased intermediary attractive? One is the extent to which bargaining with the intermediary forces one's adversary into a weaker bargaining position. This condition is likely to be met when the adversary is more dependent on the intermediary than you are. Your adversary may recognize this consequence but have little choice if it wishes to retain the previous relationship of cooperative association with the intermediary.

A second condition is that the very entry of the third party into the intermediary role promises to work to dilute the previous special relationship with the adversary, and to improve the relationship with you. Such consequences become more likely after rough parity of bargaining assets has been achieved between you and your adversary. So long as the biased intermediary can be kept in the third party role, the intermediary is less likely to enter into, or to fully activate, a hostile coalition with your adversary. Both of these reasons are particularly compelling to the primary party that has previously had less cooperative ties with the intermediary.

A third condition has more general appeal. The biased intermediary can potentially provide the political, military, and economic contributions that each primary party wants, and can prevent states of affairs that neither wants. To realize that potential, it becomes highly desirable to draw the biased intermediary into the bargaining process in such a way that the focus of bargaining comes to involve the intermediary's concessions to each primary party at least as much as it does the parties' adjustments to each other. Once this happens, there is incentive for the primary parties to collude, or at least tacitly cooperate, in order to maximize extractions from the intermediary. Success at bargaining for intermediary concessions offers an additional advantage to the primary party against whom the intermediary was previously biased, and some compensation to the primary party who was previously favored.

This perspective makes explicable the role of Kissinger and the United States when impartiality and independence conditions were not met. It provides a general rationale for the situational behavior of Sadat and accounts for the acceptance of Kissinger's role by the Israelis. It explains the provision by the United States of numerous contributions to both Egypt and Israel beyond face-saving assistance, and it explains the greater aloofness of Syria from the whole process. Indeed, the failure to meet the independence condition was crucial to whatever success Kissinger had.

Some Implications

If we relate the perspectives of Touval and Young, several other implications follow that seem to be manifest in the Kissinger case. First, the primary parties will be attracted to a biased intermediary if they have the ability to interfere directly, or through their backers, in the intermediary's internal affairs (oil and the Israeli lobby). Paradoxically, vulnerability to interference of this sort may limit the effectiveness of an impartial intermediary while making a biased intermediary seem more attractive. Second, the biased intermediary role will be particularly important between primary parties who highly value what the intermediary has to give them. Third, instability in the intermediary's own political system renders doubtful the prospect of meaningful implementation of concessions to the primary parties; one should expect the momentum of an intermediary intervention to decline as perceptions of instability become more salient. Fourth, while unobtrusiveness may have value in other intermediary situations, the primary parties find obtrusiveness highly attractive for a biased intermediary.

Public commitment by the intermediary to a highly visible, important role makes it easier for the primary parties to focus on their relationship with the intermediary rather than on their relationship with the adversary. Such a focus does have some of the face-saving advantages that Young attributes to impartial intermediaries; it also makes it easier for the primary parties to push the intermediary into matching and possibly raising the concessions made to each in order to match the intermediary's previous concessions and commitments to the other. To the extent that the intermediaries find themselves behaving accordingly, the previous special relationship with one of the primary parties obviously becomes less disparate from the emerging relationship with the other. Finally, as the reference to face saving illustrates, a biased intermediary can still use many of the tactics, and draw on many of the resources, pertinent to an impartial third party. However, an examination of the goals of the primary parties, as well as the structure of the situation in which the intermediary operates, will show that they are being used in a context where the behavior of the intermediary has itself become a prime focus of bargaining and negotiation. Analysis confined to the tactical level of intermediary behavior can easily miss this key political point.

The linkage of the oil weapon to the Arab-Israeli dispute worked to increase the acceptability of the United States and Kissinger as an intermediary. So, too, did Sadat's preference for U.S. over Soviet support and Israel's absence of alternatives to the United States. The increased difficulties in securing agreements that Kissinger experienced—after all, momentum was another possibility—could be anticipated. His contravention of Young's unobstrusiveness consideration comes to appear as something that the primary parties would value. Taken as a whole, the achievement of agreements seems to attest at least as much to the effectiveness of the primary parties as it does to Kissinger's own effectiveness.

SUPERPOWER DECISION-MAKING TENDENCIES

The premises stimulated by the works of Young (1967) and Touval (1975) were combined in my approach to Kissinger's activities with some observations of American, and other superpower, foreign policy decision making to yield several conclusions. I will state these as general tendencies, with the caveat that they need not operate for all high foreign policy officials in all situations. Unfortunately, the probability of their holding true is extremely high.

First, the local parties—their stakes, commitments, aspirations, and fears—are not taken very seriously. Even the language used to discuss them has that flavor: third world, peripheral, local, small. Accordingly, the superpowers not only treat regional outcomes as instrumental to "more important" ends, but also consider themselves justified in doing so. Statesmen are warranted in combining the persuasion of pressure and reassurance to bring leaders of "minor" nations to subordinate their "selfish" and "parochial" interests to the "larger" issues of the superpower's foreign policy. Of course, it is desirable to avoid doing so in ways that involve the diasppearance of the minor nations. That might be morally embarrassing and, more importantly, might suggest to great power competitors that they could expand their sphere of influence through proxy aggression. The proper emotion, therefore, for small power allies that require superpower intervention is gratitude. Such propensities may partially explain Kissinger's delay in addressing the Arab-Israeli dispute prior to the October War, and his occasional irritation with the Israelis and Syrians during the course of his subsequent diplomacy.

Second, the international bargaining skill of small nations is inferior to that of the superpowers. The leaders of small nations are more emotional and more shortsighted, less well informed and imaginative. It often seems to be assumed that the skills of leaders are in some sense proportionate to their nation's gross national product and military capacity. Accordingly, little attention is given to the possibility that the leaders of nations in crisis and conflict, as in the Middle East, may be better informed about their regional adversaries than the intermediary, and at least as capable at operating simultaneous multiple strategies and channels of communication. Little credence is given to their capability to turn weakness into strength in a bargaining situation, to the possibility that leaders of nations with less strength (according to the customary aggregate measures of national capability) will manipulate the vastly more powerful intermediary to gain significant leverage. Perhaps this bias explains why accounts of Kissinger's intervention give little evidence that he had a clear understanding of the ways in which Sadat and the Israelis may have been using him and the United States as a tool in pursuit of their own respective designs.

Third, in spite of their ostensible limitations relative to superpower statesmen, the leaders of small nations are supposed to be unencumbered by domestic constraints. Their internal political base is assumed to be firm or, if not, of "petty" concern, and to be prevented from distorting regional outcomes attractive to the superpower intervenor. Surely the superpower need not pay much attention to the possibility that intervention activities will bring to power in the small nation an even more recalcitrant regime, or deprive existing leadership of the political standing to make agreements that the regional adversaries will expect to last. Kissinger's relative lack of attention to Israeli political repercussions, and his apparent assumption that the Jordanian option for dealing with the Palestinian problem would not recede, may well be cases in point.

Fourth, high level foreign policy officials of a superpower are unable to devote their full attention for an extended period of time to any particular regional conflict. Whatever their short-term ability to focus on crises and secure credits for crisis management, the pressures on officials to turn to other issues are inexorable. As these mount, the initial high stemming from dramatic crisis management is replaced by irritation at having to divert one's energies to what is no longer a high priority matter, while matters that were or are more pressing are made to suffer. It soon becomes important to find some way of bringing the regional situation to a point where the local parties or subordinates can take charge of it for awhile. This need may well be known in advance because of other planned initiatives and programmed events at the international and domestic levels. From this perspective, the episodic, step-by-step nature of Kissinger's diplomacy was almost inevitable. More specifically, it implies that the primary parties' leverage on him would increase, if anything, during the course of his prolonged venture in shuttle diplomacy.

Finally, some points specific to the U.S. political system since World War II need to be taken into account. American presidential administrations seek to arrange foreign policy "accomplishments" in order to divert attention from domestic shortcomings. No American administrations in recent memory have needed a foreign policy success more than those of Nixon and Ford during the period under review. Consider the combined effects of Watergate, Vietnam, energy dependence, and inflation. Standard ingredients of a foreign policy "success" are a show of force that can be presented as causing an adversary to back down, the personal involvement of high officials, and an international agreement. These ingredients also have to fit with the media definition of news. This means that events and human interest have to be provided on a continuing basis; drama and visibility are requisites. It is also true that correspondents with a particular foreign policy venture to cover, who are removed from other sources of information, have substantial incentives to find drama in the doings of a political personality (a form of "publish or perish"). They can easily find themselves co-opted at the time into an attempt to focus the attention of the U.S. public and political elites (Cohen 1963).

In addition, the positions of National Security Advisor to the President and Secretary of State provide relatively weak bureaucratic bases of power in the U.S. national security/foreign affairs system. Their incumbents have influence primarily to the extent that they are seen as having the strong backing of an effective president, as having skills that make them indispensable as individuals, or as being able and willing to deal with issues that other high officials (particularly the Secretary of Defense) would prefer to avoid. One need not be familiar with Kissinger's Middle East activities to be alert to the importance for him of enhancing an image of personally unique competence and establishing the primacy of detailed face-to-face negotiation with heads of state.

CONCLUSIONS

The notion of biased intermediaries, combined with the above characteristic tendencies of superpower (and particularly American) foreign policy decision making, leads to the following interpretation: The regional parties believed that extraordinary measures were necessary in order to secure high priority attention to the Middle East area of conflict. American involvement soared in the context of grand foreign policy issues with great domestic implications. The U.S. intermediary tended to view the security concerns of the primary parties as exaggerated. For their part, initially it was important to exploit any available means to constrain the intermediary from acting accordingly. For the Israelis, constraints on Kissinger involved pressures in the United States and escalatory actions; for the Arabs, they involved the oil weapon and personal bonding (Sadat's "my Dr. Henry"). The regional parties in all likelihood sought to turn Kissinger's strength into weakness by pursuing complex direct and indirect strategies with the intermediary—an intermediary who perhaps only recognized the growth of his own stakes after the fact. Kissinger probably was also inattentive to the domestic politics of the parties and based his timing on a continuation of their domestic and inter-Arab status quo.

While Kissinger found it increasingly difficult to disengage, he felt increasing pressure to do so as well as decreasing benefit from continued maximum involvement. One result was a growing preference on his part for steps with clear stages and intervals of stability rather than a more generalized process. The U.S. intervention tended to be conducted in ways that made news, and the news slighted the strategy and tactics of the regional parties. Kissinger himself needed to present and define the situation as one in which negotiations between the parties had to be conducted by him through face-to-face diplomacy. All of these tendencies made Kissinger more acceptable as a biased intermediary to the parties in the region because their effect was probably to strengthen the parties' bargaining hand. Of course, it would have been self-defeating for them to trumpet those implications.

At the same time, these tendencies implied that long-term, highly contingent commitments by Kissinger were probably seen to have little value in themselves. The reasonable option set, from the point of view of the parties, was limited to U.S. commitments that were in some measure self-enforcing and difficult to revoke. With regard to each other, the regional parties were interested in specific arrangements that were sustainable without the continued high level attention of Kissinger. Interests therefore converged on measures providing short-term conflict abatement. No party pushed hard to start processes that Kissinger could not complete or that could be dangerous to the local parties, given the fleeting and biased nature of Kissinger's participation.

REFERENCES

Brenner, M. J. "The Problem of Innovation and the Nixon-Kissinger Foreign Policy." *International Studies Quarterly*, 1973, 17, 255-94.
Cohen, B. C. *The Press and Foreign Policy*. Princeton: Princeton University Press, 1963.
Dickson, P. *Kissinger and the Meaning of History*. London: Cambridge University Press, 1978.

Golan, M. *The Secret Conversations of Henry Kissinger.* New York: Quadrangle, 1976.

Herzog, C. *The War of Atonement: October, 1973.* Boston: Little, Brown, 1975.

Kalb, M., and Kalb, B. *Kissinger.* Boston: Little, Brown, 1974.

Kass, I. *Soviet Involvement in the Middle East: Policy Formulation, 1966–1973.* Boulder: Westview, 1978.

Kissinger, H. *White House Years.* Boston: Little, Brown, 1979.

Liska, G. "Tripartism: Dilemmas and Strategies." In Laurence Martin, ed., *Neutralism and Nonalignment.* New York: Praeger, 1962, 212–21.

Quandt, W. B. *Decade of Decisions: American Policy toward the Arab-Israeli Conflict, 1967–1976.* Berkeley: University of California Press, 1977.

Safran, N. *Israel: The Embattled Ally.* Cambridge: Belknap Press of Harvard University Press, 1978.

Sheehan, E. R. F. *The Arabs, Israelis, and Kissinger: A Secret History of American Diplomacy in the Middle East.* New York: Reader's Digest Press, 1976.

Touval, S. "Biased Intermediaries: Theoretical and Historical Considerations." *Jerusalem Journal of International Relations,* 1975, 51–69.

———. "Mediators in the Israeli-Arab Conflict: Requisites for Success." In Asher Arian, ed., *Israel: A Developing Society.* Assen: Van Gorcum, 1980, 59–93.

Walker, S. G. "The Interface between Beliefs and Behavior." *Journal of Conflict Resolution,* 1977, 21, 129–61.

Young, O. R. *The Intermediaries: Third Parties in International Crises.* Princeton: Princeton University Press, 1967.

8

HENRY KISSINGER AS STRATEGIST AND TACTICIAN IN THE MIDDLE EAST NEGOTIATIONS

P. Terrence Hopmann and Daniel Druckman

INTRODUCTION

In several messages to Egyptian National Security Advisor Hafez Ismail in 1973, Henry Kissinger took pains to offer Egyptian President Anwar Sadat a lesson in realistic statecraft:

> We live in a real world and cannot build anything on fancies and wishful thinking. Now in terms of reality you are the defeated side and shouldn't, therefore, make demands acceptable only from victors. . . . You may be capable of changing existing realities—and consequently, our approach to the "solution"—or you may not. If not, certain solutions have to be found which *follow from* your position, and these will be different from the solutions you now suggest. I hope my meaning is clear . . . (Sadat 1977, p. 288).

This statement reveals Kissinger's underlying belief that negotiations must reflect and follow from the strategic relations of parties engaged in a dispute. In the case of the negotiations in the aftermath of the 1973 Arab-Israeli War, he particularly believed that any negotiated outcomes would have to be based upon the strategic relations among not only the parties within the Middle East region, but also the major actors outside of the region, especially the two superpowers. Therefore, prior to his mediation,

The authors are grateful for the advice and comments of Mary Ellen Lundsten, whose expertise on the Middle East was of invaluable assistance in writing this chapter.

Kissinger emphasized the importance of structuring the particular relations among the parties involved in order to facilitate negotiation success.

This chapter shall first examine some of the ways in which Henry Kissinger intervened strategically in the Middle East during the period of his stewardship over U.S. foreign policy, in order to establish the basis for his mediation. This will be followed by a consideration of negotiating tactics, to document the ways in which these followed from the strategic situation in order to create a partial and temporary order in the area of conflict. More specifically, the next section will examine the ways in which Kissinger manipulated the balance of power, while the following two sections will provide a more specific analysis of Kissinger's mediational tactics. Although Kissinger received considerable praise for the success of the negotiations, much of it well deserved, the concluding section will provide a critique of some of the inconsistencies that developed between these two aspects of his intervention in the Middle East. In the final analysis, it will be argued that Kissinger failed to achieve the sort of strategic solution to the problems of the Middle East that is essential for long-term, peaceful settlement of conflict in this most important region of the globe.

KISSINGER'S GRAND STRATEGY IN THE MIDDLE EAST

As noted by Kalb and Kalb (1974, p. 102), the basis of Henry Kissinger's theory of international relations was the concept of linkage, which "was an up-to-date application of Kissinger's theories about the balance of power." He had consistently held the view that world order and regional order depended upon a balance of rival claims, rather than the imposition of one upon the other. Consequently, he believed that every problem was linked with every other, so that progress on one issue would affect progress on another. Kissinger applied this formulation primarily at the global level, where it implied a set of policies designed to meet the Soviet Union's challenge through direct action, whether that action took the form of threats to employ force or the use of arms control as a device to induce cooperation. Kissinger also believed this approach should be applied at the regional level, where the ideological appeal of revolutionary movements might appeal to the disorder and uncontrollable war that threatened Kissinger's conception of world order. Linkage also meant that small power alignments within various regions of the globe would have to be brought into equilibrium to complement the great power balance at the global level. Furthermore, all elements of strategy— political, economic, social, and military—were viewed as intertwined rather than as autonomous tools of manipulation.

In the Middle East, Kissinger was especially interested in manipulating the domestic political situation in a number of Arab states in the hope of taking advantage of propitious trends within these countries' domestic factions. While encouraging such trends within Arab factions, particularly in those Arab countries that were trying to recover from the devastation of the 1967 war, Kissinger also sought to strengthen Israeli military forces. Since the war, the Labour government in Israel had been accumulating stocks of U.S. weapons in order to be able to demonstrate Israel's overall military superiority in the region. Therefore, U.S. intervention in the politics of the region appeared to offer the possibility of creating the kind of balance of power that Kissinger sought.

At the time of his appointment as Special Assistant for National Security Affairs to President Nixon, Kissinger cited the continuing Arab-Israeli conflict as his major regional concern. Although his involvement was largely unpublicized until fall 1973, Kissinger maintained contact through regular use of those U.S. national security bureaucracies whose work he was responsible for coordinating. Chief roles in these back-channel communications were assigned to the Central Intelligence Agency and to Assistant Secretary of State Joseph Sisco, with whom Kissinger had formed a close bureaucratic alliance (Kalb and Kalb 1974, pp. 218–20). In addition, a wider network of business friends and members of the press, as well as other national leaders friendly to U.S. interests, kept Kissinger in touch with personalities and developments in the region.

Just as Kissinger had delayed the SALT negotiations in 1969 until he could "control all of the strings," so did he also try to forestall an active mediating role for himself in the Middle East until he could develop an alignment of interests that would serve U.S. objectives. Such alignments necessitated gaining Arab acceptance of Israel as a Zionist state, precluding radicals from positions of power in the Arab states neighboring Israel, and expanding U.S. investments and markets for high technology weapons in the region, with the concomitant political leverage over the recipients that accompanied such sophisticated weaponry.

At the heart of Kissinger's strategic intervention in the Middle East was his policy toward Egypt and Syria. In Egypt the United States played upon a number of events that opened up possibilities for greater U.S. economic influence. Ever since the Arab States Summit Conference in Khartoum, Sudan, in August 1967, Egypt had been receiving grants of over $350 million annually from conservative oil-producing states in order to replace revenues lost due to the closure of the Suez Canal. Although Nasser's regime relied primarily on trade with countries in the socialist bloc, in early 1969 Egypt began talks with representatives from the International Monetary Fund and the International Bank for Reconstruction and Development (IBRD). Furthermore, it initiated discussions about a special relationship with the European Economic Community. All of these activities signalled greater Egyptian economic reliance upon actors with whom the United States had considerable influence, rather than upon sources primarily under Soviet influence.

With Nasser's death in 1970, the domestic political situation in Egypt also took a turn in a direction favorable to U.S. influence strategies. After Anwar Sadat, Nasser's successor, had eliminated the pro-Soviet Ali Sabri faction from his government in 1971, he enacted a more liberal foreign investment code and established the Egyptian International Bank for Trade and Development. Later that same year Egyptian officials signed a new agreement with the United States for debt rescheduling, as well as an agreement with the IBRD to establish new procedures for settling foreign investment disputes. As a result of these actions, the United States was able to influence Egyptian policy in ways that had not been possible during previous peace initiatives, such as the abortive attempt to mediate the Middle East conflict under the terms of the Rogers Plan in 1970.

Similarly, in 1969 a noteworthy shift took place within the Baathist regime of Syria. Defense Minister Hafez Assad rose to ascendancy in the Syrian cabinet. Furthermore, it was known that Assad's faction favored economic reorganization and more intensive industrialization. In order to promote these goals, Assad began to seek vital funds from the oil-producing states under the leadership of Saudi Arabia. Within a year after taking power, Assad and other Syrian officials began to develop economic ties with the European Community as well. Once again, changes in Syrian domestic politics were favorable to a more extensive application of U.S. influence in the region.

In order to strengthen and reinforce the trends that were emerging in Israel's two key neighbors, Kissinger made particular use of close ties with the United States' friends in two of the major oil-producing states of the Middle East, namely King Faisal of Saudi Arabia and his monarchical confrere, the Shah of Iran (Heikal 1978, p. 239). While Kissinger held out to Egypt and Syria the possibility of recovering territories lost in the 1967 war as an outcome of negotiations, he made use of these two key Arab leaders in an effort to supplement his influence in the region. In his view, the United States' objectives would best be advanced by deepening its economic influence, by preventing a new outbreak of violence that might bring an end to Israel's military superiority, and by trying to reassure and strengthen the conservative dynastic order in the states bordering the Persian Gulf.

Even so, both of these regimes were threatened domestically and internationally in the early 1970s. Saudi Arabia's King Faisal several times voiced his concern about isolation from the other Arab states because of his close attachment to the United States. In 1969 there had been an abortive coup attempt within the Saudi military. Since 1968 the PLO, under the leadership of Yasir Arafat, had taken up the banner of the Arab revolution, threatening the popular support of all the Arab regimes. The

PLO appealed to Arab populations, maintaining that it constituted the sole force of Arab nationalism and Arab opposition to control by neocolonial powers. This appeal contrasted with the objective conditions of military defeat and economic shortage in which many of the Arab states involved in the 1967 war found themselves in the aftermath of that confrontation. Leftist groups within the many unstable regimes in the region played upon the fervor of Arab nationalism that survived after the 1967 Khartoum Conference. These forces threatened to change the political map of the region, especially if they were successful in such weakened states as Jordan and Lebanon. Successful revolutions in these states would have increased both Soviet domination in the region and Saudi isolation from the other Arab states. Finally, it might have led to a growing pattern of instability in Iran, which until that time had been relatively stable domestically.

From Kissinger's perspective, these events could have led to a nightmare for U.S. interests in the Middle East (Kalb and Kalb 1974, p. 222). His immediate goal was to block revolutionary movements from coming to power in Jordan, a U.S. client state. In addition, more subtle and complex tactics were required. These included using Israel and Iran as bases for punitive military action where necessary, in order to keep Arab radicals on the defensive. At the same time, he increased U.S. military support for the two most favored states in the region, Israel and Saudi Arabia. He continued both security assistance and economic subsidies to U.S. client states, such as Jordan and Lebanon. As noted previously, Kissinger made use of growing economic ties with Egypt, and the increasing role of funds from the oil-producing countries, in order to gain influence in Syria. By linking Egypt more closely with the United States, and by linking Syria with U.S. allies in the region such as Saudi Arabia and Iran, he could gain some influence over their policy. Finally, all of these combined actions tended to isolate the most militant actors in the region, especially the PLO and Iraq, from the other major Arab states.

Thus prior to the outbreak of the 1973 war, the situation in the Middle East had become restructured so as to provide greater opportunities for successful U.S. influence. Under these conditions, Kissinger felt that a negotiated outcome could be reached that would better reflect U.S. interests than would have been possible several years before. Kissinger undoubtedly would still have preferred negotiations in which the Soviet Union played an active role in order to enhance the prospects for long-term stability in the region. On the other hand, if agreement could not be reached at the superpower level, regional negotiations were more likely to be amenable to U.S. influence. American mediation in the region would seek to promote Egyptian negotiations with Israel, and the prospect of possible recovery of lost territory could also be held out to the Egyptians as a further incentive to negotiate seriously. This might also serve as an example to Syria, especially if linkages between Egypt and Syria could be strengthened.

This latter linkage was finally strengthened by the 1973 war itself. As Israel's common opponents, Egypt and Syria were drawn closer together. By enhancing the solidarity of the Arab states, at least for the short run, the war also increased the influence of Saudi Arabia (and therefore indirectly the influence of the United States) over Egypt and Syria. These two countries became increasingly dependent upon their wealthier Arab neighbor in the aftermath of the war. One final effect of the war was felt in Israel where early defeats, even though they were eventually reversed, had destroyed the image of Israeli infallibility on the battlefield. This image of Israel's declining overall military superiority, coupled with its renewed dependence on U.S. military assistance, both enhanced Israel's willingness to negotiate with somewhat greater flexibility than before and made the Israeli government even more susceptible to Washington's influence.

Thus, when the 1973 Arab-Israeli War was brought to a halt, the conditions were ripe for the exercise of U.S. influence in ways that had not been possible as recently as two or three years before. Even if Kissinger could not "control all of the strings," he was able to manipulate a substantial number to serve his ends. By this time the interests of the states in the Middle East conflict—especially Egypt, Israel, and Syria—had been realigned so as to provide the basis for at least a partial settlement of the long-standing conflict. In 1969 Kissinger had noted that "given the influence and intransigence of the Soviets, the militance of Nasser, and the power of the fedayeen, . . . the Middle East was not ready for a comprehensive American initiative" (Kissinger 1979b, p. 357). It was largely for this reason that Kissinger never had much hope for the success of the Rogers Plan when it was introduced in 1970, an initiative that Kissinger considered inopportune. By the end of the 1973 war, however, conditions had changed sufficiently that the President's National Security Advisor had become committed to personal mediation of the conflict in this explosive region.

THE BARGAINING PROCESS WITHIN THE STRATEGIC ENVIRONMENT

This section will discuss the ways in which Kissinger's intervention in the Middle East conflict influenced the bargaining process among the participants. Specifically, it will indicate some of the ways in which Kissinger, acting as an interested mediator, helped the conflicting states both to acknowledge their common interests and to codify them through concrete agreements. Throughout this process Kissinger tried to create additional common interests by manipulating the strategic environment, while also occasionally creating enmities that he deemed tactically necessary. He tried to maintain the negotiation process so that some of the parties could reach concrete agreements. To do this, he had to make their common interests appear to be more salient than the elements of conflict, so that the parties would believe that the positive gains to be derived from agreement outweighed any related costs. In order to explicate more fully how Kissinger accomplished this end, it may be useful to discuss briefly some basic theories of the bargaining process.

Theories of the Bargaining Process

Most theories of the bargaining process are based upon some fundamental assumptions derived from models of two-person, nonzero-sum games. These models assume that negotiations occur under "mixed motive" conditions, when elements of both conflict and cooperation are present. Therefore, the objectives of negotiations are to promote the recognition of common interests and to transform those congruent interests into concrete agreements.

Figure 8.1 illustrates the basic dimensions of a bargaining problem as conceived within the framework of two-person, nonzero-sum game theory. The horizontal and vertical axes represent the gains and losses of two players, and the polygon represents the environmentally determined set of possible agreements. This simple model suggests two basic axioms

FIGURE 8.1

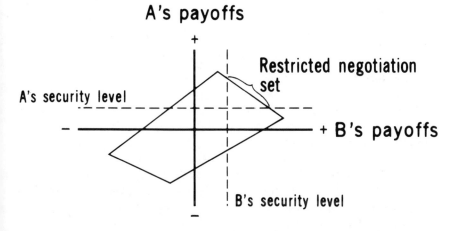

The Restricted Negotiation Set

that form the foundation of bargaining theories. First, agreements should be reached at some point along line in the upper right quadrant, generally called the negotiation set. Along the polygon this line both players in a game are unable to improve their joint payoffs. Since externally dictated conditions prevent the players from moving outside of this polygon, when the parties find themselves situated along this line it is not feasible for them to move in a northeasterly direction, the only direction in which moves would be jointly profitable. Any move back and forth along the line would benefit one player at the other's expense. Any move off this line in any direction within the polygon would make both parties worse off. Thus both have a common interest in seeking agreements that fall along this negotiation set. Of course, they also have divergent interests concerning the exact location where an agreement should be struck along this line. It is at this point that the conflictual elements in bargaining enter into the process.

The second axiom of the negotiated game states that no party should agree to an outcome that leaves that party worse off than would result from acting alone. A negotiator compares the payoffs that his or her side would receive from an agreement at any point along the negotiation set with the outcome that would be received in the absence of any agreement. The limit, the point beyond which the net payoffs from an agreement fall below the payoffs associated with no agreement, is called the security level. This is depicted by the broken lines in Figure 8.1; the points where these broken lines cross the negotiation set represent the points of minimum acceptable agreement for each player. Thus the possible outcome in a negotiation game between two rational players falls within the restricted negotiation set, that is, along line A-B between the security levels of the two players. Although both parties seek to maximize joint benefits, there is no incentive for them to accept an agreement that falls below their respective security levels, since they would then be worse off with the agreement than without it.

These two axioms may also be depicted in a slightly different way, as in Figure 8.2. The horizontal axis represents an issue dimension along which the negotiating parties are assumed to have conflicting interests. Examples of these issues in the Middle East negotiations are both tangible (including kilometers of territory and militarized borders) and less tangible (including national independence and status in both the international and regional political systems). Lines A-A' and B-B' in this figure represent the payoffs that two nations, such as Egypt and Israel respectively, would receive from agreements at any point along those lines. These payoffs are scaled on a vertical dimension that is subjectively standardized as the relative gains or losses that a party would receive relative to the status quo. On the horizontal line, 0 represents the neutral point or the point of indifference, where an actor such as Israel would

FIGURE 8.2

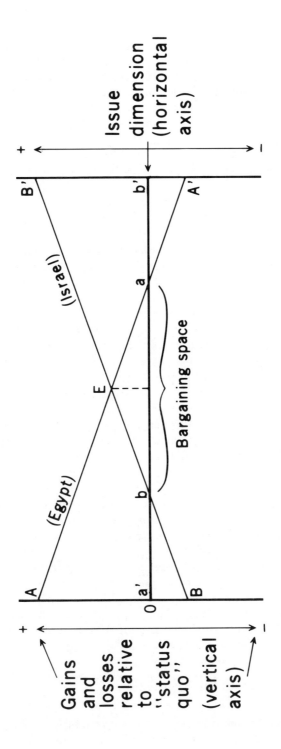

A Simple Bargaining Model

perceive that the net payoff from an agreement is virtually identical to that attainable in the absence of an agreement. In Figure 8.2, Egypt clearly stands to gain considerably from agreements that fall to the left of the diagram, whereas Israel stands to gain more as the settlement point moves to the right. However, as stipulated by the second axiom, neither country will settle for an agreement that falls into the negative category (below the horizontal line). Therefore, the range of possible outcomes is restricted to the bargaining space that falls between points a and b on the issue dimension. These points represent the security levels of Egypt and Israel respectively.

In this model the joint utilities of the two players may be maximized at point E. However, this point does not represent a stable equilibrium, since either Israel or Egypt may still be tempted to maximize its own national utility within the available bargaining space. Egypt has an incentive to move the outcome to the left of point E, whereas Israel has an incentive to move toward the right. The parties thus have conflicting interests in that each seeks to make the greatest gains possible within the available bargaining space at the other's expense. On the other hand, Egypt and Israel each have a common interest in finding an agreement that falls somewhere within this bargaining space, since this will leave them both better off than they would be without any agreement.

In a bargaining process like the one depicted in this model, the functions of a mediator such as Kissinger include trying to enhance cooperative interests by making the available bargaining space as large as possible. Kissinger did this largely through his manipulation of the strategic environment. He tried to increase the potential rewards of agreement for all of the parties engaged in the conflict, so that there would be a wider potential range of mutually profitable agreements. A second function is to promote the process of compromise within the available bargaining space so that negotiators would tend to converge on an agreement at a relatively central point, such as point E. In this way it is possible to avoid highly asymmetrical outcomes that might not endure. Such covergence allowed Kissinger to avoid unequal outcomes that could have disrupted the sensitive balance he had achieved previously in the external, strategic system of linkages among the parties. Successful agreement would not only be acceptable to the parties in the short run, but it also would head off any long-run instability or realignment of interests that could disrupt the existing strategic balance within the region and possibly lead to renewed warfare.

The Preconditions for Negotiation

The model summarized above seems to be broadly applicable to the Arab-Israeli conflict in the aftermath of the 1973 war. The basic precondition for its applicability is that the issues must contain elements that are both conflictual and cooperative.

The three most central states in the conflict—Israel, Egypt, and Syria—had developed a limited set of common interests. Foremost among these was the shared desire to avoid a renewed and prolonged regional war. Not surprisingly, these common interests arose from somewhat different strategic and domestic interests. For Israel these desires particularly reflected the strategic jolt that resulted from military losses sustained early in the war. Although Israeli forces had penetrated well into Egyptian and Syrian territory by the end of the war, the Egyptian recapture of land held by Israel in a surprise attack had demoralized the Israeli army. Furthermore, the effort to push back the Egyptian attack across the wide Sinai Peninsula had been costly for Israel both in lives and in destroyed military hardware.

The Egyptians and even the Syrians, despite the latter's urgings for Egypt to continue the fighting, also had strong incentives to negotiate. Further fighting against a rearmed Israel could be successful only if it were conducted by means of a "popular struggle" that neither regime could endure. Both Syria and Egypt had already restored some military honor, enabling them to negotiate without feeling disgraced. By attacking Israel, Sadat had stolen the thunder of Palestinian and Iraqi radicals and had thus retained Egyptian leadership among the Arab states. However, because of Egypt's limited aims in the war and because of Israel's successful counterattack, in the end both Arab armies were in retreat. Egypt's Third Army was nearly surrounded, and Syrian tank losses were devastating. For Sadat, a favorable settlement on at least some of the territorial issues was crucial in order to justify his claim of leadership over the Arab system. Furthermore, this had to occur before a new atmosphere of disillusionment could settle over the Arab world.

Finally, as an involved external party, the United States had its own vital interests in preventing renewed warfare. The United States had suffered several negative consequences as a result of the 1973 war. Relations with the Soviet Union had worsened over the military alert President Nixon had called to head off any potential Soviet involvement in the war. American relations with Israel had been strained by the United States' slow response in resupplying Israeli forces. In addition, the oil production cutbacks by Arab states were clearly designed to put political pressure on the United States through control over energy supplies. Therefore, in the months following the war it was critical for the United States to intervene more directly in the conflict in order to secure a set of agreements that might restore stability and reinvigorate the U.S. strategic system in the reigon.

While the 1973 war had also advanced the realignment process that Kissinger wanted to bring to the Middle East, many elements of conflict remained. The military lines of demarcation at the end of the war corresponded neither to Israel's original borders nor to the limit of post-1967 Israeli-occupied territory. Thus, at least in certain parts of the Israeli perimeter, the withdrawal of troops and the establishment of new demarcation lines remained issues of conflict with Israel's neighbors. Even on a bilateral basis, these issues were essentially zero-sum in character, since territorial gains for Egypt and Syria by definition implied territorial losses for Israel. However, these issues affected the overall strategic balance within the region on a multilateral basis as well.

In addition to these issues of sovereignty, there were other important disputes that Kissinger referred to as security issues. For example, although Israeli defense analysts viewed the advance deployment of forces as being essential for their safety, these were viewed as threats to both the national security and stability of the domestic political regimes in Egypt and Syria. There was also a clear and dramatic clash between the Israeli desire to exist as an independent Zionist state within the region and the Palestinian demand for self-determination in all of the territory formerly under British mandate. These latter issues were so fundamentally conflictual that they had already resulted in over 50 years of fighting in the region. While various U.S. diplomats had successfully modified Egyptian attitudes on this question, the Palestinian demands were a serious factor that had to be taken into account by all Arab regimes. Therefore, in spite of the many common interests among the parties, the issues that divided them ran very deep.

The issues at stake in these negotiations can be roughly grouped in three categories according to the relative mix of cooperative and conflictual elements. The three sets of issues, going from those with the most cooperative elements to those that were most fundamentally zero-sum in character, are as follows:

Issue Set I: Cease-fire
    1. Lines of demarcation
    2. Humanitarian assistance to opposing forces
    3. Logistics, monitoring of demarcation lines

Issue Set II: Disengagement
    1. Troop movements, redeployments, and force levels
    2. Temporary national boundaries
    3. Reopening of the Suez Canal
    4. Reconnaissance

Issue Set III: Conflict Settlement
    1. Diplomatic recognition and political legitimacy for Zionist Israel
    2. Sovereignty of Golan, Gaza, Sinai, and West Bank

3. Self-determination for Palestinians
4. Palestinian rights to repatriation and compensation
5. Status of Jerusalem

Related to the range of cooperative and conflictual interests in each of these issues was the question of the tactically most appropriate forum for dealing with these issues. The issues in Set I were clearly most appropriately treated in bilateral negotiations between the parties to the military conflict. The issues in Set II were also primarily bilateral issues between the competing parties, although the settlement of these issues had implications for other patterns of relationships among states in the Middle East. Finally, the issues in Set III, because of their complexity and their impact on so many actors, could only be dealt with adequately in a multilateral forum. Specifically, the relationship of all parties in the Middle East to the Palestinian question would seem to have rendered nugatory any negotiation in which most or all of these states were not directly involved.

The Mediation Process

The mediation process itself began within the confines of the bargaining space depicted in Figure 8.2. Within this space, Kissinger could seek agreement through paired negotiations, first between Egypt and Israel and then between Syria and Israel. In each effort to mediate, his role was to help the parties find an agreement point as close as possible to an equitable midpoint on each issue dimension. This required two broad kinds of intervention.

First, Kissinger sought to manipulate the timing and sequence of negotiating moves, encouraging each party to make concessions toward the position favored by the other. Concession-making, however, confronts each party with a tactical dilemma: although concessions often generate counterconcessions in a mutually reinforcing process, if the party initiating concessions appears to be too soft, the other party may exploit this by toughening its own position, possibly leading to stalemate. This dilemma has sometimes been referred to as Stevens' (1963) "inherent paradox" of negotiating, namely that the negotiator must be firm without appearing too rigid, while at the same time being willing to yield without appearing too conciliatory. In order to resolve this paradox, Kissinger encouraged each party to make concessions only when he felt that the other party was ready to respond with counterconcessions. By contrast, he might encourage one nation to hold back in its concessions so as not to appear too soft.

Another technique employed by Kissinger was to identify trade-offs, in which exchanges could be made across several issues to create packages of agreements. Particularly when issues are discrete, as in the recognition or nonrecognition of the state of Israel, incremental concessions may not be possible or appropriate. In these instances, Kissinger tried to create package agreements by encouraging one party to take a loss on an issue of lesser importance to it in exchange for winning on another issue of higher priority or value. For example, in the first Sinai disengagement negotiations, Egypt took a loss in its opposition to force limitations, while Israel accepted a symbolic rather than a formal pledge of nonbelligerence from Egypt. So long as Egypt's gain on the issue exceeded its loss on the force limitation issue, and Israel's gains on the force limitation exceeded the loss of accepting only a symbolic pledge, the trade-off was perceived to be mutually profitable. Kissinger's additional offer of secrecy for these arrangements also helped to make the package more acceptable to Egypt.

The second kind of intervention employed by Kissinger was less tactical and more strategic in nature. In the Middle East negotiations Kissinger tried to manipulate the strategic environment in order to influence the parties to move in directions he preferred. Three tactics were employed in this regard. First, commitments were manipulated so that one party was made to appear firmly identified with a particular position from which further concessions were impossible. If the other party could be convinced of the credibility of this commitment, and if the commitment fell within the bargaining space, then the second party would be forced to accept agreement at that point rather than risk stalemate. Second, threats were employed as conditional statements by which Kissinger indicated that the United States would either apply punishments or remove rewards to the parties if they failed to reach agreement along the lines he preferred. Finally, promises were used in a similar fashion, in this case to provide rewards or remove punishments conditionally in exchange for a party's agreement to settle at a point preferred by the United States.

In his first role of encouraging mutual concessions within the available bargaining space, Kissinger acted very much like a traditional mediator; he helped the conflicting parties to converge toward agreement at a mutually acceptable point. In the second role, however, Kissinger played the part of strategist, a part that was most appropriate to someone with both a distinct interest in the nature of the outcomes and possessed of the resources to exert influence on the negotiators. These same tactics were also available to the negotiating parties. In these negotiations, however, Kissinger as a third party also had access to tactical instruments, and he used them often to affect the parties' perceptions of the negotiating framework and to modify the utilities subjectively assigned to various agreement payoffs. Thus Kissinger functioned both as a mediator and as a directly involved strategist. In these roles he promoted convergence between the parties by carefully controlling the timing and sequencing of negotiating moves. He moved the more negotiable issues to the forefront, while forestalling those issues in Set III that were too strategically sensitive to permit rapid results. As Quandt (1977, p. 212) writes:

> It was important to create the proper balance of incentives first; then to reach limited results at an early stage without making commitments to the final goal; eventually, when a mutuality of interests had emerged, more substantial areas of agreement would be possible.

The ways in which Kissinger manipulated the timing of moves, serving as both mediator and strategist, may be demonstrated most clearly by briefly reviewing his handling of some of the major issues throughout the course of the negotiations.

KISSINGER'S MEDIATION IN THE MIDDLE EAST CONFLICT

As was suggested previously, Kissinger initially wanted to limit the issues under negotiation. Therefore, the first bilateral negotiations between Egypt and Israel concerned the relatively limited issues of the cease-fire and its maintenance. Although Kissinger made his first visits to the region in the aftermath of the war in early November 1973, a large portion of these early negotiations were conducted directly between Egyptian and Israeli military officers at Kilometer 101 on the road from Cairo to Suez. Golan (1976, pp. 120–21) notes that substantial progress was underway through direct, bilateral negotiations on a wide range of issues such as disengagement provisions.

Israeli Major General Yariv and Egyptian Lieutenant General el-Gamasy dealt not only with the immediate terms of a cease-fire and its enforcement, falling within Set I of our typology; they also treated Set II issues, especially the disengagement of the opposing military forces. Egypt began by demanding the return to the prewar borders, while Israel at first wanted to maintain its troops on the West Bank of the Suez Canal. However, according to Golan (1976, p. 97), the two men behaved very much like "merchants in an oriental bazaar" and rapidly exchanged compromise proposals. Egypt proposed a withdrawal of Israeli forces to 35 kilometers east of the canal, with Egyptian forces stationed no further than 10 kilometers east of the canal. The territory in between would become a United Nations buffer zone. Although the Israelis were at first receptive to these proposals, in the end they reversed their position and the negotiations were broken off.

Golan (1976, pp. 120–21) suggests that it was Secretary Kissinger who was responsible for this because of his plan to reserve these issues for later in the negotiations. Kissinger felt that Set II issues could be addressed most effectively within the Geneva forum, where some visible progress would have to be made in order to develop the Arab consensus that he considered essential for a viable agreement. Kissinger wanted to keep certain issues out of the bilateral forum so that they could form the basis of this politically necessary forward movement in Geneva. Furthermore, he wanted to avoid precedents that might be applied too readily to disengagement on the Syrian front, since the latter issue would almost necessarily become linked with the most sensitive aspects of the Palestinian issue, that is, with the core of Set III disputes. Quandt (1977, p. 220) observes that Kissinger wanted to avoid an Egyptian-Israeli disengagement arrangement that would serve as a precedent for demands by Assad that Israel would not oblige. Therefore, from Kissinger's vantage point, Yariv was moving too quickly toward agreement before the linkages had been established for following through with the negotiations on Set II and Set III issues. Furthermore, it was doubtful that Yariv's offer had the support of the Israeli cabinet.

Kissinger also wanted the United States to retain a central role in the negotiation process. Initial success in purely bilateral negotiations might preclude Kissinger's own role on behalf of the United States. This role was essential since he believed that he was the only participant in the process with a view of the entire system rather than just a portion of it. For these reasons he encouraged the Israelis to pull back, thereby breaking off the Kilometer 101 negotiations.

Similar motivation seems to have influenced Kissinger's behavior in response to a proposal by Israeli Defense Minister Dayan advanced on December 7, 1973. Dayan proposed that Israel withdraw to a line just west of the Mitla and Giddi passes, in exchange for demilitarization of the forward areas and a commitment by Egypt to reopen the Suez Canal. Kissinger's response, however, was to urge the Israelis not to move too fast in making concessions. He particularly wanted to create the impression among the Arab states that Israel was neither weak nor excessively subject to U.S. influence (Quandt 1977, p. 221). Such a perception might have led the Egyptians to believe that they could exploit Israel's initial concessions, thereby forcing the Israelis to accept outcomes near the latter's security level or minimum position. Once again the negotiations were slowed in comparison with what might have occurred in the absence of Kissinger's intervention. The effect of this intervention was to assure Kissinger that the negotiations would be structured along his preferred lines, regardless of whether these coincided with the interests of the parties immediately involved.

By slowing down the process in the region, Kissinger was also able to proceed with his preferred strategy, which was to use the Geneva negotiations as a larger forum after initial agreements had been achieved bilaterally. For this reason it was important that the bilateral negotiations not reach a conclusion too rapidly, prior to Kissinger's determination of the proper conditions for success within the larger strategic framework represented by the Geneva forum. It was with this consideration in mind that Kissinger went to the Middle East early in 1974 in order to secure a disengagement between Israel and Egypt.

On January 11, 1974, Kissinger visited with President Sadat in Aswan to promote an agreed-upon basis for further negotiations in Geneva. However, according to Golan (1976, p. 158), Kissinger was surprised to find Sadat encouraging him to stay in the Middle East to work out the details of an agreement himself. Sadat, of course, wanted to avoid pressure from either the Soviet Union or Arab radicals. This motivated him to reach an Egyptian-Israeli disengagement without having to submit to the pressure that would have inevitably occurred at Geneva (Sheehan 1976, p. 110). After Sadat had helped him to achieve rapid and concrete successes in the bilateral format, Kissinger's preoccupation shifted. Instead of reserving his energies for the more distant role of supervising the overall negotiation and keeping it in line with his global linkage strategy, Kissinger became enmeshed in the details of three bilateral negotiations. Although he tried to keep alive the prospect of Soviet participation at Geneva, as well as the possibility of broader Arab ratification of an agreement through this forum, his attention focused almost exclusively on the step-by-step negotiating process.

Since any disengagement agreement dealing with the Israeli-Syrian border could not avoid the sensitive security issues dividing these two states, especially because of the impact of an agreement on the Palestinian question, Kissinger decided to pursue an Egyptian-Israeli disengagement first, in the hope of achieving rapid success. The first round of shuttle diplomacy began on January 11, 1974, with two major issues dividing the parties: the direction and extent of withdrawals, and the number of troops allowed to remain at the lines of demarcation.

Egypt wanted Israeli forces withdrawn east of the Mitla and Giddi passes, a position that Israel opposed. Israel wanted Egyptian forces east of the Suez Canal limited in number, while the Egyptians were opposed to such a limitation. Although the Israelis also demanded a formalized end to Egypt's state of belligerence, this was an opening demand that was soon modified in favor of less explicit but nonetheless effective indications of Egypt's nonbelligerence. Kissinger's main role in this phase was to shuttle back and forth between Israel and Egypt, seeking concessions on both the point of Israeli withdrawal and the limitations on Egyptian forces in the region east of the Suez Canal. Kissinger functioned here as a go-between, conveying an Israeli map of the proposed disengagement line to the Egyptians. When the latter accepted this proposal, except for its southern extremeties, Kissinger encouraged Israel to modify the map slightly in the direction favored by Egypt. Golan (1976) reports that although Sadat accepted the positions demarcated by this redrawn line, he was psychologically unprepared to accept a disengagement map that had been drawn by the Israelis. Kissinger thus presented this map as an American one in order to gain Sadat's concurrence.

Similarly, the force levels to be retained by Egypt in the region were settled through incremental compromises. Initially the Israelis favored keeping the demilitarized zone free of tanks, while the Egyptians wanted to be able to station up to 200 tanks in the zone. After one trip Kissinger was able to persuade the Egyptians to reduce the number of tanks to 100, and after still another trip the overall figure came down to a final total of 30. Thus this agreement was reached largely through a series of incremental concessions by both competing parties. The main role of the mediator in this phase was to encourage each party to make concessions without risking either loss of face or the exploitation of their concessions by the other party.

In his second effort at force disengagement, Kissinger turned his attention to the more difficult Syrian-Israeli border. Here Kissinger had less leverage, though he knew that the inclusion of Syria in the negotiation process was essential if an Arab consensus were to be achieved in an ultimate set of agreements. In Syrian President Assad, Kissinger encountered a personal negotiating style that was very different from Sadat's style. Although Assad was willing to strike bargains about troop withdrawal and disengagement zones, he continued to insist that the Palestinians be compensated as the major victims of Israeli injustice. Disengagement was ultimately secured by Kissinger not only through a series of compromises, but also through the use of strategic manipulation of the Arab political environment. It was in these negotiations that Kissinger began to emerge in his role as strategic manipulator as well as mediator.

The precise line of disengagement and the nature of postdisengagement force limitations were the main issues providing opportunities for trade-offs, just as they had been in the Egyptian-Israeli negotiations. The city of Quneitra became the first major obstacle to agreement. In early May 1974, Kissinger succeeded in securing Israeli concessions that would have returned all but the western parts of the city to Syria. However, when he presented these proposals to Assad on May 8, 1974, Kissinger held back some of the Israeli concessions so that he would have something to concede in future trips. He was clearly interested in maintaining his own personal control over the timing of the negotiations, so that he could demonstrate gradual, steady progress without making either side too optimistic at the outset. At the same time he resorted to more threatening tactics in order to pressure the Syrians into making appropriate concessions. These included the use of U.S. leverage with other states more closely tied to the United States, including Egypt, Saudi Arabia, and even the influential radical Arab leader, Boumedienne of Algeria. Perhaps the promise of further Israeli concessions would have been more effective in moving the negotiations along quickly than these more threatening tactics. Nevertheless, Kissinger was less interested in the speed of the negotiations than he was in maintaining momentum, keeping the pace of the negotiations under his control rather than letting it be determined by the direct, conflicting parties in the bilateral negotiation.

Kissinger's centrality was further asserted in the Israeli-Syrian negotiations by the tactic of presenting the proposals of each side as if they were his own, thereby making compromises more palatable. In the end it was Kissinger's own commitment on behalf of the United States that was decisive with the Israelis. According to Quandt (1977, p. 243), Kissinger promised the Israelis that Palestinian commandos would be denied access to the Syrian side of the disengagement line. Similarly, Kissinger had to assure the Syrians that the hills west of Quneitra, which were to be left under Israel's occupation, would not be allowed as sites for the emplacement of heavy weapons with which the Israelis could inflict new damage on the city below (Golan 1976, p. 204).

Even at this point, when promises and threats had been required to encourage the parties to redefine their conception of minimum security positions in the negotiations, several diplomatic observers have reported that a final punitive measure and implicit threat was needed in order to obtain Syrian acceptance of Israel's proposal concerning the Golan Heights. According to these reports, Kissinger manipulated aid that was channeled by the Central Intelligence Agency to the Kurdish rebels fighting against the Iraqi government. This was probably a decisive element in silencing the opposition of the Baathist majority in Iraq to Assad's Baathist regime in Syria reaching a disengagement with Israel. Syria thus found itself relatively free of pressure from an Arab neighbor, Iraq, that might have proven to be an obstacle to a settlement.

The final set of negotiations in the aftermath of the 1973 war involved the Sinai disengagement. Having achieved agreement bilaterally between both Egypt and Israel, and again between Syria and Israel, Kissinger found himself confronted with two alternatives. On the one hand, he could push for a third bilateral negotiation between Israel and Jordan. Although this offered considerable advantages from a strategic point of view, Kissinger believed that this alternative would encounter considerable tactical difficulty. The issues at stake in this bilateral relationship fell mainly in Set III; these included issues such as the future of the West Bank and Palestinian sovereignty, each of which contained a substantial element of zero-sum conflict. Furthermore, these were the very issues that Kissinger would have preferred to address in a multilateral forum, since they involved larger strategic questions that could not be treated adequately in bilateral negotiations. Finally, at a time when the

U.S. government had been dramatically weakened back home by the resignation of President Nixon, Kissinger seemed to be especially caught up in the success of his shuttle diplomacy.

For each of the above reasons, Kissinger decided to forgo the possibility of dealing with these issues in the immediate future in favor of a second, less risky, alternative: renewed negotiations between Egypt and Israel over disengagement in the Sinai. Although this choice may have maintained the momentum of negotiations as Kissinger wanted, it also indicates that he had begun to lose sight of his larger strategic objectives in the glare of the publicity surrounding his tactical successes as a mediator. In the long run, this disregard for strategic considerations may have resulted in a lost opportunity to achieve a more durable solution to the Middle East conflict.

The actual negotiations on the disengagement in the Sinai took place during the summer of 1975. The major issue involved the extent of Israeli withdrawal in the Sinai. Kissinger tried to secure Israeli abandonment of the disputed Mitla and Giddi passes in exchange for an Egyptian agreement to confine its military emplacements to the western slopes of these passes. However, the negotiations succeeded primarily because of agreement upon a United-Nations-supervised buffer zone that significantly revised the security situation for both parties. In addition, the United States became directly involved in monitoring any violations of this buffer zone by agreeing to provide and man some of the electronic warning devices placed in this zone. This U.S. presence provided an additional guarantee to both Egypt and Israel. It also provided the United States with strategic rather than merely symbolic leverage, should future developments ever require action by the United Nations Security Council. Furthermore, the United States pledged economic aid and additional military assistance to both parties, a factor that proved decisive in getting them to reinterpret the security concerns on their common frontier. Specifically, Kissinger pledged $2.25 billion in aid to Israel for fiscal year 1976, and he promised a favorable response to Israel's request for F-16 all-weather fighters and Pershing I missiles. President Sadat was granted aid amounting to $750 million, mostly to cover the cost of installing an early-warning system in the Sinai.

Kissinger supplemented this aid with promises of U.S. policy commitments that were designed to render the 1973–75 negotiations less reversible. The best known of these was Kissinger's pledge to the Israelis not to enter into discussions with the PLO without Israel's prior approval. Similarly, the pledge of continued oil for Israel over the coming five-year period exemplified the use of a "promise." This commitment was likely to be considered binding on the United States even beyond the five-year period specified in the formal U.S. statement. The United States, finally, was not at all reluctant to employ threats as well as promises in order to induce the parties in the second Sinai negotiations to reach agreement. For example, President Ford sent the Israelis a letter on March 21, 1975, threatening to suspend U.S. military and economic aid—as part of an overall reassessment of American policy in the region—if Israel did not show greater flexibility in those negotiations.

In short, Kissinger was anything but a passive and neutral mediator in most of the Arab-Israeli negotiations. He represented a nation with a distinct interest in the outcomes of these negotiations. He also represented a country with the resources to issue credible commitments, threats, and promises, and to execute them if necessary. This gave him far more influence over the negotiations than most mediators traditionally have. He not only facilitated compromises between the extreme positions of the two parties; he often proposed compromise solutions and then used tactical manipulation to ensure that these proposals were accepted by all of the parties. His role in the bargaining process was central, and the outcomes of the negotiations directly reflect the nature of the dual role as mediator and strategist that he assumed on behalf of U.S. interests.

AN EVALUATION OF KISSINGER'S ROLE IN THE MIDDLE EAST NEGOTIATIONS

Henry Kissinger has primarily thought of himself as a strategist of international politics. Indeed, he has prided himself on his role in formulating and implementing policy derived from a broad strategic framework, thereby differentiating himself from most of his contemporaries in the world of diplomacy and placing himself in the same framework as such great historical strategists as Metternich and Bismarck. For Kissinger, therefore, tactics must both reflect and follow from strategic ends. It is with this view in mind that he entered personally into the negotiations for a settlement of the Middle East conflict.

How successful was Kissinger as a strategist and tactician? It will be argued here that Kissinger's performance in the Middle East negotiations was characterized by a basic irony. Although he entered the negotiations with a strategic framework foremost in view, he became engrossed with bargaining tactics and enthralled by his success as a mediator with both national leaders and the mass media. Paradoxically, this involvement and success made Kissinger lose at least partial sight of his overall strategic goals. The result was that the "grand strategist" met with considerable success as a tactician, while failing to provide any lasting or durable solutions to the conflict at the strategic level. Therefore, we shall first examine Kissinger's effectiveness as a mediator, and then turn to some of his limitations as designer of an overarching solution to the problems of the Middle East.

Kissinger the Tactician

As a tactician, Kissinger placed a good deal of emphasis upon the function of the negotiation process as a means for generating solutions from the bottom up, a phenomenon often referred to as the construction of packages of agreements. These packages were developed by Kissinger largely through the effective use of four tactical devices, all of which may also prove effective in other similar efforts at mediation.

First, Kissinger focused the negotiations on negotiable issues so that results could be produced at an early date. This required him to determine which of the several possible issues appeared to provide considerable bargaining space, with the interests of the parties potentially overlapping. Kissinger focused the negotiators' attention on concrete issues; he pursued these issues in a bilateral rather than multilateral forum. This procedure, sometimes referred to as issue control, has been found to be effective in laboratory bargaining situations where agreements can more readily be achieved on "smaller" issues (Deutsch, Canavan, and Rubin 1971, pp. 258–67). Our analysis of the negotiations in the Middle East indicates that Kissinger was able to induce convergence between the parties by concentrating on negotiable (Set I) issues that could readily lead to early agreements. The key to his success here was his ability to separate these issues from the more sensitive dimensions of difference (Set III issues).

Kissinger's style of mediation was largely effective in shaping the bargaining space to serve his ends. Rarely in his discussions with the principals did he raise Set III issues for consideration. He made clear at the outset what he was prepared to discuss, mentioning the sensitive issues only in response to questions raised about them (Sheehan 1976, pp. 96–97). Such decoupling did not apply, however, to those broader issues that transcended regional concerns. When it was necessary in order to provide motivation for agreement, he would refer to linkages between the negotiation process and such broad concerns as global stability or the international economic order (Quandt 1977, p. 223). This tactic was intended to remind the participants of the importance of his efforts, without drawing implications for the resolution of more sensitive issues.

Second, Kissinger was particularly effective in influencing the other parties' perceptions of him as a mediator. Although Kissinger had impressive credentials when he entered the negotiations, he had to overcome considerable concern about his neutrality on Middle East issues and great skepticism about his understanding of the regional situation into which he interjected himself. To overcome these doubts, Kissinger had to gain personal acceptance by establishing close relationships with each of the principal actors. Only through such relationships could he induce the parties to modify their perceptions of the situation and their irreconcilable differences. In a survey of conditions affecting the success of mediation efforts, Frei (1976) has placed considerable emphasis upon the relationships between the mediator and the conflicting parties. The best prospects for mediation occur when the mediator is perceived as belonging to the reference groups of both parties and when he does not have a tense relationship with either party. A symmetrical pattern of sentiments toward the mediator renders him effective in his attempts to influence both parties. Kissinger's challenge was to create such a pattern.

Genuine personal relationships did develop between Kissinger and his two principal Arab clients. He employed a technique sometimes referred to as impression management in order to enhance this relationship in spite of the considerable differences between himself and Sadat and Assad. Most notable, perhaps, was his success in creating the impression that he was needed, that only he knew what the sides were saying and thinking. He controlled the process in order to focus his clients' attention on himself, without competing demands or offers being presented by other interveners. In addition, relentless discussions with the parties enabled him to demonstrate a willingness to be immersed in details, a penchant for nuance, and a disarming manner. He was able to use these qualities in order to influence the actual negotiations, as when he succeeded in overcoming Sadat's reservations about force limitation proposals by presenting an Israeli plan as if it were an American proposal. Actions like this made Kissinger appear to the parties as an indispensable element in the peace process.

Third, Kissinger maintained secrecy as a tactic to facilitate the concession-convergence process. Although there is considerable debate about the utility of secrecy as a diplomatic tool, in this instance Kissinger used it effectively to enhance the negotiation process. This helped him to reduce the influence of domestic political forces at undesirable junctures in the process, to avert the intervention of other outside parties, and to enable the parties to make concessions without substantial loss of face or credibility.

For example, Kissinger excluded Fahmy and Gamasy from some of his discussions with Sadat in order to build a strong personal relationship with the Egyptian president and to convince Sadat of his views (Sheehan 1976, p. 112). By keeping the Soviets out of the Syrian-Israeli disengagement talks, Kissinger was able to resist Soviet pressure to return prematurely to multilateral negotiations in Geneva, which might have weakened progress made up to that point (Quandt 1977, pp. 236–37). Also, Kissinger's offer of secrecy for arrangements made in the first Sinai negotiations increased Sadat's willingness to accept the package, because secrecy enabled Sadat to make public his own interpretation of this agreement at a later time. Therefore, the tactical use of secrecy often served to sustain momentum in the negotiation process and to produce turning points that led to the disengagement agreement.

Fourth, Kissinger managed to overcome "Stevens' paradox," referred to previously, in which a negotiator must be firm without appearing too rigid, while also being willing to yield without appearing too conciliatory. Brown (1977, p. 278) has argued that this paradox requires a negotiator to build "pressures toward face-maintenance into the structure of a negotiation." By reducing these pressures to save face, a mediator may facilitate the exchange of concessions that can provide momentum for the process of convergence in bargaining. Several examples may illustrate how Kissinger dealt with these pressures.

Kissinger's sensitivity to the perils of giving too much too soon was evident in advice he gave to the Israelis and in his presentations to the Syrians. In response to a disengagement proposal offerred by Dayan, Kissinger urged the Israelis not to move too quickly in the negotiations. It was important that Israel not look weak and for the Arabs to conclude that it was difficult for the United States to influence Israel (Quandt 1977, p. 221). Later, while assailing Dayan for making an "inadequate" proposal, Kissinger emphasized that Israel should not give up any settlements at that stage. Then, being aware of Assad's "substantial appetite" for Israeli concessions, he decided to disclose some concessions but withhold others. The withheld concessions were to be used on later trips in order to show continued progress (Quandt 1977, p. 241).

Unrealistic expectations may also be created by the bargainer who appears rigid. Aware of this, Kissinger attempted to soften the image of the other parties. For example, while telling Eban and Allon that he did not expect them to give Assad's proposal serious consideration, he said that he was convinced that this was not the last word from Damascus (Golan 1976, p. 182). When talking to Sadat, he would complain that "it is unbelievable what the Israelis are demanding," while reminding him that he was making progress in extracting more concessions (Sheehan 1976, pp. 180ff.). Kissinger's control of the process enabled him to convey these impressions. By convincing each party that the other was neither too conciliatory nor too firm, he was able to create expectations about an eventual agreement.

In short, Kissinger helped to move along the negotiation process in the Middle East through the judicious use of a number of effective bargaining tactics. By focusing attention upon the negotiable issues, he was able to separate these from the underlying ideological differences. Rather than enhancing tensions, these tactics tended to promote agreement. The increased credibility that resulted from his personal role enabled him to gain acceptance for proposals presented under the guise of an American plan. By maintaining secrecy he could control the process and elicit concessions without loss of face. Control over the process also permitted him to convey expectations, thereby facilitating the exchange of reciprocal concessions. Together these tactics served to create and sustain a dynamic bargaining process. The effects of these tactics are summarized in Table 8.1.

There were, however, several limitations to Kissinger's tactical role in these negotiations. First, he tended to rely very heavily upon the use of threats in order to create his desired equilibrium. As Boulding (1978, p. 157) has observed, the long-term stability of an equilibrium based on threats is doubtful because the dynamics of such systems tend "constantly to expand far beyond the optimum into highly pathological states, whether this is in the international system or in the human learning process." While Kissinger broke the spiral of threats in the short run, his strategy failed to create those confidence-building measures that would assure stability over the long term.

Second, Kissinger's step-by-step approach failed to provide a basis for communication and exchange following the disengagement agreements. Missing was a plan for creating structures that could sustain the realignments fostered by his intervention. One such structure is a communication and information regime that enables the parties to develop the conventions and rules that they believe are applicable, and that can also define violations of the implied agreement (Bobrow 1979). Another structure might consist of a mediational mechanism designed explicitly to reduce ideological polarization. Examples include strong coalitions of moderates from each nation who are linked by superordinate regional identifications, and cross-cutting identifications between members of the different societies (Druckman and Zechmeister 1973).

Third, Kissinger's substantial ego became strongly involved with the process of step-by-step diplomacy, especially when it thrust him into great international prominence. In this light, success in the individual steps started to become ends in themselves, rather than linked steps to a larger solution. These limitations became critical when they affected Kissinger's role as a strategist.

Kissinger the Strategist

Kissinger's conception of U.S. objectives in the Middle East placed prime emphasis upon the creation of a system of global and regional alignments. At a minimum, this system would counterbalance Soviet influence and provide for a U.S. stronghold in one of the vital regions on the periphery of the central area of Soviet-American confrontation. To establish such a stable system in the Middle East, Kissinger would have to go well beyond reinforcing the U.S. alliance with Israel. It was essential to include Egypt within this system, due to its manpower at Israel's back

TABLE 8.1

Effects of Kissinger's Tactics on the Negotiation Process and on the Region

Tactic	Purpose	Effects	Regional Impact
Decoupling issues	To focus attention on negotiable issues	Limited agreements; reduced antagonism between parties	Avoided polarization of conflict along one line: increased frames of reference for conflict
Manipulating perceptions of mediator	To increase mediator's credibility	Increased trust; increased acceptance of mediator proposals	Reduced the asymmetry of the tensions between mediator and parties
Maintaining secrecy	To ensure mediator control of process	Elicited concession without loss of face	Increased parties' dependence on the United States
Resolving Stevens' paradox	To shape expectations for other's concessions	Facilitated coordination of concession exchanges	Made further negotiations and interventions feasible

door, its geographic centrality within the region, as well as its historic role as guardian of the Suez Canal and spokesman for the Arab states. This core structure also had to be reinforced by the silent participation of Saudi Arabia, especially to support Egypt's participation in the revised regional alignment. In his efforts to create this system of alliances, Kissinger was largely successful.

However, to insure his long-term objectives, another more complex system of alignments was needed in the region. Dominance over this system would bring with it a broader range of U.S. influence. Once again Kissinger wanted to make use of the Saudis as silent partners in order to enlist the cooperation of the reluctant Syrian Baathist regime. This more subtle client system could be used by Kissinger to obtain ratification of the agreements formalizing the system in this region. While the Saudis did help to bring Syria into the settlement process, this arrangement worked only so long as such Set III issues as restored Arab rights on the West Bank, Gaza, and Golan could be put off for the future. As these issues became more salient, the inevitable conflict between Arab interests and the Israeli desire to maintain a military strategy of defense-in-depth would have to be confronted. Kissinger was successful in achieving a disengagement agreement with Syria, aided by tactics employed outside the negotiations. These included punitive measures against radical Arab groups within Syria, against similar elements in Iraq, and against the PLO in Lebanon. But any more far-reaching settlement would run up against Kissinger's limited ability to influence these domestic and international factors within the Arab countries.

These strategic difficulties were compounded by some of Kissinger's tactical weaknesses, noted previously. Kissinger's step-by-step diplomacy, due particularly to its excessive reliance on threat systems, did not provide a basis for communication and exchange among the parties following the disengagement agreements. Missing also was a plan for creating structures that could sustain the realignments fostered by his intervention. If Kissinger had sought to establish an ongoing regime of interaction in the region, with built-in mechanisms to facilitate long-term mediational efforts, conceivably his short-term successes could have turned into long-term regional solutions. But Kissinger was afraid that any such efforts to deal with these issues on a multilateral basis would slow the bilateral success rate. Consequently, his ego involvement and perception of the timing of events prevented him from striving to build a structure that might survive in the long run.

In *A World Restored*, Kissinger (1979a, p. 286) quoted Metternich's appraisal of his own strategic system:

> I feel as if I were in the middle of a web, like my friends the
> spiders whom I love. . . . I have brought to bear my moral means in all

directions . . . but this state of things forces the poor spider to remain in the centre of its fine web. These webs are beautiful to behold, artfully spun and capable of resisting light attacks; but not a gust of wind.

Kissinger's careful strategic system in the Middle East survived the puffs of the debilitated Arab revolutionary movements that had emerged after the 1967 war. But the structure was so fragile, and consisted of so many essential components that were left untouched, especially those dealing with the problems of the Palestinians, that it seemed unlikely to survive the gusts of future winds. Subsequent events, such as the political and religious upheaval in formerly conservative Iran, and interjection of Soviet forces into Afghanistan, may serve as warnings of gusts that lie on the horizon.

Within the core system itself, the Israeli moves to consolidate military control over the Golan and the West Bank, the increasingly sophisticated tactics employed by a frustrated Palestinian movement, and the potential instability in the economic regeneration of Israel and Egypt, all threaten the stability of the region. Conflicts may be even more difficult to resolve, and opportunities to settle the fundamental conflicts may become even more elusive in the years ahead. In this regard, Kissinger's conservative tactics of phasing and sequencing events may have proven successful in securing short-term agreements, but at the price of long-term regional stability. Thus, both the immediate rewards that Kissinger received from playing his tactical role as mediator, and the temporary stability of his strategic system, may prove to be as ironic in the long run as Metternich's spider caught in its own web.

REFERENCES

Bobrow, D. B. "Arms Control through Communication and Information Regimes: Report from the Bureau of Governmental Research." University of Maryland, 1979.

Boulding, K. E. *Ecodynamics: A New Theory of Social Evolution.* Beverly Hills, Calif.: Sage, 1978.

Brown, B. R. "Face-Saving and Face-Restoration in Negotiation." In *Negotiations: Social-Psychological Perspectives*, ed. D. Druckman. Beverly Hills, Calif.: Sage, 1977.

Deutsch, M.; Canavan, D.; and Rubin, J. "The Effects of Size of Conflict and Sex of Experimenter upon Interpersonal Bargaining." *Journal of Experimental Social Psychology*, 1971, 7, 258–67.

Druckman, D., and Zechmeister, K. "Conflict of Interest and Value Dissensus: Propositions in the Sociology of Conflict." *Human Relations*, 1973, 26, 449–66.

Frei, D. "Conditions Affecting the Effectiveness of International Mediation." *Papers of the Peace Science Society (International)*, 1976, 26, 67–84.

Golan, M. *The Secret Conversations of Henry Kissinger*. New York: Quadrangle, 1976.

Heikal, M. *The Sphinx and the Commisar: The Rise and Fall of Soviet Influence in the Middle East*. New York: Harper and Row, 1978.

Kalb, M., and Kalb, B. *Kissinger*. Boston: Little, Brown, 1974.

Kissinger, H. A. *A World Restored: Metternich, Castlereagh, and the Problems of Peace, 1812–1822*. Boston: Houghton Mifflin, 1979a.

———. *White House Years*. Boston: Little, Brown, 1979b.

Quandt, W. B. *Decade of Decisions: American Policy toward the Arab-Israeli Conflict, 1967–1976*. Berkeley, Calif.: University of California Press, 1977.

Sadat, A. *In Search of Identity*. New York: Harper and Row, 1977.

Sheehan, E. R. F. *The Arabs, Israelis, and Kissinger: A Secret History of American Diplomacy in the Middle East*. New York: Reader's Digest Press, 1976.

Stevens, C. A. *Strategic and Collective Bargaining Negotiation*. New York: McGraw-Hill, 1963.

9

KISSINGER IN THE MIDDLE EAST: AN EXPLORATORY ANALYSIS OF ROLE STRAIN IN INTERNATIONAL MEDIATION
Kenneth Kressel

MEDIATION AND THE PROBLEM OF ROLE STRAIN

Human behavior is powerfully affected by obstacles to the enactment of prescribed social roles. The theoretical nature and consequences of these obstacles have been described by Sarbin and Allen (1968) and Deutsch and Krauss (1965) among others. More recently, this notion has been fruitfully applied to an explanation of negotiators' behavior (Walton and McKersie 1965; Druckman 1977), as well as to the diverse orientations of attorneys in negotiations between divorcing spouses (Kressel, Lopez-Morillas, Weinglass, and Deutsch 1979). It is the purpose of this chapter to extend this analysis to the process of mediation, with particular reference to Henry Kissinger's role as mediator in the Arab-Israeli conflict.

The discussion is organized around the concept of role strain, defined as felt and/or latent (not fully recognized by the actor) difficulties in role performance (Komarovsky 1976). Three components of role strain are particularly important in the present analysis: role conflict, role hindrance, and role ambiguity.

Role conflict refers to the difficulty in role performance produced by the direct clash of two legitimate role expectations such that complete fulfillment of both expectations is realistically impossible (Parsons 1951). For example, the role of instructor in a military academy may involve a direct conflict between military and educational norms regarding the

I would like to thank Morton Deutsch and Jeffrey Z. Rubin for their helpful reactions to earlier drafts of this chapter.

appropriate behavior of teacher toward student (Getzels and Guba 1954). Role conflict may also be occasioned when parties with whom the role occupant interacts hold contradictory expectations for the actor's behavior. Negotiators may be pressured by their constituents into presenting the constituents' demands vehemently and without backing down, while their opposite numbers across the bargaining table may expect these same negotiators to adhere to norms of moderation and compromise (Walton and McKersie 1965). Role conflict has received considerable research attention; perhaps that is why the concept has often been used interchangeably with that of role strain. Role conflict, however, is but one variant of role strain.

Role hindrance, a second subcategory of role strain, refers to the difficulty in role performance produced when the enactment of a given role expectation is blocked, either totally or partially, by situational obstacles to role performance. The strain of a doctor called upon to treat a disease for which there is no available cure, or the strain of the man socialized to demand of himself that he be the intellectual superior of his wife in a society that does not provide men with the special privileges to ensure such superiority, are cases in point (Komarovsky 1976).

Role ambiguity refers to uncertainty about whether a norm governs a situation, and if so, which one. It may also refer to uncertainty about the expectations that others hold. The college male in a quandary about whether he should pay for dinner on a first date, in a dating culture in which clear guidelines governing the relations between the sexes are absent, is experiencing the stresses of role ambiguity.

Role conflict, role hindrance, and role ambiguity were each important obstacles to Kissinger's effective enactment of his role as mediator. Although Kissinger's performance suffered accordingly, the principal purpose of this chapter is not evaluative but analytic: to describe the important role pressures that may hem in mediators, and with which they must struggle fully as much as with the dispute that they have been asked to help resolve.* The following discussion is divided into two major sections. In the first, the context of the Kissinger's mediation will be examined in order to illustrate the nature of his role difficulties. In the second section, Kissinger's efforts to cope with these role problems will be discussed, as well as the implications of role analysis for an understanding of mediation. Before proceeding to these matters, however, it is necessary to consider the nature of a mediator's role obligations.

---

*Role conflict, role hindrance, and role ambiguity do not exhaust the varieties of role strain. Other types include role inadequacy (where the personal characteristics of the role occupant mesh poorly with the requirements of the role) and insufficient rewards for role conformity. See Komarovsky (1976) for a discussion of these and other variants of role strain.

There is no precise catalog of the behavior and attitudes that are expected of a mediator. There are, however, certain recurrent themes in the reflections of practitioners and students of the art that may serve as useful guideposts (Kressel 1972; Deutsch 1973; Rubin and Brown 1975; Meyer 1960). With regard to the parties, the mediator is expected: to establish and maintain trust and confidence; to demonstrate empathy and understanding for the positions of each side; to be highly expert on substantive and procedural issues, but to use that expertise to guide and counsel, not to impose personal views or take sides. With regard to the process, the mediator is expected to foster a procedure of dispute resolution: in which neither party gets all that it is asking, although neither ends by feeling humiliated or defeated; that engages all parties in an active process of give and take, albeit one that is sufficiently controlled so that the risks of conflict escalation are kept to a minimum; and that is based on an objective and realistic assessment of the forces and interests at play. With regard to the settlement, the mediator is expected to promote agreements: that both sides can defend publicly; that each can view as reasonably fair; and that lay the groundwork for improved interaction.

Fulfilling all of the requirements of the mediator role is a task of no mean accomplishment, especially in conflicts of any intensity. This is partly because the role requirements are individually difficult and challenging. In larger measure, however, it is because at various points the different role requirements are in direct opposition (role conflict); are blocked by situational obstacles (role hindrance); and are inadequately defined in scope (role ambiguity). In the case of Kissinger's intervention in the Middle East, these components of role strain can be traced to two major sources: the parties and the structure of their dispute, and Kissinger's position as U.S. Secretary of State.

THE PARTIES AND THE STRUCTURE OF THE DISPUTE AS OBSTACLES TO MEDIATOR PERFORMANCE

The most obvious source of role difficulty is that, by definition, the mediator occupies a boundary role position between two or more antagonists. Loyalty to the interests of one party is likely to be perceived as disloyalty to the interests of the other. This is role conflict of the clearest kind. Since the Arab-Israeli dispute is among the more intractable of the twentieth century, Kissinger's problems in maintaining rapport were bound to be considerable. The sheer intensity of the conflict, however, was not the only feature of the dispute that may have created problems of role enactment for the mediator. The number of disputants, the power balance between them, and the degree of factional conflict within each party may have contributed additional elements of role strain.

Conflicts Involving Multiple Parties

The degree of role strain a mediator encounters, especially with regard to maintaining rapport, is frequently increased when more than two parties are involved in a dispute. Role conflict is likely to be greater because loyalty to many masters is even more difficult to maintain than loyalty to two. Role hindrance will also increase for various reasons. At the simplest level, the demands on the physical and intellectual energy of the mediator and the mediator's staff are likely to be higher in multiparty disputes. For Kissinger, the necessity of constantly shuttling among Israel, Egypt, Syria, Saudi Arabia, and Jordan—each with its different dramatis personae and somewhat different issues—can hardly have provided the most favorable circumstances in which to function.

When a conflict involves multiple parties, the mediator's success with one pair of belligerents may generate significant pressures on the mediator to resolve issues in another subconflict along lines that threaten impartiality. As Golan (1976) points out, Kissinger pressed the Israelis to make territorial concessions to Syria, similar to those already made to Egypt, on the grounds that it would be difficult for Assad to refuse the conditions that Egypt had already agreed to—or to accept anything less (p. 191). The Israelis, understandably, did not see the wisdom of this point of view and resented Kissinger's pressure. They were concerned about maintaining secure and defensible borders, not with making evenhanded concessions to their enemies.

The mediator's success in one subconflict may also exacerbate the problem of maintaining rapport by giving the mediator a stake to protect, thereby undermining any unequivocal claim of being a disinterested party. Thus, as Quandt (1977) notes, Kissinger's success in arranging the first Israeli-Egyptian disengagement appears to have increased his investment in an Israeli-Syrian settlement. Kissinger now viewed an agreement between Israel and Syria as necessary in order to protect both Sadat's position in the Arab world and the flourishing relationship between the United States and Egypt. If war were to resume on the Syrian front, Egypt might well be drawn in and Kissinger's own painstaking efforts in the first Israeli-Egyptian disengagement would have been for naught. In order to arrange a settlement with Syria, the Americans applied considerable pressure on Israel that resulted in a clear worsening in the relations between Kissinger and the chief Israeli negotiators. The strained climate with the Israelis was not an asset for Kissinger during the second round of Israeli-Egyptian negotiations.

It is also noteworthy that the level of role hindrance Kissinger encountered in attempting to maintain rapport was increased by the significant discrepancy in the intensity of the subconflicts. For a variety of reasons, the dispute between Egypt and Israel was much more prone to resolution from the outset than the dispute between Israel and Syria. Had the Israeli-Syrian dispute not been linked to the simultaneous conflict between Israel and Egypt, the kinds of pressure generated on Kissinger by his successes on the Egyptian front would have been absent from the Israeli-Syrian entanglement. We have here an inverted illustration of Coleman's (1957) "Gresham's Law of conflict resolution": the "good" conflict exacerbates the "bad," and the "bad" conflict, in turn, worsens the "good." Although this formula is surely an oversimplification, it alerts one to an important aspect of mediation in multiparty disputes: the mediator's activities and successes in one arena may seriously affect the mediator's activities, attitudes, and prospects in another—and not always in a manner that is immediately obvious or straightforward.*

Conflicts Involving Parties of Unequal Power

For a mediator, power inequality between the disputants is another important source of role hindrance. The mediator's goal is often to get the parties to compromise. However, when one party is markedly superior to the other in its control of tangible resources, achieving that goal is made more difficult. Among other things, the higher power party is bound to be sensitive to the implied premise upon which negotiations (and the mediator's activities) will be based; namely, that as the party controlling more of the pie, it will nonetheless be asked to do less of the eating.

In the present instance, although both sides had countervailing power, Israel was considerably more powerful. Its military superiority had been demonstrated in each of the three preceding wars, and it held large chunks of Arab territory as a result of its crushing defeat of the Arabs in 1967. Once the cease-fire was in place, Kissinger became convinced (and tried to convince the Israelis) that an Israeli withdrawal from occupied Egyptian territory, however unfair it might appear in the short run, was a prerequisite for building a stable peace (Kalb and Kalb 1974, p. 504). While this argument may have been fundamentally sound in terms of the long-range interests of the parties, it required the Israelis to give up something tangible immediately for intangible benefits in the future, which they found very difficult to do. Kissinger, as the broker of this psychologically problematic arrangement, again paid the price in the all-important coin of mediator rapport (Quandt 1977, p. 215).†

---

* Variations in subconflict intensity also had some positive consequences. The mutual, if implict, desire of Israel and Egypt to reach some accommodation probably provided a needed psychological and strategic respite for the mediator as well as the parties when Israeli-Syrian negotiations became unduly frustrating. Certainly the example of the first Israeli-Egyptian disengagement seems to have been good for morale, demonstrating to Kissinger, no less than to the parties, what could be achieved.

† This situation is analogous to one the author has observed to be a major strategic obstacle to mediation with divorcing husbands and wives over the terms of their settlement

Conflicts Involving Parties with Multiple Constituencies

According to Kalb and Kalb (1974, p. 502), Kissinger's greatest successes occurred when he worked with dictators or other strongmen, while he encountered the greatest difficulties working with popularly elected leaders. Kissinger's preference for strongmen reveals at least as much about the issue of mediator role strain, when one or more of the disputants is responsible to numerous (and not necessarily united) constituents, as it does about any authoritarian predilections in Kissinger's makeup. Examination of the Middle East case suggests that under such conditions, significant degrees of role hindrance occur for the mediator both in the orchestration of a constructive negotiating process and in the maintenance of good relations with the parties.

The presence of numerous negotiator constituencies makes the task of inducing compromise more difficult by increasing the demands on the mediator's energies, diagnostic skill, and powers of persuasion, and by making it harder for negotiators to make concessions without losing face. Policymakers must often consult a variety of constituencies before offers and counteroffers can be made in the external negotiations. The kind of posture that emerges from such diliberations may become increasingly difficult for the mediator to predict as the number of such constituencies increases. For a mediator concerned with orchestrating the momentum of settlement, this time-consuming, enervating, and uncertain process can easily produce frustration. Thus, while Kissinger had only to win over Sadat and Assad in his negotiations with Egypt and Syria, in Israel he had to convince not only the prime minister, but often the cabinet, the political opposition, and the press as well (Kalb and Kalb 1974, p. 502).

Numerous constituencies also provide negotiators who are unwilling to compromise with a convenient excuse for resisting the mediator's efforts to produce movement. The greater the number of such constituencies, the easier it is for negotiators to invoke them in order to justify intransigence, and the more difficult it is for the mediator to assess whether the claim is truthful or primarily a bargaining ploy. For example, Golan (1976) describes the interesting byplay that occurred when Kissinger complained to the Israeli bargaining team that they were making his job harder by allowing details of their bargaining position to be published in the Israeli press before Kissinger had conveyed them to the Arabs. Allon responded that the leaks had probably come from the foreign affairs committee of the parliament. Kissinger inquired if the negotiators could report less to the committee. Dayan replied that that

---

agreements. There is a distinct possibility that the mediator will lose his acceptability with the husband since it is the husband who has the greater knowledge and control over the couple's resources, and who therefore tends to regard the mediator's efforts to foster an equitable negotiating process as a sign of favoritism toward the wife (Kressel et al., 1977).

would be impossible under Israeli law. Kissinger then asked Prime Minister Meir if the press could be censored. She turned to Chief of Staff Gur, who claimed that the military censor had said it would be illegal to do so. Kissinger, whom Golan describes as furious by now, was finally dispatched by Allon with the reminder that Israel was a democracy whose numerous parts did not always cooperate. The Arabs would simply have to reconcile themselves to that fact.

The existence of constituencies also makes it harder for negotiators to compromise, even if they wish to do so, because of the negotiators' concern about maintaining an image of strength before actual or potential rivals in their own camp. When both parties to the external conflict are preoccupied in this way, the mediator may judge that the chances for fruitful intervention are precluded altogether. This appears to have been the case in the aborted Israeli-Jordanian negotiations.

When negotiators representing one side are responsible to more numerous constituents than are the negotiators for the ōtherside, the mediator's task of maintaining rapport and a spirit of evenhandedness is made more difficult. To some degree, the highly tempestuous and frustrating climate that existed between Kissinger and the Israelis was undoubtedly a reflection of the greater obstacle that their internal divisions presented to the efficient and focused decision-making role to which Kissinger was inclined. Kissinger was far more comfortable with Sadat and his ability to make "command" decisions than he was with what he came to consider the fruitless "haggling" of Meir, Dayan, Rabin, and company; he occasionally even implied as much to the Israelis.

One may argue that dealing with a high level of factional conflict among both disputants rather than only one, would be even more onerous for a mediator. This may be so, but in the former situation the mediator is at least likely to experience similar levels of annoyance and frustration with both sides. Therefore, although the effect on his judgment and empathy for the parties may not be entirely salutary, at least its negative aspects are more likely to be evenly distributed.[*]

It should also be noted that role hindrance may easily become a source of role conflict. When the mediator encounters obstacles in an effort to produce movement in the negotiations (obstacles such as those generated when negotiators have multiple constituencies), the mediator faces an uneasy choice between exerting pressure at the risk of losing rapport, or maintaining rapport at the risk of being ineffectual. This

---

[*] Note that the preceding is not an argument for the inferiority of democracies in the sphere of international negotiation. There are other values to be served besides the ease or convenience of mediators. One could easily enumerate several distinct advantages of a process that, however slow and demanding, involves all of the relevant constituencies in an effort to hammer out a bargaining stance. Not the least of these is the increased likelihood that any agreements reached will carry with them a firm degree of commitment.

dilemma is a reflection of still another component of role strain: role ambiguity about how much of a change the disputants desire in their relationship and how much initiative in producing that change they consider appropriate for a mediator to exercise.

Parties' Ambivalence about Change and Mediator Initiative

A serious invitation to a mediator to enter a dispute constitutes implicit acknowledgment by the parties that changes in their relationship are necessary and that assistance is required to negotiate those changes. The invitation to intervene has another side, however, since change carries with it the unknown risk of altering unpleasant but predictable arrangements. The parties want some change, but how much?

At the outset of negotiations, neither the parties nor the mediator may be able to give a precise answer to such a question. One might expect, therefore, that mediators would be prone to err on the side of caution and relative passivity; better to let the parties gradually discover for themselves the desirability of abandoning old arrangements. That mediators often take risks in just the opposite direction is a result of the strong, implicit pressures on them to exercise initiative. In conflicts of any intensity, these pressures may come from the parties, who may view the mediator as having special knowledge or expertise, and therefore as having an obligation to make forceful interventions. Pressures also may emerge from the mediator's own belief that a more objective observer can see the necessary but hidden contours of a viable settlement more clearly than the parties. Pressures on the mediator to act forcefully may also arise from the mediator's face-saving function (Pruitt and Johnson 1970; Brown 1977). Because of the fear of looking weak, it is often easier for the parties to make concessions when the idea and pressure for the compromise can be attributed to a third party. Unfortunately, it may be difficult for a mediator to know when a proposal is required in order to help the parties save face, and/or how forcefully such a proposal should be promoted. How much initiative will rob the parties of a sense of ownership in the settlement? At what point will it lead them to resent the mediator? Thus, to the ambiguity of desired change must be added the ambiguity of desired initiative, thereby creating an additional dimension of mediator role strain.

KISSINGER'S POSITION AS U.S. SECRETARY OF STATE AS AN OBSTACLE TO MEDIATOR PERFORMANCE

Consideration of the pressures generated by the parties, as well as the structural dimensions of their conflict, does not exhaust the sources of mediator role strain. As the U.S. Secretary of State, Kissinger not only brought assets to the conflict, but also some decided liabilities. Examination of this issue is predicated on a fundamental distinction between nonrepresentational and representational forms of mediation.

In nonrepresentational mediation, third parties represent nobody but themselves. They are retained by the parties to settle their dispute and are paid by them. When the dispute is resolved to the principals' satisfaction, the third party's relationship with them ceases. This form of mediation most commonly occurs in interpersonal peacemaking such as marriage counseling. In representational mediation, third parties are representatives of some group, organization, or institution. Their intervention is embedded in an ongoing relationship between their employer and the disputing parties that does not end with successful mediation of the conflict. Industrial and international mediation are prime examples of the representational form of third party intervention. There is good reason to believe that the level of role strain is generally much higher for representational mediators than for their nonrepresentational counterparts. This is so because of the conflict of interest and the high degree of power that are typically associated with representational mediation.

Problems Caused by Representational Mediator's Conflicts of Interest

Although conflicts of interest between mediators and disputants are by no means unheard of in nonrepresentational mediation, in representational mediation there is an inevitable, if unannounced, expectation that mediators will attempt to advance the aims and interests of their own constituents as well as those of the belligerents. When the interests of Party A, Party B, and the mediator's own party diverge—as they almost certainly will—the mediator is likely to find the degree of role conflict raised to an extremely uncomfortable level. After all, how can the mediator maintain the trust and confidence of the belligerents, while simultaneously achieving the goals of his or her own party? It is not even necessary that a clash of interest actually exist. The parties' very suspicion that the mediator is acting to safeguard some personal objectives is sufficient to create a serious obstacle to rapport. Labor mediators employed by public sector agencies, for example, are quite aware of the tensions that result from the actual or imagined pressures on them to protect the public welfare by keeping settlements within government guidelines, for instance (Kressel 1972).

In the Kissinger mediation, the principal conflict of interest was between Israel's concern with its national security and the U.S. desire to build ties with the Arab world in order both to protect its oil interests and to reduce the influence of the Soviet Union in the Middle East. To the

Israelis, U.S. interests did not always seem compatible with their own. Israel's military and economic dependence on the United States, however, made it difficult to resist determined U.S. mediation efforts, while it gave Kissinger a potentially valuable lever with which to further the American goal of rapprochement with the Arab world. Indeed, the linchpin of the entire mediation was Sadat's strategic calculation that Egyptian aims could best be achieved through the good offices of the United States; that is, by acknowledging and putting to use the United States' very considerable influence with Israel. The point was by no means lost on Kissinger, who summarized it neatly: "[The Egyptians] can get weapons from the Soviet Union. But they can get territory only from us" (Kalb and Kalb 1974, p. 502).

The statement is equally apt, however, as a summary of Kissinger's strategic dilemma throughout the negotiations: how to maintain Israel's goodwill and susceptibility to influence in the face of its realization that the United States had interests in the area to which its own might be sacrificed. Kissinger never did solve this dilemma satisfactorily. Probably it was insoluble. The Israelis were suspicious and resentful of his activities from the very outset, and no amount of personal charm could change these attitudes for very long. The Arabs had their own reasons to be distrustful of Kissinger's goals, but they had much less to lose by accepting his services. He could hardly ask them to relinquish territory to Israel, and their dependence on U.S. material assistance was relatively small. Therefore, if mediation failed they would not be much worse off than before.

Problems Caused by Representational Mediator's Power

Representational mediation has one outstanding and impressive advantage over its nonrepresentational cousin: access to power and the motivation to use it. At the organizational or international level, only a mediator whose own constituency is highly interested in the outcome of a dispute is likely to be able to summon the necessary motivation and resources to effect a resolution. As Quandt (1977, p. 279) notes, the high degree of U.S. self-interest in the Arab-Israeli dispute did more than provide the initial impetus to intervene; it also served to ensure the continuation of Kissinger's activities in the face of high levels of frustration and difficulty, and to guarantee that the considerable economic and military leverage that had to be supplied would be forthcoming. A mediator with less investment in the outcome of the dispute might have been unwilling to use all the resources available; or, muttering a plague on both houses, the mediator might have chosen to retire from the dispute altogether. Moreover, from the perspective of the parties, the mediator is an instrument for the achievement of certain ends. Kissinger was an attractive instrument precisely because of the power to which he had access. Had he intervened and then refrained from drawing upon that power, one or both of the parties might have inferred that he was unmotivated, inept, or actually hostile to the resolution of the conflict. This would almost certainly have been the case with Sadat.

However, although the representational mediator benefits from power and is under an obligation to put that power to use, the possession of power is a decidedly mixed blessing. Its exercise may bring the mediator into conflict with the role obligations of maintaining rapport and promoting settlements that are viable, not merely expedient. Kissinger's rapport problem arose from the one-sided nature of his leverage. It was the Israelis who most often bore the brunt of U.S. power whenever Kissinger applied it to produce a change in the momentum of negotiations, because it was the Israelis to whom this power flowed most directly and easily. Inevitably they resented this, especially when they suspected that a major goal of U.S. intervention was to compel Israel to cede territory to Egypt and Syria (Quandt 1977, p. 229).

The conflict between the exercise of mediator power and the mediator's obligation to produce a satisfactory (and not simply a quick) settlement is more difficult to establish, partly because the definition of a "satisfactory" settlement is by no means simple or obvious. There are, however, two defects in the quality of settlement that are likely to result when the exercise of mediator power has been high. First, the parties may experience an insufficient sense of ownership in the settlement and therefore may be less likely to live up to its terms. Thus, although the application of mediator power may make it easier for the parties to settle, it may be at the cost of reducing their reliance on their own resources and problem-solving skills, with all that this implies for the future instability of the agreement—particularly if the motives and/or power of the mediator should shift). Second, the parties may settle too quickly, without due deliberation about the possible effects of the settlement upon both the relationship with the opponent and important constituents. At the time of this writing, for instance, it appears that the isolation of Sadat from his Arab compatriots (an outcome that followed in the wake of the signing of the Egyptian-Israeli peace treaty brokered by President Carter), may be due in part to the possibility that the wheels of settlement were unduly greased by a well-intentioned but far from omniscient mediator.

These risks associated with the wielding of power are to be contrasted with the difficulties that representational mediators may encounter in trying to engage and mobilize the power that is nominally theirs. Just as the parties may be constrained by their constituents, so may representational mediators be constrained by their constituents when they attempt to seize the initiative in the external dispute. The difficulty is compounded by the disputants' awareness that this is the case. They know that a potentially useful weapon exists for resisting mediator initiatives, by appealing to audiences who monitor the mediator's behavior and on whom the mediator is dependent for the exercise of authority. From the parties' perspective, this is handy; from the mediator's vantage point it is primarily a headache. Thus, although no Secretary of State since John Foster Dulles has had as much governmental authority as Kissinger, both U.S. public opinion and the U.S. political bureaucracy created problems for Kissinger when he attempted to forcefully orchestrate the negotiations between Israel and the Arabs.

Public opinion is a nebulous concept with very real, albeit insufficiently understood, effects on policymakers (Druckman 1977). Sources vary in the degree to which they emphasize the role that U.S. public opinion had on Kissinger's mediation efforts, but all agree that it was a factor of some importance. For example, American mediation became more problematic after the first Egyptian-Israeli disengagement, in part because the Arab oil embargo set in motion by that intervention undercut popular support for an Arab-Israeli peace; after all, why help the Arabs when they are harming us? (Quandt 1977, p. 259). Similarly, Kissinger's move toward abandoning the piecemeal orientation of step-by-step mediation, in favor of a more global approach involving direct pressure on Israel to negotiate with the Palestinians, appears to have been thwarted by congressional opposition fueled by the power of pro-Israeli public sentiment (Quandt 1977, p. 270).

Kissinger's mobilization of U.S. power was also heavily dependent on the domestic political bureaucracy. On the whole, Kissinger appears to have been successful at bending the machinery of government to his wishes, but the task was not always easy. The problems were partly attributable to the sheer complexity of communication in a vast bureaucratic network; they also may have reflected differences of policy perspective between Kissinger and executives in other branches of government, notably in the Department of Defense, and the attendant resistance to following orders.

The stresses on the mediator caught in a cross fire between the pressures of public opinion and the resistance of a governmental bureaucracy are conveyed in the Kalbs' (1974) account of the U.S. military resupply of Israel during the October War. This was a ticklish issue because Kissinger wished to prevent both an Israeli defeat and an Israeli victory. According to the Kalbs, Israeli Ambassador Dinitz did not hesitate to remind Kissinger that if the United States did not immediately begin a military resupply of Israel, the Israelis would go public about the American foot-dragging. Kissinger was fearful of what such a public Israeli attack would do to a seriously weakened Nixon administration. But getting the Pentagon to move on Kissinger's orders was not easy. Calls from Kissinger to the president's aide, General Haig, a meeting with

Nixon himself, and a National Security Council confrontation with Secretary of Defense Schlesinger, were all needed before Kissinger could be assured that his orders regarding military resupply of Israel would be carried out in timely fashion (Kalb and Kalb 1974, pp. 475–76). These efforts were costly in both energy and goodwill, and the uncertainty of their result was an added source of tension for the mediator.*

The representational mediator's subordinate status in a hierarchy of power is disadvantageous as well. Thus, it may be argued that Kissinger's ultimate dependence on presidential authority placed an inherent limitation on what he could accomplish as a mediator in an international conflict of such scope and intensity. The hallmark of truly superior mediation is that it not only resolves the immediate issues, but also creates a new and more viable framework for the parties' relationships with one another. A fair global assessment of Kissinger's intervention is that he worked principally on the periphery, arranging a cease-fire, the disengagement of forces, and the reduction of tensions. Untouched were the central issues defining the parties' relationships with each other. Thus Kissinger did not tackle the crucial Palestinian issue, nor did he seriously work to bring about a full-scale peace treaty. To some extent, this was because the parties were not ready to take such far-reaching steps. In addition, however, Kissinger's behavior appears to reflect the fact that at this high level of international politics, only a president has the legitimate authority to make the kinds of fundamental commitments in U.S. foreign policy that mediation with such comprehensive objectives would necessitate. The fact that the peace treaty that was ultimately arranged in January 1979 between Egypt and Israel was mediated by President Carter, rather than by one of his subordinates, is very much to the point in this regard.

TACTICS OF INTERVENTION

The preceding analysis has made the point that a mediator is the occupant of an inherently stressful social role. Coping with these role stresses constitutes an important task for the mediator, a task that is related to but distinguishable from the task of helping to resolve the conflict between the disputants. Three major strategies of role-related coping may be identified in the Kissinger mediation: strategies of direct role strain reduction; strategies focused on building a commitment to mediation; and strategies aimed at reducing the parties' expectation for gain.

---

*The veracity of the Kalbs' account of this incident is less important than its plausibility. See Quandt 1977, p. 203, however, for alternative constructions of the episode.

Although the dissection of mediator activity into discrete strategic categories is useful, it can also lead to oversimplification. It is desirable, therefore, to preface the discussion of Kissinger's behavior with several general observations and caveats.

First, we are in no way suggesting that strategies of reducing role strain are self-conscious. Indeed, mediators are likely to be at least partially unaware of the role problems they face, if for no other reason than that such ignorance is itself a protective psychological mechanism. Ignorance of one's own motives is often costly, however. By alerting mediators to the unconscious springs in their own behavior, role analysis also points the way to a greater measure of mediator self-awareness. In principle at least, such awareness should result in more controlled and effective intervention.

Second, separating the strategies by which mediators handle role stress from the strategies by which they attempt to help resolve the conflict between the parties is an analytic device, not a reflection of what actually occurs in mediation. Any intervention may serve the multiple purposes of handling the external dispute while simultaneously addressing the mediator's inner conflict. Kissinger's preference for private meetings with Sadat, for instance, may be viewed as a mechanism for reducing role strain by establishing rapport with a key figure, as well as providing a private forum in which Sadat could be helped to understand some of the constraints of a representational mediator. However, private meetings also served the process of resolving the external conflict by reducing the influence of Sadat's more hawkish advisors, and by increasing the probability that Kissinger's preference for a settlement would be accepted.

The multipurpose nature of mediator activity has an important functional consequence, related to the concern in any social activity of keeping the costs of behavior low in relation to possible gains. Given the mediator's ambiguous mandate to pressure the parties and to change the terms of their relationship, one of the serious costs that the mediator may incur is the suspicion and resentment generated by his or her activities. From this perspective, the multiple aim of many mediator interventions is an extremely economical method, serving to keep interventions to a minimum while maximizing the movement toward conflict resolution. Indeed, one may hypothesize that an intervention is adroit to the extent that it does accomplish more than one tactical purpose at a time. It may be that what distinguishes the brilliant mediator from the merely good or downright poor one is the ratio of such multipurpose acts to the total number of mediator interventions.

A final related point is that mediation is best viewed as an organized gestalt, a process of ever-widening circles of connected activity. This characteristic of Kissinger's approach to mediation has been largely omitted from this chapter in order to isolate the various tactical responses to role strain. It needs to be kept in mind, however, that a classification of mediator behavior into discrete units, however accurate, is of only limited value if one loses sight of the organic nature of the process.°

Strategies of Direct Stress Reduction

The psychological mechanisms by which individuals cope with obstacles to successful role enactment have long been of interest to role theorists. Like any other frustrated role occupant, the mediator may employ a variety of psychological tactics in order to reduce role tension. Among the more prominent tactics of stress reduction are cathartic responses of various kinds (the blowing-off-steam approach) and cognitive-perceptual distortion of the parties and their conflict.

Catharsis

Cartharsis is not commonly discussed by mediators, probably because it appears to contradict the notion that the mediator is one who resolves conflict rather than adding to it. Peacemakers are not supposed to have tantrums. The reality, nonetheless, is that mediators may deal with their frustrations in ways that are not always polite or adroit.

The Kissinger mediation is replete with emotion-laden outbursts, primarily aimed at Israel. Israel's divided and numerous internal audiences, its power advantage over the Arabs, and its ready access to U.S. opinion were the source of extraordinary role tension for Kissinger. His position as Secretary of State compounded the difficulties, since U.S. strategic interests were not identical with those of Israel. Given this incompatability, it is not surprising that Kissinger's efforts to deal with his frustrations sometimes took a rather primitive form. His angry outburst at the Israeli negotiating team during the disengagement talks with Syria is a good example. Golan (1976, p. 195) describes Kissinger screaming at the Israelis, in a fit of sheer pique, that it was undignified for an American Secretary of State to plead with them for compromises:

> I am wandering around here like a rug merchant in order to bargain over 100 to 200 meters! Like a peddler in the market: I'm trying to save you, and you think you are doing me a favor when you are kind

---

° This is one of the problems with the increasing number of laboratory studies of mediation within social psychology that employ an experimental design to evaluate this or that tactic of mediation (see Rubin 1980 for a useful review of this literature). Such a piecemeal evaluation of mediation misses the essential nature of the process and is bound to be seriously misleading.

enough to give me a few more meters. As if I were a citizen of El
Quneitra! As if I planned to build my house there!

Golan's account may be biased or inaccurate, but Kissinger's outburst is
consistent with an understanding of the competing pressures under which
he was acting.

Cognitive and Perceptual Distortion: The Significance of Diagnosis

Diagnosis of a conflict and the parties to it is essential for effective
mediation. Such understanding provides the mediator with a set of
objectives and a basis for organizing intervention. Unfortunately, diagnosis also provides the mediator with an excellent opportunity to reduce the
stresses engendered by role conflict, role ambiguity, and role hindrance.
The higher the role strain, the more likely the mediator is to misperceive
or misconstrue the conflict in such a way as to relieve or minimize role
tension. This observation is in keeping with the research of Janis (1972;
Janis and Mann 1977) and others, who have shown repeatedly that
distortions in the gathering and processing of information are common
among decision makers under conditions of high stress. (See Kinder and
Weiss 1978, for an excellent review of this literature in the realm of
international politics.) Diagnostic activity is all the more available as an
avenue for reducing role strain because of the absence of clear-cut
guidelines by which the mediator may check wishful thinking.°
Very little is known about the nature of Kissinger's diagnostic
activity. This absence of detail has many possible causes, including the
lack of salience the subject may have had for various sources, and the
unwillingness of Kissinger and his aides to talk about potentially explosive
and secret matters involved in his assessment of the parties. However, the
lack of diagnostic details in this case parallels the absence of such
information in studies of less sensitive types of conflict (Kressel 1972;
Kressel and Deutsch 1977), and may therefore reflect a more fundamental
issue, namely the ignorance of mediators of their own actual diagnostic
decision rules. Research in other areas of decision making is supportive of
this possibility (Brehmer and Hammond 1977).
In the absence of details, an analysis of the ways in which Kissinger's
diagnostic efforts may have fallen short of the ideal is necessarily speculative. However, two possibilities of misdiagnosis in the interest of role
strain reduction may be cited.
First, the mediator may believe that the needs of the parties are

---

°Even in seemingly simpler arenas of human conflict, such as that between divorcing
spouses, expert practitioners have little to say about the indicators on which one should rely
in deciding whether one or another line of action is appropriate (Kressel and Deutsch 1977).
The absence of such criteria is also responsible for the "mediation as an art" perspective that
is so popular among industrial mediators (Kressel 1972).

consistent with the needs of the mediator's own constituents when, in fact, they are not. Early in the conflict, Kissinger acted forcibly to discourage the unassisted talks between Egyptian General Gamasy and Israeli General Yariv concerning a military disengagement on the banks of the Suez Canal. The move can be justified as a structural tactic designed to help establish a mediation function that would surely be needed later, even if it was not essential at the time. Moreover, as Quandt (1977, p. 220) notes, the Israeli cabinet did not reject Kissinger's pressure to desist from direct talks, which suggests that Yariv may have been ahead of the Israeli government in his willingness to reach an accommodation. There is little question, however, that the discouragement of direct talks also fit nicely with certain U.S. objectives that were quite removed from those of Israel. For one thing, the United States wanted the Arab oil boycott lifted, and a U.S. role in promoting a settlement between Egypt and Israel could be used as evidence that the United States was not indifferent to Arab interests. Also, if the United States remained firmly in control of the negotiations, the prestige and involvement of the Soviet Union would remain low.

These factors may well have militated against a careful and thorough evaluation of the evidence in favor of permitting direct talks to continue. Nonetheless, there are several reasons why direct talks should have continued. In the first place, the final agreements that were reached several months later with Kissinger's assistance were not substantially different from what Gamasy and Yariv were about to conclude on their own. Had they been allowed to reach those accords unassisted, not only might Kissinger have saved his efforts for more intractable issues, but more importantly, the parties' autonomy, and hence their investment in the settlement, would have been increased. That the principal negotiators were high ranking military officers is of note in this regard, since the military on both sides represent powerful constituents in any international conflict. Anything that can be done to increase the military's enthusiasm for a negotiated settlement, particularly one involving the deployment of troops, would seem desirable for the future integrity of the agreements. Finally, although the issue of direct talks seems to have been structured by Kissinger and his staff as a choice between active mediation and no mediation, there is nothing compelling about this formulation. Kissinger could have encouraged direct talks while still maintaining some contact with the parties and alerting them to his willingness to take a more active hand should their own efforts break down.

The second possibility of misdiagnosis can be stated as follows: a mediator may fail to vigorously gather and evaluate certain kinds of information because a line of action may be generated that appears fraught with even more role strain than the one that is currently being pursued. Perhaps the most far-reaching decision Kissinger made was to avoid pressing vigorously for a settlement between Jordan and Israel.

Thus Kissinger did not pressure Sadat very strongly to support Jordan as the representative of the Palestinians at the Arab summit meeting in Rabat in October 1974. He also apparently accepted at face value the findings of a preliminary diagnostic excursion that Hussein would accept nothing less than an Israeli withdrawal from the Jordan River, and that an alternative Israeli withdrawal from the town of Jericho and the important Nablus area was improbable since neither side was enthusiastic (Quandt 1977, p. 256). This occurred despite the fact that it is the give and take of bargaining that is often the only means of ascertaining, for the parties no less than the mediator, where the real lines of compromise may lie.

The upshot of Kissinger's weak efforts at probing the possibilities for Israeli-Jordanian talks was that Hussein had nothing to support his legitimacy as a bona-fide spokesman for the Palestinians. At Rabat, the Arabs therefore named the PLO as the sole legitimate representative of the Palestinian people. An opportunity was thereby lost to handle the explosive Palestinian issue in a context more acceptable to Israel, with repercussions that continue to this day.

Kissinger's failure to proceed with the necessary diagnostic vigor may be attributable to the increased role strain he might have anticipated in Israeli-Jordanian negotiations. As has been noted, one important source of such mediator role strain is the pressure on negotiators to appear strong before their respective constituents. This was clearly the situation in Israel. At the time that the possibility of talks with Jordan was under consideration, Israel's cabinet was divided, and Prime Minister Rabin was new and not a commanding figure. The official Israeli position toward Jordan was therefore rigid. Analogously, King Hussein, despite his genuine acceptance of Israeli statehood, was fearful of making concessions of his own lest he appear weak and traitorous to his Arab allies. Moreoever, the possible introduction of the Palestinians into the negotiations raised an even more complicated and potentially explosive constituent question: If Hussein were to represent the Palestinians in negotiations, how strong would the pressure be to appear tough to the Palestinians and other Arabs? Since even the commanding Arafat of the PLO was driven by such pressures (Sheehan 1976, p. 46), would Hussein fare any better? In light of these considerations, it is not hard to see why no thorough evaluation was undertaken of the negotiating possibilities on the Jordanian front. How much easier for Kissinger to return to the Sinai negotiations and the relative security of dealing with Sadat, a man more thoroughly in control of his own house.

Strategies of Building a Commitment to Mediation

Under conditions of high role strain, representational mediation is a very unstable form of social interaction. Occupying a position midway between fervent enemies, uncertain of how much pressure these enemies will tolerate, and shackled by their own constituent responsibilities, representational mediators stand on slippery ground. Consequently, shoring up the parties' commitment to mediation is a primary and continuing task that may be accomplished in a number of ways.

First, the mediator may increase the parties' commitment to mediation through the exercise of personal charm, tact, and discretion. Such efforts are designed to increase the parties' liking and respect for the mediator, thereby increasing their tolerance for other mediator activities about which they may be fearful, suspicious, or ambivalent. Somewhat more cynically, it may be said that to the extent that mediators can successfully create the trappings of a personal, spontaneous relationship with disputants, they divert attention from the very impersonal and role-bound nature of the ties that form the true basis for the interaction, and that are also the source of much of the parties' distrust of them.

Kissinger was both adept and active in the exercise of such personal tactics. He was skillful at flattery (Kalb and Kalb 1974, p. 511); he made frequent and effective use of humor (Golan 1976, p. 98); he could act both with restraint and discretion (Kalb and Kalb 1974, p. 590); and he went to great lengths to demonstrate his empathy for, and understanding of, each side's position (Sheehan 1976, p. 42). Kissinger was eager to establish a direct one-to-one relationship with key figures in the conflict, especially Sadat. With the Arabs, at least, he was able to maintain a posture of respect and deference, even when their mode of expression and the content of their views were strongly antagonistic to his own (Sheehan 1976, p. 70). Where possible (and again, primarily with the Arabs), he made skillful use of the media in order to develop a sympathetic image (Kalb and Kalb 1974, p. 516).

Second, the mediator may employ technical or material incentives in order to augment or substitute for personality, thereby building commitment to mediation. Material incentives are especially likely to be employed with the party most antagonistic to the mediator's efforts, that is, the party with higher power. The Israelis were more anxious about the immediate consequences of Kissinger's mediation than were the Arabs. Consequently, they were more immune to the exercise of personal charm. When charm failed, Kissinger relied on heavy doses of U.S. military and technical aid in an effort to reconcile Israel to U.S. negotiation pressures that they otherwise found unpalatable (Quandt 1977, p. 188; Sheehan 1976, pp. 76–77). This assistance did not particularly create a climate of trust and confidence; indeed, the assistance sometimes became a battleground in its own right, as when Israel made its agreement to a second Sinai accord contingent upon more military assistance than the United States was prepared to offer.

Third, the mediator may increase the parties' commitment to

mediation though the use of structural tactics that are designed to enhance the value and importance of mediation in the parties' eyes. Kissinger's early push for a Geneva conference may be viewed as a tactic of this kind. The primary value of Geneva was to legitimize the settlement process, to give the Soviet Union enough of a role to prevent it from disrupting the talks, and to meet the complex physical and administrative requirements of a multinational negotiation (Quandt 1977, p. 213). In short, the Geneva conference stood to enhance the prestige, visibility, and seriousness of the mediation process in the eyes of all concerned. As matters evolved, no real use was made of Geneva, but in the chaos and uncertainty of the days immediately following the cease-fire, its appeal to Kissinger is not hard to fathom.

Another structural tactic employed by Kissinger was to maintain an unbroken string of agreements, no matter how small, thereby avoiding at all costs anything that might be regarded as a mediation failure. Such a procedure was not only directly helpful, but kept the parties' morale and confidence in the negotiating process at a high level, even when the specific agreements were relatively unimportant. This was a central part of the rationale of step-by-step diplomacy. The essence of step-by-step was to focus the parties on matters that, in Kissinger's judgment, had the best chance of being resolved. In practice this meant shifting attention from large, abstract issues to smaller, concrete ones (Quandt 1977, p. 209).

Strategies of Reducing the Parties' Expectations for Gain

One of the principal sources of mediator role strain is the cross fire of conflicting aspirations in which the mediator may be caught. It is therefore very much in a mediator's interest, and in the interest of effective intervention, that those aspirations be lowered. The Kissinger record contains some notable examples of this strategy.

An extremely important cause of Kissinger's role conflict was the Arab expectation that he would use his leverage with Israel to effectuate the return of conquered Arab territory. A principal tactic Kissinger used to reduce these expectations was to educate the Arabs about the nature of his role dilemma. Early in the negotiations Kissinger explained the situation to Sadat, partially by appealing to Sadat's own experience: just as Sadat had to cope with his generals, he (Kissinger) had to contend with the pro-Israeli lobby in the United States. Sadat must understand that Kissinger could not pressure the Israelis in public without exposing himself to a powerful Israeli counterattack that could undermine his support at home (Sheehan 1976, pp. 49–50).

An even more effective tactic was to manipulate Israeli negotiating behavior in a fashion that would simultaneously reduce Arab expectations and reassure Israel that it would not always be asked to make concessions. Thus, when Dayan indicated early in the negotiations with Egypt that Israel was prepared to immeidately withdraw its troops from part of the Sinai, Kissinger discouraged the move. "Israel should not look weak," Quandt (1977) writes of Kissinger's position. "It was important for the Arabs to see that it was difficult for the United States to influence Israel; otherwise their expectations would soar" (p. 211).

Perhaps the most fundamental strategy for dampening the parties' ambitions was to orchestrate a favorable balance of forces between them so that neither side would feel overly self-confident. The requisite balance of motivation was initially affected by the orchestration of events on the battlefield. To insure that neither side emerged with an unequivocal victory of defeat, U.S. military assistance to Israel was systematically manipulated—increasing when Egypt became overconfident and inflexible in its demands regarding the terms of a cease-fire, and decreasing when the military tide began to turn too far in Israel's favor (Quandt 1977, pp. 173–98).

Influencing events on the battlefield was only the initial, although perhaps the most dramatic, way in which Kissinger strove to orchestrate a balance of negotiating incentives. Once the negotiations had begun, it was necessary that the proper balance of flexibility and willingness to compromise be established and maintained. An important mechanism for doing so was controlling the flow of communication between the parties. Thus we find Kissinger selectively transmitting the least conciliatory part of an Israeli proposal to Egypt, omitting the Israeli clarification that this was only an initial position, in order to produce an immediate Egyptian rejection. Kissinger's goal was to make it clear to Israel, without saying so directly, that its stance in the negotiations was too rigid (Golan 1976, p. 230). The procedure could also be used on Israel's behalf, as when Kissinger intentionally withheld some Israeli concessions from Assad while transmitting others during the difficult negotiations with Syria. "Kissinger felt that he had to avoid whetting Assad's already substantial appetite for Israeli concessions, while at the same time being able to show continued progress" (Quandt 1977, p. 241).

Masking

Mediators occasionally conceal, deny, or obscure their true motives, knowledge, or feelings. Such behavior is referred to as masking. Masking may range from the subtle to the blatant and can occur in all three of the strategic areas that have already been considered. Its advantages over these more direct methods of handling role strain are several. In the cathartic domain, masking constitutes a more tactful and effective manner of discharging anger and frustration; the mediators protect their credibility by maintaining their poise in front of the parties, yet achieve some discharge of feeling. In more instrumental areas, masking allows mediators greater latitude to exert pressure and achieve their own objectives, while at the same time, adhering (at least superficially) to the mandates of impartiality, evenhandedness, and disinterest.

Masking has its disadvantages, however. The most obvious is that the mask may be suspected or penetrated by the parties, with the result that trust and confidence in the mediator may be seriously damaged. In addition, because it threatens to undermine trust and confidence, mediators are motivated to remain partially or totally unaware of their deceptiveness. The discrepancy between the mediator's belief that his or her behavior is open and aboveboard, and the contrary inference made by observers or the parties, may become an additional source of annoyance and frustration for the mediator. In these ways masking is both a response to role strain and one of its significant contributors.

Masking in the Interest of Catharsis

Humor is an effective mask for the expression of frustration since it simultaneously permits the expression of annoyance and exerts pressure for compromise in a manner that is not distasteful to the intended audience. An example of this is Kissinger's joke to the Israeli negotiators about the masseur at the King David Hotel who would give up ten years of his life for peace, but not an inch of captured territory (Sheehan 1976, p. 41).

Strategic withdrawal from a dispute also provided Kissinger with an opportunity to mask annoyance. For instance, "reassessment" was the official motive for the temporary suspension of talks and Kissinger's return to the United States. But as Quandt (1977, p. 268) notes, reassessment, however justified, became in part an instrument for Kissinger to vent his exasperation toward Israel. This particular mask was unsuccessful, partly because its aggressive intent was insufficiently hidden from the Israelis.* The failure of this instance of strategic withdrawal is especially instructive since it illustrates the disadvantageous position in which the representational mediator is placed when a public (unmasked) performance cannot be avoided.

The sequence of events developed in the following way. The Israelis were angered by reassessment because they sensed that its purpose was to picture them as uncooperative, thereby providing Kissinger with do-

---

*Sheehan (1976, pp. 164–65), provides an account of the semipublic forms that Kissinger's exasperation with the Israelis took once he had returned to the United States.

mestic support for his efforts to extract further Israeli territorial concessions to Egypt. They responded to this reassessment by "going public"
with a convincing and simple appeal to various American audiences. In
return for making major territorial concessions in the Sinai, the Israelis
argued, they had asked only for an elementary courtesy: Egypt's renunciation of belligerency. Was this so unreasonable and inflexible? Kissinger
responded with public declarations of his own. He argued that a new
balance of forces was necessary in order to stabilize relations in the
Middle East, and that this required further territorial concessions from
Israel. He also argued that the Israelis understood perfectly well that, for
reasons of face, Sadat could not agree to nonbelligerency; they were
therefore insisting on it in order to retard the settlement process (Quandt
1977, p. 268). Kissinger lost this debate. Two months after it began, 76
United States senators sent a letter to President Ford urging him to be
responsive to Israel's economic and military needs.

    This episode illustrates one reason why representatiohal mediators
are likely to prefer the mask of secrecy to a performance in the public
spotlight: the age of instant replay is more flattering to positions that are
short, simple, and easy to digest than to those that are complicated.
Belligerents are much more likely to be comfortable with the invocation
of principles that promote their positions. These principles, with their
simplicity and immediate propaganda appeal, are most useful in winning
audiences over. To the extent that mediators are beholden to constituents
of their own, are identified to some extent with the perspective of both
sides, and are concerned with the requirements of a constructive settlement, they are likely to be burdened with positions that are more subtle,
more complex, and therefore more difficult to defend in public.

Masking to Build a Commitment to Mediation

    One of the parties whose commitment to mediation Kissinger had to
increase were his constituents in the U.S. political bureaucracy. A method
of defusing internal opposition to his policies involved camouflaging
those policies behind a screen of nuance and complexity, thereby disarming potential critics. As Quandt (1977) comments: "The Nixon-
Kissinger policy . . . could be seen as pro-Israel, pro-Arab, pro-dentente,
or anti-Soviet depending on what one was looking for. Those who
disagreed with one element of policy were likely to support other aspects.
This left the president and Kissinger in a commanding position" (p. 205).

    The selective transmission of information is another step along the
continuum of masking. Its use in reducing the parties' expectations for
substantive gain was referred to above. Controlling the flow of information was also used by Kissinger to avoid failures that might shake the
parties' confidence in him and in the procedure of step-by-step. Thus he
intentionally withheld from the Syrians the details of an Israeli proposal

that he was certain would lead to the collapse of negotiations. Instead, Kissinger requested the Syrians to consider some general matters on which no immediate responses were required, and got them to agree to further talks with him in Washington. The momentum of negotiations was thus preserved.

The mask of secrecy was also useful when it came to channeling material aid to Israel. The problem with doing so openly was the possibility of stirring up domestic opposition in the United States and of embarrasing Sadat with his Arab compatriots. A partial solution was to embody promises of aid to Israel in secret memoranda of understanding. However, these memoranda created their own problems. Although Kissinger told Sadat about most of the U.S. commitments to Israel, he neglected to mention a promise regarding Pershing missiles. This raised suspicions among the Egyptians about other secret agreements that Kissinger might not have mentioned (Quandt 1977, p. 275).

Masking to Reduce Parties' Expectations for Gain

In some respects the need to reduce the parties' expectations is the most ticklish assignment the mediator faces. It is an essential task because it helps reduce the mediator's role conflict and because it is the principal vehicle that makes compromise possible. The job is delicate, however, because of the mediator's highly ambiguous mandate when it comes to pressuring the parties to change their positions. A prominent solution to this dilemma is for the mediator to engage in strenuous efforts to conceal from the parties the degree to which pressure is being applied and influence exerted. For Kissinger, a prominent means of doing so was to misrepresent his role or motives. He sometimes attempted to hide behind invocations of presidential authority. It was the president, Kissinger would claim, not he, who was insisting on certain moves that Israel found unpalatable (Golan 1976, pp. 84–85).

On other occasions, Kissinger gave inaccurate descriptions to the parties of what he conceived his function to be. For example, although Kissinger often presented himself as little more than a go-between (see, for example, Kalb and Kalb 1974, p. 536), this was untrue. As matters progressed, Kissinger became an increasingly active proponent of each side's perspective and position to the other. In doing so he was following more or less faithfully the mandate of the mediator role: to orchestrate the necessary balance of incentive and pressures that would make a settlement possible.

The use of certain verbal formulas that regularly occurred during Kissinger's more forceful efforts at persuassion was another device designed at least partly to mask the application of mediator pressure. Here, for example, is what Kissinger had to say at the height of his exasperation with Israeli reluctance to make further concessions in the

Sinai: "I'm not angry at you and I'm not asking you to change your position. It's tragic to see people dooming themselves to a course of unbelievable peril" (Sheehan 1976, p. 52). The first sentence in this quotation is an obvious falsehood if taken literally. Kissinger was angry—steaming, according to some accounts (cf. Golan 1976)—and he certainly was asking the Israelis to change their position. The disclaimer was a verbal pirouette whose function was to reduce the appearance of coercion. Similar disclaimers probably also occurred during other moments of pressure. The cumulative effect of such a tactic, no matter how understandable it was in light of the other pressures impinging upon Kissinger, may have been to create an unflattering image of Kissinger's Machiavellianism.

The mask of concealment may extend to mediators themselves. When Kissinger was asked at one point whether he had to do any arm-twisting with the Israelis, Kalb and Kalb (1974) report him as snapping: "Both parties feel their essential interests are being protected. There was no arm-twisting of any kind" (p. 539). There is a natural tendency for an observer to dismiss statements such as these as cynical and transparent falsehoods. That may be. However, we have learned to expect similar denials as a routine component of interviews with both labor mediators and divorce therapists, even though these denials are not corroborated by the respondents' own detailed accounts of their intervention nor by the recordings of mediation sessions (Kressel 1972; Kressel et al. 1977). This discrepancy between a mediator's words and deeds is best regarded as a defensive maneuver designed to protect the mediator from the inherent contradictions of the role. Another possibility is that we may be dealing with attributional differences between actors and observers. Mediators know, even if they cannot articulate, the conflicting pressures under which they operate. This knowledge is more than sufficient to convince them that they have engaged in no violations of their role. The observer, deprived of such knowledge, finds the attribution of deliberate misrepresentation and deviousness on the part of the mediator far easier to make.

SUMMARY AND CONCLUSION

Freud once remarked that there are three tasks that are more or less impossible to do well: govern a country, raise a child, and conduct a psychoanalysis. To this list we may be tempted to add: mediate a dispute—especially an international one. The problematic nature of mediation is clearly more than a reflection of the recalcitrant nature of the human and institutional forces involved. As this chapter has attempted to demonstrate, it is also the result of certain implicit conflicts in the things that are demanded by virtue of the mediator's special social role, the way in which these role demands articulate with the needs and circumstances of the parties, and the mediator's own position as a representative. Mediators may wish and strive to be impartial, evenhanded, impeccably trustworthy, empathic, and clear-sighted. These objectives will soon be found to conflict with the need to overcome resistance, promote compromises, represent and manage the needs of their own constituencies, and promote settlements that cause nobody undue pain.

The problems faced by mediators are conceptually similar in some respects to the boundary role conflicts of negotiators that Walton and McKersie (1965) have so ably described, but the mediator's difficulties extend even further. First, in representational mediation the third party occupies not one boundary role position but several, depending on the number of disputants to the external conflict. Second, the mediator is burdened with role obligations to be impartial and evenhanded that are not part of the obligations of a negotiator.

In light of these considerations, one hesitates to be determinedly critical of Kissinger's mediation of the Arab-Israeli dispute. His indisputable accomplishment was to strengthen the alliance between the United States and Egypt, thereby increasing the prospects of a new and potentially valuable role for the United States as an intermediary, rather than a partisan, in the Middle East. The groundwork he laid also was invaluable to President Carter's subsequent mediation efforts. Kissinger does get poor marks for not promoting the parties' autonomy or institutionalizing a process of accommodation (via the exchange of ambassadors, the formal renunciation of a state of belligerency, and so forth). Perhaps his biggest failure was leaving the Palestinians out of the negotiations. One suspects, although it is difficult to prove on the basis of the information available, that the weakest procedural aspect of his intervention was its insufficient diagnostic vigor and acumen. As noted, however, these shortcomings are partially attributable to the contradictory things that are expected of a representational mediator and the situational factors that may complicate the role.

To date, most empirical research on mediation has occurred in the confines of the laboratory where few, if any, of these complex realities are at issue. We need to focus more attention on the activities of expert practitioners, who function in the real world, in order to increase an understanding of how mediators cope with the internal conflict that is inherent in their role, and the price that they and the parties have to pay in exchange.

REFERENCES

Brehmer, B., and Hammond, K. R. "Cognitive Factors in Interpersonal Conflict." In D. Druckman, ed., *Negotiations*. Beverly Hills, Calif.: Sage, 1977.
Brown, B. R. "Face-Saving and Face-Restoration in Negotiations." In D. Druckman, ed., *Negotiations*. Beverly Hills, Calif.: Sage, 1977.

Coleman, J. S. *Community Conflict*. New York: Free Press, 1957.

Deutsch, M. *The Resolution of Conflict*. New Haven: Yale University Press, 1973.

Deutsch, M., and Krauss, R. M. *Theories in Social Psychology*. New York: Basic Books, 1965.

Druckman, D., ed., *Negotiations: Social-Psychological Perspectives*. Beverly Hills, Calif.: Sage, 1977.

Getzels, J. W., and Guba, E. G. "Role, Role Conflict, and Effectiveness: An Empirical Study." *American Sociological Review*, 1954, 19, 164–75.

Golan, M. *The Secret Conversations of Henry Kissinger*. New York: Quadrangle, 1976.

Janis, I. L. *Victims of Groupthink*. Boston: Houghton Mifflin, 1972.

Janis I. L., and Mann, L. *Decision Making*. New York: Free Press, 1977.

Kalb, M., and Kalb, B. *Kissinger*. Boston: Little, Brown, 1974.

Kinder, D., and Weiss, J. A. "In Lieu of Rationality: Psychological Perspectives on Foreign-Policy Decision Making. *Journal of Conflict Resolution*, 1978, 22, 707–35.

Komarovsky, M. *Dilemmas of Masculinity*. New York: Norton, 1976.

Kressel, K. *Labor Mediation: An Exploratory Survey*. New York: Association of Labor Mediation Agencies, 1972.

Kressel, K., and Deutsch, M. "Divorce Therapy: An In-depth Survey of Therapists' Views." *Family Process*, 1977, 16, 413–43.

Kressel, K.; Jaffe, N.; Tuchman, B.; Watson, C.; and Deutsch, M. "Mediated Negotiations in Divorce and Labor Disputes: A Comparison." *Conciliation Courts Review*, 1977, 15, 9–12.

Kressel, K.; Lopez-Morillas, M.; Weinglass, J.; and Deutsch, M. "Professional Intervention in Divorce: The Views of Lawyers, Psychotherapists, and Clergy." In G. Levinger and O. Moles, eds., *Divorce and Separation: Context, Causes, and Consequences*. New York: Basic Books, 1979.

Meyer, A. S. "Function of the Mediator in Collective Bargaining." *Industrial and Labor Relations Review*, 1960, 13, 159–65.

Parsons, T. *The Social System*. Glencoe, Ill.: Free Press, 1951.

Pruitt, D. G., and Johnson, D. F. "Mediation as an Aid to Face-Saving in Negotiation." *Journal of Personality and Social Psychology*, 1970, 14, 239–46.

Quandt, W. B. *Decade of Decisions: American Policy toward the Arab-Israeli Conflict, 1967–1976*. Berkeley: University of California Press, 1977.

Rubin, J. Z. "Experimental Research on Third Party Intervention in Conflict: Toward Some Generalizations." *Psychological Bulletin*, 1980, 87, 379–91.

Rubin, J. Z., and Brown, B. R. *The Social Psychology of Bargaining and Negotiation*. New York: Academic Press, 1975.

Sarbin, T. R., and Allen, V. L. "Role Theory." In G. Lindzey and E. Aronson, eds., *Handbook of Social Psychology*, Vol. 1. Reading, Mass.: Addison-Wesley, 1968.

Sheehan, E. R. F. *The Arabs, Israelis, and Kissinger*. New York: Reader's Digest Press, 1976.

Walton, R. E., and McKersie, R. B. *A Behavioral Theory of Labor Negotiations*. New York: McGraw-Hill, 1965.

10

KISSINGER AND THE MANAGEMENT OF COMPLEXITY: AN ATTEMPT THAT FAILED

Donald B. Straus

The assessment in this chapter of what Henry Kissinger accomplished in the Middle East in the aftermath of the 1973 Yom Kippur War is based on two themes.

The first theme is that he was confronted with a problem of immense complexity. In order to reduce this complexity into manageable proportions, he invented step-by-step diplomacy, a technique that sought to move toward an overall agreement one step at a time. Although this technique allowed Kissinger to achieve several remarkable successes, he was unable to string these successes together to form the structure of a total peace.

The second theme is that the role of Secretary of State of the United States is incompatible with the role of mediator. In playing both roles, Kissinger developed a technique I have called mediation-with muscle. Again, the record shows that skillful use of this technique led to the achievement of a number of short-term objectives. Even so, the contention is that Kissinger's attempt to play both Secretary of State and mediator roles decreased the long-term effectiveness of each, to the detriment of both the country he served and the region he was trying to help.

A balanced assessment of Kissinger's performance during this period must be made in the context of his service to the country as Secretary of State. This chapter does not presume to do that. Written from the viewpoint of a professional mediator, its focus is much narrower: it considers only Kissinger's progress toward a peaceful resolution of the many Middle East conflicts.

KISSINGER AND COMPLEXITY

There is nothing new about complexity. Those who have sought to govern and manage the affairs of humanity have been confronted with complexity from the very beginning of time. But complexity has grown exponentially in recent years, and is itself a product of the various explosions that have characterized the last half of the twentieth century: the technological explosion, the population explosion, the knowledge explosion, the word explosion, and many others.

Complexity has a way of camouflaging (even anesthetizing) one's perception of its existence. In the face of complexity, people tend to oversimplify and to revert to previously held prejudices that obscure the essence of the problem being confronted. It is unnerving, perhaps even psychologically damaging, to confront for too long a chaotic scene out of which one can make no sense or logic. As a result, people tend to deny complexity and to obscure it with an overlay of steroctyped simplifications. For these reasons, the Middle East problem is often seen in simple bold headlines: ARABS HATE ISRAELIS; PALESTINIANS DEMAND WEST BANK; SAUDI ARABIANS THREATEN OIL BOYCOTT; SOVIETS CHALLENGE U.S. ROLE IN MIDDLE EAST.

It is naively tempting to assume that Kissinger's goal in the Middle East was simply that of peace between the Arabs and Israelis. Peace was surely a goal, but it was only one among many. Merely to list some of these objectives provides perspective on the complexity Kissinger faced: preserving detente with the Soviets while diminishing their relative influence in the Middle East; increasing United States influence among the Arab countries without alienating or weakening the Israelis; maintaining support by the American Jewish electorate for the Nixon administration; reconciling his own Jewishness with his duties as Secretary; coping with and seeking to eliminate the Arab oil embargo; maintaining an unstable balance of power between Israelis and Arabs in order to deter both Arab acts of desperation and unilateral Israeli ventures into territorial aggression; balancing his own desire to remain acceptable as a mediator with his need to represent U.S. interests; bolstering a doomed president under pressures from Watergate; and finally, but not insignificantly, feeding his own demanding ego. For Kissinger, mediation and peacemaking may have been mere preludes to these often larger tasks.

Step-by-Step: A Tool to Manage Complexity

Despite Kissinger's intelligence, experience, and immense prestige, even he was unable to unravel the tangle of complexity listed above. He was never fully able to comprehend or manage the Middle East problem as a whole. Instead he did the next best thing, and used his step-by-step approach as a device for breaking the problem into manageable parts.

Through step-by-step diplomacy, Kissinger attempted to identify manageable problems and to solve them one at a time, realizing that he had neither the tools nor the ability to handle larger problems. He hoped that if smaller problems could be resolved, these small successes would eventually lead to an overall solution. Like those who criticized him of losing sight of the big picture, Kissinger was aware that Middle East peace could not be based solely on an Israeli-Egyptian agreement; but try as he might, he was never able to put all the pieces together at one time. For Kissinger, the Middle East was a scene of piecemeal triumphs and large-scale frustrations.

All who seek solutions to large-scale problems immediately face a dilemma: to confront the entire problem boggles the mind and frustrates a rational approach; on the other hand, solutions to occasional pieces of the problem are of minimal value unless they can be strung together in a way that will eventually produce a whole solution. Kissinger did make several attempts to put it all together. One of these was in November 1975. This occasion was just after the United Nations had passed a resolution defining Zionism as a form of racism. Kissinger assigned the Deputy Assistant Secretary of State for Near Eastern Affairs, Harold H. Saunders, to make a statement to Congress in which he indicated that the Palestinian dimension of the Arab-Israeli conflict was at the heart of the conflict. While there was little new in this statement, it symbolized the U.S. determination at that moment to work for a total peace settlement that included the Palestinians. Israeli hostility to Saunders' remarks was so great that Kissinger had to withdraw his support for this ambitious goal and return once again to efforts at solving more manageable pieces of the problem.

Kissinger in the Middle East was like the sorcerer's apprentice: everywhere he turned there was more to do than he could do himself. In his constant search for a possible (as opposed to the theoretically best) course of action, he discovered, as did his successors in the Carter administration, that Egypt appeared to be most susceptible to mediation among the Arab nations. The Israelis were as reluctant as Kissinger to take on the issue of the PLO and the West Bank because of its sensitivity at home. As Rabin constantly reminded Kissinger, any softness with regard to this issue might result in the fall of Rabin's party and its replacement with leadership that would be even less willing to negotiate.

Therefore, when Kissinger chose in August 1974 to continue efforts for an Egyptian-Israeli disengagement in the Sinai rather than to push for a Jordanian-Israeli settlement in the West Bank, he was motivated more by what he deemed possible than by a deeply held philosophical conviction about the importance of issues or the order in which they should be tackled. He would have preferred to address the tougher and more central issue of the West Bank (Sheehan 1976, p. 176), but he was persuaded that he simply did not have the strength to do so. In hindsight, it now seems that the Palestinian issue should have been tackled head-on at a far earlier date, but it was characteristic of Kissinger's style to move along the path of least resistance rather than adhere to a rigid plan. Similarly, at Geneva in early 1974, Kissinger marched up the hill to the big problem, became appalled at its magnitude and the intransigence of the parties, and marched right back down again.

Kissinger was remarkably successful at isolating manageable pieces of the Middle East puzzle, and combining his prestige as Secretary of State with his personal talent as a mediator in order to achieve a steady flow of cease-fire arrangements and partial agreements. Nor should these achievements be minimized. They led to an uneasy and unstable cease-fire; they kept the parties talking; they produced the steady stream of proposals that are the lifeblood of any mediation effort; they maintained the dominant role of the United States (and Kissinger) in the area; and they generated favorable headlines at a time of desperation in the Nixon administration.

Furthermore, in theory step-by-step was a sound mediation tactic. It removed from the complexity of the whole those identifiable parts that were manageable; it generated small successes that should have moved (and to some extent did move) attitudes and expectations away from that of "battles to be won" to "problems to be solved." But movement from piecemeal settlement to overall Middle East peace was disappointing. The steps in step-by-step diplomacy were more like the motions in a square dance than a march toward some clearly specified goal. Over and over again, Kissinger found himself moving a step ahead in one successful negotiation, a step sideways in another negotiation, then a step backward after an unsuccessful attempt, and finally back again to the original starting point of Israeli-Egyptian relationships. In retrospect it is obvious that forward progress was limited by lack of attention to the problem of the Palestinians. Because it was so resistant to solution, Kissinger kept sweeping this critical issue under the rug. As a result he was unable to use his step-by-step successes as stepping-stones toward a total peace.

In principle, step-by-step seemed like a fine idea, one that should have worked as readily as the stepwise construction of a complex model airplane. Anyone who has spent Christmas week at such a task knows that the instructions are quite explicit. First, one sorts out the individual peices and assembles them in some order or relationship. Then small subassemblies are glued together. After awhile, and with a little luck, one has the pieces of a wing, the fuselage, the undercarriage, and so forth, in neat little piles. Finally, there comes the grand moment of total assembly, as the completed design emerges from the chaos that first tumbled out of the packing box.

Unfortunately, large-scale, complex problems of the sort confronted by Kissinger in the Middle East do not lend themselves so neatly to this sort of approach. No instructions come with the box, and there are no easily recognizable first steps. Because the appearance of the total finished model is still unknown, the small pieces that have been assembled do not easily or necessarily fit together, nor is the eventual configuration of a solution readily apparent. Furthermore, unless one keeps working on the small pieces, especially those that at first seem to defy solution, things may disintegrate into chaos. On the other hand, if one tries to assemble the smaller pieces into something that does not fit together or conform to perceptions of what is acceptable, such futile efforts can also turn to chaos. Kissinger never did get all the pieces to fit together.

THE SECRETARY AS MEDIATOR

Peace in the Middle East was an important item on the United States foreign policy agenda during Kissinger's term as Secretary of State. Whether or not this objective warranted as much of his personal time as Kissinger devoted to it is less clear. Also debatable is whether the Secretary of State should have undertaken the role of mediator in matters that were, and are, vital to U.S. interests. In any event, it is clear that a mediator who possesses both the carrot and the stick of U.S. financial and military resources is not practicing mediation as usually defined.

A mediator is typically a person with no direct interest in the outcome of a dispute. In labor relations, an acceptable mediator would not be an owner or executive of a business, nor a member of a labor union, and certainly not one involved in the case. In no event would the mediator stand to gain or lose personally as a result of the agreement that was reached. In contrast, virtually every detail of the agreements on which Kissinger worked was of interest to his chief client, the president of the United States, and therefore of interest to him. An issue was of concern to voters at home because of the voters' ethnic background or personal preferences, or it affected the potential flow of oil, or it cost money in direct transfers of military equipment or in foreign trade, or it otherwise affected the fragile balance of power in the Middle East: issues that were all of great concern to the makers of U.S. foreign policy. At no time was Kissinger impartial as Secretary of State. He sought the image of impartiality and at times achieved it, but he never allowed (nor indeed should he have allowed) impartiality to temper his duty as the negotiator for the United States' goals.

Mediation-with Muscle

Mediation implies the impartial application of those skills that are necessary to induce the parties in a dispute to reach agreement of their own accord. Resolution of a dispute through peaceful means is the sole objective; classic mediation injects no value judgments and contains no hidden agenda. The skills of persuasion are the only tools available in order to achieve results.

As has already been observed, Kissinger, as Secretary of State, clearly had many concerns other than peace in the Middle East that were vital to his conduct of U.S. foreign policy. He never hesitated to use mediation as a negotiating tool by wielding the carrot and stick of U.S. power. In short, Kissinger was a staunch advocate of mediation-with-muscle.

In another era, perhaps even as recently as just prior to the outbreak of the Vietnam War, mediation as a tool of diplomacy would have been buried at the bottom of the State Department's tool chest and little used. As a major world power, there were so many more direct ways to achieve United States objectives than for the Secretary of State to devote a major share of his time to mediation. But in the aftermath of Vietnam, and in the anteroom of Watergate, the potency of more traditional American power tools was reduced or unavailable, and the value of mediation increased.

As an experienced negotiator, Kissinger understood that mediation could often be transformed into a powerful negotiating tool. Mediation and negotiation have several features in common. A mediator must listen with care and empathy in order to fully understand the positions of both sides and to diagnose the points at which a compromise might be reached; a skilled negotiator must be able to do much the same thing. A mediator must also be inventive at assembling different proposals in such a way that they accommodate the needs and desires of the opposing parties; similarly, a negotiator who can construct a proposal that will meet both his own needs and those of his opponent will be all the more successful. In these respects, as well as in others, the tasks of mediator and negotiator are similar indeed.

Mediation-with-muscle is a very special art. The objective is not merely to promote peace, but to do so only when this objective, and the most effective tactics for achieving it, coincide with other policy consider-ations. When these objectives did coincide, Kissinger achieved agree-ments that seemed miraculous to many observers. However, when a conflict existed between the consequences of pure mediation and the other goals on Kissinger's agenda, the mediator's impartial role was often subordinated.

Aborting the Talks at Kilometer 101

Nowhere is Kissinger's ambivalence as a mediator more clearly illustrated than in his attempts to abort the apparently successful direct negotiations between Arabs and Israelis at Kilometer 101 in November 1973. It is not entirely clear how active Kissinger's role was in derailing these negotiations just when they appeared to be making progress. What is certain, at the very least, is that Kissinger did nothing to encourage these direct talks. From the narrow perspective of mediation theory, this was and is most unorthodox behavior.

Conventional mediaton wisdom holds that direct negotiations between parties should be encouraged whenever possible. If direct negotiations can lead to agreement, then this is the sine qua non of mediation success, since the "pure" mediator has no agenda other than to promote settlement. At Kilometer 101, however, Kissinger appeared to have a number of other items on his agenda. Among these were the following:

> Kissinger believed the negotiators were ahead of their constituents, and that they might have difficulty later selling the agreement reached at the bargaining table to these constituents.
>
> Kissinger feared the possibility that Syria might insist on a similar agreement, thereby delaying the Geneva talks.
>
> Kissinger wanted to make certain that the U.S. role in Middle East mediation remained dominant. He believed that he, both personally and as Secretary of State, was indispensable to the mediation efforts and wanted to keep things that way; agreement negotiated directly by Israel and Egypt would not contribute to his record of personal success.
>
> Kissinger believed that if the Geneva conference were to open with an agreement negotiated directly by Israel and Egypt without his assistance, the U.S. role in Geneva could be more easily subordinated; moreover, the continued demonstration of an a U.S. role in Middle East mediation was necessary in order to deflate Soviet prestige.

Other and more positive motives may be attributed to Kissinger as well in an effort to explain his attitude toward the talks at Kilometer 101. As has been seen, Kissinger was wedded to the tactic of step-by-step, and was both skeptical and pessimistic about the possibility of tackling the problem as a whole. Yet, as he explained to Abba Eban (Israeli delegate to the United Nations), by moving the talks from the tent at Kilometer 101 to Geneva, it would be possible to bring to the conference a settlement that was not burdened with disagreements in principle and was not linked to other sensitive issues such as the Jordanian-Palestinian question. Geneva constituted Kissinger's only attempt to bring all the parties together, and it is entirely possible that he wanted an agreement that appeared imminent at Kilometer 101 to be consummated in Geneva, where it might encourage further, more widespread agreement.

Sheehan (1976) writes of Kissinger's action: "The format, the process, the context of the disengagement were as important to Kissinger as the disengagement itself—even though, as events proved, Geneva was not to prosper as the site of substantive negotiations" (p. 81). If indeed, Kissinger's purpose was to move the talks from a forum where progress was being made into a larger forum where the areas of agreement would be widened and deepened, then this was mediation at a most sophisticated level.

Certainly there may have been many legitimate reasons for Kissinger to have derailed the direct negotiations at Kilometer 101. But even if there were, Kissinger might have ahcieved his objective in a number of ways other than the abrupt and insulting action he is reported to have taken. Direct talk between Israeli and Egyptian negotiators was, in itself, a remarkable event, one that should certainly have been cherished and cultivated at almost any cost. It surely would have been possible for Kissinger to have injected himself into these discussions, probably toward the end, thereby taking some of the credit for their success. This would not have been beyond his capabilities as a diplomat and as a manager of events, nor would it have been entirely unjustified, as it is doubtful that these discussions could have taken place without his prior intervention to bring about a cease-fire. Had Kissinger intervened and taken a hand in the final stages of these discussions, he could easily have tailored the public content of an agreement so as to preclude some of the concerns that may have been on his mind vis-à-vis the other Arab countries. Given the advantage of hindsight, it would also appear that the momentum achieved at Kilometer 101 might have been directed constructively toward fortifying the forthcoming meetings in Geneva, and might have led to earlier direct negotiations between Sadat and the Israelis.

In an interview with Mohammed Hassanenin Heikal in November 1973, Kissinger clearly indicated that he was aware of the ambiguities inherent in the roles of mediator and Secretary of State. In this interview, Heikal asked Kissinger to explain the role that he thought he was playing. It could not be the role of a mediator, Heikal suggested, because he was not perceived as neutral by all of the parties; could it be the role of a negotiator, since the United States was not a direct party in the negotiations. Kissinger replied that he understood the ambiguity of his position, and suggested that perhaps it could be best explained as representing the "concern" of the United States for a grave crisis that was taking place in an area in which it had strategic, political, and economic interests that it wished to protect. Kissinger further admitted that he brought to the Middle East his own agenda: he hated failure and was compulsive about maintaining a record of success. He expressed confidence that the force of his personality would assure success in the Middle East as it had in other areas of the world. Despite this moment of insight, Kissinger usually responded to a challenge of his impartiality with a burst of anger. It was all very well for him to admit to Heikal, in a moment of frank introspection, that he was not impartial; it was quite a different matter for one of the active parties in the negotiation to accuse him of partiality to one side or the other. On such occasions, Kissinger reacted with proclamations of injured innonence.

How Muscle Can Change Mediation Tactics

It is not unusual for a mediator to advise the parties about bargaining tactics that might improve their chances of reaching agreement. For example, a mediator may occasionally suggest that one party be allowed to present only a portion of the next negotiating offer in order to test its acceptability. Subsequently, the mediator may be able to bring back a counteroffer from the other party matching the concession that the first was originally prepared to give. It is also not unusual or unethical for a mediator to use his powers of persuasion to get one side or the other to change its offer to be more to the liking of the other side. A skillful mediator can take credit for, and thus increase his credibility by, moving the parties toward the zone of potential agreement. However, when a mediator withholds information to the detriment of one side or the other, he is behaving in an unethical manner that will eventually undermine his effectiveness. Finally, a mediator-with-muscle must be concerned with the possibility that one of the parties is moving toward agreement too quickly. Since the mediator has already demonstrated an ability to extract concessions, there is always the danger that muscle or inducements (rather than powers of persuasion) will be perceived as responsible for the mediator's effectiveness, thus inflating the currency of carrots and sticks required in the next round of negotiations.

There were a number of occasions when Kissinger had to weigh considerations such as these. During the first weeks of December 1973, Kissinger was just beginning to try his skill at mediating in the Middle East. An uneasy truce prevailed, with Israeli troops on the western shore of the Suez Canal, Egyptian troops on the eastern shore, and the rest of the quarrelsome states (including the Russians) poised to take advantage of any opening or mistake that might occur. It was also during this period that Kissinger was trying to choose between a multiparty conference in Geneva and the step-by-step, two-party tactics that were just beginning to be formulated in his mind. It was in this setting that Israeli Minister Dayan offered to withdraw to a line west of the Mitla and Giddi passes in an effort to obtain arms as well as other concessions from the United States. At this point Kissinger is alleged to have urged the Israelis not to offer this particular concession for fear that Israel would look too weak. According to Quandt (1977), "It was important for the Arabs to see that it was difficult for the United States to influence Israel, otherwise their expectations would soar" (p. 221). On the other hand, were it to become known (as did in fact happen) that it was Kissinger who prevented Dayan from yielding these passes, then this could only reinforce the Arab perception of Kissinger's power over the Israelis.

On another occasion, on May 8, 1974, as Kissinger was nearing the end of his mediation effort to establish a semipermanent cease-fire line between Israel and Syria in the Golan Heights, he left Jerusalem with a number of new concessions that had been given to him by the Israelis. He disclosed some of these concessions to Assad, but withheld others in order to leave more room for bargaining. On May 16, 1974, Syrian President Assad countered with an even larger concession than Kissinger had expected, and these concessions were the ones that made the final Syrian-Israeli agreement possible. Once again Kissinger was hesitant about fully disclosing these concessions (although he did in fact transmit them) because, according to Golan (1976):

> On one hand, he was glad that the ice was broken. On the other hand he expressed fear, half seriously, half humorously, that from now on the Israelis would believe in his power to wrest concessions from the Syrians and this would toughen their position (p. 204).

Once again, in March 1975 when Kissinger was still trying to convince the Israelis to withdraw from the Mitla and Giddi passes, he allegedly told reporters that he was carrying new Egyptian proposals to Israel. According to Golan (1976), Kissinger had no new proposals but was merely trying to create an impression of Egyptian moderation and Israeli obstinacy. Even after Rabin discovered his ruse, Kissinger feigned innocence, laying all responsibility for the report on the journalists who wrote the story. It is difficult to understand why Kissinger used this kind of obvious falsehood, one that was bound to be discovered sooner or later. For a mediator without muscle, such behavior would be tantamount to commiting suicide.

How Lasting Are Agreements Produced by Muscle?

As has been observed, when Kissinger mediated he could, and did, push the parties in the direction he wished with inducements far more powerful than pure persuasion. He could directly effect the consequences of delay or recalcitrance by a particular party by withholding or promising vast amounts of arms or other kinds of aid. There were also all the other less tangible but nonetheless potent implications of being in the favor or disfavor of a superpower. For example, offers of arms shipments to one side or the other were apparently made for reasons other than an interest in maintaining a balance of military power. There were instances when such offers appeared to be inducements (actually bribes) designed to get one party or the other to go along with a mediation proposal. As a result, the level of armaments in the Middle East increased dramatically. Kissinger himself recognized that he might have been "whipsawed" into causing this increase. Thus, Sheehan (1976) quotes him as saying:

> When I ask Rabin to make concessions he says he cannot because Israel is weak. So I give him more arms, and he says he does not need to make concessions because Israel is strong (p. 66).

By using the various carrots in his mediation tool kit, Kissinger in effect provided the Middle East countries with a ratchet to extract ever higher tributes from the United States, in exchange for their agreement to go along with mediation proposals.* One is left wondering about the extent to which these infusions of ever-higher levels of arms capability (ostensibly made at the time to produce small pieces of an overall agreement and to stabilize the balance of military power) might eventually lead to the potential for armed conflict at a more terrible level of destruction. Another issue, perhaps even more difficult to address, concerns the economic and political cost to the United States of providing this massive military assistance to the Middle East combatants.

Even if one acknowledges that Kissinger used mediation-with-muscle primarily as a diplomatic instrument to forward U.S. objectives, it is clear that his intervention also was a powerful instrument for deterring war in the Middle East. Unfortunately, the absence of armed conflict, as important as that may be, is simply not the same as peaceful coexistence. A more difficult question to answer, therefore, is whether or not the Kissinger brand of mediation-with-muscle contributed to, or actually detracted from, long-term peace in the area. The concrete manifestation of the muscle exerted generally took one of two forms: arms that flowed both to the Israelis and the Arabs; and in lesser amounts, aid in goods and money for other purposes. Arms shipments were presumably designed to maintain some rough balance of power and to reduce both a sense of helplessness that could lead to acts of military desperation, and a sense of military superiority that could lead to acts of aggression. Whatever the short-run impact on military and psychological stability in the region,

---

* This pattern, once set, proved to be resistant to change. More recently, on a three-day trip to the Middle East, President Carter "persuaded" Israel and Egypt to conclude the Camp David agreement—at a cost of over $5 billion.

however, the long-run effect was certainly to elevate the area's ability to wage war.

It is also interesting to speculate on the effect that mediation-with-muscle had on the peace prospects for the United States itself, particularly vis-à-vis the Soviet Union. Clearly a high Kissinger priority was to neutralize and reduce Soviet influence in the Middle East and therefore, presumably, its ability to upset detente or wage war against the United States. Even in Kissinger's mind, however, using muscle to achieve a mediation goal, while not upsetting or impairing detente, was something of a juggling act. Others will have to judge the effect that his mediation activities had upon Soviet-American relations.

Assume for a moment that mediation-with-muscle is the only form of intervention that will prove effective in political disputes like that in the Middle East. Assume further that this is the only kind of mediation that the United States can or will engage in now and in the future. Given these assumptions, a number of questions remain about the process and its consequences that have not yet been addressed.

First, even if mediation-with-muscle fails to produce the quality of agreement generated by pure persuasion, is not such mediation preferable to many other forms of diplomacy, such as the gunboat diplomacy of the pre-Vietnam era?

Second, assuming that mediation-with-muscle becomes an accepted tool of diplomacy, as well as dispute resolution, what are the pragmatic ground rules that should be observed? For example, should it be used if the parties are reluctant or unwilling to participate? How much muscle is effective? At what point does additional muscle, in the form of either implied force or quantities of funds, produce diminishing returns or actually become ineffective?

Third, assuming that only a voluntary agreement can result in a lasting peace, how effective is muscle at producing such voluntary agreement?

Fourth, how open should mediators-with-muscle be in stating their objectives and priorities? Assuming that these objectives will be discovered eventually, and may differ from what the mediators have stated publicly, wouldn't they lose credibility?

Fifth, which tactics in the use of muscle are apt to be effective, and which are not? To take but one example, in view of Kissinger's apparent willingness to lie and his ability to get away with it, should future practitioners of this new form of mediation assume that such behavior is acceptable and effective?

Sixth, what are the ethical and other consequences of using the gift of military hardware to help produce short-run agreements, even at the expense of escalating the parties' armed potential? What are the long-run implications for peace and for the diplomatic and ethical health of the mediator's own nation if, in the course of mediation, the economic well-being of the mediator's home arms industry is enhanced?

Finally, to what extent will (and should) mediation-with-muscle by a superpower be perceived as a new form of colonialism? To what extent will such a perception diminish the diplomatic benefits of successful mediation?

Mediation-with-muscle in international affairs is still new and as yet unproven.* It has both clear benefits and certain dangers. Before the technique can be used with greater confidence, questions of the sort posed above will have to be addressed.

ANOTHER LOOK AT MANAGING COMPLEXITY

A major thesis of this analysis is that Kissinger's failure to manage the complexity of the Middle East problem contributed to the very limited success of his total effort. At issue here is neither Kissinger's talent nor his energy in pursuit of his goal; rather it is the ineffectiveness of the tools that have thus far been developed for the purpose of managing complexity.

The management of complexity has received far too little attention in past and current research on dispute resolution. The rest of this chapter will therefore speculate a bit by suggesting a model that might be useful. The framework has been divided into nine steps, more for ease of discussion than to suggest that these steps would necessarily be followed, let alone followed in the order suggested, in any one dispute.

First, the international community—either the United Nations, neighboring states, or a superpower—would become aware of an incipient dispute. The evidence could be an actual outbreak of fighting, the exchange of diplomatic notes, or any other manifestation of international strife.

Second, a mediator would become part of the process. This person could be appointed by a body such as the United Nations, could be mutually selected by the parties (a rare occurrence in international affairs), or could be self-elected, as in the case of Kissinger and the United States in the Middle East. Ideally, all the participants would be willing to negotiate under the auspices of the mediator, would regard the mediator

---

*Variations of mediation-with-muscle have been used in labor relations, particularly in cases of national emergency; the power and prestige of a president, a governor, or a mayor are often used to break or prevent a strike. Similarly, parents and teachers also use force-cum-persuasion to separate quarreling children. When used in international diplomacy, however, the complexity of issues and the magnitude of consequences render mediation-with-muscle a totally different activity.

as competent and impartial, and would openly avow their intention to cooperate in the process. Of course, few of these ideal conditions ever occur; the best that could be expected would be a close approximation.

Third, the mediator would try to identify the participants necessary for a lasting solution, and would then seek to win their confidence and willingness to participate in the process. Kissinger knew who the participants were; however, because of Israel's refusal to recognize the Palestinians, and the Palestinians' refusal (along with most of the Arabs) to recognize Israel as a legitimate state, he felt compelled to ignore the Palestinians. This made good short-run sense in his early step-by-step efforts, because it seemed to bypass a most contentious issue. Unfortunately, this decision did not remove the issue, and may have escalated the amount of terrorism and reprisal. An early effort by Kissinger to recognize the Palestinians, or at least the legitimacy of their human rights, would have been preferable to neglect—even if the result had been short-run Israeli disapproval and distrust. Underlying this retrospective opinion, admittedly voiced in the absence of the pressures to which Kissinger was subjected at the time, is the strong belief that if a major issue of some complex problems is ignored, the issue will only fester and become more troublesome at a later time.

Fourth, the analysis of the problem proper would now begin. A listing of separate facts would be developed and examined, and an early determination made as to those facts that are agreed to by all the parties, and those that are in dispute. It is at precisely this point that data mediation could occur, by assembling a file of agreed-upon facts on which the remainder of the negotiations could be based. Values would also be examined at this point. The mediator could help the parties to understand how these values differ, what their various goals and fears are, and how the values, goals, and fears relate to the developing file of facts and patterns of separate but related problems.

Looking into the future, it is my belief that this is the point in the intervention process where mediators will begin to develop, with the participation and assistance of the parties, a computer model that assists in the management of complex issues. Such a computer-based arrangement could be in the form of a simple computerized file of facts available for quick retrieval. It could also take the form of a more complex model that not only helps store and retrieve facts, but also supplies additional aids such as detailed maps or calculations of the interrelationship among such divergent factors as population movement, natural resource requirements, labor supply, and other economic factors deemed pertinent to the deliberations. Since one of the primary activities of a mediator is to submit proposals for the parties' consideration, computer-based assistance would enable mediators to develop these proposals more quickly; moreover, it would permit the parties to evaluate the proposals in greater detail and with a greater sense of reality, particularly if they had participated in the original construction of the models.

Fifth, the smaller and more manageable pieces of the problem (for example, the matter of individual demilitarized zones) would be assembled in a pattern so that their interrelationships might begin to be understood more easily. The detailed analysis of such interim decisions would be stowed away (either manually or with the aid of a computer) so that they could be retrieved and assembled in different stages and patterns as the negotiating process continues. At this point, the mediator and the negotiating parties could shift back and forth from an aggregated macroview of the problems to a detailed microview.

Sixth, the mediator would begin the slow and painful process of refining the model. Because of the care with which the mediator assembled the parts and made them easily accessible, both the mediator and the parties could dip into the organized and accepted data bank and remove from it those chunks of the problem that seem capable of discussion across the bargaining table. These are the human-sized chunks that are amenable to negotiation, mediation, and consensus. For each of these chunks, the mediator would attempt to elicit agreement on the facts, a mutual understanding of values, and a list of alternative solutions that should be considered.

Seventh, the mediator then would focus the negotiations on a particularly contentious chunk. In many respects, this step is very similar to the process adopted by Kissinger in the Middle East, and in fact reflects his step-by-step tactic enacted at a later, more mature stage of the process.

Eighth, the mediator would seek to wire the mediated chunk(s) back into the totality of the problem. It is at this point that Kissinger encountered the greatest difficulty. In fact, there is little evidence that he either saw this as an important step or tried to accomplish this objective.

As an example of the process at this eighth step, imagine that the chunks selected for mediation were the Israeli-Syrian dispute, the Israeli-Jordanian dispute, the Israeli-West Bank (Palestinian) dispute, and the Israeli-Egyptian dispute. If partial agreement had been achieved in the Israeli-Egyptian dispute, then the problem here would be to take this consensus and determine its effects on each of the other three parts of the total problem. If an Israeli-Egyptian settlement included an agreement by Israel to withdraw from the Sinai, what possibilities would this present for accommodating some of the Palestinians now residing on the West Bank? What effect would self-government by the Palestinians residing in the Sinai have on the Palestinians residing in the West Bank? What aspects of the Israeli-Egyptian settlement could affect the future negotiations between Israel and Syria, and Israel and Jordan? What reciprocal opportunities for trade and industrial development would this open up?

The step described above is the most speculative link in this forecast of future efforts at international mediation. Similar uses of the computer have occurred in other areas of human activity, but not in dispute resolution.* That a computer is technically capable of handling this order of complexity is not in doubt. What remains to be developed is some way to motivate disputing parties to cooperate to the extent necessary for the development of a common model. Also in need of understanding is the extent to which the very act of developing a common model would (as I suspect) be an effective mediation technique in and of itself—or, as others have suggested, might be a deterent to consensus. These questions cannot be determined until the process is tried under live conditions.

Ninth, assuming that each of the separate chunks of the total problem has been subjected to mediation, with agreements resulting therefrom, total or partial agreement would now be reached on all (or a majority) of the human-sized chunks of the problem. At this point, the total dispute (beyond the capability of mediation in step five) would now be ready for mediation, leading toward a peace treaty that encompasses the totality of the problem.

The framework described above, designed to attack the problem of complexity, is admittedly a speculative and rough conceptualization. It seeks to break the problem into pieces that can be resolved across a bargaining table, and then to assemble the different ensuing agreements into a model representing the whole that permits mediation efforts designed to encompass the total dispute. There is nothing really new about this process. We engage in it more or less unconsciously every day of our lives, as we are forced to address one problem or another without the aid of computers. Although present computer technology is still not ready for easy application of this process to a negotiating situation, rapid strides are being made in this direction. It is both interesting and useful to consider the directions these strides must take to permit the power of computers to augment mediation efforts.

At present, the computer is best at performing the huge volume of computations that are routine and repetitive, and can therefore be programmed so that no changes are required during the program's operation; such programs are used routinely in business operations for accounting and billing purposes. However, when used to solve problems, as an aid in mediation, or in other creative activities, the gap between what the computer can now do and what a mediator might like it to do remains wide. The computer can outperform all of us in storing and retrieving facts (memory), in handling a volume of mathematical compu-

---

*The author is currently engaged in a project to use a computer model as an aid to mediation in conflicts over the siting of power plants.

tations (arithmetic), or in finding correlations according to previously given instructions. But it is slow learning new instructions or shifting between different models of the same problem. A programmer must feed into the machine, in the most minute detail, any changes in a program. Then the effect of the new instructions must be carefully checked to be sure they have been properly understood.

The human brain leaps with split-second speed to the new and creative solutions that are developed in negotiations. The participants in this human process are often impatient to test their new proposals with one another or to see their impact on a physical or mathematical model. The computer of the future must therefore be capable of absorbing these shifts in perception and insight if it is to be truly useful as an aid in negotiation and mediation. In solving problems, the human mind also jumps between the macro- and microlevels with great agility. Kissinger's attention was continually shifting from such microdetails as the terms of a cease-fire during the Yom Kippur War, to a macroconcern with the impact of a cease-fire on Arab-Israeli or U.S.-USSR relations. Each such shift in focus demands the application of a huge number of different facts and assumptions previously collected, as well as the intuitive insights and facts that grow out of new developments. In this process, the action of the mind is like a zoom lens moving close-up to examine and adjust details, then moving back to study the impact of the changes on the whole problem.

No computer today is programmed to keep up with this rapid-fire human activity, for the mind is simply too sophisticated and nimble in its operation for current computer technology. Nevertheless, it is well to remember that the human mind has its limitations as well; for instance, it contains relatively small storage and integrating capacity for facts. As a result, only a small and highly aggregated amount of available data and assumptions can be considered by negotiators at any one time, leading to the possible omission of some very important facts and assumptions at every point in the process. It soon will be technically feasible to build into a computer sufficient flexibility to permit rapid interaction with negotiators at various points in the process, supplying at least reminder checklists of facts and assumptions that should be considered while different options are explored at both macro- and microlevels of a complex problem. By reexamining Kissinger's activities in the Middle East, it is possible to identify weaknesses in our current ability to handle complexity of this kind and to speculate on ways of overcoming these difficulties. Eventually the interactive use of computers in some form or another will become an important, practical part of the new technology of mediators and negotiators on the international scene. Research is badly needed to discover how this future capability can best be used.

REFERENCES

Golan, M. *The Secret Conversations of Henry Kissinger.* New York: Quadrangle, 1976.

Quandt, W. B. *Decade of Decisions: American Policy toward the Arab-Israeli Conflict, 1967–1976.* Berkeley, Calif.: University of California Press, 1977.

Sheehan, E. R. F. *The Arabs, Israelis, and Kissinger: A Secret History of American Diplomacy in the Middle East.* New York: Reader's Digest Press, 1976.

PART IV

DISCUSSION

11

INTEGRATION AND COMMENTARY
Jeffrey Z. Rubin

This chapter is designed to begin the important work of integrating the book's eight core essays. By commenting on various points of similarity and contrast among these pieces, it is hoped that a process can be initiated that will lead eventually to a clearer understanding of both Secretary Kissinger's intervention in the Middle East and, of even greater importance, the general nature of the third party intervention process. Unfortunately, a chapter of this sort can do little more than touch upon a few of the authors' many interesting and provocative ideas. As the editor, I can only hope that readers will come to share my enthusiasm for the contributed chapters and will be motivated to continue the effort to move toward a more integrative framework.

In keeping with the authors' own organizational assignment, this chapter consists of two sections: the first summarizes the authors' collective analysis of Kissinger's third party intervention in the Middle East; the second section summarizes and comments upon the contributors' assumptions about the nature of conflict, negotiation, and the intervention process.

ANALYSIS OF KISSINGER'S INTERVENTION:
AUTHORS' GENERAL COMMENTS

The contributors were asked to describe and evaluate Kissinger's mediation both generally and in the context of several specific questions. The general issues the authors addressed included: an overall characterization of the distinguishing features of Kissinger's step-by-step diplomacy; appraisal of the degree to which the particular outcomes in the Middle East would have obtained had someone other than Kissinger intervened, or had there been no intervention at all; and finally, an evaluation of Kissinger's intervention effectiveness. The authors' comments on each of these issues are considered in turn.

The Distinguishing Features of Kissinger's Intervention: What Did He Do and Why?

Virtually all of the contributors agree that Kissinger's primary objective in the Middle East was the achievement of a series of small-scale, short-term agreements rather than the more general framework for an overall peace settlement; he may have been interested in moving toward a more general peace in the region, but his activity was focused almost exclusively on a set of bilateral disengagements. Although there is considerable divergence regarding the merits of Kissinger's decision, the authors agree that he was fundamentally interested in securing a chain of relatively small successes.

But why did Kissinger become involved in the pursuit of these disengagement agreements in the first place? Several contributors conclude that Kissinger was primarily interested in protecting or enhancing the power and reputation of the United States in the Middle East, particularly in relation to the perceived interests and objectives of the Soviet Union. Fisher observes that Kissinger's highest priority was the maintenance of global political balance with the Soviet Union, with the interests of the regional participants being secondary; he argues that Kissinger wished to exclude the Russians from the Middle East, while simultaneously increasing U.S. power in the region. Similarly, Bobrow contends that Kissinger took the initiative in the Middle East because he wanted to demonstrate American strength and resolve vis-à-vis our Western European allies, the Soviets, and the Chinese. Hopmann and Druckman point out that Kissinger was interested in manipulating the domestic political situation in a number of Arab States in order to serve American interests and objectives, for example by preventing revolutionary movements from coming to power in the region. As they observe: "conditions were ripe for the exercise of U.S. interests in ways that had not been possible before." Other reasons cited in explanation of Kissinger's pursuit of the disengagement agreements include Bobrow's observation that Kissinger wanted to divert attention from the White House and the unraveling of the Nixon presidency, while at the same time performing a "rescue operation . . . on his own tarnished image as a manager of crises." Taken together, these comments suggest that a third party's intervention must be understood in the context of that party's own particular interests in a conflict and its resolution.

And what of Kissinger's step-by-step diplomacy? What function was this unique, piecemeal approach to international mediation designed to serve? The explanation cited with greatest frequency, described in greatest detail, and clearly of the greatest importance in most authors' judgment, was Kissinger's desire to generate and sustain momentum. The sense of this argument is that Kissinger believed that the only effective way to move the principals along the road to a comprehensive peace settlement was by engineering a series of relatively small successes that would help generate the momentum necessary for continued work. As Fisher points out, "the technique was to seek agreement where agreement was most likely." Similarly, Zartman quotes President Sadat on step-by-step: "It is the idea of eating bit by bit what cannot be swallowed all at once." The effect of step-by-step diplomacy, writes Zartman, was to build trust by convincing the principals that "compromise was theoretically possible and was preferable to the dire alternatives of unilateral action and inaction." Pruitt points out that step-by-step diplomacy was designed to sustain the belief that agreement is possible, and was facilitated by providing the negotiators with a steady diet of concessions and agreements, as well as by placing less controversial issues early on the agenda. Other explanations for Kissinger's adoption of step-by-step include: Straus' observation that Kissinger invented the technique in order to reduce complexity to more manageable proportions; Kressle's similar conclusion that step-by-step enabled Kissinger to handle the external dispute while coping with his own role strain; and Kochan's observation that this method helped Kissinger to "whittle away at the number of unresolved issues."

The authors generally agree that Kissinger was a highly directive, even aggressive mediator who tried to control events and dictate strategy. Rather than sit back and wait for events to unfold before intervening, Kissinger preferred to help engineer these events in ways that, in his judgment, made a negotiated settlement more likely. Zartman makes the interesting point that Kissinger deliberately helped to create a military and political stalemate in the Middle East in the aftermath of the October War, so that the parties would subsequently be motivated to concede.° Kissinger's tactic, writes Zartman, was "to cultivate an awareness of stalemate by heightening each party's understanding of the other's

---

°Nadav Safran, in his important book *Israel: The Embattled Ally* (1978), makes an interesting point in this regard. He indicates that Kissinger attempted to influence relationships and outcomes not only after the October War, but during the war itself. Like a Greek god in the Trojan War, Kissinger tinkered with the actors. He manipulated the flow of arms to Israel, the timing of U.S. pressure to declare a cease-fire, and the declaration of a worldwide alert, all in order to create a stalemate that he believed was in the best interests of the United States and his own forthcoming role as mediator.

inability to meet the first's terms, while at the same time cultivating a preference for a negotiated solution."

Apart from his tactical use of stalemate, Kissinger attempted to enhance the parties' motivation to reach a negotiated settlement in a number of other ways. Fisher, Hopmann and Druckman, and others point out that Kissinger often acted as a go-between, trying to educate each side about the other's concerns. Pruitt observes that Kissinger tried to persuade each side to make concessions on the grounds that such concessions were necessary (because the other seemed intransigent), were in the party's own interest, and were likely to generate concessions by the other side. Pruitt, Fisher, and others also point out that by encouraging the principals to direct their conciliatory offers at him rather than each other, and by initiating a number of his own proposals, Kissinger was able to deflect many of the parties' face maintenance concerns onto his own shoulders. Similarly, Hopmann and Druckman observe that Kissinger was able to manipulate skillfully the timing and sequence of negotiating moves in such a way that concessions could be made without appearing too conciliatory. They point out that Kissinger was a master of "issue control," able to identify possible negotiating packages and trade-offs in such a way that the parties were increasingly motivated to reach agreement. Finally, Zartman describes Kissinger's talent for developing an overall plan (formula) that provided the disputants with the basis for subsequent resolution of the detailed points of conflict.

In order to maintain the tempo of negotiations, the contributors agree, Kissinger found it necessary to continually press the disputants for concessions by utilizing a technique that Straus aptly describes as mediation-with-muscle. Time and again Kissinger linked concession making by the principals to the promise of additional U.S. military and/or economic aid and the threat of withholding such support in the absence of movement. Zartman correctly points out that it was largely after Kissinger's threats "began to wear thin" that he resorted increasingly to promises of U.S. assistance in order to maintain the pressure for agreement. As shall be seen, several authors believe he relied too heavily on the use of power in order to achieve his ends, and that his mediation effectiveness suffered accordingly.

Finally, a number of contributors point to the uniquely personal quality of Kissinger's third party diplomacy. Fisher observes that Kissinger preferred to deal not with governments but with individuals. Struas, Pruitt, and Kressel describe Kissinger's self-deprecating humor and his ability to exploit this humor for tactical ends; Kressel also comments on his talent for building commitment to mediation through the timely use of personal charm. Conversely, as Pruitt points out, Kissinger also knew how to serve as the target of angry displays by the disputants, thereby deflecting anger that was really directed at the other side. As Fisher and Kressel observe, Kissinger's personal involvement with the principals may have led him to become too emotionally involved, occasionally leading to angry outbursts of his own that may have reduced his effectiveness as a mediator.

The Causal Responsibility for Kissinger's Intervention: Was He Necessary?

Some of the authors believe Kissinger was indeed necessary, that the particular outcomes of U.S. intervention in the Middle East would not have resulted had someone other than Kissinger been at the helm. Kochan contends that Kissinger was able to "move the peace process in a more significant way than any of his predecessors," while Pruitt observes that Kissinger "was a strong man representing a powerful country. . . . One suspects that there would have been no agreements in the absence of U.S. pressure." Similarly, although Fisher and Zartman diverge about the effectiveness of Kissinger's intervention, they agree that this intervention was of instrumental importance in determining the particular outcomes that resulted. Indeed, because these four authors fundamentally share the view that Kissinger's performance as an actor was of critical importance, and have analyzed his intervention from this vantage point, their chapters were grouped together in Part II of the book.

Although the remaining authors obviously also believe that Kissinger's third party intervention had an important effect on outcomes in the Middle East, their analytic framework is strikingly more contextual. These authors are acutely sensitive to the situational constraints and pressures within which Kissinger's intervention emerged, and their chapters have therefore been grouped together in Part III. Although Bobrow believes in the importance of Kissinger's involvement and the uniqueness of his contribution, he also points out that the disengagement agreements were possible because: the Soviets found U.S. success tolerable, the Israelis wanted to buy time, the Egyptians wanted to look attractive to the United States, and the Syrians wanted to prevent the Israelis from engaging in a revenge attack. Quite apart from anything that Kissinger said or did, the principals seem to have had their own special reasons for accepting movement toward settlement. Hopmann and Druckman observe that the parties had already achieved the "preconditions for negotiation" by the time Kissinger intervened, and were therefore ready for agreement. Kressel's point of view appears to be that Kissinger was probably not responsible for what happened (and did not happen) in the Middle East. Instead, the outcomes were a result of the role strain and competing pressures to which Kissinger was subjected. His shortcomings as a mediator, Kressel writes, "are partially attributable to the contradictory things that are expected of a representational mediator." Finally, Straus likens Kissinger to the sorcerer's apprentice, with more informational complexity to manage, and more to do, then he or any one person could do himself. Straus observes: "At issue here is neither Kissinger's talent nor his energy in pursuit of his goal; rather it is the ineffectiveness of the tools that have thus far been developed for the purpose of managing complexity." The implication here is that had the tools been better, the imprint of Kissinger's talent and energy would have been more likely to come to the fore.

Overall Evaluation of Kissinger's Intervention: Was He Effective?

The authors' appraisal of Kissinger's intervention effectiveness may be understood in relation to two primary themes: the use of step-by-step diplomacy in order to achieve a series of bilateral disengagements, and the exercise of mediation-with-muscle.

Comments on Step-by-Step

It has been seen that the contributors differ in their assessment of the functions step-by-step diplomacy was designed to serve. Disagreements also exist regarding the overall effectiveness of this technique of tackling the issues a little bit at a time, beginning with the relatively easy ones. Arguments in support of the effectiveness of step-by-step come from a number of quarters. Bobrow points out that "Kissinger's intervention showed creativity, determination, boldness, even courage . . . Kissinger rescued himself and his policies from what could easily have been massive setbacks." Fisher observes that step-by-step diplomacy allowed Kissinger to accomplish several objectives: "He bought time; he excluded the Soviet Union from most Middle East diplomacy; and he obtained widely hailed diplomatic successes." Kochan concludes that the decision to embark on the step-by-step approach "appears to have been based on a realistic appraisal of what was possible—the mark of an effective mediator."

Perhaps the strongest argument in support of step-by-step diplomacy is that it helped pave the way for President Sadat's visit to Jerusalem in 1977 and the subsequent talks among Israel, Egypt, and the United States at Camp David in 1978. Without Kissinger's patient and painstaking effort to extract disengagement agreements from the principals, it is contended, the machinery of peacemaking would not have been set in motion, and insufficient momentum would have been generated to keep the process going at Camp David three years later. We thus have

Kissinger to thank for where we are today.* "Even Kissinger's harshest critics," writes Kochan, "must regard his intervention as a partial success, a necessary step on the road to a permanent peace." Similarly, Pruitt observes that "the momentum generated by Kissinger's success between 1973 and 1975 bore fruit in Sadat's dramatic visit to Jerusalem in November 1977." Finally, Zartman has the following kind words of support:

> Kissinger mediated effectively because he well understood the negotiation process. . . . He recognized and, in part, engineered a situation propitious for negotiation; encouraged and, in part, created a formula for settlement of the important issues; and used elements of power, deadline, trust, and momentum first to bring a process to fruition and then to leave it in a situation propitious for a new cycle of negotiation.

Offsetting the arguments in support of the effectiveness of step-by-step diplomacy are several critical concerns. Perhaps the most powerful of these is the argument that by tackling only the more peripheral issues in the Middle East, the central and most thorny problems were left untouched and no easier to address (perhaps even more difficult to address) at a later time. Fisher analyzes Kissinger's objective as "holding his thumb in the dike," a solution that does little more than stave off disaster for a while. Similarly, Zartman observes that "Kissinger was all process. He indicated neither a goal toward which he was moving nor one that he thought likely." Kressel argues that Kissinger failed to proceed "with the necessary diagnostic vigor," being content instead to work on the periphery. Finally, Hopmann and Druckman point out that Kissinger's intervention was characterized by a fundamental irony: "the 'grant strategist' met with considerable success as a tactician, while failing to

---

* Note that this argument is a two-edged sword, depending upon where one thinks we are at present. Should Camp David be regarded as a success or as a long-range failure? There is no doubt that the talks produced a series of bilateral agreements between Egypt and Israel, calling for Israeli return of the Sinai Peninsula, the normalization of relations between the two nations, and so forth. But at what cost were these agreements achieved? As of this writing, in late July 1980, the Israelis are continuing to develop new settlements in the West Bank, Jerusalem has been declared the one and only capitol of their country, and the government of Prime Minister Begin appears to be in danger of collapse. Over in Egypt, President Sadat is more isolated than ever from the other nations of the Arab world, remains in uncertain health, and continues to be plagued by domestic economic and political problems that are in danger of pulling him down. In short, it is not at all clear that the Camp David meetings succeeded in moving the principals in the Middle East toward a comprehensive peace agreement. To the contrary, Camp David may have raised the parties' expectations for a quick and easy settlement, only to have these expectations dashed all the harder on the rocks of political reality.

provide any lasting or durable solutions to the conflict at the strategic level. . . . Missing was a plan for creating structures that could sustain the realignment fostered by his intervention." In the long run, they argue, Kissinger's structural machinery for sustaining peaceful exchange was so fragile, leaving so many elements untouched (especially the fate of the Palestinians), that "it seemed unlikely to survive the gusts of future winds."

Comments on Mediation-with-Muscle

Straus' term, mediation-with-muscle, readily captures the sense of Kissinger's ability to couple traditional mediation with the carrots and sticks necessary to generate movement toward agreement. Several of the authors point to the importance of this technique in first helping to create, and then sustaining, the momentum required to continue the concession-making process. Offsetting this argument, however, are several levels of concern.

First of all, a number of authors point to the sheer financial cost associated with Kissinger's increased willingness to couple concessions with U.S. promises of military and economic assistance. Zartman and Straus, for example, argue that the Israelis were given an excessive commitment to military aid in exchange for the second Sinai disengagement with Egypt.

Second, quite apart from the financial consequences of Kissinger's promises is the fact that these commitments progressively locked the United States into what Zartman describes as a "hamstrung policy in the Middle East." As he points out, in exchange for Israel's willingness to reach agreement during the second Sinai negotiations, Kissinger promised to tolerate Israeli retaliation for Palestinian attacks across the cease-fire line in Lebanon, and to accept an Israeli veto of contacts between the United States and the PLO.

A third extremely interesting and important consequence of Kissinger's mediation-with-muscle is that the United States may have become increasingly vulnerable to manipulation by the regional participants. The line of reasoning here is that Kissinger was apparently so committed to obtaining peace in the Middle East that he was willing to have the United States pay almost any price to accomplish this objective. The regional parties understood this commitment to settlement as well as the clear U.S. dependence it implied, and used this dependence to their advantage. Bobrow describes Kissinger and the United States as "needy," pointing out that the regional parties' already considerable leverage increased dramatically with the possibility that Kissinger's diplomacy might end in failure. Similarly, Kressel observes that Kissinger became trapped in the Middle East, as when his success in managing the first Egyptian-Israeli disengagement increased his investment in achieving a settlement between Israel and Syria. Finally, Straus comments: "Kissinger in effect provided the Middle East countries with a ratchet to extract ever-higher tributes from the United States, in exchange for their agreement to go along. . . ." The general point is that Kissinger's single-minded pursuit of disengagement, and his reliance on whatever muscle was necessary in order to achieve this objective, may have created the conditions of overcommitment to a policy that trapped Kissinger and the United States in an increasingly costly spiral. Indeed, it may be argued that the effects of this policy are being felt even today, as the U.S. government continues to attempt to cement a Middle East agreement with ever-increasing offers of assistance.

A fourth critical consequence of mediation-with-muscle is, as Straus points out, that U.S. arms shipments to the Middle East served "to elevate the area's ability to wage war." The question thus remains of whether the U.S. decision to act as arms merchant to the nations of the Middle East—and indeed the world—will help or hinder the chances of peace.

Fifth, Fisher argues that Kissinger's use of power in order to achieve his objectives led him to be too concerned with power as an end in itself. "To be so concerned with the power that comes from success," writes Fisher, "is to be too little concerned with making the world a better place." Kissinger should have paid more attention to being a person of integrity, and less attention to protecting an image of success.

Finally, Pruitt points out that one of the important negative consequences of a third party's undue reliance on power in order to achieve certain ends in that the change induced by the third party may not last. Pruitt writes: "Traditional mediation without muscle is a weak reed when issues are . . . deeply felt. . . . However, it must also be acknowledged that a mediator who exercises too much power may induce an agreement that will crumble when the mediator from the scene." As seen in the discussion of advisory versus directive roles in the Introduction, although a directive third party may elicit speedier agreement in the short run, it may be the agreement reached through the intercession of an advisory third party that proves to be more enduring.°

° Although this chapter is devoted to the authors' analyses rather than my own, it may be appropriate to add a brief note at this point regarding my own characterization of Kissinger and his effectiveness. In the language of the typology of third party roles that was described in the Introduction, I would characterize Kissinger's set of roles as informal, representative, more noninvited than invited, partial, directive (advisory "with teeth"), an uncomfortable mixture of interindividual and intragroup, content-oriented, conflict managing, temporary, and relationship inhibitory—with all the pros and cons that each of these roles implies for third party effectiveness.

ANALYSIS OF KISSINGER'S INTERVENTION: AUTHORS' ANSWERS TO SPECIFIC QUESTIONS

The contributors were asked to respond to questions regarding Kissinger's intervention in four specific situations. A summary of these questions, and the authors' answer to each, will be presented below.

Direct Talks between Israel and Egypt

In late November 1973, Egyptian General Gamasy and Israeli General Yariv began to negotiate a Sinai disengagement directly. Kissinger attempted to abort this experiment in direct negotiations. Was his intervention appropriate? What would you have advised him to do?

Several of the authors responded to these questions by arguing that Kissinger's intrusion was inappropriate and that he should have been advised to stay out. Fisher, Kressel, and Straus comment that Kissinger should have been advised to encourage direct talks, and should have coupled this encouragement with an offer to be available for assistance if the parties desired; Kressel adds that a direct agreement would have increased the parties' investment in making the settlement work. Bobrow also concludes that Kissinger should not have discouraged direct negotiations, although he points out that the principals may have deliberately attempted to negotiate directly in order to "spur Kissinger on," to keep the United States involved so that U.S. concessions could be extracted at a later time. The interesting assumption here is that the principals were actually playing a rather different game, with a rather different objective in mind, than Kissinger may have suspected.

Virtually all the authors agree that Kissinger's decision to discourage direct talks was based on a desire to maintain control over the tempo of negotiations and the centrality of U.S. involvement. Moreover, those contributors who conclude that Kissinger's intervention was appropriate in this situation consistently cite the importance of control and American centrality. Hopmann and Druckman, Kochan, and Zartman all comment that Kissinger wisely called off the direct talks in order to preserve his intermediation and U.S. influence—both of which were necessary, they argue, if agreement was to be reached. Pruitt adds the similar observation that Kissinger did what he did out of a concern that the parties might be moving too rapidly, leading each side to explain the other's concession making as a sign of weakness and thereby encouraging intransigence and eventual loss of momentum.

Israeli Initiatives to Disengage in the Sinai and in the Golan Heights

In December 1973, Israeli Defense Minister Dyan advised Kissinger of a unilateral Israeli offer to withdraw from the strategic Mitla and Giddi passes in the Sinai in exchange for Egyptian agreement to reopen the Suez Canal to Israeli ships. Kissinger advised the Israelis against this course of action, urging them to move more slowly and thereby maintain an appearance of strength. In another similar situation, during the May 1974 negotiations between Syria and Israel regarding a disengagement of forces in the Golan Heights, Kissinger elected to disclose to Syrian President Assad only some of the concessions that the Israelis were willing to make. The authors were asked, regarding each of these situations: Do you agree with Kissinger's analysis? What would you have advised him to say or do? Because the authors' analyses proved to be strikingly consistent from one of these intervention situations to the next, their comments regarding the situations have been combined.

Although most of the authors believe that Kissinger made the correct recommendation in these situations, a few are critical of his intervention. Bobrow and Fisher argue that Kissinger should·have encouraged the Israeli initiatives; Fisher adds that in order not to weaken the Israelis' bargaining position, Kissinger might have proposed converting their proposals into "suggestions" that could have been introduced for discussion by the United States. Straus takes the position that by not conveying the Israeli proposals as intended, and by attempting to deter the Israelis from their initiative, Kissinger behaved unethically.

The arguments in support of Kissinger's intervention come from a number of quarters. Pruitt and Hopmann and Druckman contend that the principals were in danger of moving too quickly, and that Kissinger wisely slowed them down in order to keep in motion the willingness to continue making concessions. Similarly, Kressel points out that by discouraging the unilateral Israeli initiatives, Kissinger was able to lower the Egyptians' and Syrians' respective aspirations and expectations for gain, thereby reducing his own role strain and making agreement at a lower level more likely. Kochan regards Kissinger's intervention as a good example of how an effective mediator can go about building credibility with one side (the Egyptians and the Syrians, respectively) by being seen as "responsible for obtaining whatever concessions were wrung out of the opponent"; that is, rather than have the Israelis initiate concessions, Kissinger preferred to lead the Egyptians and Syrians to believe that these concessions were made at his own behest. Finally, Zartman makes the interesting point regarding the Dayan initiative in the Sinai that had the Israelis been encouraged to proffer their offer, and had it been accepted by the Egyptians, momentum for a subsequent Egyptian-Israeli disengagement might have been destroyed. The idea here is that the particular disengagement line proposed by Dayan (near the Mitla and Giddi passes) was so stable—so prominent a settlement point, in effect—that the parties would have converged on this solution and would have had little room left for concession making in subsequent negotiations; it was not agreement, but the sense of movement toward agreement, that was important in sustaining momentum.

Second Sinai Disengagement versus Movement in the West Bank

In August 1974, Kissinger had to decide which of two settlements to pursue next: a relatively easy and less far-reaching second disengagement between Egypt and Israel in the Sinai Desert, or an extremely difficult but critically important agreement between Israel and Jordan regarding the fate of the West Bank. Given that Kissinger did elect to pursue the former agreement, what choice would you have advised him to make, and why?

Most of the authors seem to believe that Kissinger made the wrong choice, although several contend that he did the best he could under extremely difficult circumstances. Kochan and Pruitt take the position that Kissinger was, as Pruitt puts it, "simply bowing to political realities in Israel and the Arab world." Similarly, Zartman argues that "the West Bank was to ride on momentum, not on stalemate," and this momentum simply did not exist at the time. (Indeed, wonders Zartman, does it exist even today?)

Those authors who are critical of Kissinger's decision regarding the West Bank take the position that the Middle East and the world had far more to gain than to lose by a mediated effort to forge agreement on the West Bank, and that an important opportunity was lost in 1974 when Kissinger elected to look the other way. Hopmann and Druckman write of Kissinger's decision: "he had begun to lose sight of his larger strategic objectives in the glare of the publicity surrounding his tactical successes as a mediator." In a similar vein, Fisher observes that "he should have been less concerned with United States prestige and somewhat more concerned with the human beings caught up in the Arab-Israeli conflict," while Straus comments that Kissinger was motivated more by what he deemed possible than by what he believed to be right or important. Finally, Bobrow contends that the costs of a failed initiative on the West Bank were probably not so great for the regional participants (in contrast to Kissinger and the United States) "as to make the risk prohibitive." In other words, had Kissinger done a more objective job of analyzing the risks and rewards associated with pushing for movement on the West Bank, and had he been less invested in protecting his reputation as a successful mediator, he might have made a decision that would have been in the greater long-term interests of the regional participants.

AUTHORS' ASSUMPTIONS ABOUT CONFLICT, NEGOTIATION, AND THE INTERVENTION PROCESS

Perhaps the most direct way of uncovering the points of similarity and contrast among the contributors' assumptions is by addressing some of the authors' individual and collective statements, both implicit and explicit, about the nature of effective third party intervention. In pursuing this analytic tack, it is my own assumption that the authors' underlying views regarding the nature and functions of conflict and negotiation will, in turn, be revealed. Furthermore, in order to impose a modicum of conceptual structure on the authors' assumptions about intervention effectiveness, their comments have been organized in relation to the third party functions that were presented in the Introduction: the modification of physical and social structures, the modification of issue structure, and increasing the motivation to reach agreement.

The Modification of Physical and Social Structures

The authors touch upon three themes that may be subsumed conveniently under this heading. The first of these is the assumption that an effective third party may be able to generate significant movement toward agreement through improvement of the quality of communication between the disputants. Both Bobrow and Fisher comment on the importance of communication; Fisher, in particular, develops the point in some detail. His thesis is that a third party can help each side to understand better how the other sees things and, in so doing, may be able to break a conflictual impasse. "In any conflict," writes Fisher, "it is highly likely that each adversary has a one-sided view of the problem.... Adversaries, even face-to-face, rarely find the words that are most persuasive to each other." One of the most important things an effective third party can do is to help the disputants to communicate directly with each other and, if necessary, to act as a go-between of sorts—clarifying and illuminating positions and preferences in ways that make them more acceptable to the other side.

Second, Hopmann and Druckman point to the importance of increases in the available bargaining space. The effectiveness of intervention, they argue, is influenced by the third party's ability to manipulate the strategic environment in ways that increase the number of possible settlement points. By enlarging the size of the conflictual pie through the infusion of additional resources, an effective third party can produce a "wider potential range of mutually profitable agreements," thereby enhancing the disputants' cooperative interests.*

Finally, Hopmann and Druckman, as well as Kressel, make the assumption that one of the hallmarks of effective intervention is the creation of new structures that survive any agreement reached. Kressel writes: "Truly superior mediation . . . not only resolves the immediate

---

*One should not lose sight of the fact, noted earlier in this chapter, that the injection of additional resources also carries with it a number of risks and possible costs.

issues, but also creates a new and more viable framework for the parties' relationships with one another." Effective intervention requires the elaboration of procedures that are likely to sustain the disputants' good working relationship even after a settlement has been reached and the third party has ridden off into the sunset. Hopmann and Druckman, as well as Bobrow, suggest several such procedures: the development of a "communication and information regime" that permits the principals "to develop the conventions and rules that they believe are applicable and define violations of the implied agreement"; and the creation of a coalition composed of members of each side that, by crosscutting the traditional lines of antagonism, introduces the possibility of superordinate goals and identifications that are likely to have a binding and enduring effect.

The Modification of Issue Structure

The contributors converge on three major ways of modifying issue structure, each of which is assumed to be related to intervention effectiveness. The first of these involves helping the disputants to find a formula that enables them to move toward agreement. Zartman points out that many negotiations—particularly those containing multiple parties and multiple, complex issues—are characterized by a two-stage process: the disputants first seek a formula that groups the issues under discussion in such a way that agreement is possible in principle; they then set about the task of implementing the detail associated with their particular formula by exchanging concessions and proposals until agreement is reached. An effective third party should be able to help the disputants to discover the integrative formula that shapes the nature of an eventual agreement. Moreover, the third party should be able to present the formula in ways that allow the disputants to retain and apply it to the narrower issues that arise in the course of negotiations. Zartman expresses this point in relation to Kissinger as follows: "Kissinger's useful role consisted of reapeatedly finding, or helping the parties to find, narrower applications of the formula that were true to its original meaning and resolved the issue at hand." By helping the principals to develop a negotiating formula, an effective third party can modify the principals' perception and organization of the issues in dispute, and can generate movement toward agreement.

A second major theme that emerges regarding issue structure concerns Fisher's observation that a third party can help the disputants to find better games to play. Fisher points out that in many (perhaps most) conflicts, the disputants engage in hard bargaining, a process characterized by mutual suspicion, the use of threat, and commitment to immediate victory at the expense of the parties' long-term relationship. One of the things a skillful third party can do in such a situation is to encourage the principals to engage instead in friendly bargaining. This process is characterized by mutual trust and a willingness to compromise; perhaps of greatest importance, it involves shifting the disputants' attention away from the merits of any single substantive issue toward the matter of their own ongoing relationship. Unfortunately, writes Fisher, "hard bargaining is a dominant strategy over friendly bargaining"—meaning that if two bargainers have been playing a friendly game and one begins to play hard, the game will eventually be played hard by both. Therefore, if the disputants are to engage in something other than hard bargaining, an alternative to friendly bargaining must be found.*

The alternative Fisher suggests is principled problem solving, a negotiating strategy in which "the commitment is to principle and the necessity of a solution based on the merits of the matter at issue." Principled problem solving is characterized by objectivity, willingness to respond to reason, treatment of all personal issues as independent of substantive differences, and, most generally, by what may be described as a legal/judicial outlook. By shifting the disputants' game from hard bargaining to principled problem solving, a third party can thus attempt to modify the issue structure—transforming a commitment to positions into a commitment to principle. Fisher contends that principled problem solving is a dominant strategy in relation to hard bargaining: "When the hard bargainer discovers that pressure does not produce results but that the principled negotiator is flexible and willing to respond to good arguments on the merits, then he, too, begins to emphasize objective arguments on the merits." Would that this were so! Unfortunately, it is all too often the case that reason and principle fail to elicit reason and principle in return.

A third theme that emerges concerns the importance of interventions that are designed to help the disputants manage complexity. Straus observes that many bargaining relationships are characterized by a welter of informational complexity, including multiple issues that differ widely in their difficulty and centrality. All too often, such complexity leads to

---

*Issue can be taken with Fisher's argument regarding the dominance of hard bargaining over friendly bargaining. The friendly bargainer is characterized a bit naively by Fisher as a passive, yielding, easygoing sort of person who is likely to react to pressure from the other side by simply turning the other cheek. Surely a bargainer can be friendly without also being a fool, as when a bargainer indicates that friendship is contingent upon evidence that the other party has similar intentions. In fact, social psychological research (for example, Deutsch, Epstein, Canavan, and Gumpert 1967) has indicated that a contingently friendly strategy elicits cooperation more readily than a strategy resembling hard bargaining.

oversimplification, stereotypy, and distortion both on the part of the disputants and the third party. Straus suggests that a third party can manage complexity effectively and, in so doing, can help the disputants to reach a comprehensive agreement. In his chapter he develops an intervention framework that argues for the management of complexity in stepwise fashion. With a third party's assistance, the disputants develop both a macroview of the problem(s) at hand (a big picture of sorts that is reminiscent of Zartman's notion of formula) and a microview of the smaller and more manageable issues. As agreement begins to be reached on some of these smaller issues (what Straus refers to as human-sized chunks), the third party attempts to wire these agreements back into the totality of the problem by studying the effects of such agreements on each of the overall problem's other facets. Agreements are thus reached on a tentative basis, subject to an appraisal of their fit with remaining issues. An important assumption in Straus' analysis is that in proceeding step-by-step through the negotiation of a set of issues, one must be vigilant regarding the implications of such negotiations for the overarching settlement that may eventually result.

Increasing the Motivation to Reach Agreement

The contributors have developed at least five sets of ideas that may be understood in relation to the theme of motivation. The first of these concerns the enormous importance of intervention timing. Virtually all of the authors agree that for intervention to be effective, the third party must enter the conflict at some optimal point—ideally, says Kochan, the point at which the disputants' motivation for settlement is "ripe." Both Pruitt and Zartman describe this intervention point in relation to the concept of stalemate. When a stalemate has been reached (sometimes, as we have seen, with a bit of assistance from the third party), neither side can force additional concessions out of the other, and each therefore realizes that the only way to get a portion of what one still wants is by moving toward a negotiated settlement. It is at this point, when the disputants are ready to take seriously the work of dispute resolution, that an effective third party should intervene.

A second, related assumption of several authors concerns the judicious exercise of power. On the one hand, in order for the disputants to be motivated to reach agreement, Zartman, Pruitt, and Kochan point out that it may be necessary for third parties to use, or threaten to use, some of the power they may have available. On the other hand, as Fisher and several others comment, the most effective intervention is the one that relies on the least force necessary to generate movement toward agreement. Kochan elaborates upon this idea by observing that the harder third parties press for agreement—beyond some point—the more their credibility is apt to decline. Similarly, Pruitt points out that one of the risks of pushing too forcefully is that the disputants may regard the third party as having a vested interest in a particular outcome, at the sacrifice of their own best interests; as a result, the disputants may choose to resist the third party's influence attempts.

How much power, then, is the right amount? Kressel suggests one interesting possible answer to this question when he discusses the importance of third party moves that are as economical as possible, thereby "serving to keep interventions to a minimum while maximizing the movement toward conflict resolution." He continues: "it may be that what distinguishes the brilliant mediator from the merely good or downright poor one is the ratio of multipurpose acts to the total number of mediator interventions." So the right amount of power in effective intervention is the amount necessary to exert the greatest leverage with the least necessary force.

A third theme that pertains to the disputants' motivation to reach agreement concerns the third party's management of role strain. It is Kressel who has developed this idea most completely, pointing out that "a mediator is the occupant of an inherently stressful social role." By coping with role strain in appropriate and productive ways, an effective third party may be able to generate movement toward settlement. Among the many factors that are likely to increase third party role strain, Kressel observes, are the existence of conflicts that involve multiple parties who are of unequal power, ambivalent about change, with ties to multiple constituencies, or who are assisted by a third party occupying a representational role. In order to reduce role strain effectively, a third party can do a number of things, including increasing the disputants' commitment to third party intervention. As Kressel points out, by skillfully coupling personal charm with the timely introduction of various incentives and a sense of movement toward agreement, a third party can increase the disputants' motivation to settle while simultaneously managing to cope effectively with any personal role strain.

A fourth set of relevant issues pertains to various third party attributes that are assumed to be associated with intervention effectiveness. Kochan argues that an effective third party must be mutually acceptable to the parties, high in credibility, and capable of inspiring trust and confidence. Pruitt adds that intervention effectiveness is more a matter of how the third party is regarded than what any particular personal attributes happen to be. An effective third party, he says, is likely to be regarded as expert in the issues at hand, as having great concern for the disputants' welfare, and as having rapport with the other side. This last point is particularly interesting because it suggests that it is not rapport per se that is of interest to the principals, but rather the third party's ability to persuade the other side to concede. Bobrow adds to this potpourri of third party attributes the observation that an effective third party takes the needs of the disputants seriously. All too often, he points out, third parties mistakenly assume that the disputants' needs are trivial and that their bargaining skill is inferior.

Perhaps because of the specific case they were asked to analyze, several contributors consistently directed their attention to a single third party attribute: impartiality. The sense of their observations is that a third party need not be impartial in order to be effective. Kochan makes precisely this point (as does Pruitt) when he contends that impartiality has been overemphasized as a third party virtue. Similarly, Bobrow draws on Touval's (1975) earlier analysis to indicate the important and effective role that biased intermediaries can perform in the resolution of conflict. Finally, Fisher observes that although an ideal mediator is typically seen as "a kind of eunuch from Mars who happens to be temporarily available," a third party can function effectively as an individual who is clearly partial to the interests of one of the disputants. Far more important than the third party's impartiality, the authors agree, is the ability to induce concessions; and when the third party happens to be partial to the disputant who must make the first or larger concession, this ability to generate movement is likely to be enhanced.

A final consideration relevant to the matter of increasing the motivation to reach agreement concerns the third party's ability to encourage the disputants to explore positions without commitment. Throughout the book the authors repeatedly observe that bargainers in the midst of intense conflict are reluctant to make concessions lest they give up terrain that cannot be recovered subsequently, and lest they lose face.[*] One of the most important things a third party can do to offset such concerns is encourage the disputants to "come clean without prejudice," as Kochan puts it: to make proposals informally and on a tentative basis, with no commitment to adhere to the positions expressed until a final agreement has been reached. Fisher has developed a full-blown analysis of this theme in his chapter. Because the alternative he describes is particularly controversial and important, his analysis deserves closer attention.

Fisher contends that bargainers typically engage in what he describes as a concession-hunting minuet. By this he means that bargaining traditionally involves a mutual and sequential search for the concessions that the other side is willing to make. He argues that this process has several consequences that slow the pace of dispute resolution: first, the parties tend to develop extreme opening positions so that they will have

---

[*] These concerns correspond to the concepts that Pruitt (1971) has described elsewhere as position loss and image loss.

room to make subsequent concessions; second, the process "encourages obstinacy by rewarding it"—since the less each side gives, the more it will get; third, the process directs attention to the parties' relative willingness to make concessions rather than to achieve a reconciliation of their conflict.

As an alternative to conventional bargaining, Fisher recommends the "single negotiating text" strategy, a plan he contends was implemented successfully at the 1978 Camp David meetings. Rather than encourage the principals to draw up separate, extreme positions from which concessions are made until a common position is developed, a third party should "listen to the parties, try to understand their basic interests, and then make a preliminary sketch" that is criticized, revised by each party, and finally accepted or not. The essence of Fisher's interesting and important idea is that "it is much easier for a party to criticize a draft than it is to make a concession." The disputants can explore positions without commitment, placing the onus of creative and integrative responsibility in the hands of the third party.

Fisher argues that the merits of the single negotiating text strategy far outstrip its drawbacks as a mediation technique. I remain a bit skeptical, however, for several reasons. First, by enormously increasing the pivotal importance of the mediator role, the disputants' ability to resolve their conflict is made to depend upon the third party's own effectiveness. While a creative and talented mediator may be able to work wonders with Fisher's strategy, an ineffective one could conceivably foul things up far more than would have occurred in the absence of any intervention at all. Second, the single negotiating text strategy ignores the possibility that the disputants' underlying motivation may occasionally be not to reach agreement, but rather to be able to extract concessions that allow each side to look good in the eyes of various constituencies. The very movement toward convergence that Fisher proposes to eliminate is thus an important source of data by which bargainers can demonstrate their ability to function effectively. Finally, there is something quite comforting about the sheer predictability of the concession-making process; indeed, Fisher's minuet metaphor exactly captures this quality. Steps are made in a known, overlearned sequence, providing the disputants with a structure in which they can comfortable move about. The single negotiating text procedure, in contrast, contains far less structure and certainty; one never quite knows for sure whether movement has really been accomplished until the very end of the process, when the third party's final draft is accepted by both parties or not. For each of the above reasons I suspect that, given some choice, bargainers may be quite reluctant to accept Fisher's intervention strategy and to work seriously within the confines it imposes.

CONCLUSION

It has been my intention in this chapter to be as honest as possible to the authors' individual words, while at the same time moving a step closer to a synthesis of their ideas. Although I have tried not to quote contributors out of context, and I have tried to avoid attributing views to them that they disown or find repugnant, it is always possible that I have erred along the way. Inductive movement toward a more general conceptual framework requires the use of a procrustean bed, I suspect, and it is not always fun to stay the night with an innkeeper who may have procrustean intentions. Therefore, if you have not already read the contributors' fine chapters I urge you to do so, both in their interest and in the interest of understanding better the general contours of the intervention process.

Finally, let us not lose sight of the fact that the contributors, in turn, have been asked to do a bit of procrustean work of their own. Although they have tried to analyze Kissinger's intervention in the Middle East without misrepresentation or distortion, they have undertaken the extremely difficult task of simplifying and reducing their analysis to a systematic array of principles; the sources they were asked to work from should therefore be read in the original. Kissinger was invited to comment on the preceding essays, and although he was unable to accept this invitation, I am confident that his memoirs of the step-by-step era will be published eventually. We look forward to reading Kissinger in his own words.

REFERENCES

Deutsch, M.; Epstein, Y.; Canavan, D.; and Gumpert, P. "Strategies of Inducing Cooperation: An Experimental Study." *Journal of Conflict Resolution*, 1967, 11, 345–60.

Pruitt, D. G. "Indirect Communication and the Search for Agreement in Negotiation." *Journal of Applied Social Psychology*, 1971, 1, 205–39.

Safran, N. *Israel: The Embattled Ally.* Cambridge, Mass.: Harvard University Press, 1978.

Touval, S. "Biased Intermediaries: Theoretical and Historical Considerations." *Jerusalem Journal of International Relations*, 1975, 1, 51–69.

INDEX

ABOUT THE EDITORS AND CONTRIBUTORS

JEFFREY Z. RUBIN is Associate Professor of Psychology at Tufts University and Director of its Center for the Study of Decision Making. He received a Ph.D. in social psychology from Teachers College, Columbia University. He is the author of articles on bargaining and negotiation, conflict escalation and entrapment, decision making, and dispute resolution through third party involvement. Rubin is the coauthor of *Social Psychology: People in Groups; The Social Psychology of Bargaining and Negotiation*; and *Making Decisions: A Multidisciplinary Introduction*.

DAVIS B. BOBROW is Professor of Government and Politics at the University of Maryland, where he has also served as Chairman of the Department of Government and Politics, and Director of the Bureau of Governmental Research. He received a Ph.D. in political science from MIT. He is the author of numerous articles on public policy, international affairs, political communication, and China, and has authored, coauthored, or edited the following books: *Components of Defense Policy; Computers and the Policy-Making Community: Applications to International Relations; Weapons System Decisions: Political and Psychological Perspectives on Continental Defense; International Relations: New Approaches*; and *Understanding Foreign Policy Decisions: The Chinese Case*.

DANIEL DRUCKMAN is the Mathtech Social Scientist at Mathematica, Inc., in Bethesda, Maryland. He received a Ph.D. in social psychology from Northwestern University. He is author of articles in the areas of interparty conflict resolution, policy decision making, simulations, and negotiations. Druckman is the editor of *Negotiations: Social-Psychological Perspectives*, and the author of *Human Factors in International Negotiations: Social-Psychological Aspects of International Conflict*.

ROGER FISHER is Samuel Williston Professor of Law at Harvard Law School, where he also received an LL.B. His numerous articles span the areas of international conflict, public international law, and negotiation. He is the author of *International Conflict for Beginners; Dear Israelis, Dear Arabs: A Working Approach to Peace; International Mediation: A Working Guide; International Crises and the Role of Law: Points of Choice*; and *Improving Compliance with International Law*.

P. TERRENCE HOPMANN is Director of the Quigley Center of International Studies at the University of Minnesota, where he is also Associate Professor of Political Science. He received a Ph.D. in political science at Stanford University. He has published widely in the areas of international conflict and negotiation, alliance cohesion, international politics, and American and comparative foreign policy. Hopmann is coauthor of *Unity and Disintegration in International Alliances: Comparative Studies.*

THOMAS A. KOCHAN is Professor of Industrial Relations in the Sloan School of Management at MIT. He received a Ph.D. in industrial relations from the University of Wisconsin. He is the author of articles in the areas of public sector mediation, collective bargaining, and organizational behavior. He is coauthor of *Public Sector Labor Relations: Analysis and Readings,* and author of *Collective Bargaining and Industrial Relations: From Theory to Policy to Practice.*

KENNETH KRESSEL is Associate Professor of Psychology at Rutgers University. He received a Ph.D. in social psychology from Teachers College, Columbia University. He has written articles in the areas of labor mediation, marital conflict, and divorce therapy, and is the author of a forthcoming book, *The Dynamics of Divorce Negotiations: A Social-Psychological Analysis of the Role of Lawyers, Therapists, and Mediators.*

DEAN G. PRUITT is Professor of Psychology at the State University of New York at Buffalo. He received a Ph.D. in social psychology from Yale University. He is the author of numerous articles on decision making, interpersonal bargaining, mediation, and group behavior. Pruitt is the author of *Negotiation Behavior,* and coeditor of *Theory and Research on the Causes of War.*

EDWARD R. F. SHEEHAN is a journalist, novelist, and dramatist. He has contributed major articles to publications in the United States, Great Britain, Europe, and the third world, including the *New York Times Magazine, Harper's, Saturday Evening Post, Reader's Digest, Foreign Policy,* the *Sunday Telegraph* of London, *Nouvel Observateur* and *Jeune Afrique* of Paris, the *Journal of Palestine Studies* of Beirut, *Maariv* of Tel Aviv, *Jiji Press* of Tokyo, and many others. Sheehan won an award from the Overseas Press Club for distinguished interpretation of foreign affairs. He served until recently as a research fellow at the Center for International Affairs at Harvard University, where he conducted seminars on the Middle East.

DONALD B. STRAUS is the former president of the American Arbitration Association and president of its Research Institute. He received an MBA from the Harvard Graduate School of Business Administration. He is a consultant and arbitrator with extensive experience in the areas of labor-management relations, health insurance, nuclear energy, world population, and international trade.

I. WILLIAM ZARTMAN is Professor of International Studies at The Johns Hopkins University. He received a Ph.D. in political science at Yale University. He has written extensively in the areas of comparative government (North Africa, the Middle East), international relations, world politics, and negotiation. Zartman is the author of *The 50% Solution, The Practical Negotiator, Ripe for Resolution: Conflict and Intervention in Africa, Africa in the 1980s: A Continent in Crisis,* and editor of *The Negotiation Process: Theories and Applications.*